THE BROTHERS KARAMAZOV

Fyodor Dostoevsky

AUTHORED by Kendrick Strauch
UPDATED AND REVISED by Adam Kissel

COVER DESIGN by Table XI Partners LLC
COVER PHOTO by Olivia Verma and © 2005 GradeSaver, LLC

BOOK DESIGN by Table XI Partners LLC

Published by GradeSaver LLC, www.gradesaver.com

First published in the United States of America by GradeSaver LLC. 2007

ISBN 978-1-60259-119-6

Printed in the United States of America

For other products and additional information please visit http://www.gradesaver.com

Table of Contents

Table of Contents

Biography of Fyodor Dostoevsky (1821-1881)

Fyodor Mikhailovich Dostoevsky was born October 30, 1821, in Moscow's Hospital for the Poor. He was the second of seven children born to a former army surgeon, who was murdered in 1839 when his own serfs poured vodka down his throat until he died.

Following a boarding school education in Moscow with his older brother Mikhail, Fyodor was admitted to the Academy of Military Engineers in St. Petersburg in 1838. He completed his studies in 1843, graduating as a lieutenant, but was quickly convinced that he preferred a career in writing to being mired in the bureaucratic Russian military. In 1844 he published a translation of Balzac's *Eugenie Grandet*, and he followed this two years later with his first original published work, *Poor Folk*, a widely-acclaimed short novel championed by the influential critic Vissarion Belinsky.

His works over the next three years were not as well accepted. The "literary lights" whose acquaintance he had made started to treat him with contempt and mockery. Under the influence of Belinsky, Dostoevsky turned to a materialist atheism. In 1847, he broke with Belinsky's group to join the socialist Petrashevsky group, a secret society of liberal utopians, where he associated himself with the most radical element.

On April 23, 1849, Dostoevsky was arrested with other members of the Petrashevsky circle and was sentenced to death. He was placed in solitary confinement in the Petropavlovsky Fortress for eight months. During this time, Tsar Nikolai I changed his sentence but ordered that this change only be announced at the last minute. On December 22, Dostoevsky and his fellow prisoners were led through all the initial steps of execution, and several of them were already tied to posts awaiting their deaths when the reprieve was sounded.

Dostoevsky's sentence of eight years' hard labor in a Siberian prison was reduced to four, followed by another four years of compulsory military service. During the latter, he married the widow Marya Dmitrievna Isaeva, with whom he returned to St. Petersburg in 1859.

Dostoevsky's harrowing near-execution and his terrible years of imprisonment made an indelible impression on him, converting him to a lifelong intense spirituality. These beliefs formed the basis for his great novels.

After his release, Dostoevsky published a few short works, including "Memoirs from the House of the Dead" (1860-1861), which was based on his prison experiences, in the journal *Time*, which he had co-founded with his brother Mikhail. In 1862, he made his first trip abroad, to England, France, Germany, Italy, and Switzerland.

While abroad, he had an affair with Apollinaria Suslova, a young and attractive student whom Dostoevsky considered an intellectual equal. He also made observations on Western society that fueled his rejection of Western philosophies as models for Russian society.

In 1863, *Time* was banned, so Fyodor and Mikhail founded another magazine, *Epoch*, which in 1864 published the complex Notes from Underground, generally considered the preface to Dostoevsky's great novels.

In that same year, both Marya Dmitrievna and Fyodor's beloved brother Mikhail died, leaving Dostoevsky saddled with debts and dependents. Apollinaria Suslova declined a marriage proposal, and in an attempt to win money through gambling, Dostoevsky mired himself further in debt. With creditors at his heels and with debts of around 43,000 rubles, Dostoevsky escaped abroad with 175 rubles in his pocket and a "slave contract" with bookseller F. T. Stellovsky. This agreement stipulated that if Dostoevsky did not produce a new novel by November 1, 1866, all rights to Dostoevsky's past and future works would revert to Stellovsky.

Time passed, and Dostoevsky, preoccupied with a longer, serialized novel, did no work on the book he had promised Stellovsky until at last, on the advice of friends, he hired the young Anna Grigorievna Snitkin as his stenographer. He dictated *The Gambler* to her, and the manuscript was delivered to Stellovsky on the very day their agreement was to expire. Through November, Dostoevsky completed the longer novel Crime and Punishment, which was published that year to immediate and abundant success. Fyodor proposed to Anna, and they soon were wed on February 15, 1867.

This second marriage brought Dostoevsky professional and emotional stability. Anna tolerated his compulsive gambling, managed his career, and nursed him through depression and epilepsy. His great works, notably *The Idiot* (1868), *Demons* (1871-1872, also known as *The Devils* or mistranslated as *The Possessed*), and The Brothers Karamazov, were all written in this last phase of his life.

Despite this relative success, the Dostoevskys were dogged by the massive debts left by Mikhail's death and Fyodor's gambling until about 1873. At this point, Anna became his publisher and he (according to his wife) gave up gambling. Their newfound financial stability enabled the Dostoevskys to purchase the house they had been renting in 1876, and between 1877 and 1880, Dostoevsky worked on The Brothers Karamazov, regarded by many as the apex of his career. During these last years of his life, he enjoyed prominence in his public life as well as his literary career.

Fyodor Dostoevsky died on January 28, 1881, of complications related to his epilepsy. At the funeral procession in St. Petersburg, his coffin was followed by thirty to forty thousand people. His epitaph reads, "Verily, verily, I say unto you, except a corn of wheat fall into the ground and die, it abideth alone: but if it die, it bringeth forth much fruit," which is the quotation Dostoevsky chose for the preface of The Brothers Karamazov.

Dostoevsky is one of the first writers to explore the ideas of psychoanalysis in his works. His religious ideas are still relevant in theological debate. He also is one of the seminal creators of the ideas of existentialism. Despite his varying success during his lifetime, today Dostoevsky is considered to be one of the preeminent Russian novelists—indeed, one of the preeminent novelists—of all time.

About The Brothers Karamazov

Dostoevsky lived in Russia in the mid-19th century, a particularly tumultuous time in the country's long and chaotic history. The agitation, despair, and pride of the time worked their way into much of Dostoevsky's prose. Thus, understanding Dostoevsky's context and personal life is extremely valuable in interpreting his work.

When Dostoevsky was born in 1821, Russia saw a bright future ahead. In 1812, Napoleon had tried to invade the massive country, but Russia had repelled the attack. Around the world, Napoleon was viewed as a rampaging tyrant, and Russia was admired and cheered for having halted such a dangerous force. Alexander I was called the "savior of Europe."

During the Industrial Revolution, Russia was on the verge of Westernizing and becoming more technologically advanced, and its people were becoming increasingly progressive. It was truly an exciting time for the people, especially in the cities. In 1825, there was a revolt later named "The Decembrist Revolt," which was intended to install a constitutional monarchy (with more protections than before), but Nicholas I became more protective of his government. Instead of becoming more liberal, the country adopted the slogan "Autocracy, Orthodoxy, Nationality." Russia slid back into its traditions and moved away from Westernization. Many in the country, however, remained sympathetic to revolutionary influences, including anarchy and nihilism.

In the 1860s, nihilists rose to prominence. After being stymied when they appealed to the government for reform, they decided to take a much more grassroots approach and go straight to the people. The "Narodnik Movement," as it was called, was not harmless. The nihilists in the Narodnik Movement committed acts of terrorism and even assassination. Most famously, they carried out the assassination of Alexander II in 1881, the year Dostoevsky died.

The most important change in Russia during Dostoevsky's lifetime was the emancipation of the serfs in 1861 by Alexander II. This grand shift in the socioeconomic hierarchy turned out to be nominal, from the point of view of material conditions, for the most part. Many of the serfs did not leave the land they had worked, choosing to stay on the land and work for pay. A low pay scale and special taxes for former serfs meant that their situations stayed relatively stagnant. Thus, the revolutionary tensions that Alexander had been trying to avoid continued to grow; the liberation of the serfs kept paving the way for further reformist movements.

Russia's battles during the 19th century were not restricted to its internal affairs. Russia fought several wars during this time. In 1853, Turkey declared war on Russia, beginning the Crimean War. In 1875, Russia clashed with the Ottoman Empire because Russia wanted to extradite the Balkan Christians from their Ottoman rulers. In 1877, just four years before Dostoevsky's death, the Ottoman Empire and Russia went to war. This was the second time during the 19th century that Christian Russia had gone to war with a nation (or empire) of a different faith. It is no wonder, then, that Russians took their religion as seriously as their nationalism.

Russia's political turmoil, its religious battles, and its constantly shifting world status kept its citizens from gaining a sense of stability. Its material strife and its ideological crises meant that no aspect of life was safe from constant challenges. This is the Russia that Dostoevsky wrote about, and Russia's struggles were his struggles. His works reflect how man can survive and comprehend life in a troubled nation. The Brothers Karamazov, a long and complex novel (see the themes in this ClassicNote), engages with his contemporary Russian experience even while it speaks beyond his time and place.

Character List

Fyodor Pavlovich Karamazov

The aging patriarch of the Karamazov family. He is surly and emotional, generally disliked by everyone. He is eventually murdered by Smerdyakov.

Dmitri Fyodorovich Karamazov

Fyodor's oldest son (whose mother is Adelaida). He is impulsive and quick to anger like his father, but he has a faith in God that Fyodor does not share. He is convicted of killing Fyodor.

Ivan Fyodorovich Karamazov

Fyodor's second son (his first by Sofia). He is intellectual and cynical, and he becomes very ill when his father is murdered because he feels that he is very much to blame.

Alexei (Alyosha) Fyodorovich Karamazov

Fyodor's youngest son (his second by Sofia). He is deeply religious and caring, and he tries to follow in the footsteps of Father Zossima, the elder at the monastery whom he respects very much.

Pavel Fyodorovich Smerdyakov

Rumored to be Fyodor's illegitimate son by Lizaveta, he has grown up as a servant to Fyodor. This epileptic boy is enamored of Ivan's ideas about life, and he murders Fyodor.

Adelaida

Fyodor's first wife and Dmitri's mother.

Sofia

Fyodor's second wife and Ivan's and Alyosha's mother.

Father Ferapont

Another monk at the monastery. He serves as a foil to Father Zossima, disagreeing with Zossima's ideas of love and compassion.

Grigory Vassilyevich

Fyodor's servant; Smerdyakov's adopted father.

Agrafena (Grushenka) Alexandrovna

The "she-devil" whom Fyodor and Dmitri both pursue.

Madame Hohlakov

Lise's mother.

Lise

The young girl who gets engaged to Alyosha.

Ilusha

The young boy with whom Alyosha becomes close. His illness is a catalyst that brings the other boys together.

Katerina Ivanovna

The girl who is in love with Dmitri and is determined to marry him.

Nikolay (Kolya) Ivanovich Krassotkin

A young boy who looks up to Alyosha.

"Stinking" Lizaveta Smerdyaschaya

The town idiot who gives birth to Smerdyakov (rumored to be Fyodor's son).

Marfa Ignatyevna

Grigory's wife.

Mussyalovich

Grushenka's former lover, who returns to see her.

Mihail Ospovitch Rakitin

A young friend of Alyosha whom Grushanka bribes to bring Alyosha to her.

Captain Snegiryov

Ilusha's father. He was severely beaten by Dmitri, and Alyosha brings him money from Katerina.

Father Zossima

The elder who takes Alyosha under his wing and urges him to leave the monastery.

Major Themes

Duality and the Clash of Ideas

Dostoevsky is fascinated by the idea of opposites. He sets characters in opposing, contrasting roles, and he pits ideas and philosophies against each other. In The Brothers Karamazov, he illustrates many foil relationships between characters, which places each character in a complex position on a multidimensional grid of ideology and philosophy. For instance, Father Zossima and Father Ferapont are rivals because of their stances on Christianity. Father Zossima's loving attitude toward all things contrasts sharply with Ferapont's acerbic cynicism. At the same time, Zossima is a foil to old Fyodor, for Fyodor has no faith in God and has no sense of responsibility. Each of the Karamazov brothers is also a foil to Fyodor in his own way; for instance, Ivan's thoughtfulness contrasts with Fyodor's impulsive nature, and Alyosha's loving manner contrasts with Fyodor's meanness. By highlighting the opposing natures of his characters, Dostoevsky creates a forum for debate, sometimes expressed explicitly among the characters, sometimes in a presentation of the characters that seems designed to get the reader to debate the issues in his or her own mind. In this way, the novel addresses such sweeping issues as morality, responsibility, nihilism, murder, and love through the characters, what they frankly discuss, and what their words and actions represent.

The difficulty is that Dostoevsky's characters are not flat characters who represent simple opinions, being two-dimensional embodiments of arguments expressed in the grand scheme of the novel. The characters themselves embody conflicts and arguments; their position on any particular issue can develop and change. Dmitri is the best example of this inner conflict. Instead of being a pristine religious fanatic or a depraved profligate with no conscience, he is a guilty pleasure-seeker, a sinner who yearns for God's grace. He spends very much of his time and energy trying to pay Katerina money he owes her, a rather honorable pursuit. He initially spent this money, however, on an affair with another woman. He feels that he is destined to "plunge into the abyss" of "degradation" headfirst, but he feels that even if he is "following in the devil's footsteps, [he is] still [God's] son." Dmitri embodies an important conflict in the novel: the desire for earthly pleasures and the struggle to control such desire. Dostoevsky shows that there is good and evil in every person—a person has moral choices to make. Even though Dostoevsky deals with such grand issues as good and evil, he very astutely creates characters who display human virtues, vices, and fallibility.

Christianity's Place in Society

Dostoevsky believed that having faith in God and embracing "Mother Earth" constituted the only path to personal salvation and peace. He also believed that Christianity in a society makes it strong and capable. Hence, much of the novel centers around the struggle for faith and the anti-religious ideas that threaten Christian society. The desire for sexual and sensual pleasure that both Dmitri and

Fyodor feel runs counter to traditional Christian attitudes.

Ivan's life runs on his intellectuality and sympathy rather than religion, which poses a threat to a view of faith as the only path to peace. Ivan has integrity. He writes so that he can support himself. In a novel where debt and money hold such great import, Ivan's financial responsibility is noble. He also has great empathy, feeling repulsed (as almost everyone does) by the suffering of innocent children. His sense of justice is strong, and he cannot tolerate affronts to it. This intolerance actually creates a rift between his ideas and the religious ones held by characters such as Alyosha and Father Zossima. He cannot "accept this God-made world," and therefore Ivan does not fit with Dostoevsky's ideal of someone who accepts God and all his creation. Ivan ends up choosing not to do what he can to protect his father from a potential murder, however, and the guilt he feels from his inaction drives him insane. This major mistake reveals human fallibility despite the intellectual's best intentions, undermining the notion that the intellectual life is enough for peace. If Dostoevsky's novel shares the didactic tendencies of a fable, Ivan's insanity can be considered his punishment or a consequence of his rejection of the God-made world. Alyosha, in contrast, leaves the monastery to live in the world and do good in it. The novel ends with him being applauded for his Christian teachings of love and acceptance, his reward for his religious fervor. The fates of the two brothers end up reinforcing the importance of Christianity in the world, despite or in spite of the world's frequent lack of peace.

Voluntary Suffering

The novel suggests, as Christians sometimes do, that suffering can purify people and bring them closer to salvation. Suffering is thus primarily a personal experience, defined not by outside forces but by its role in self-development. Father Zossima believes that punishment by the state or by an authority figure has no effect on the soul. The only type of productive punishment is when one's conscience admits a sin and copes with it. In the novel, the desire of characters to find salvation is expressed sometimes as an illness, sometimes as a self-imposed punishment, and sometimes as a simple desire for humiliation. When Ivan believes he is guilty of letting old Fyodor be murdered, he has a mental breakdown and falls ill, having to be confined to bed for long periods of time. Ivan's behavior is reminiscent of Raskolnikov's behavior in Crime and Punishment—Raskolnikov periodically falls ill, wracked by guilt over his murder.

Dmitri, though technically innocent of the murder of his father, wants to accept the suffering that prison will afford him because he believes it will enable him to change and begin a new life. While this may offend the reader's sense of justice, it should be made clear that, according to the novel's outlook, suffering for any reason, not simply when it is just in the particular instance, can help a person find salvation. Other characters yearn for humiliation. Dmitri says that he might "find a certain pleasure in falling in such a humiliating way." Similarly, Katerina wants to be with Dmitri, who shuns her in return. He is very openly trying to be with

Grushenka, and Katerina's fidelity contrasts sharply with Dmitri's infidelity. Perhaps Katerina is simply loving unconditionally, but it is also possible that she longs for the disgrace that Dmitri will bring her. Dostoevsky's fascination with suffering very likely was enriched during his long imprisonment and faux execution. Perhaps he found redemption in his suffering, but many of his characters seem simply masochistic, having lost the connection between suffering and the purification of character that it can effect.

Shared Responsibility

Father Zossima states that every man is partially responsible for the sins of his fellow man. Fyodor's murder is a pivotal plot point, so determining who is to blame for his murder is very pertinent to the novel. Is Smerdyakov alone guilty, or did all the characters in the novel contribute in some way to the murder? Ivan is an obvious candidate for partial guilt, since he feels so strongly that he is partially guilty of Fyodor's murder that he has a mental breakdown. Dmitri is also an interesting case; even though he is wrongly convicted of the crime, he wants to suffer so that he may find peace and a new life. Both brothers encounter self-motivated suffering as if they are actually guilty of the murder. We thus see that responsibility can be a matter of character; it can be internal, not merely a result of external actions. Since humans are fallible, we might be able to connect a wide complex of individual character flaws to a crime such as a murder, even blaming "society" at least in part.

In the novel, the feeling of responsibility for the sins of others also expresses a Christ-like perspective—responsibility even if one sees no actual culpability in oneself. Alyosha does not simply feel guilty for the sins of others; he actively involves himself in their affairs because he believes that the affairs of the world are his, too. Father Zossima helps him come to the conclusion that his place is not in a secluded monastery but in the world, for he has work to do there. This underscores Alyosha's strongly-held sense of responsibility for others. Many of Dostoevsky's characters feel the weight of responsibility for their fellow man, which supports Dostoevsky's view that man should be "married" to the world around him, inextricably connected to all of God's creation.

The Importance of Money

Many of the characters in The Brothers Karamazov are fixated on money. They attach great importance to the exchange of rubles, and owing a debt is extremely stressful and shameful. Dostoevsky spent a great deal of time in debt because of his propensity for gambling, and he knew well how poverty could wreak havoc on a man. In Russia at this time, serfdom was a very recent memory (it was only abolished in 1861). Even when the serfs were emancipated, the disparity in wealth was very great, and many former serfs still lived in primitive, impoverished situations. When a character like Fyodor or Dmitri spends money recklessly, it is not portrayed as charming or silly but as selfish and indicative of weak character. Dostoevsky's characters are not all greedy thieves and profligates, however. The fact that money is imbued with great importance makes it a weighty currency of respect and of honor.

Dmitri, for instance, is obsessed with paying Katerina back a sum he owes her. He feels that he cannot go ahead with his plans to marry Grushenka before his debt is paid. Though he is essentially breaking an engagement and running off with another woman, his sense of honor and duty compel him to return the 3,000 rubles she has loaned him, and the desire to do so consumes him.

Ilusha's father is a complicating example. He is a poor man who was badly beaten by Dmitri, humiliating his son Ilusha. Because she pities him, Katerina offers to give him 200 rubles, a sum that will dramatically improve his family's situation. But since Alyosha is the messenger who offers it to him, he decides he cannot take it from a Karamazov. He wants to earn his son's respect, and refusing money from the family that shamed him is more important to him than helping his family out of poverty. When Rakitin accepts money to trick Alyosha into seeing Grushenka, he becomes very upset and guilty. This Judas-like act of accepting money to betray a friendship weighs on his conscience. Although money carries such gravity in the novel, characters with integrity still prefer principles such as friendship; honor goes beyond its financial characteristics.

Generational Divide

There is a strong sense of generational influence in The Brothers Karamazov. Even if Fyodor does not exert direct control over his sons, his presence is definitely a large influence in all their lives. Father Zossima is even more clearly a paternal figure, for he teaches Alyosha how to think and act from his position at the top of the hierarchy in the monastery. And as Father Zossima was a teacher to Alyosha, so is Alyosha a teacher to the young boys of the town. Since Sofia, Adelaida, and Lizaveta are all dead, the older generation has a distinctly paternal character.

This is not simply a story of "passing the torch" and coming of age, however. The younger generations are not simply growing to fulfill the roles left vacant by the passing older generation; they are trying to extricate themselves from the sins and burdens left by their elders. (Recall that the Russian nation was, in some ways, under revolutionary ferment.) Dmitri feels that "since he is a Karamazov," he is doomed to fall into "degradation" and "humiliation" as his father has. Ivan, trying to set himself apart from the father he disdains, becomes his father's opposite–a rational, thoughtful man who pays all his debts. The idea of repaying old debts and finding justice for sins long since committed is another way the generations are connected. When Dmitri loans Katerina's father money, she takes it on herself to repay him and offer him her hand in marriage to repay her father's debt. Smerdyakov, the son of Fyodor's rape of "Stinking Lizaveta," is bitter and mean. Despite his rationalizations for murder based on Ivan's cold logic, his murder of the old man is in part retribution for the sins committed against his mother.

Similarly, Ilusha bites Alyosha's hand when he meets him because he is defending his father's honor; his father was severely beaten by Dmitri, and Ilusha deems it fair to treat all Karamazovs with hostility.

The generations in The Brothers Karamazov thus are distinct from each other yet inextricably linked. Most importantly, the younger generations represent hope. When Alyosha goes into the world to do good, he cannot stop his father's murder, Ivan's insanity, Dmitri's indictment, or Smerdyakov's suicide. He is not a failure, however, because he focuses on teaching the younger generation the ways of love and acceptance so that they will create a better world. The younger generations can redeem the sins of past ones.

Passion for Life

At one point in the novel, Ivan proclaims that if nothing else, the Karamazovs all share a "passion for living." In Fyodor's case, this passion consists of a constant appetite for sensual gratification. Alyosha, however, simply desires to be connected to the world and its creatures, spreading love and understanding. Such disparate attitudes all spring from this "passion for living," so it seems to be a neutral energy that can be used for good or ill. Dostoevsky places great importance on religion, and his religious attitude is that a person should be "married" to the world. This idea of spirituality is very tangible and corporeal. This leads the reader to believe that Dostoevsky considers "passion for living" a good thing when informed by religion.

At the same time, it leads to hedonistic behavior by characters including Fyodor and Dmitri. Consider Dmitri's brief consideration of suicide. When Grushenka's ex-lover returns and Dmitri's affair with her seems thwarted, he decides to kill himself. This implies that his desire or passion for life is waning, a feeling based on the outcome of events and relationships. His ardor is conditional. This conditional passion is inconsistent with Father Zossima's view that one should love everyone and everything in the world. Dmitri's passion expresses a selfishness that can be confused with a desire for life. When Dmitri goes to prison, however, he realizes he wants to begin anew. He gains perspective and realizes his mistake. He decides he wants to be with the woman he loves, "till the soil," and die in his own country. Desire for life should be unconditional, it seems; his former course was misguided. "Passion for living" is necessary for a good life, though it easily can be redirected through selfishness.

Glossary of Terms

Agnosticism

A philosophy that holds that one cannot know whether God exists.

Allegory

A story that acts as an extended metaphor; a parable.

Asceticism

An austere, simple lifestyle associated with the pursuit of spiritual discovery.

Atheism

The belief that God does not exist.

Avarice

Greed.

Benefactor

One who offers financial help to another.

Cana of Galilee

The site where Christ performed his first miracle, changing water into wine, at a wedding celebration.

Catharsis

The dramatic purging of feelings of guilt or tension.

Consumption

A colloquial term for tuberculosis.

Ecclesiastical

Pertaining to a church.

Elder

A high-ranking monk.

Epilepsy

A disease of the neurological system characterized by violent seizures.

Faro

A card game where the players bet on what cards will turn up.

Freemasonry

A mysterious fraternity, originally of stone workers, that is dedicated to helping one another and society.

Friedrich Schiller

A German philosopher and poet in the late 18th century.

Mysticism

A set of spiritual beliefs centered on the idea that one can experience spiritual clarity, not through rationality but in other ways such as, in the Christian mystic tradition, by praying, fasting, and imitating Christ.

Nihilism

A philosophy based on the belief that religion and morality are meaningless. Nihilists believe that God does not exist and that life has no meaning.

Oedipal Stage

Freud believed that there is a stage of development where a child will feel competitive with his father for his mother's love.

Parricide

Murder of one's own father.

Paternal

Fatherly.

Penance

A voluntary punishment undergone to show penitence for a sin.

Pestle

A grinding tool used to crush varied things such as food or mortar.

Preconsciousness

Latent memories that can be accessed by the conscious mind.

Profligate

Immoral or debauched.

Rationalism

The belief that one can find truth through reason and deduction.

Requiem

A service or hymn for someone who has died.

Ruble

The unit of Russian currency, worth 100 kopecks.

Sensualist

A person who pursues sensual enjoyment.

Serf

In the feudal system, a serf is a peasant who does forced labor, usually working for a landowner.

Spanish Inquisition

In the fifteenth and sixteenth centuries, non-Catholics were persecuted by the Catholic Church. Recent converts to the church were interrogated for blasphemy.

Tirade

An outburst of violent invective.

Troika

A Russian cart pulled by three horses.

Short Summary

The Brothers Karamazov is a family tragedy centered around a father and his sons. Fyodor, the eldest Karamazov, has three sons: Dmitri, Ivan, and Alyosha. Ivan and Alyosha have the same mother, but Dmitri, the oldest, has a different mother. Fyodor is a greedy landowner, a bawdy lecher, and a neglectful father. Hence, the Karamazov brothers end up growing into young men under the care of various other people. But they all have returned home to visit their father, and it is the first time they all have been together for quite some time.

Dmitri has a dispute with Fyodor over his inheritance, and Alyosha, who is living in a monastery, suggests that they see Father Zossima, Alyosha's mentor. Alyosha believes that the wise old man can settle the dispute peacefully. Father Zossima is patient and kind, but Fyodor and Dmitri end up quarreling anyway. After Fyodor drives the men to frustration, they leave the monastery separately, and Alyosha worries about their family's future. Alyosha talks to Dmitri, who confesses his complicated situation with women and money. Dmitri promised to marry a girl named Katerina, and she lent him 3,000 rubles. Instead of paying it back, he spent it on another girl named Grushenka. He wants to run away with Grushenka, but he feels that he needs to pay Katerina back before he can do so. This is why he is so interested in getting the money from Fyodor.

Back at Fyodor's house, Smerdyakov is talking to the Karamazovs. Smerdyakov is an epileptic servant who was adopted by Grigory and Marfa, Fyodor's other servants. He was born to a woman named Lizaveta who died in childbirth. She was the town idiot, and she lived off charity from the other townspeople. Everyone called her "Stinking Lizaveta," and when the town found out she was pregnant, they were furious at whoever could do such a thing to a helpless girl. They decided Fyodor must have been the culprit. Grigory and Marfa gave birth to a deformed child, and when they buried the child, they found Lizaveta, who had just given birth to Smerdyakov. They adopted the child immediately, and Fyodor named him

Father Zossima is dying, and Alyosha is distraught. Instead of asking Alyosha to stay with him during his last days, however, Father Zossima tells Alyosha he should leave the monastery to be with his family. His life gets even more complicated when a young crippled girl named Lise expresses that she has feelings for him. Alyosha visits Katerina, the girl who is engaged to marry Dmitri. Ivan is in love with her, but he feels that Dmitri is a better match for her. Frustrated and disgusted with his family's situation, Ivan says he is going to leave town. Alyosha sees a boy being picked on by his schoolmates, and he tries to talk to the boy, but he bites Alyosha's hand and runs away. Later, when Alyosha is bringing money to a man named Captain Snegiryov, who has been beaten by Dmitri, he recognizes the man's son. It is Ilusha, the boy who bit his hand. The family is poor, but Captain Snegiryov refuses to take the money because he feels that he needs to earn his son's respect after being humiliated by Dmitri—and accepting charity, especially from a

Karamazov, is out of the question.

When Alyosha goes back to see Katerina, he finds Lise, Madame Hohlakov's daughter. The two realize that they love each other, and they decide to get married. Alyosha goes to visit Ivan, and he finds him in a restaurant. Ivan has gone there to get away from his father, and Alyosha sits down with him to have an intimate talk. Ivan tells his brother about his thoughts regarding God and the world. He recites to Alyosha a poem he has written called "The Great Inquisitor." The poem describes Christ returning to earth in the sixteenth century. The Church throws him in jail, and The Great Inquisitor explains to him that his presence is problematic for the world. The Church has spent years trying to replace the sense of freedom Christ gave man with security. He talks about how cruel the world is, especially to innocent children. After their meal, Alyosha and Ivan part ways, feeling closer than ever. Ivan sees Smerdyakov when he goes back to his father's house, and Smerdyakov tells him he is worried about Fyodor. He is worried Dmitri will come to kill him and the old man will be helpless to save himself. Ivan goes to sleep very troubled.

Father Zossima is on his deathbed, and Alyosha goes to visit him. The Elder tells those around him how much Alyosha reminds him of his older brother, a boy who died when he was a youth. He talks about being a profligate youth in the army. One day, he challenged another man to a duel because of a girl. Before the duel, however, he had a change of heart. He did not shoot and, after the duel, he retired from the army and joined a monastery. He talks about how much the Bible has affected him and says that everyone should embrace the world and the people in it. He dies. Many predicted that a miracle would happen upon Father Zossima's death, but his body begins to putrefy, filling the monastery with an awful smell. This fills the other monks with doubt that Father Zossima was the saintly man they thought he was. Alyosha is shaken by the news. He goes to see Grushenka, who has sent for him, and she admits to wanting to "ruin" him. When he tells her that Father Zossima has died, however, she becomes contrite about her callousness. She says she thinks she is a wicked person, and the two comfort each other. When Alyosha leaves, he has a renewed faith in Father Zossima and his teachings because Alyosha feels how wonderful it is to love and be loved in return.

Meanwhile, Dmitri has become desperate. He wants to be with Grushenka, but he wants to pay Katerina back first. He goes on an odyssey, hoping that he can depend on the charity of others. He visits a man named Samsanov, a man who used to pursue Grushenka, and he hates Dmitri. He sends Karamazov to see a surly drunk, tricking Dmitri into thinking this man may be helpful. The man is practically incoherent, however, and Dmitri goes to find Madame Hohlakov. She tells Dmitri that the only way he will find 3,000 rubles is in the gold mines. In confusion, Dmitri concludes that Grushenka has gone to visit his father, and he goes to his father's house in a rage, carrying a brass pestle. When he arrives, he does not find Grushenka, but as he is leaving, Grigory, his father's servant, thinks he has come to murder Fyodor. The two scuffle, and Dmitri hits Grigory on the head with the pestle.

After determining that the man is not dead, Dmitri flees the scene and looks for Grushenka. She is with Kalganov, a former lover who had treated her poorly. Dmitri decides that he will not end up with Grushenka and decides to kill himself after seeing her one more time. He crashes her party and sits down with her gentleman friend and some other men. The situation becomes tense, and after the gentlemen make some disparaging remarks about Russians and Dmitri, Grushenka decides she does not want to be with such an insulting and vicious man. She decides that she loves Dmitri, and as the two are coming to terms with their love, the police come to arrest him for the murder of Fyodor. As the police question Dmitri, it becomes clear that the facts all support the conclusion that he did indeed murder his father, even though he did not commit the crime. He was at the scene of the crime, wielding a weapon, the night of the murder. He had said he would kill his father on several occasions. He publicly announced he was looking for 3,000 rubles and was desperate to find them, and Fyodor reportedly had an envelope with 3,000 rubles that was stolen the night of the murder. Dmitri is carried away, and very few people believe that he is innocent of Fyodor's murder.

Meanwhile, Alyosha is visiting Ilusha, the boy who bit his hand, in the hospital. The boy has fallen quite ill, and Alyosha has gotten to know many of the boy's friends, who are also visiting him. One boy, Kolya Krassotkin, is a leader among the boys. He and Ilusha were friends, but they had a falling out because Ilusha fed a pin to a dog, and Kolya did not approve of his cruelty. When Alyosha comes to visit, he and Kolya talk for quite some time. The boy looks up to this wise man about which he has heard so much from the other boys, and he wants to impress him. The two become friends, and Alyosha treats all the boys as equals. When Kolya goes in to see Ilusha, he gives him a dog as a present. He reveals that the dog is none other but the dog Ilusha gave the piece of bread with a pin in it. Kolya has nursed the dog back to health and has fully trained him as a gesture of friendship to Ilusha. The mood is dampened, however, when the doctors go in to see Ilusha. Without even saying it, everyone understands that the boy does not have much time left. Ilusha is brave, and he tries to lift the spirits of those around him.

Later, Alyosha visits his brother in jail. Dmitri tells Alyosha that Ivan has concocted a plan for his escape from jail. Alyosha goes to talk to Ivan, who feels strangely guilty about his father's death. Alyosha tells his brother that he should not feel responsible for a crime that he did not commit, but Ivan stalks off angrily. He meets Smerdyakov, who tells Ivan he thinks the Karamazov brother is guilty as an accomplice to the murder. He says that Ivan wanted his father dead and left the night of the murder to try to free himself of the responsibility of protecting his father. Ivan is angry and troubled by this, and when he talks to Smerdyakov later, Smerdyakov flatly admits to hilling Fyodor. He says that Ivan's theories and ideas were the basis for his crime and that Ivan's talks with Smerdyakov basically rationalized the deed. When Ivan returns home after this meeting, he sees a devil in his room. The devil chastises him for being a wicked person with weaknesses and foibles that have led to disastrous circumstances. Alyosha bangs on the door and finds his brother in a feverish state, muttering about a devil and Smerdyakov. Alyosha stays the night with his brother to take care of him.

Dmitri's trial begins. Many people from all around come to see the spectacle of the parricide trial. Dmitri has an excellent lawyer, but it is a hard case to win. The prosecution brings many witnesses who testify to seemingly damning evidence against Dmitri. The defense, however, discredits one after another of these witnesses, showing ulterior motives or mitigating circumstances. Alyosha defends his brother from the stand, and Katerina gives a moving account of Dmitri's honorable nature. Then Ivan comes into the courtroom, waving money and implicating Smerdyakov. Since he is yelling nonsense, disrupting the trial, and generally acting crazy, the court does not believe him. Suddenly, at the end of the trial, Katerina stands up again, showing a letter from Dmitri that clearly states Dmitri's intention to kill Fyodor as a last resort. She has a change of heart and no longer wants to lie to protect a man who has hurt her so much. Word comes to the courtoom that Smerdyakov has hanged himself. After final statements are made, the verdict comes back: guilty. Dmitri is sentenced to jail. Dmitri welcomes this chance to become a new man, but he does not want to be in exile in Siberia for the rest of his life; he wants to return to his home country before he dies.

Ivan is still sick, and Katerina takes care of him. Alyosha visits the boys with whom he has become friends. They are sad because Ilusha has died. Alyosha passes along Father Zossima's teachings of love and understanding, and they all embrace his words, cheering him.

Summary and Analysis of Book 1

Fyodor Karamazov and his three sons have just been reunited after many years, and the novel's first chapters concern themselves mostly with the family's backstory. We meet Fyodor, a "muddle-headed" eccentric who has led a reckless and selfish life. Though many thought him too impulsive to be crafty, he died with 100,000 rubles, proving that he must have been keen in some ways. He has few friends and many enemies, and he is an enigma to all. He married a fiery, romantic woman named Adelaida, who thought his lifestyle was "bold." After bearing him a son whom they named Dmitri, she ran off with a tutor. Fyodor was crushed by her desertion, but he also relished the idea of his humiliation so much that those who heard him talking about his situation thought that he somehow enjoyed his position as a cuckold.

Neglected by his father, young Dmitri fell under the care of various servants and relatives through the years. He grew up "unruly" and "impatient." When he was old enough, he joined the military. His impassioned character led him to be demoted for dueling, but he was re-promoted for "gallantry." His extravagant lifestyle had put him far into debt by the time he left the military, and he came home to collect his inheritance from his father.

After Adelaida left him, Fyodor married a beautiful innocent named Sofia. He was won by the sixteen-year-old's innocence, and he said of her, "those innocent eyes of hers slit my soul open like a razor." She had two sons, Ivan and Alyosha. Because Fyodor felt that she should be "indebted to him" for saving her from a bad situation, he felt justified in treating her cruelly, sleeping with other women in the house, sometimes in front of her. His mistreatment of his young wife eventually led to her having a nervous breakdown. With both parents unsuitable for taking care of their children, General Vorohkov's widow—Sofia's former benefactress—took in the children. She left each of the boys 1,000 rubles for his education. Ivan grew up sullen and quiet, embarrassed about living on charity from others and more embarrassed about his father. He was a fiercely intelligent boy, and he made money by tutoring, freelancing, and reviewing books for money. He wrote a relatively famous article about the ecclesiastical courts that was debated in political and religious circles alike. He came to town rather unexpectedly.

The youngest boy, Alyosha, was well-loved by Fyodor. He was popular, fearless of others, and, unlike his brothers, unconcerned with money. Instead of finishing school, he became quite taken with an elder named Father Zossima in the nearby monastery. He decided to join the monastery, and Fyodor gave him his blessing. Alyosha was the sort of boy who believed in miracles, but he was curiously very much a realist. Alyosha was a "member of the younger generation." Many believed that studying under an elder in a monastery was a "terrible apprenticeship"—by self-annihilation, one might achieve self-realization. Father Zossima was sixty-five years old and a former officer in the army. He was kind to even the worst sinners, and he was locally famous for his saint-like status.

When Alyosha meets his brothers for the first time, he quickly takes a liking to Dmitri. He finds Ivan "absorbed in something within himself, something very important, that he was pursuing some goal, perhaps a very difficult goal, which left no room for Alyosha in his thoughts." Dmitri, however, likes Ivan. Because of the dispute between Dmitri and Fyodor over Dmitri's inheritance, the newly reunited family decides to see Father Zossima to help resolve the issue. Alyosha, who is very close with Father Zossima, fears that the family is going to make a ridiculous scene and treat a serious occasion like a farce. But Dmitri assures his brother that he will act respectfully and calmly and that everything will go fine.

Analysis

In this first book, the reader gets to know the Karamazovs. The eldest Karamazov is a licentious old curmudgeon and a bad father. Readers begin to wonder how his behavior and treatment of his sons will be reflected in their own personalities and lives. These early chapters serve as introductions, and they do not focus much on the present. Interestingly, Fyodor and his three sons have not been together for some time, so the reader knows that any interactions they have will not be the tried, worn conversations of longtime acquaintances. Instead, it is clear that the conversations the family share will be new and telling of future relationships. There is drama and suspense leading up to the meeting with Father Zossima, for not only will a family dispute be mediated, but all four Karamazovs will be in the same place. This will be the first legitimate gathering at which the reader will see all the Karamazovs.

Dmitri seems very much his father's son. His inconsistent nature and his inclination to violence and sex remind the reader very much of Fyodor. Still, he seems to have a noble streak that is absent in Fyodor. Even though he was demoted in the army, he was re-promoted "for gallantry." The disparity between Dmitri's extremes is great. He seems like he will be a loose cannon, and the reader is anxious to see how he will deal with a formal meeting about a hotly-contested issue; he seems capable of both civility and wild rage.

Ivan is less obviously observable. He is quieter than his older brother, and he is very much ruled by his intellect, not his viscera. He seems to be very proud, refusing to ask his father for money and working very hard to make it. He and his older brother are also the sons of different mothers, and the significance of this detail is undeniable. It is not entirely clear yet how his personality is different from his brother's because of this fact, though. His mother was an innocent woman, not a passionate woman like Dmitri's mother. Ivan does not seem innocent, for he seems to understand the world enough to find a way to fend for himself. He also seems to understand the concept of reputations, for he is deeply embarrassed by his own father. Dmitri does have a predilection to follow his whims that Ivan does not have. Ivan seems very measured and in control of himself. He is the brother whose story is most concise. Alyosha and Dmitri are described at length, but Ivan has only a small section devoted to him. This is not because he is a lesser character—his role becomes clear later—but because he is more of an enigma. His motivations and actions are not as open and forthright as his brothers'. Dostoevsky thus leads us to want to unlock Ivan's mysterious character.

Alyosha seems to be the hero of the novel even at this early stage. In fact, most of the novel will revolve around his experiences, for he is involved in everyone's problems. When a character is described as having very few flaws, jaded modern readers suspect that one of his flaws might hurt him by the end, and we become interested to see how Alyosha might fall. But Alyosha never fully compromises his character. He retains a grand love for all mankind throughout the novel, and any missteps are minimal. He remains likeable and admirable throughout the novel, and his integrity is constant.

The three brothers thus may represent three distinct ideologies. Dostoevsky is prone to making his characters embody certain ideas, and at this point in the novel, we can start to make such identifications. While it is very interesting to see how these different "character-ideologies" will cope with the situations presented to them, it is even more interesting to see how characters who might seem two-dimensional and clearly pigeonholed will become more complexly human. The introduction to this novel makes every character's future a fascinating one.

Summary and Analysis of Book 2

The Karamazovs go to the meeting with Father Zossima to resolve the dispute between Dmitri and Fyodor over Dmitri's inheritance. Ivan and Fyodor arrive with Ivan's former benefactor, Peter Miusov, but Dmitri is nowhere in sight. Even though the group contains very influential citizens, no fuss is made upon their arrival. No monks rush to greet them. Instead, they are surrounded by beggars. Eventually, a monk invites them into the monastery, and they are all invited to dine with the Father after the meeting. Fyodor exclaims, "I wouldn't miss it for anything!" Old Karamazov calls Zossima "Holy Elder," "Your Reverence," "angelic man," and "blessed man." He gets down on his knees and kisses the father's hand. It seems as if he is playing. Peter Miusov is very annoyed by Fyodor's ironic demeanor, and he bickers with the elder Karamazov, showing his embarrassment at his presence, chastising him for his inconsiderate nature in front of a respected man. After such pleasantries, Father Zossima leaves to greet some visitors for a moment.

The visitors are peasant women except for a more well-to-do pair: Madame Hohlakov and her sickly and paralyzed daughter Lise. All the women ask Father Zossima for advice. Many of them behave quite strangely, "wailing in ecstasy ...barking like dogs," as if "shocked" by the "host" himself. The narrator explains that this is the behavior of suffering women with an "intensely unhappy life, full of brutality and ill-treatment." Father Zossima is patient with each woman, listening to her problems and offering thoughtful advice. When he gets to Madame Hohlakov, she thanks him profusely for "healing" her Lise. When the Father talks to Lise, instead of shedding tears she bursts into giggles. She blames her outburst on Alyosha, to whom she has taken a liking. Madame Hohlakov tells Father Zossima that she lacks faith in God and is not altruistic; instead, she expects gratitude for her good deeds. He advises her to "avoid lying, especially to yourself." Again Lise laughs, then suddenly begins to cry, pining for Alyosha. Father Zossima tells her that he will send Alyosha to visit her.

When Father Zossima and Alyosha return to the Father's cell, Ivan is talking to the monks about the separation of church and state. He advocates no separation, for he believes that if the church were the institution punishing crime, crime would be virtually nonexistent. Criminals would be more afraid of excommunication than jail time. Alyosha, who is still trying to figure out his intellectual brother, is impressed by Ivan's respectfulness and lack of condescension toward the monks. Father Zossima responds to Ivan's ruminations by saying that the only effective punishment is one's "awareness of one's own conscience."

Before they can debate this issue, however, Dmitri bursts into the room. He apologizes for his tardiness, saying that Smerdyakov told him the wrong time for the meeting. Father Zossima is not angry, and he greets Dmitri warmly. Dmitri sits down, and the men continue their theological debate. Ivan argues that "there is no virtue if there is no immortality." Men will cannibalize each other, figuratively and literally. Without belief in immortality, crime becomes inevitable. Dmitri and old Fyodor begin bickering. Karamazov accuses Dmitri of owing him money and attacking a captain in the army. Dmitri accuses old Karamazov of chasing after Grushenka, a girl he has been pursuing. Karamazov becomes so worked up that he challenges Dmitri to a duel, and an infuriated Dmitri exclaims, "why should such a man live?" As everyone bickers and shouts, Father Zossima bends down and kisses Dmitri's feet. Everyone is shocked; they do not know what to make of this. Everyone exits and continues on to a luncheon with Father Zossima except Fyodor. He decides not to attend the luncheon.

While Alyosha is walking the Father back, Zossima tells him he should leave the monastery and rejoin the world. He tells Alyosha to "stay close to your brothers—not just one of them, but both." Alyosha is very upset by this because he wants to be with Father Zossima, who is very ill. Disturbed by Father Zossima's advice, Alyosha continues on. He discusses the father's bow with Rakitin, a "career-conscious divinity student." Rakitin is skeptical of Father Zossima's motives. During Rakitin's rant, he predicts the murder of old Karamazov by Dmitri. Alyosha is a bit shocked. Rakitin hypothesizes that Ivan would like to marry Katerina for her dowry. Alyosha refuses to believe this. He says that Ivan is after "higher things … perhaps it's suffering and torment he's after." Rakitin does not like Ivan. The two see that the luncheon is breaking up, and they rush over excitedly to see what has transpired. Fyodor changed his mind and decided to go to the luncheon, a five-course feast. He decided, "since it was not in his power to regain their respect, why shouldn't he go on and disgrace himself altogether?" After telling distasteful stories and attacking the monks for taking advantage of believers, saying that they "suck the blood of the poor," Ivan puts him in a carriage. As they drive away, Fyodor yells at Alyosha to leave the monastery and move back in with Fyodor. As the father and son drive back, Fyodor promises Ivan a drink.

Analysis

The much-anticipated meeting is, in fact, extremely telling about the personalities of the Karamazov men. Fyodor's mischievous manner is very much in keeping with the stories about his past from the first book. It seems that he causes trouble arbitrarily, not because he is particularly angry or disgruntled but because he feels like causing trouble. He is not respectful of anyone or anything, and he is not afraid to embarrass himself or those around him. The accusation that Fyodor might be trying to bed the same girl whom Dmitri has been courting adds another dimension to their dispute. Fyodor and Dmitri are the two most undependable and explosive members of the Karamazov clan. Dmitri shows up late and quarrels with his father in front of a respected man. But he is also gracious, listening closely to Father Zossima's advice. Their dispute is not resolved, and they part on bad terms. It seems unlikely that, if a calm and reasonable man such as Father Zossima could not help resolve their dispute, they will not be able to do so independently.

Father Zossima acts as a foil to Fyodor, matching the elder Karamazov's vulgarity with quiet integrity, combating his acerbic remarks with patience and love. He is as much a father to Alyosha as Fyodor is, setting up an interesting duality for Alyosha's character. Alyosha seems to align his actions and ideas wholly with Father Zossima's, even though he is caring and understanding toward his biological father. Whereas Dmitri's character may be an amalgam of his parents' characters, bolstering the idea that one cannot escape his own genes, Alyosha is completely different from his father, affected more by his teachings than by his blood.

Both Father Zossima and Alyosha are very noticeably devoid of hatred and temper. Neither character is a simple embodiment of Dostoevsky's ideas; each is individually human. Father Zossima has a sense of humor; he jokes with Fyodor by telling him to try not to tell any lies while Zossima steps outside for a moment. Alyosha is also prone to emotions such as embarrassment and worry; he is not the picture of calm holiness. It remains to be seen if Alyosha's and Father Zossima's reason and love will triumph over the hot-bloodedness of Dmitri and Fyodor.

Madame Hohlakov and Lise are interesting additions to the mostly all-male cast thus far. Lise's girlish adoration for Alyosha reminds the reader how young Alyosha is, and it also brings up the possibility of a romance between the two. While making Alyosha seem more human, this budding romance could serve to compromise his pious status as a monk. Along with the other women who visit the monastery, Madame Hohlakov's adulation for the man borders on infatuation. While he remains humble, his fame precedes him and his followers worship him. It is unclear if these women actually feel legitimately helped by him or if they are simply gravitating toward an icon. Father Zossima's sensitive, loving manner puts to rest the fear that he may be a manipulative attention-seeker, but this does not mean his devotees come to him with wholly pure intentions. Father Zossima's status is fascinating. The fate of a man surrounded by such hysteria is uncertain.

Ivan remains an enigma. While the rest of the characters are caught up in an emotional dispute, Ivan remains aloof and distant, instead talking about larger issues. He is very quiet and difficult to read, but he is polite and agreeable for most of the interview. When Maximov tries to get in the coach as it is leaving, however, he violently pushes him off, showing a shockingly violent streak. He seems very dangerous. When Rakitin hypothesizes that Dmitri will kill Fyodor and Ivan will benefit, it seems plausible that Ivan could have a hidden agenda. Alyosha defends his brother, and Alyosha's honesty and thoughtfulness lead the reader to agree with him. The candid conjecture about murder is unsettling, as is Father Zossima's bow. Such a vague and grand gesture seems to portend something. The final impression of this book is a feeling of foreboding. From Ivan's covered smoldering to the impassioned feud between Fyodor and Dmitri, there are many clues that a great drama–perhaps a great tragedy–is to come.

Summary and Analysis of Book 3

Book Three begins with an introduction to Fyodor's servants, Grigory and Marfa. Grigory has been Fyodor's servant for years. He is "stubborn ... honest ... incorruptible." For instance, his loyalty to Fyodor is inextinguishable. When the serfs were emancipated in 1861, Grigory was free to do as he pleased. His wife Marfa asked to leave Fyodor, but Grigory would not hear of it. He decided that they would not leave old Karamazov. Years ago, Grigory and Marfa had a child. The poor boy had six fingers and died after only two weeks, devastating his parents. While Grigory was burying the child, he heard a baby crying. Puzzled and thinking he was hallucinating, Grigory followed the sound. He found a dying woman lying on the ground. Next to the woman he saw a baby boy. The woman was known as "Stinking Lizaveta," the town idiot. She was abnormally short, unable to speak, and the daughter of a violent, drunken man. Everyone liked her; she was like an orphan whom the town collectively cared for. The citizens in the town would give her food and clothes, and when they realized that she was pregnant, they were furious. Rumors flew that the only person depraved enough to take advantage of one so innocent and helpless was Fyodor Karamazov. After Grigory and Marfa found the baby, Lizaveta died. They adopted the little boy and Fyodor named it Smerdyakov, "the stinking one."

Alyosha leaves the monastery and is worried about his meeting with Katerina. Though he believes that she has noble intentions toward Dmitri, Alyosha cannot put his finger on the vague sense of dread he feels about the meeting. Coincidentally, Alyosha runs into Dmitri on the way to see Katerina, and Dmitri wants to talk. He has been drinking. He wants to tell Alyosha all his troubles and thinks that only Alyosha will understand. Dmitri proceeds to confess to Alyosha, intermittently quoting Schiller's *Hymn to Joy*. He tells Alyosha his history of seducing women, spending money with abandon, and generally acting with "insect sensualism." Then he tells Alyosha the story of how he met Katerina.

The daughter of a commanding officer of the camp, Katerina was a haughty and gorgeous girl who had always ignored Dmitri's advances. One day, Dmitri found out that the commanding officer had lent 4,500 rubles to a man who would not pay him back. Dmitri told Katerina's older sister that the military would come asking for the money, and if her father did not want to be court-martialed or jailed, he should send Katerina to visit Dmitri's room. Dmitri planned on having his way with the girl, but when Katerina visited him, Dmitri did not try to sleep with her or do anything wayward. Instead, he gave her the money with no strings attached. He found her "noble and generous" while he was just a "bedbug." He gave her the money with reverence, and she left without another word.

Later, Katerina's father dies. When she comes into a large inheritance from a relative, she visits Dmitri again, deeply grateful for his generosity toward her father. She offers him the money he had lent her father and offers him her hand in marriage.

He accepts. When Dmitri returns to Fyodor's town, however, he becomes obsessed with a girl named Grushenka. Katerina remains faithful to him even though she has heard rumors of his relationship with Grushenka. She gives him 3,000 rubles and asks him to give the money to her half-sister, but he spends it on a bacchanal with Grushenka instead. Dmitri's financial and moral indebtedness to Katerina makes him unable to bear Katerina's love, so he asks Alyosha to break off his engagement with Katerina. Then he tells Alyosha he wants him to go to Fyodor and ask for 3,000 rubles for him. He knows that Fyodor has an envelope with 3,000 rubles for Grushenka, but he feels that Fyodor is morally indebted to him for his ill treatment of Dmitri's mother. Dmitri wants to repay Katerina and never ask for money again.

We now meet Grigory's and Marfa's adopted son Smerdyakov. He has grown up to be an angry, epileptic cook of Fyodor, and he has a penchant for debate and intellectual discussion. He is talking to Fyodor and his foster father Grigory about his views about God. He says that it is hardly a sin to renounce God, for man can always repent and come back to God if he feels the urge. After he and Grigory leave, the Karamazovs continue to talk about their views of God. Ivan says that God does not exist—and neither does immortality. Alyosha disagrees.

Fyodor, who has been sitting through this lofty conversation for too long, decides to talk about "wenches." When his tirade turns on Alyosha's mother, however, Alyosha faints and has a seizure. Ivan is angry at his father for hurting his brother and verbally attacking his mother. Dmitri runs into the room at this instant looking for Grushenka, who is not to be found. When Fyodor begins chastising Dmitri for stealing money from him, Dmitri, already in a fit of rage, attacks the old man and kicks him in the temple. As he leaves, he threatens his father once more.

As Ivan and Alyosha are looking after their wounded father, Ivan's hostility toward his brother decreases. Alyosha visits Katerina, who thinks that Dmitri will get over Grushenka. To Alyosha's surprise, Grushenka comes out from behind a curtain; she has been there all along. Grushenka admits that she is going back to a former lover, and Katerina is ecstatic at the news. She compliments Grushenka profusely, but Grushenka does not return her affection. In fact, she says that she may not reunite with her old lover and may pursue Dmitri instead. Katerina becomes furious and screams at Grushenka as she leaves.

As Alyosha is returning from Katerina's, he receives a letter from Lise. He sees Dmitri again, and the two talk about Alyosha's visit with Katerina. Dmitri becomes sad about how cowardly he has been in his relationships toward the two women. Alyosha returns to the monastery to find that Father Zossima's health is declining, and that Zossima will not live for much longer. Alyosha resolves to stay by the side of the man who has acted more like a father to him than Fyodor has. He reads the letter from Lise, which says that she is in love with him and that she wants to marry him one day. She apologizes for her earlier jokes at his expense, and she asks him to visit her. Exhausted from his day, Alyosha falls into a deep sleep.

Analysis

Grigory and Marfa are less complex than the characters who have already been established. They do not have the verve of Dmitri or Fyodor, the high-minded intellectualism of Ivan, or the depth of purpose of Alyosha or Father Zossima. They lead simple lives with a singular purpose, staying faithful to their master. They are good, dependable people. They care for all of Fyodor's children, and when their desire for their own child is thwarted by fate, they are rewarded with Lizaveta's orphan. They both are very caring and compassionate.

Grigory acts as a third father figure in the novel. In addition to the biological paternity of Fyodor and the spiritual guidance of Father Zossima, Grigory acts as a father to the Karamazov boys and Smerdyakov in purely logistical ways. He spends time with them, feeds them, and cares for them. It is unclear whose method of paternity has the largest effect on a boy's growth, or if they all have an equal effect. Interestingly, Smerdyakov, the one boy Grigory and Marfa raise as their own, is resentful and bitter. Their compassion does not turn him into a loving person. Perhaps it is Fyodor's influence that makes him like he is.

Alyosha, on the other hand, seems unaffected by his biological lineage. This suggests that a person is responsible for his own personality. His reactions to the influences in his life depend on his own strengths, weaknesses, and proclivities.

This book also sheds more light on Dmitri's character. He is quite likeable despite his foibles, since he is clearly well-intentioned but deeply fallible. His actions with the captain and Katerina are very complicated. He shows a manipulative streak, uncovering a depravity that is similar to Fyodor's. Then he undergoes a complete change, acting nobly toward Katerina, feeling guilty about his former actions. But instead of learning from his mistakes, Dmitri does not continue to treat Katerina with respect. He spends her money and takes up with another woman after they get engaged. He becomes guilty about this, too, and feels that repaying Katerina is the only honorable course of action. Dmitri is perpetually caught between his desire to do good and his appetite for gratification. He seems unable to break the cycle of guilt and longing for redemption. He is too cowardly to ask his father for money again or to break off his engagement with Katerina in person. Nevertheless, he was re-promoted during his time in the army for "gallantry." Dmitri is full of contradictions. He embodies many of the arguments in the novel, showing how one man can contain multitudes.

Grushenka is very much what the reader expects her to be, capricious and mischievous. Katerina is less transparent. It is unclear if Katerina loves Dmitri or if she is obsessed by the idea of being a martyr. Dmitri has shunned her, but she remains faithful to him. She does not even expect his love in return, though. She feels relatively complacent about the idea that Dmitri may never return her love. Perhaps she relishes suffering.

Indeed, yearning for suffering is a motif in the novel. Dostoevsky himself wrote most of his important works after spending years of hard labor in Siberia. He felt that suffering changed him, and many of his characters are either changed by their suffering or desire suffering. The value of this suffering is not based on the justice done, however. Katerina does not want to suffer because she deserves retribution for some sin. Instead, she wants to suffer for suffering's sake. Katerina is not the only one who yearns for pain. Later in the novel, Dmitri and Lise express similar feelings. Aside from this, Katerina seems honorable. She has quite a temper, but she seems to be motivated mostly by love and the desire to do right.

Alyosha continues to get along well with his brother Dmitri, who clearly returns his affection. Alyosha has earned Dmitri's trust, and Alyosha does what he can to help him out. It seems that everyone needs Alyosha's help, and Alyosha is very willing to offer his services.

Ivan, however, has not warmed up to Alyosha yet. They represent two theological extremes. Simply put, Alyosha is a believer while Ivan is not. They very plainly disagree about faith, but not hostilely. They are civil as they discuss immortality and the existence of God. Since Alyosha has been proving time and again that he is thoughtful, helpful, and loving, Ivan is taking the position of a villain by disagreeing with his brother. The only way Ivan has revealed his character thus far, however, has been through his opinions about intellectual matters; his emotions and motivations are still veiled. It is curious that he is becoming a foil to Alyosha given that they both have the same mother. The only two characters who have the same parents have the widest disparity in their opinions about God.

Ivan does respect Alyosha, though at first he was suspicious that Alyosha's opinions were the opinions of a thoughtless religious fanatic. The brothers have learned to understand each other, and they all are starting to be able to tolerate each other. The same cannot be said for Fyodor's and Dmitri's relationship. As expected, the first conversation they had since the meeting with Father Zossima turned violent. Their situation has worsened, and a resolution for them is nowhere in sight.

Summary and Analysis of Book 4

Father Zossima is dying, and his devotees huddle around his bed. He tells them his theory of shared responsibility. A man is not responsible for his sins alone; he bears a portion of the burden for the sins of all other men. Alyosha is very upset at Father Zossima's condition, so he leaves. He knows that everyone expects a miracle when Zossima dies. Many think that Father Zossima is almost saint-like—except a few detractors such as Father Ferapont. Ferapont hates all the other elders, Father Zossima most of all. He advocates severe asceticism. He believes that the devil is at work in all things. Father Zossima asks to see Alyosha in his cell. He tells Alyosha that the boy's place is not in the monastery but alongside his brothers and father. They need his help more than the monastery does. When he goes back to town, Alyosha finds his father sitting by himself. Fyodor says he wants to live much longer. He says he needs money to make women sleep with him in his old age—thus he needs to be frugal in order to continue his lifestyle of debauchery. He vows that he will be a hedonist until he dies.

Alyosha leaves and sees some schoolboys throwing rocks at a delicate nine-year-old boy, who throws rocks back and then runs away. Alyosha runs after the boy, fascinated about what would make a nine-year-old so angry. He finds the young boy, but the youngster will not answer Alyosha's questions. He eventually picks up a rock and hits Alyosha with it, bites his hand, and then runs away, leaving Alyosha confused. Alyosha goes to visit Katerina again, but he is surprised to find Ivan upstairs with her. He asks Madame Hohlakov for something for his bitten hand, and Lise comes to talk to him. She wants her letter back, telling him she wrote it as a prank. Alyosha says he does not have the letter, so he cannot give it back. Then he talks to Ivan and Katerina. Katerina tells Alyosha she will never leave Dmitri even if he wants Grushenka or marries her. She does not mind if her love goes unrequited, even though she understands the craziness of such a gesture.

Alyosha cannot take this anymore, and he tells her that they clearly love each other and should follow their hearts, not their intellectualizations. Ivan says he loves Katerina but that she and Dmitri are more complementary. He is unhappy about this fact, but he is resigned to the fact that he will not be with the woman he loves. Ivan declares that he is leaving for Moscow, and he says his farewell. Katerina tells Alyosha about a certain Captain Snegiryov whom Dmitri has beaten. She feels very bad about this and takes pity on the man. She tells Alyosha that she wants to help him in some way and that she has two hundred rubles that she would like to give him as a token of her sympathy. She asks Alyosha to deliver this money to the man, and he accepts. Alyosha continues to be a messenger for others, proving his willingness to help, but acting without his own volition. He goes to visit the man, troubled about what has happened to him during the day.

Captain Snegiryov lives in an old, dilapidated house with his wife and two daughters—one of whom is handicapped—and his son. His son Ilusha is the boy who bit Alyosha's hand. Ilusha immediately assumes that Alyosha is there to bemoan his injured hand. Alyosha suddenly realizes that this boy felt such rage against him because he is Dmitri's brother. Captain Snegiryov goes outside with Alyosha and tells him that Dmitri traumatized his poor son by beating him badly. He makes clear that his family is excessively poor, and Alyosha becomes very excited that he can help. He tells Captain Snegiryov that he came to give him money. The captain is overjoyed at first, telling Alyosha all the ways he can help his family with the money. But he changes his mind and suddenly throws the money on the ground, explaining that he cannot dishonor himself by accepting money from the brother of a man who has humiliated him; this would destroy his son. Alyosha takes the money and goes back to Katerina.

Analysis

Alyosha encounters the two strongest father figures in his life at the beginning of this book. They both talk of old age, of dying, and of what Alyosha should do with himself. Father Zossima wants Alyosha to be with his family to help them through a difficult time, and Fyodor also wants Alyosha to leave the monastery and stay with him.

This may be the only area where the two men agree. Father Zossima knows he does not have long to live, and, according to rumors and hypotheses of men like Rakitin, Fyodor is about to be murdered.

The men have a parallel relationship regarding Alyosha, though they are quite different. Whereas Father Zossima is most concerned about his disciples and Alyosha as he nears his death, Fyodor talks mostly about himself. Zossima wants to make sure he has spread the word about living with love and understanding to as many people as he can before he passes; Fyodor is only concerned with sleeping with as many wenches as possible.

Alyosha does not try to change Fyodor; he simply listens to him. Alyosha is passive in the way he tries to help everyone around him. He does not change anyone's behavior. Instead, he does their bidding, usually giving others messages for them, and he listens. He is loving and understanding, but he does not change the course of what they are doing. Just as he wants to be by Father Zossima's side as he lays dying, Alyosha is there for his brothers and father, talking with them and aiding them when they need assistance. Alyosha provides comfort and support without actively protecting those around him. While this is a service that is much needed, it may not prove to be enough to keep his family from disasters ahead.

Alyosha encounters a boy, the first character who is of an even younger generation than the Karamazov brothers. The emphasis has been on the relationship between the older generation and the younger one, but this boy adds another generation to the mix. The boy has a strong sense of the connectedness of families. He feels responsible for his father's honor, and he believes that any relative of someone who has wronged someone should be treated with as much disdain as the person who has committed the offense. His father also makes a great financial sacrifice by not taking Katerina's money to gain his son's respect. This family sees little generational divide; the Snegiryovs see a family as one unit, and all its members are inextricable from each other. Alyosha treats Ilusha with interest and care, but the boy clearly does not appreciate the attention. Alyosha reaches out to him, and he does not try to punish the boy's violence; instead, he tries to understand his motives and feelings. Father Zossima tried to pass along salutary teachings to Alyosha, and now Alyosha is passing along those teachings to others, at least by example.

Katerina is proving to be a very active character who tries to make things right. After her father's death, she made sure to find Dmitri and repay him for his loan. She also repaid him for his kindness by offering herself to him. She felt as if Captain Snegiryov had been wronged, and her instinct was to compensate him in some way. She actively tries to see justice done. She is also very kind. Earlier in the novel, it seemed as if she might try to gain a sort of karma by her actions. Even though she knew Dmitri was in love with another woman and had disgraced her, she vowed to stay by his side. This seemed less of an expression of her love for him and more of a gesture showing her fidelity and steadfastness. She seems to relish the obvious disparity between her actions and Dmitri's. The worse he is, the better she seems to be. Katerina's motivations continue to be mysterious. She may long for humiliation, or she wants to prove to the world that she is upstanding and honorable—or perhaps she simply is very loving. She trusts Alyosha very much, and she entreats him to help her often. Alyosha believes that she has good intentions, so he is very willing to help her.

Captain Snegiryov is a living reminder of the damage that can be done from living a reckless, profligate life. Dmitri not only hurts his conscience if he sins; he hurts those around him. He also reminds the reader what abject poverty existed in Russia in the 19th century. The fact that 200 rubles is a large sum to him puts the 3,000 rubles Dmitri spent with Grushenka into new perspective. Dmitri is obsessed with money, and not having his 3,000-ruble inheritance drives him to rage and violence. Dmitri acts as though this money is essential to his life, but he is far from the poverty in which the captain and his family live. The quarrel over Dmitri's inheritance now seems like a battle characterized by greed and privilege. They are concerned with impressing women, and 3,000 rubles is an amount that will allow them to continue their courting. To a family like the Snegiryovs, however, 3,000 rubles would provide a great deal of food and medicine. They could repair their pathetic house and alleviate their misery. Captain Snegiryov refuses the money that could help his family because honor and dignity mean more to him than his or his family's material situation. These circumstances show that money remains of great importance in this novel.

Summary and Analysis of Book 5

When Alyosha returns to see Katerina, he finds that she has fallen ill. Alyosha explains to Lise what happened with the captain because Katerina is asleep. Lise is affected by Alyosha's loving compassion for the man, and she is moved to confess to Alyosha that the letter was not a joke and that she did mean what she said. Alyosha confesses that he has lied; he does have the letter, and he keeps it near to his heart because it is so meaningful to him. They realize that they care for each other, and they decide to get married.

Lise's mother has been listening to their conversation, and she tells Alyosha she does not approve of the marriage. She thinks Lise is too young. Alyosha tells her that the marriage is still a long way off, so she does not have to worry about Lise's age. Alyosha goes to find Dmitri. He decides that it is more important to help his brother than to hurry back to Father Zossima's side. Instead, he finds Smerdyakov, and he asks him if he has seen Dmitri. Smerdyakov tells Alyosha that Ivan is going to meet Dmitri at a restaurant, so Alyosha goes to meet his two brothers there.

He cannot find Dmitri—only Ivan is there. Ivan says he has grown to like and respect Alyosha. He tells Alyosha that he has a desire for living, but the world seems to be an unfair, ugly place. Alyosha is too preoccupied with the situation between his father and Dmitri, however, to focus on this conversation. He is worried that something dreadful might happen between the two of them if Ivan goes to Moscow. Ivan responds that it is not his responsibility to take care of his brother or his licentious father. He tells Alyosha that he hates even being around his father; this is why he came to the restaurant.

Ivan lays out his theological opinions for Alyosha. He says what he "[does] not accept and cannot accept is the God-created world." He believes that the mystery of God does not make sense to him; man should be able to comprehend God if he is God's own creation. Ivan ponders that this means he necessarily has to reject God. Alyosha wonders why Ivan cannot accept the world. Ivan adds that he has "never been able to understand how it is possible to love one's neighbors." He cannot stand the barbarism that seems to be inherent in man. He hates the suffering of children the most. He says that the only rationalization for the suffering of children is that they are "paying for the sins of their fathers who ate the apple." He cannot accept a God that allows this sort of injustice. He feels that loving God is like loving one who tortures you. Alyosha is appalled by all this, and he asks how Ivan can be so pessimistic about the world. Ivan responds that he is not being pessimistic; he simply does not think that anything is worth the suffering of an innocent like a child. He asks Alyosha if he would "torture just one single creature" if, by doing so, he could establish peace and tranquility for all mankind. Alyosha says he would not.

Ivan begins to recite to Alyosha a poem that he has composed, "The Grand Inquisitor":

In the sixteenth century, during the Inquisition, Christ returns to the world, healing and preaching in the streets. As he is healing some gatherers, a cardinal realizes who he is and has him arrested. In prison, Christ is visited by the Grand Inquisitor, who admonishes Christ for reappearing; he says that Christ's presence is interfering with the church. When Christ resisted temptations from Satan in the desert, he cursed man with liberty. Ever since, the church has had to work to reverse the damage. For instance, human nature dictates that man will not give up nourishment or safety for the promise of something as ill-defined as a heavenly reward. Thus, given a choice, man will always fail to follow a heavenly path. The Grand Inquisitor argues that "security" is preferable to "freedom." Also, if Christ had demonstrated his heavenly ability by performing a miracle instead of humbly resisting temptation, man would "have something to worship," which is "man's greatest need on Earth." The Grand Inquisitor also says that since Christ did not accept the power offered him by the devil, he forced the church to assert power over man. The church has finally gotten man to give up his Christ-given freedom in exchange for "happiness and security." The Grand Inquisitor says he realizes that this puts him on Satan's side of the argument, but he asserts that the precedent that Christ set when he resisted the temptations is very high. It is very difficult for man to achieve this level of strength, and only a few can do so. If only a few strong men can be saved anyway, at least the Grand Inquisitor's plan grants pleasure and satisfaction on Earth. Christ kisses the Inquisitor, never saying a word. Inexplicably, the Grand Inquisitor sets him free and tells him never to return. Ivan concludes his story and looks to Alyosha for his reaction. Alyosha only kisses his brother, and Ivan says, "That's plagiarism!" They conclude their meal happily and part ways.

Ivan is troubled after he leaves Alyosha. He starts to feel physically ill, but he does not understand why. When he sees Smerdyakov sitting outside, however, he realizes that this "miserable wretch" has been weighing on his mind. Instead of lashing out at him, he approaches him very amiably, and the two begin to talk. Smerdyakov says that he is worried by the love triangle consisting of Grushenka, Fyodor, and Dmitri. Both Dmitri and Fyodor are so worked up about the girl that they have both threatened Smerdyakov. He says that he might have an epileptic seizure because of the stress, hinting that he may even fake a seizure for his own safety. He then admits that he is burdened with the knowledge of what Grushenka's "signals" to old Karamazov will be when she visits him. He knows that if Grushenka goes to Fyodor, it will throw Dmitri into a rage, and he will come after his father. Smerdyakov fears that Fyodor will be helpless because Grigory and Marfa will not be able to protect him. They are both ill. In addition, Smerdyakov will not be able to help if he is incapacitated by a seizure.

This information is alarming to Ivan, and he is skeptical of Smerdyakov's intentions for telling him all of this. He asks Smerdyakov if he has intentionally created a situation where Dmitri will have free reign to murder his father. Ivan realizes that he cannot protect his father (he made clear earlier that he is not his father's keeper) since he is going to Moscow. Smerdyakov unsuccessfully pleads with Ivan not to go to Moscow, and they both retire. Ivan lies awake, distressed by his talk with

Smerdyakov. When morning comes, he meets with Fyodor, who also pleads with him to stay home with him. Ivan, worn down, decides to stay in town. He informs Smerdyakov that he will indeed stay at home. Later on, Smerdyakov in fact has a seizure and falls down the stairs. As Smerdyakov foresaw, Fyodor is left unprotected, waiting for Grushenka.

Analysis

Ivan reveals much more of his character in these chapters. For the first time, he talks about what he truly cares about, and though he is still speaking about sweeping issues, he is no longer detached and aloof. He is admitting his deepest concerns and principles. He longs for a world without cruelty, but he feels that most people are cruel. Children are the only ones who are innocent. Even though Ivan says he cannot love his neighbor, it is not because he hates people; he thinks people, on the whole, do not live up to their potential.

Ivan is not the cold-hearted intellectual he seemed at first. He is a frustrated idealist. He feels that he is not responsible for his father's safety or his brother's actions. Whereas Father Zossima thinks that every man shares part of the responsibility for the sins of all other men, Ivan feels independent of his fellow men. This is one of many ways that Ivan tries to assert his independence. Since he has been a child, he has felt embarrassed about his father, and he does not like to be associated with him. He did not like living off other people's charity, and he tried to become financially independent. Now, just because he is related to Dmitri and Fyodor, he does not feel compelled to help them as Alyosha does. He feels that he is responsible only for his own actions. His opinion will change after his father is murdered, when his realization of his complicity drives him insane. The lesson Ivan learns about responsibility serves as a sort of parable.

Ivan is uneasy about Smerdyakov, but he is not immediately sure why. The servant expresses concern for his own safety and that of his master. He tells Ivan all of the reasons why Fyodor will be vulnerable to an attacker, and the list sounds like too many coincidences to be true. When Smerdyakov explains to Ivan that it is possible to fake an epileptic seizure, his motives become slightly more suspicious. The idea that Smerdyakov can fake a seizure shows Ivan that Smerdyakov is not as helpless as he seems. Perhaps the pathetic servant is capable of manipulating a situation instead of simply commenting on it. He is not the harmless servant he first appeared to be. It also seems that Smerdyakov looks up to Ivan. Smerdyakov's motives are unclear, but his adulation of the Karamazov brother does not seem purely innocent. Smerdyakov's mix of weakness, bitterness, and manipulation is a disturbing combination.

The story of the Grand Inquisitor is an allegory for the difference between Ivan's and Alyosha's world views. Like Ivan, the Grand Inquisitor only wants peace and happiness for mankind. He disagrees with Christ, however, about how to achieve this goal. Even though Ivan and Alyosha disagree, they both want the same thing.

The most interesting thing about this chapter, however, is that Dostoevsky has included a parable in the middle of the novel. Why would he do this? What could Ivan's poem express that could not be expressed in the story? For one thing, the novel has a deep reverence for storytelling. The whole novel is told as a story recounted by an outside observer. Countless references are made to townspeople and citizens talking about each other, telling stories they have heard about one another. The trial is itself an excuse to tell the story of the Karamazovs in front of an audience. This poem adds another layer of mythology, theology, and philosophy to the novel. The parable deserves an essay in itself, and it will repay a close reading.

Ivan brings up an interesting point. He says to Alyosha that if children suffer, it is because they "are paying for the sins of their fathers who ate the apple." This is the first time a character in the novel has directly referred to the concept of the "sins of the father." Ivan does not believe that one should suffer for something someone else has done. He believes that a man should be accountable for his actions and his actions alone. He must acknowledge, however, that the world does not quite work this way. It seems as though people are unfairly punished for their predecessors' or others' mistakes. Sometimes, though, it may not be nature or God enacting an unjust penalty on the innocent. Perhaps the suffering one experiences is internal, self-generated. For instance, Ivan feels embarrassed about his own dependence on others, and he tries to stay independent of those around him. He is not being punished from above for Fyodor's neglect; he has made a decision based on his own feelings. He may have developed these feelings in part because of his father, but his desire for independence is his own.

Sometimes, then, one learns to be concerned about poignant issues from the concerns of his ancestors. Perhaps Dmitri does not feel doomed to become an amoral fiend because he is a Karamazov and cannot escape it; or perhaps he feels worried about becoming a bad person because he knows this stigma has plagued his father, and he has developed an irrational fear of this result himself. In any case, Fyodor's actions weigh heavy on each of his sons, and whether Heaven is exacting torture on them for his sins or whether they have individual battles to fight, they are all haunted by Fyodor's ghost.

Summary and Analysis of Book 6

Father Zossima is dying, yet he is still talking to those gathered around him. Alyosha comes back to the monastery after his other visits, and he goes to Father Zossima's side. Father Zossima is happy to see him, and he explains to Alyosha the meaning of his bow to Dmitri during their interview. He says that he bowed to Dmitri because he prophesied great misfortune for him, a fate he does not believe that Alyosha will share. He urges Alyosha to go back to his brothers and help them, for helping them with their difficulties will show Alyosha how to embrace all of humanity and show those in anguish how to appreciate life. Father Zossima then begins talking about his older brother. Father Zossima says that he looked up to his brother. He then tells Alyosha that he reminds him of his dear brother, which is part of the reason why Zossima has taken such a liking to Alyosha.

Father Zossima's brother, who was some eight years older than he, fell into the company of an intellectual with liberal ideas. He disagreed with his religious mother, and she became very saddened by his beliefs. One day, he fell ill with tuberculosis, and the doctors told him that he had only several months to live. He began acting very loving, and he handled his incapacitation very bravely. He became very interested in every living being around him. He talked incessantly about the need to love all of nature and humanity. He had a great effect on those around him in his last days, and his younger brother never forgot the lesson he learned from his teachings. Father Zossima calls his late brother "a message from above."

Father Zossima pauses to tell those around him how greatly the Bible has affected him. It captured his imagination as a young boy, and he never lost his fascination with it. He wishes that all men could find the meaning he found in the book as a boy. He says, "it is like a sculpted model of the world, of mankind, and of the characters of men; everything is there and it contains guidance for us for all ages. How many mysteries are solved in it, how many revealed!"

Father Zossima then talks about his wayward life as a young man. He says of his youth, "drunkenness, debauchery, and rowdyism were almost matters of pride." When he graduated from military school, he was a free spirit. He spent money "with the total recklessness and abandon of youth." He became quite enamored of a girl, but he did not ask to marry her because he was having too much fun as a bachelor. Then, after being gone for several months, he found out that the girl had married another man. Hot-blooded Zossima was incensed, losing "all sense of reality." He decided to challenge her new husband to a duel. The morning of the duel, however, Zossima was musing on his brother's last wishes. He realized that his hot-headedness was not consistent with the message of love his brother had advocated. He went to the duel anyway, revived by his new outlook on life. He let the other man shoot, bravely facing his opponent, looking at him "with love." The other man shot, but the bullet just nicked Zossima, who turned and tossed his pistol away before asking the man's forgiveness. After the duel, he decided to retire from military service and go to a monastery.

When he told his fellow officers about his resignation, they teased him, but they did not reproach him. In fact, they admired his bravery and liked his honesty. He talked about the duel with people from around the community, and he became quite famous for his duel. News about Zossima's actions reached many people, and one night Zossima received a visitor. The man was a famous philanthropist who was respected throughout the town. The man said he had heard Zossima's story and was rather impressed. He asked about what had prompted Zossima's change of heart, and Zossima told him about it, his decision to strike out in a new direction in life, and the exhilaration of that realization. The two continued talking, and they met and talked for nights on end. After many of these meetings, the man told Zossima that he had killed someone but another man had been blamed for the crime. Even though the man died before his trial, Zossima's visitor always felt the need to confess, despite becoming a good citizen and an essential member of his community. One day, overcome by guilt, he confessed to his crime in the open, but everyone chalked it up to temporary insanity. They could not believe that such a good man was capable of committing such a terrible act. Zossima's visitor became sick after his many talks with Zossima, arguably because he felt so guilty. Father Zossima visited him, and he never told anyone of the man's crimes. Before the man died, he told Father Zossima he was at peace with the world for the first time in years.

Zossima then tells Alyosha his theory about the importance of monks in Russia. He knows that often, monks are derided in society for being "shameless beggars living off other people's labor." Zossima feels that monks and the true Russian folks are the key to the salvation of the Russian people. The regular folks are ultimately the most important agents of change, but the monks lead them by example. He feels that the monk is actually very near to the common people, and he believes that all men should be equal; the hierarchy among masters and servants should not exist. If hierarchy between a master and a servant can be abolished, they can become true "brothers in spirit." Zossima goes on to tell all those around him that all men are intertwined, so man should love all those around him, and he should also feel that he is culpable for the sins of others. God is mysterious. Man should not judge his brethren; only God can judge. There is no Hell; there is only man's conscience to torment him. This is a "spiritual Hell." Suddenly, in the middle of his speech, Father Zossima lowers himself to the ground, spreads his arms, and embraces the Earth. In a state of "ecstasy," he dies. Those in the monastery quickly find out about his death. By morning, even the townspeople know. Father Zossima, the famous elder, is no longer.

Analysis

Father Zossima is the sole focus of Book Six. In very plain terms he tells those around him his beliefs and gives them spiritual advice. This section of the novel reads like a theological text or a piece of apologetics, and it is perhaps the most didactic installment of The Brothers Karamazov. In many novels, extracting characters' true beliefs from their words and actions can take a great deal of analysis and inference. In this novel, however, many characters speak their minds plainly and clearly. At one point in a discussion with Alyosha, Ivan explains that all "good Russians" are most concerned about their relationship to God and country. Why should a man shy away from these grand issues if they are so close to every Russian's heart? Zossima's words from his bed, for his part, are not simply his views. They are the views that he believes all men should share. He is not content to love humanity; he wants others to feel the same way about humanity that he does, for he believes it to be morally, psychologically, and spiritually healthy to do so. Father Zossima is the character whose words and deeds influence Alyosha, the hero of the novel, the most. Thus, his sage words are central to the theme of the book. It is almost as if Dostoevsky is speaking directly to the reader—not that this is Dostoevsky's final word on these matters, but it is a perspective he wants readers to take seriously.

A common trope in The Brothers Karamazov is that each character has a foil or doppelganger in some respect. Ivan's atheism is very much defined against Alyosha's piousness, Dmitri's sensualism is a reflection of his father's. In keeping with this pattern of doubling, Father Zossima tells Alyosha how much he reminds the old man of his late brother. Unlike the story about the Grand Inquisitor that Ivan told, the story of Zossima's brother is based on fact. Alyosha is very much like Zossima's brother, as he is like Christ in *The Grand Inquisitor*.

Alyosha is thus being established as the successor protagonist in a couple of dramatic religious traditions. He is likened both to Christ and the brother who Zossima saw as a role model. Alyosha is still a young man, but high expectations are set for him. Dostoevsky lends him storied weight by associating him with almost mythical characters. Zossima's brother, however, is not perfect like Christ, nor is he unwavering in his beliefs. In fact, he undergoes a complete change during Zossima's description of him, going from liberal intellectual to reverent mentor. This implies that Alyosha too has an internal conflict with which he struggles. Alyosha does not seem to have the wayward streak of Dmitri or the skepticism of his brother Ivan, however, so what is his struggle? It seems that Alyosha feels very concerned about his father and brothers, and he does not know how to help them most. He also wants to stay in the monastery with Father Zossima but knows he must go into the world. This is a key moral struggle for people of faith, who feel responsible both to the Church and to the world.

Alyosha is not the only character with an internal struggle. Father Zossima describes his younger days as an army officer. He was not always the paragon of love and understanding that he is now. He was a hot-headed profligate. The almost saintly Zossima now seems incapable of any feelings outside of love and charity. The idea that he once recklessly challenged a man to a duel may seem impossible, but this is the standard material of testimonial apologetics.

Until now, Alyosha and Zossima have seemed insufficiently three-dimensional. Knowing that they have struggles and weaknesses helps us see them as more human. Just because Father Zossima has gained a bit of humanity, however, his status as an acclaimed icon is not shaken. Zossima's spiritual conversion before the duel gained him fame, and people from all around heard about him. Even now, he is famous for his religious fervor. Fame does not require singularity of purpose and character; the more interesting protagonists overcome conflicts and serve as examples to others.

Conflict is not necessarily weakness in a world of uncertainty; it can lead to realization, understanding, and prudent action. Just because Dmitri is deeply conflicted, for instance, on that basis alone he is not necessarily worse morally than Alyosha and Zossima. Dmitri means well, at least, and he is struggling with conflicting impulses. He is capable of a deep understanding of the complexity of an issue, and this is why he tends to be ambivalent. Feeling conflicted is more honest than having a steadfast opinion and sticking to it uncritically. A strong, unwavering opinion can be stubbornness, yet for Alyosha and Zossima, it is integrity.

Summary and Analysis of Book 7

Father Zossima's body is prepared for burial. Alyosha is stricken with grief, and Father Paisii tries to comfort him. He assures Alyosha that Father Zossima is in Heaven and that this day is Zossima's most glorious day. Father Zossima is given a customary requiem service, and by dawn, people have come to see his body. They bring sick children with them because they are certain that great healing powers are being released upon his death. It is widely held that Father Zossima was a saint. People gather around the corpse, waiting for a miracle to happen.

Instead, his body begins to decompose, and those around fear that the decomposition belies a flaw in his holy constitution. This disproves the hypothesis that Father Zossima was a saint. Alyosha does not understand how such a holy man could be degraded in such a way. The monastery is polarized by differing opinions about the fate of Zossima's body. The camp against Zossima is headed by Father Ferapont, who rushes around trying to exorcise demons from Zossima's room. He ridicules the late Father for demanding that men "worship [him] like an idol." Father Paisii confronts him, angry that he is disrupting the peace. He asks Ferapont to leave, and Ferapont makes a dramatic exit, screaming, "this is an unholy, unholy place!"

Alyosha leaves. He does not understand why God has allowed Father Zossima to be shamed in this way. He meets Rakitin who, in his characteristic fashion, sneers at Alyosha's anguish and Father Zossima's humiliation. With a glint in his eye, Rakitin asks Alyosha if he wants some vodka or some sausage. Even though he should not accept them because it is Lent, Alyosha takes them. Aimless and broken down, Alyosha also accepts Rakitin's offer to visit Grushenka with him. Rakitin is taken aback at Alyosha's indifference and quick acceptance of the offers, but he is delighted at the idea of watching Alyosha compromise himself.

When they arrive at Grushenka's place, she is waiting for a message from a former lover who has returned for her. She is excited that Alyosha has come. She is ebullient and loud, but Alyosha believes she is actually happy to see him. Grushenka flirts with Alyosha and teases him, asking why he looks so glum. She sits on his lap, and he does not ask her to get up; in his state, he is "immune" to such attempts at seduction—but he is also "paralyzed" by his grief. When Grushenka learns that Alyosha is sad because Father Zossima has died, she feels remorseful for flirting with Alyosha and acting so disrespectful. Alyosha is grateful for her pity and her respect, and he thanks her for it, pleading with Rakitin to do the same instead of mocking him.

Overcome with self-reproach, Grushenka castigates herself for being an amoral wretch. She tells Alyosha she has not done any good deeds in her life, and she adds that she bribed Rakitin to bring him to her. She had the intention of "ruining" Alyosha. She had become fascinated with him because he seemed so pure, yet he never seemed to notice her. She then tells Alyosha about a young captain in the military who once seduced her and left her. Recently, this captain became a widower and sent for her again. She admits that she has been seeing Dmitri purely as a distraction from this man. She also asks if Alyosha can tell Katerina not to be angry with her. Rakitin occasionally interrupts her to say rude things to her. Alyosha finally yells back that Grushenka is a caring girl with a great capacity for forgiveness. He says her soul could "have treasure in it." She kneels at his feet, saying she feels that he has taken pity on her and forgiven her for her many sins, and she is thankful. They both burst into tears. Talking to someone so forthright and compassionate lifts Alyosha's spirits. Before he can respond, Grushenka receives the message for which she has been waiting. She is ambivalent about seeing the man who treated her so badly long ago; she fears for her dignity. Regardless, she decides to see the man, so she says her farewell. Rakitin is upset, and he cannot seem to get a rise out of Alyosha. He suddenly exclaims that Alyosha should not be angry because of the bribe Rakitin took, for, he says, "you are no Christ and I am no Judas." Alyosha stays fairly calm, but Rakitin storms off in frustration, clearly annoyed at the events of the night.

Alyosha goes back to pray in Father Zossima's old cell, feeling that his experience with Grushenka has corroborated the value of Zossima's teachings. He experiences fulfillment from responding to others with love and sympathy, and he feels that he can make a positive difference in their lives. Grushenka has revitalized him, has saved him from "walking toward [his] perdition." He did not expect to find such a noble and loving person; he thought he would find a "wicked soul." Realizing that even those who appear wicked can be loving, caring people gives Alyosha new strength. He overhears one of the monks recounting a verse from John about the wedding at Cana.

Exhausted from his day, Alyosha falls asleep. He dreams of being in the wedding at Cana, and Father Zossima is there. He tells Alyosha not to despair; even on this gloomy day, Alyosha has helped Grushenka find redemption. There is good that comes out of every situation, and Alyosha should be cheerful. Alyosha realizes that no miracle can be as important as the necessity of loving all of humanity. Alyosha wakes and leaves the monastery, refreshed and filled with hope.

Analysis

This section seems like a grand turning point in the novel. Father Zossima represents all that Alyosha loves and aspires to be. He has dedicated his life to following this man, but when Father Zossima's body decays, it feels as if Alyosha's adulation has been nullified. The man he has emulated and admired may not be a saint but just another person. If Alyosha has been wrong about Father Zossima's sainthood, his entire life's purpose is thrown into question. To this point, Alyosha has been the most steadfast, consistent character in the novel. He is calm and straightforward, helping those who need help and selflessly taking on responsibility. When Zossima dies, however, he seems a bit lost. Without the guiding hand of a mentor, Alyosha's stability is shaken. Without the assurance of his divine purpose, Alyosha's momentum is temporarily stalled, and he falters. He becomes quiet and sullen; he agrees to immoral behavior such as visiting a woman of questionable character, eating sausage, and drinking vodka. The hero of the novel seems to have lost hope.

At this point, the story could move in a new direction. Alyosha could withdraw, leaving all the characters to their own vices. Without Alyosha's helpful hand, these characters would hardly communicate peacefully with each other, tempers would not be calmed, and everything could fall apart.

But Alyosha finds faith again. He regains hope and embraces the world anew. His interaction with Grushenka reminds him that his spiritual strength comes from within, from his tradition, and from God, not merely from Father Zossima. This realization is a testament to Alyosha's strong character, and it becomes a saving grace for all the characters in the novel.

One could argue that things do not turn out so well for many of the characters in The Brothers Karamazov. Ivan has a nervous breakdown, Dmitri goes to jail, and Smerdyakov commits suicide. Alyosha's help does not significantly improve anyone's situation, it seems; he does not focus his effort on improving the material conditions of those around him. Instead, he focuses on showing everyone love, which does improve their situations. His continued love helps characters such as Dmitri and Grushenka find peace and direction, and though they have not avoided tragedy, their lives are more meaningful because of Alyosha.

Grushenka does undergo quite a change in this book. To this point, she has been something of a discursive presence. Fyodor and Dmitri are in love with her, and everyone seems to know gossip about her. The reader has met her once before in person, but this meeting is more telling of her character. Her coy, flirtatious side gives way to a more sensitive impulse toward Alyosha. Like Dmitri's, Grushenka's character is pulled in opposite directions by competing desires. She is sweet and good-natured, but she can be hot-tempered. She can be loving and cruel. Alyosha draws out the good in her, and she saves him, for all intents and purposes, from spiraling into despondency. Though she can seem manipulative and calculating, playing men off each other for fun, she is actually quite sad. She feels trapped by her situation and is considering turning to a man who left her years ago, humiliating her, because her will has grown weak from her life's strife. She has had a difficult life and does not hope to gain respect, only money and power over men. She tells Alyosha she thinks she is wicked. Her contrition reminds the reader of Dmitri's guilty confessions. Perhaps the two are a good match for each other, for both try to do good but are sometimes swayed from the righteous course by their impulsive natures.

Grushenka asked Alyosha to come to her because she wanted to "ruin" him. She desired to conquer a pious, good person. In reality, she ended up conquering him in a different way. She conquered his despair and gave him new life, simply by offering him sympathy and honesty. It is she, not Father Zossima, who confirmed Alyosha's desire to embrace humanity.

After years of being taught the importance of love and compassion, the first thing Zossima's gathered followers look for after Father Zossima's death is a miracle. Zossima taught practical love of one's fellow man, but once he passes away, the emphasis immediately shifts to mysticism. His sainthood is discussed in terms of how fast his body is decomposing. Sadly, his years of compassion and patience are not much discussed. Even Alyosha feels distraught. He knows that Father Zossima is a great man because of what he believes, but he yearns for some divine confirmation of Zossima's greatness. As practical-minded as Alyosha is, he is still a Christian who believes in a reality beyond the physical world.

The fact that Zossima's death is surrounded by so much superstition is not necessarily a sign that people do not understand his teachings (for even Alyosha, his greatest disciple, does not mind the talk of miracles and sainthood). Rather, it shows that the Russian people have a strong desire to experience something greater than their everyday experience of life. Theirs is a standard expression of a spiritualized hope among people living in strife. The church not only represents a way of living on earth but also offers an account of the afterlife, a second chance to be at peace, free from misery and the struggle for survival.

Some express this hope for a better life with piety. Others, like Ivan, wish merely for changes in this world. Ivan criticizes religious institutions, political institutions, and even human nature, but this is because he hopes for a better life, just as the most superstitious, God-fearing Russian peasant does. The difference is in what they ground their hopes on. Father Zossima was a physical embodiment of this hope, and the lack of a miracle following his death threatens that hope. Their spiritual beliefs are not challenged just because the physical world turned out to be different from what they expected, yet Ivan does not need to face such challenges. The craze after Zossima's death is less about religion that about desperate persons longing for something remarkable.

Summary and Analysis of Book 8

Dmitri is desperate. He is obsessed with Grushenka, and even though she "loved him for an hour," she often treated him "cruelly, and at times with complete ruthlessness." He does not know what she wants. He wants Grushenka to marry him, and he is optimistic that she will be his. He muses that Grushenka is probably deciding whether to be with him or with Fyodor; the thought that she might want to be with another man does not cross his mind. Still, he feels that it is necessary to reimburse Katerina before doing anything with Grushenka. He decides to sell some of Fyodor's land to a rich landowner named Samsanov for 3,000 rubles.

Samsanov does not want to receive Dmitri, but after Dmitri pleads with him, he agrees to meet him. Samsanov is hostile toward the desperate Karamazov, and he listens to Dmitri's offer with cold indifference. Samsanov is widely considered a "wreck"; he was once a suitor of Grushenka, but his relationship with her is now more of a relationship between a father and a daughter. Finally, Samsanov says he will help Dmitri, who is overjoyed to hear it. He tells Dmiti to visit a man known as "the Hound," who he says can help Dmitri.

Samsanov has no intention of helping this man whom he sees as competition for his former lover. Instead of helping him, he sends Dmitri on a wild goose chase to see a "cold, cruel, mocking man" named Lyavgeny. Samsanov says that the man is interested in the piece of land that Dmitri is offering, though he knows that the man will not be able to help Dmitri. Dmitri visits Lyavgeny, but he cannot do business with the man, for he is too drunk. Dmitri angrily tries to shake the man out of his drunken delirium, but it is no good. Dmitri is despondent and jealous, worried about Grushenka's fidelity and imagining "God knows what horrors about her deceiving him." Finally, Dmitri is forced to turn to Madame Hohlakov for the money. He realizes that if she will not give him the money, he may be forced to do something desperate. She plays with Dmitri, ironically telling him that she can offer him much more than 3,000 rubles. Then she tells him he should go to the gold mines. She tells him he should forget about women and come back only after many years. When Dmitri asks her again to lend him the money, she says she will not lend Dmitri a ruble.

Dmitri, now unsure of what to do, decides to visit Grushenka. When he cannot find her, he ascertains that she has gone to visit his father. He takes a brass pestle and goes to Fyodor's house in a rage. A servant who sees him leave exclaims, "My God! He'll end up murdering somebody!" Dmitri goes to his father's house, but he does not find Grushenka. Fyodor is there alone. Grigory awakes, remembering he has forgotten to lock a gate. He has heard from Smerdyakov that this is a very dangerous time for Fyodor, and when he sees Dmitri, he yells, "You father-killer!" Before he can pursue the intruder, though, Dmitri hits Grigory with the pestle. After seeing his body lying still on the ground, Dmitri tries to wipe the blood from Grigory's head. He is afraid he has killed the servant, but he realizes there is nothing he can do about it now, so he runs away. He goes back to Grushenka's house to question her servant about Grushenka's whereabouts, and he is horrified to learn of her rendezvous with her ex-lover.

Now hopeless, Dmitri reconciles himself to the fact that he cannot have Grushenka. He decides that she is his only reason to live, and he will commit suicide after seeing her one more time. Dmitri goes to reclaim his pistols from a man named Perhotin, who is holding them as collateral for a loan. Perhotin is suspicious of Dmitri, who is covered in blood, and he watches the man order a feast, planning to visit Grushenka.

Dmitri finds Grushenka with her gentleman friend and Kalganov. He walks up and says he would like to sit with them. He is very visibly upset, blabbering incoherently and excitedly. At one point, he even bursts into tears. Despite his agitated state, he surprisingly treats the whole party cordially. He is sitting and playing faro with them when the man begins to tell unsavory stories. He is Polish, and he insults Russia, much to Dmitri's annoyance. The men begin to quarrel. Dmitri takes him aside and offers him money if he will leave, but the man is offended and tells Grushenka of Dmitri's bribe. Grushenka is upset with the man for acting so callously, however, and everyone continues to quarrel. Dmitri cannot stand it when the man begins to mock Grushenka, who is greatly offended by his remarks. Dmitri locks the man in another room. Left alone, he and Grushenka begin to talk. Disillusioned by her former lover's bad behavior, she says she cannot love him. She realizes that she loves Dmitri. At first, he is extremely happy. However, Dmitri's elation is tempered by his difficult situation. In addition to his financial burdens, he thinks he may have killed Grigory, and as he is explaining to Grushenka his difficult situation with Katerina, there is a knock on the door. Policemen have come to arrest Dmitri for the murder of Fyodor.

Analysis

This section of the novel begins comically. Dmitri is on an odyssey to find 3,000 rubles to repay Katerina, but his potential donors are all humorously unhelpful. First, he goes to Samsanov, a man who hates him. Dmitri's earnestness and urgency contrasts greatly with Samsanov's aloofness. It is a triumph for Dmitri that the man will even meet him. He sends Dmitri to Lyavgeny, who he knows will be no help. Though Dmitri is desperate and Samsanov is depressed, the scene is not oppressively bleak. The reader is in fact excited to see what buffoonery will ensue. When Dmitri meets Lyavgeny, the man is drunk and surly, and Dmitri cannot talk sense to him. While Dmitri's situation is getting more dire, his interactions only become more ridiculous. When he decides that Lyavgeny is worthless to him, he visits Madame Hohlakov, who is a quirky character. She cheerily greets Dmitri, and she leads him to believe that she will solve his problems once and for all. Notwithstanding that, her solution is for Dmitri to dig for gold. His exacerbation is tangible, and her delicate nature is offended by his gruff anger. He leaves in a huff, at a loss for a way to win the money for Katerina. This string of comic interactions between Dmitri and his possible benefactors is a reprieve from the mounting ominous tenor of the novel.

Humor exists even in the most heavy situations, and Dmitri's ineptness is revealed. He cannot solve his problems, and his attempts at ingratiating himself among his rich acquaintances make him seem pathetic.

The humor of this section soon turns grave, however, when Dmitri frantically goes to find Grushenka. Dmitri goes to his father's house looking for Grushenka, practically mad with lust and desperation. He almost escapes without any misfortune befalling him or anyone around him, but trustworthy Grigory wakes up and assumes Dmitri has come to murder his father. With one swift blow, Dmitri dramatically changes the timbre of the novel. Dmitri hits Grigory with the pestle he has in his hand, and Grigory falls to the ground, motionless. The humorous interlude is over, and violence is no longer theoretical.

It is ironic that Grigory tries to stop Dmitri when Dmitri had no intention of harming his father that night. The irony is complicated, however, by the fact that Dmitri is entirely capable of murdering his father. In fact, when he goes to his father's house, it is not unlikely that he will kill him. Not until he decides to leave peacefully does Grigory try to stop him, and Grigory's suspicion of Dmitri's violent tendencies turns out to be a self-fulfilling prophecy. When the police blame Dmitri for Fyodor's murder, the reader knows that Dmitri did not commit the crime. It is difficult to feel indignant on his behalf, though, because it seems that Dmitri could have committed the murder. He is impulsive and angry, and he has even said he will murder his father. When Dmitri strikes Grigory, it becomes explicit that he is dangerous enough to kill anyone in his path, including his father, whom he loathes.

This is a turning point in the novel. The general sense of foreboding has led to this night. Dmitri has proven that violence is indeed in the future for the Karamazovs, and his attack on Grigory is not the only violence that is to come.

When Dmitri finds Grushenka in the company of other men, the ensuing spectacle is reminiscent of his humorous pursuit of the money. He is desperate and pathetic, and the people with whom he is talking are annoyed by his presence. The tenor of this meeting is graver than that of his previous meetings, however. This time, Dmitri has vowed to commit suicide after the meeting has concluded. His desperation is no longer funny. Earlier, Ivan commented that one thing all the Karmazovs share is a "desire for life." Dmitri's desire to commit suicide therefore comes as a surprise. It seems to compromise a fundamental tenet of his character. Is Dmitri's earlier lust for life inconsistent with this new desire to kill himself?

Perhaps it is not lust for life that drives him. Maybe, like the superstitious Russian folk longing for a miracle, Dmitri has a longing for something remarkable in life. His orgies and affairs are his way of trying to break from his quotidian life. If he cannot have the romantic adventure he desires with Grushenka, suicide is another way to free himself from a menial existence. He does not have a desire for mere survival; he has a desire for an extraordinary life.

Since the beginning of the novel, the subject of Fyodor's murder has been looming over every character. Finally, after much speculation and foreshadowing, he is killed. This is the central event of the novel, and, as everything to this point has led up to it, everything in the coming chapters is tied to it. Surprisingly, Dmitri is not his father's killer. While Fyodor's murder is the expected outcome after so much suspense, the killer's identity is completely unexpected. During the preceding chapters, it was assumed that Fyodor's murder was inevitable and Dmitri would be the killer. When Dmitri reconciled with Grushenka and avoided killing his father when he went to his house, it seemed that the impending disaster had been averted. Somehow the murder that was entirely expected came as a surprise.

The one event that was expected from the beginning of the novel has become the novel's biggest twist. The structure of the novel sets up the plot in such a way as to suggest that fate is unavoidable, and no matter how characters change, their destiny is set. (Of course, the novelist does control the fate of the characters.) The strangest part about this fact is that, even though Dmitri did not commit the murder, he is still the one to blame. He is held responsible for a crime he seemed destined to commit even though he did not actually commit it. Father Zossima said that a man shares the responsibility for the sins of all other men. Perhaps guilt does not lie only with the criminal who committed a crime, and all those who are involved share in the guilt of the crime, as Zossima suggested. Perhaps Dmitri is not completely innocent of the murder after all.

Summary and Analysis of Book 9

Perhotin is determined to find out what Dmitri was doing when the two men saw each other. Agitated and restless, he retraces Dmitri's steps the night of the murder, gathering bits of information from everyone he meets. He talks to Fenya, who tells him Dmitri grabbed a pestle when he ran off to see Grushenka. When he returned, he did not have the pestle and his hands were "dripping, dripping, dripping" with blood. Perhotin thinks of visiting the Karamazov household directly, but he does not want to cause a scandal if nothing wayward has actually transpired. He decides to do more detective work before resorting to a visit to the curmudgeonly Fyodor Karamazov.

Perhotin visits Madame Hohlakov instead. He shows up late at night and, after such a disturbing earlier meeting with Dmitri, she has a migraine and is very perturbed. He asks her if she lent Dmitri 3,000 rubles. When she admits that she did not, the two surmise that he must have robbed someone, and they fear it is Fyodor Karamazov. Since he has found such incriminating information, he decides to report it to the authorities. But when he arrives at the police inspector's house, the place is in an uproar because Fyodor Karamazov has been murdered and robbed.

In the servant's quarters in Fyodor Karamazov's house, Marfa wakes up to hear Smerdyakov screaming, which always signifies one of his epileptic fits. She cannot find Grigory to come to help their adopted boy, and she begins to worry. She hears groans coming from the garden, and she remembers the night they found Smerdyakov with his dying mother. She finds Grigory covered in blood, muttering, "He's killed his father." Indeed, when she looks in on Fyodor, she sees that he is on his back, covered in blood. Confused and hysterical, she runs to their neighbor's house.

After the neighbors hear all the facts, they go to the police inspector's house to explain what has happened at the Karamazov house. Fyodor's skull has been crushed, and the envelope that he kept clearly marked for Grushenka has been torn open and emptied. Perhotin tells the police inspector that Dmitri declared that he would shoot himself. While Perhotin is worried about Dmitri and wants to find him before he commits suicide, the police inspector is assured that Dmitri is a prime suspect—he says, "that's exactly the way a desperate man of that type thinks: 'I'll kill myself tomorrow, but before I die I'll have a wild time.'" The district medical officer who goes to the Karamazov household to examine the corpse takes a particular in Smerdyakov. He notes that the length and persistence of Smerdyakov's seizures are unusual, and he specifically predicts that Smerdyakov will die by morning.

The police arrest Dmitri, who is flabbergasted by the charges. He says he "thought of killing him, but [he] didn't do it." Grushenka swears she will stay by Dmitri's side, but this does not help his situation; she assumes he has killed Fyodor, and she lovingly says she is to blame for pushing him to do it. Her good intentions backfire when she says she will "follow him to the gallows." No one, not even his beloved Grushenka, believes he is innocent. From his presence at the scene of the crime on the night of the murder to his animosity toward Fyodor to his admission that he needed 3,000 rubles—the exact amount Fyodor has set aside for Grushenka—the facts are stacked against him. He thinks he has killed Grigory, and when they tell him Grigory has recovered, he is overjoyed. His conscience is clear, and he tells the prosecutors this news has "made a new man" of him. He tells them to write down that he is "guilty of disorderly conduct, guilty of violently attacking and hurting a poor old man," but that the idea of his murdering his father is "absurd, completely absurd!" He goes on to say that he understands why he is suspected of this crime. He acknowledges that he has threatened his father, attacked his father, and promised to kill his father in front of many witnesses. He laughs, "I cannot imagine who but me could have killed him!" When they ask who else knew the secret signals that Grushenka and Fyodor had agreed upon, he names Smerdyakov. Ironically, though, Dmitri says he does not think Smerdyakov is capable of such a crime.

When he is searched, the police find 1,500 rubles on him, and he must admit the embarrassing truth that he has used only half the money Katerina loaned him on his fling with Grushenka. He saved the rest. Dmitri thinks that since he did not commit the crime, anything he says cannot hurt him. This openness has led him to admit very incriminating facts, but now that the police have found 1,500 rubles on his person, his honesty is now in question. Dmitri stated many times that he spent 3,000 rubles on the fling with Grushenka because he would not tell anyone this deeply shameful fact about himself.

After all the witnesses are interviewed, Dmitri is detained. His lawyers promise that they will work hard to acquit him of the murder. They tell him they believe that he is a good man and a "victim of unhappy circumstances." Dmitri gives a heartfelt farewell to Grushenka, who says she will remain by his side forever. In despair, Dmitri is carted off as many onlookers watch the murder suspect get taken away.

Analysis

This book focuses on the story of the Karamazovs from an outside perspective—the experiences of Perhotin, Madame Hohlakov, Marfa, police officers, and townspeople. Instead of presenting the Karamazov family firsthand, these chapters add a degree of remove. This slight distance makes the reader realize how guilty Dmitri seems to an observer with only limited information. Suddenly, the case of Fyodor's murder has catapulted from a private matter into a public one. This section of the novel illuminates how the drama reaches beyond the boundaries of the Karamazov family. Not only is the Karamazovs' story known to the other members of the community, but it affects them. Perhotin is suspicious and troubled by Dmitri's desperation. He does not want a comrade to commit suicide, and he investigates Dmitri's actions because he is worried about Dmitri. Marfa, Grigory's wife, awakes to find her husband unconscious and her master slain. Grigory incoherently mutters something about how "he has killed his father." The police question Dmitri (Dmitri is so forthright that he admits to wanting to kill his father), and everyone sees that the evidence is stacked against him. The Karamazovs are not an insular group; the entire town knows them, and the murder is quite a phenomenon. For the first time, the petty infighting of the Karamazov clan feels larger than a dispute between family members. The brothers have become quite a spectacle. This circumstance strengthens the notion of myth in the novel, and it makes the tragedy seem much more meaningful—after all, we readers are also on the outside, following the family's moves.

Dmitri, curiously, has found love and direction in his life. He feels like a new man, and his feeling of invincibility may be what makes him speak so honestly with the police. When the police knock on the door to arrest Dmitri, his fortune has changed. Up to this point in the novel, Dmitri has had a strong motive to kill his father. After winning the affections of Grushenka, however, he has little reason left to murder his competition. This night, the night when Dmitri solves his romantic problem, thereby alleviating his desire for murder, is also the night when he acts the most erratically and desperately. It is a cruel trick of fate that this is this night when Fyodor is murdered. Even though Dmitri ends the night a changed man, his dramatic actions—leading to his epiphany—damn him in the eyes of the world. His newfound strength of spirit remains undaunted, though. He has remarkable faith in justice and the legal system. He is honest and open and, knowing that he is innocent, feels entirely confident that he will be acquitted. He has the utmost faith that the truth of his heart will be apparent to everyone.

Notwithstanding that faith, everyone pays less attention to Dmitri's soul and more attention to the facts at hand, most of which point to Dmitri's guilt. Dmitri's fickle nature means that he can abruptly turn from a murderer into a harmless lover. The law, however, seeks a consistent story. Dmitri's longstanding hatred for his father is more consistent than his sudden change of heart, and therefore it is a more salient indicator of his personality to others. People cannot easily know another's heart. Often they know little more than what they see, which can be a better indicator of a man's prejudices and preconceived notions than the things he says.

Strangely, the idea of sympathy for Fyodor never seriously comes up. No character expresses much sadness at his demise, nor does anyone say that the old man was misunderstood. His sons are not even very surprised, for they have expected this murder to some degree for the entire novel. In a book about morality and religion, one would expect that murder of a man would be treated a bit more humanely, but the clear lack of humane sentiments at this point illustrates the family's sense of the perverse justice of the murder—somehow Fyodor was not innocent enough to escape what was coming to him. Dostoevsky even writes at the beginning of the novel that no one could feel bad for such a wretched creature, but can we really accept such a cold and harsh indictment?

The unassailable importance of human life is given more weight in other areas. Ivan talks about the desire to live and the tragedy of making an innocent suffer. He does not seem to feel remorse for his father, however. He only feels the burden of responsibility for a terrible crime. Not even Alyosha misses his father. He loved Fyodor while he was alive as Alyosha loves all creatures, but he feels no lasting connection to Fyodor aside from familial ties. Dostoevsky's characters treat the character of Fyodor as practically inhuman; the only problem lies with the legal and spiritual effects of committing the mortal sin of murder.

Perhaps Dostoevsky hated his own father enough to leave Fyodor as a character who seems almost to deserve this treatment upon his death, so different from that of Father Zossima. Fyodor is presented mainly as a cancer to those around him, making life worse for them without contributing in any good way. This vice is at odds with the loving religious sentiments of the rest of the novel. Perhaps Dostoevsky intends such a contrast with his more powerful theme of love and understanding.

Ivan and Dmitri have no desire to see their father alive. In fact, it seems probable that both brothers want to see him killed. Smerdyakov, in hindsight, also obviously wants Fyodor dead. In the end, Ivan is driven crazy by his own guilt, Dmitri is convicted of the murder—his life ruined—and Smerdyakov commits suicide, presumably because of his own feelings of guilt. These three, who seem pleased to see Fyodor killed, are the ones who suffer most after his death. If this is poetic justice, Dostoevsky is condemning their lack of sympathy. If Dostoevsky is in some way using this theme in relation to his own feelings about his own father, we might read these developments as his way of faulting those who do not adequately respect or like their fathers. As in Crime and Punishment, the motives and effects of the murder are very complex, involving themes of nihilism, utility, and Christianity.

If one feels both love and disgust for one's fellow humans, some murders might seem more justifiable than others. In Crime and Punishment, Raskolnikov feels guilty for killing a fairly innocent witness, but he never expresses guilt for killing the old woman, against whom he develops several reasons for the murder. In the present novel, would murdering Father Zossima have carried the same moral weight as the murder of Fyodor? The characters generally feel less upset over the murder of Fyodor, insofar as Fyodor has died, than over the natural death of Father Zossima. Feeling guilty over a death or a murder is not the same as feeling sympathetic.

Summary and Analysis of Book 10

Kolya Krassotkin is Ilusha's friend. He is a young, headstrong boy who gets teased at school for being a "mummy's boy" because his mother helps him with all his schoolwork and introduces herself to all his friends and teachers. But Kolya is unafraid of being bullied, and he is known for being "terribly strong." Instead of playing with his fellow schoolchildren, he is fond of reading. His mother sometimes accuses him of being very cold toward her because he detests "that sickening slobbery stuff." He loves his mother very much, though. He also has a mischievous streak, pushing his mother and his superiors at school—but he usually stops before he incurs any real punishment. One day, he decides to lie down as an oncoming train approaches in order to prove his bravery and daring to the other boys. This earns him their respect, and they begin to call him a "desperado." This stunt upsets his mother greatly. She pleads with him never to do such a thing again, and they both become overcome with emotion. After this episode, Kolya returns to being sullen and aloof with his mother. One day, Ilusha stabs Kolya with a pen knife because Kolya is teasing him, and their friendship becomes strained.

Ilusha falls ill with consumption. The day before Dmitri's trial, Kolya goes to visit him in the hospital. He sees a friend named Smurov, and the two talk about Ilusha's condition. Smurov tells Kolya that his classmates have been visiting Ilusha in the hospital every day and that it seems as if Ilusha will not live much longer. He says that Alyosha has been spending time at the hospital even though his brother is going to trial. Smurov says that he wishes that Kolya's dog Perezvon was another dog named Zhuchka. This would make Ilusha happy. Kolya shows off his intellect: he begins to criticize doctors, he says there is more stupidity among men than among dogs, and he comments on man's tendency to form habits. He tells Smurov, "one has to know how to talk to the uneducated." The boys walk toward the hospital, causing mischief with the townspeople along the way. When they reach the hospital, Kolya says he would like to wait outside to meet Alyosha. Smurov thinks this is a silly idea; he tells Kolya he should simply come in and meet Alyosha inside. Kolya tells Smurov he has his own reasons for meeting Alyosha in the bitter cold; he smirks, "we must sniff at each other first." Smurov goes inside, and Kolya waits outside for Alyosha.

This is Kolya's first visit to the hospital, though other boys have been visiting Kolya ever since Alyosha urged them to do so. Outside the hospital, Kolya feels nervous about meeting Alyosha. He has heard much about this remarkable man, and he wants to make a good impression on him as an intelligent, independent young man. When Alyosha comes out to meet the boy, he is smiling profusely. Kolya is put off by Alyosha's good-natured disposition, but he continues talking with him openly. Kolya tells Alyosha about his relationship with Ilusha, saying that he and Ilusha have been good friends for some time. Kolya felt bad for Ilusha, and he protected him from the boys who would beat him up. One day, in a fit of mischievous childishness, Ilusha fed a dog a piece of bread with a pin in it. Smerdyakov had taught him how to do this, but when he saw the dog yelping and running around, he regretted the prank immediately. He told Kolya what had happened, and Kolya saw that he felt contrite. Even so, Kolya punished Ilusha by ignoring him. Ilusha became very angry at Kolya over this, and he sent a message to Kolya saying he would feed pins to all the dogs in town. Then, when the boys at school were taunting Ilusha, Kolya did not step in to protect his estranged friend. Ilusha became incensed and rushed at Kolya, which is when he stabbed his Kolya with his pen knife. Their relationship remained strained, which is why the two boys did not see each other until this day.

Alyosha and Kolya visit Ilusha, and Kolya brings his dog Perezvon. Then, he reveals that his dog is indeed Zhuchka, the very dog that Ilusha fed the pin. He has been training the dog, and he did not want to visit Ilusha until the dog was fully trained. This peace offering makes Ilusha very happy, and the boys' friendship is restored, though in unhappy and dire circumstances. Kolya then produces a small cannon, which he gives to Ilusha as a present. Ilusha's demented mother demands the present for herself, and the boys concede that she may have it.

Kolya and Alyosha step outside when the doctors come to see Ilusha, and Kolya tells Alyosha his theories about life. He loves man but does not want to "coddle" him. He very much hates all forms of sentimentality. He says he is a socialist, and he quotes from many texts he has read. Instead of being impressed, Alyosha tells him he is surprised that a boy so young could already be swayed by such "wicked nonsense." They discuss matters of the mind and of the heart for a while longer and, since Alyosha treats the boy as an intellectual equal, they become good friends. The doctors come back, and all who see them know that Ilusha is doomed, including Ilusha himself. While Ilusha is talking to his father, Kolya is touched, and he tells Alyosha that he will visit Ilusha more often.

Analysis

This book focuses on a younger generation. In addition to Ilusha, whom Alyosha met earlier, there is Kolya, a willful and precocious classmate of Ilusha. They are the youngest characters in the novel, and this is the first book devoted mostly to them. After the murder–the most important event in the novel–the focus shifts to a new storyline. This acts as a breath of relief from the heaviness of the murder trial, though this is by no means a section with a great deal of levity, for young Ilusha is dying.

His death will be a parallel to Father Zossima's death. As Zossima slowly passes away in his deathbed, he is surrounded by his followers. Fyodor's death is another thing altogether. Ilusha is also surrounded by his friends and family in his last days, and his bravery is inspiring to them all. Father Zossima was an old man when he died, but Ilusha is quite young to be on his deathbed. The suffering of such a young boy reminds the reader of Ivan's outrage at the suffering of innocents.

The juxtaposition of this section with the one focusing on Dmitri's unfortunate arrest calls into question Dmitri's guilt. If an innocent child like Ilusha can suffer without reason, then suffering is not necessarily related to justice. Perhaps Dmitri is not being punished for some share of his guilt for the murder; sometimes people suffer without a discernible reason. This is one way to understand the juxtaposition of these books.

Another route to pursue is to wonder if Ilusha is not innocent after all. He has become tough and defensive from the strife he has encountered in his life, and he has tortured a dog. But unlike Fyodor, who is never good or thoughtful to anyone, Ilusha has a good heart and feels remorse. He even comforts his father, putting his own suffering below his father's peace of mind. Ilusha does seem to be innocent in that he is good at heart, even if he has made mistakes. In this way he is similar to Dmitri. Both characters suffer, but neither one has committed a crime worthy of the suffering. It seems that fate is indiscriminate; that is, there is no guarantee that virtue leads to happiness or that vice leads to suffering.

The Karamazovs do not seem to be able to extricate themselves from their past. For Fyodor there is no redemption. He dies, never changing his ways or apologizing for his sins. His sons cannot escape the specter of tragedy either. Ivan is the best example of this phenomenon. Despite hating his father, he tries not to quarrel with him. He leaves the house so as not to be around him, and he tries to leave town to extricate himself from his own family drama. But despite his best efforts, he finds himself mired in guilt over the very tragedy he tried to avoid. Even Alyosha finds himself with his brothers, dealing with the fallout from the murder. Redemption is hard to find, and even if it is difficult for the Karamazov brothers to attain, perhaps a younger generation can find it. Kolya is healthy; he has his entire life in front of him. Alyosha gives him so much attention because Kolya represents hope. While one generation can feel the weight of sin and guilt from a previous generation, it also can break free from this cycle of suffering. While the Karamazov brothers are already caught up in their own family tragedy, finding it difficult to rid themselves of their father's shadow, Kolya has a chance at living a life free from this burden.

This opportunity creates the feeling that life is more than a person or a family. Life encompasses generation after generation. Alyosha cannot help every single person in the world. He focuses on a younger generation, as many teachers do, because he realizes that they are Russia's hope. Though he did not save his father, he can save Russia, or at least he can do something toward that goal.

Just as Father Zossima was a teacher and something of a celebrity to Alyosha, Alyosha is an idol to the young boys of the town. They revere him and listen to his every word. Kolya is scared to meet him, and he tries his hardest to impress this wise and important man about which he has heard so much. Alyosha has become an important figure in the lives of the younger generation, and he became close with this generation by choosing to teach rather than spend all of his time with his brothers.

Father Zossima told Alyosha to stay with his brothers during their time of need, but Alyosha expanded this request. Father Zossima meant that Alyosha should spend his time where it is most needed, not where Alyosha has the most attachment. Thus, as

Alyosha chose to help his brothers instead of staying with Father Zossima during his last days, Alyosha now decides that his calling lies with the boys of the town who are the future of Russia, not his literal brothers. This is a large shift for Alyosha, for his family is very important to him. Perhaps he has taken Father Zossima's words to heart, separating his heart from his choices. It is difficult to follow one's heart to help others while denying one's heart in other ways in order to ensure that one is not swayed from helping those most in need.

Ilusha and Kolya are an interesting pair. Both boys have a defiant streak, and both are very complicated persons. Each has committed an act that weighs on him. Ilusha fed a dog a pin and still feels guilty. Kolya does not protect his weaker friend when the other boys jeer at him, mostly because he is trying to teach Ilusha a lesson for his treatment of the dog. Ilusha confesses his guilt to Kolya, being honest about what he has done but expressing regret for his actions. Kolya, on the other hand, does not directly tell Alyosha how guilty he feels for letting Ilusha get attacked by the other schoolboys. Still, he is very transparent, and his fixation on the topic belies his preoccupation with it. Kolya has a strong connection to Ilusha, however, and despite their violent dispute, Kolya spends hours training the recovered dog and brings him to Ilusha as a present. Kolya still feels protective of Ilusha, and Ilusha still feels close to Kolya, despite his fierce individualism.

Both boys seem equally prone to spite and love. Alyosha tips the scales on this count; he encourages the boys to love one another and do good for one another, setting an example by visiting the dying boy even though his own brother is being tried for murder. The boys are connected because they share a similar struggle between good and evil. If Alyosha did not come along, these conflicted boys could very well have been swayed negatively by others.

Alyosha's choices in a fallen world lead him to triage, that is, those who can survive without help are left alone while those who cannot be helped are also, sadly, left alone, leaving time to help those for whom help can make a difference. Although in Alyosha's Christian tradition every person deserves help, Alyosha has limited time and must act like a surgeon, spending his time on those whom he can save, not on those who are already doomed.

Summary and Analysis of Book 11

A couple of months after Dmitri's arrest, Grushenka is undergoing a heavenly metamorphosis. She tells Alyosha that Dmitri is becoming smitten with Katerina again. She also thinks that Ivan and Dmitri have been talking. She thinks the two brothers are making a plan that they are keeping secret from her. She asks if Alyosha can find out what this secret plan is, and Alyosha, her friend, agrees.

Alyosha visits Lise, who is agitated and feeling guilty about her life. She longs to experience God's retribution for her wickedness in life. She has no respect for her fellow human beings or the world around her, and she feels a very destructive impulse toward everyone and everything. As Alyosha leaves, she slams the door on her hand in a pathetic show of self-loathing.

Alyosha visits Dmitri in prison. Dmitri tells Alyosha that Rakitin wants to write an exposé about Dmitri being the victim of circumstances that led to the inevitable murder of his father. Even though Dmitri did not kill his father, he feels guilty for his reckless lifestyle and, much like Lise, feels a desire to be punished for his immorality. He believes that he will have a new lease on life if only Grushenka can come with him during his exile in Siberia. But he fears that the state will not let Grushenka follow him, and without her, he does not know what he will do.

Dmitri tells Alyosha that Ivan has visited him and told him a plan he has made for Dmitri's escape. This is the secret that Grushenka suspected. Dmitri asks Alyosha if he thinks Dmitri is guilty, and Alyosha replies that he has always believed in his brother's innocence. Dmitri greatly appreciates his brother's support.

Alyosha next visits Katerina, who has just been visited by Ivan. Katerina tells Alyosha she fears that Ivan is going crazy. He feels responsible for his father's death, and it is tormenting him. Alyosha catches up with Ivan to talk to him. He asks his brother what is troubling him, and Ivan tells Alyosha that Katerina has evidence that damns Dmitri. Alyosha wants to reassure his brother, but he is honest to a fault. Since he is convinced of Dmitri's innocence, he cannot believe that Katerina can have any evidence that proves an innocent man to be guilty. Alyosha also realizes that Ivan feels guilty for their father's death. He tells Ivan that God has given him the task of comforting him. He tells Ivan that he is not responsible for the murder–he is certain by divine knowledge. Ivan does not think that this comfort is founded in logic, however. Ivan is disgusted by Alyosha's talk of God and forgiveness. He asks Alyosha a question about the day Dmitri attacked their father. He asks if Alyosha believed that he wished that Dmitri would kill his father, that "one beast would devour the other?" Alyosha admits that he thought his brother was thinking this. Ivan thanks him bitterly and leaves.

Ivan feels sick, but his sickness has more to do with Smerdyakov than with Alyosha. Smerdyakov is still in the hospital from his seizure the night of the murder. He says he knows Ivan wished for his father's death, and he stayed out of the way to facilitate this. Ivan, enraged, hits Smerdyakov, but this does not stop the servant from torturing Ivan with his theories. He says that Ivan wanted to leave for Moscow when Fyodor was murdered because he wanted to wash his hands of what he knew would be a messy situation. Ivan tells Smerdyakov he will not report his ability to fake a seizure to the authorities if Smerdyakov will stay silent about their previous conversation before the murder. Smerdyakov says Ivan probably just wanted his inheritance, and this is why he wanted his father dead. Ivan leaves and wrestles with the idea that he may be partly guilty for Fyodor's murder if Smerdyakov did indeed kill Fyodor. He visits Katerina and confesses his contrition to her. She eases his mind by telling him she has a letter from Dmitri saying that Dmitri will kill Fyodor as a last resort to reimburse her. Ivan feels better, thinking it is his brother Dmitri who is the culprit, not Smerdyakov. He leaves, somewhat comforted.

But when Ivan talks to Smerdyakov again, Smerdyakov shatters his peace of mind by admitting to the murder. Worse, he tells Ivan that it was Ivan's words that helped him rationalize the act. "It was you who killed him all right," says Smerdyakov. He gives Ivan the 3,000 rubles he stole from Fyodor, and he begins to explain how he murdered the man. He explains how he faked an epileptic seizure the night of the murder (but that he truly had one before he was taken to the hospital). Smerdyakov tells Ivan that it was through their conversations about immorality and the nonexistence of God that he found the strength and rationalization to commit the murder. He explains that, after Dmitri attacked Grigory, Smerdyakov seized the opportunity to commit the murder. He lured Fyodor out of his room by saying Grushenka had come. Then, as Fyodor leaned out the window, he hit him with a paperweight.

After Ivan is convinced that Smerdyakov did commit the murder and that it was his words that made the murder possible, he leaves Smerdyakov. When Ivan goes back home, he resolves to tell the court about Smerdyakov's confession during Dmitri's trial. To his chagrin, he finds a devil in his room, who chides Ivan about his wickedness. Blind with tears of rage, Ivan throws a cup at the devil. Alyosha comes to his door and tells Ivan that Smerdyakov has just hanged himself. Ivan's behavior worries Alyosha, but when he asks his brother what is wrong, Ivan is too upset to describe his ordeal with the devil. Alyosha realizes that Ivan is having a nervous breakdown, and he stays with his brother for the night.

Analysis

Many characters experience intense guilt in the novel. Dmitri feels guilty for his treatment of Katerina, and Grushenka and Lise both express regret for their depravity. Ivan's guilt is even more extreme. He feels responsible for the murder he did not commit. There is a universal longing for catharsis and redemption among the characters in this novel. Though many characters feel contrition for their actions, it is not always clear if they deserve such castigation for their sins. Lise and Grushenka, for instance, are good-hearted girls, and "wickedness" is not something that obviously applies to them. Even Ivan, whose guilt is greater than any single character's guilt in the novel, feels guilty for a crime he did not technically commit. Father Zossima has laid out the idea that all men share in the sins of all other men, but many characters in this novel seems to feel the entire burden, not just a share. Ivan does not feel that he shares guilt; he feels that he is the only one responsible for his father's murder. Perhaps the characters all have inflated their own culpability. Dostoevsky puts stock in guilt and suffering. Father Zossima's lesson about men sharing each other's sins is thus somewhat misleading. One man's rightful guilt can be confused for his feelings of guilt, even if these feelings are misplaced. Some characters rationalize their internal turmoil, when in fact they are simply feeling the weight of hard times.

Smerdyakov is an exception to this widespread guilt complex. He single-handedly murders Fyodor, yet he does not blame himself at all. Despite the fact that he is the only character technically guilty of this act, he feels the least liability for it. Smerdyakov is an unfeeling aberration. Can the actual act of murder be such a small proportion of the sin of killing a man? This seems counter to Dostoevsky's feelings of murder; characters in Dostoevsky's novels sometimes commit murder because they believe that some people do not deserve to live. They are eventually punished for their sins. For instance, Dostoevsky does not make Fyodor seem sympathetic. He does not make the old Karamazov seem anything but wicked, and his murder seems at worst logical and at best imminent. The only reason his killers feel guilt is because murder is against positive law and divine law. Hence, realizing that these men hardly deserve life is not a sin, but actually taking life is a sin. It follows that Smerdyakov is the only one who is truly responsible for the murder, but everyone else suffers for their part, real or imagined.

Dostoevsky does not address the fact that characters like Ivan may be suffering without reason. Dostoevsky brings complexity to the point. He seemingly condemns the act of murder while allowing hateful feelings. He also promotes universal love toward all creatures while simultaneously portraying some characters as despicable beings unworthy of almost any kind of love. Perhaps it is this ambivalence that leads his characters to feel burdened with guilt.

One of the most shocking events in the novel occurs when Ivan returns to find a devil in his room. Since no one else sees the devil, we assume it is a figment of Ivan's imagination. The devil is very real to Ivan, however. A devil is a very meaningful symbol in this novel—but not to Ivan. When Father Ferapont sees devils in Zossima's cell after Zossima's death, he is decried as a lunatic. He is religious—but Ivan does not believe in God at all, so why would his subconscious manifest a devil? More importantly, why would Dostoevsky choose to represent Ivan's conscience as a devil? Maybe Ivan is experiencing a religious awakening, realizing that his atheism has been wrong all along. That does not seem quite right, nor is the devil intended to be real. If the novel has a moral center, it is Father Zossima and his teachings, which might permit the reality of devils in the background, yet this is not part of Ivan's ontology. Ivan may be seeing a devil because devils are part of the mythic-religious culture of his town.

If devils do exist, Father Ferapont is the only character in the novel who has an accurate conception of the world. Atheists like Ivan do not believe in God at all, and Alyosha and Father Zossima believe in a world of love and caring where devils are not needed; bad people are bad enough. The suggestion that devils do exist is quite a turn, casting doubt on the spiritual and moral center of the novel. Fyodor is not at the extreme anymore, now that devils are among the people.

Before this, all signs have led to the view that Father Zossima's teachings are the moral anchor that holds everyone together. If characters stray from this path of love and understanding, they find longing and remorse. If they adhere to it as Alyosha does, they find strength and purpose. But a devil represents not just judgment but also evil, what is often glossed over in Father Zossima's world of sympathy and compassion. Despite the new, more fragile moral center in the novel, Alyosha's faith in his purpose and understanding of the world remain as strong as ever through the end of the novel. Love and understanding continue to help characters find personal salvation.

From the point of view of an Ivan, if he could look at the whole story as we do, he might see a subtle implication that a religious lifestyle, even if deluded in some ways, is a decent and helpful one. For someone who is deeply ambivalent about religion, the introduction of a devil produces a complexity that might appeal to a rational mind that sees both good and evil in the world. Loving one's neighbor is a good thing, often producing good results even if one's motivations are misguided, and if there is something more beyond the tangible world, even if one does not understand it, it might seem reasonable to perceive devils as well as angels, a reality at least as complex as the one already on earth. When Dostoevsky brings a devil into Ivan's room, he thus sheds light on some of his own religious questions and ideas.

Summary and Analysis of Book 12

Dmitri's trial is a public spectacle. People have heard the news of the case, and the courtroom is crowded with spectators, mostly women, Interestingly, many of them are hoping for Dmitri's acquittal. Most of the men at the trial are not as sympathetic to this ladies' man, hoping for a conviction. Many people also have come to witness what they think will be a dramatic confrontation between Katerina and Grushenka. Rumors about both women are flying, and the public is hungry for a showdown. When the news is read that Smerdyakov will not appear as a witness because he has committed suicide, Dmitri exclaims, "A dog's death for a dog!" When asked how he will plead, Dmitri goes on a tirade about how he is guilty of many things. He says that he is guilty of "drunkenness and disorderly behavior … laziness and debauchery." But he says he "had resolved to become a decent man" for the rest of his life when he was arrested for this crime, which he did not commit. He pleads "not guilty" to the charges against him, but everyone, including his supporters, know that the prosecution has quite a case against him.

Dmitri's lawyer deftly discredits witnesses who testify against Dmitri, such as Captain Snegiryov, Rakitin, and Grigory, citing possible ulterior motives that each witness might have. His lawyer is very skilled, and he argues expertly for Dmitri. Alyosha is not discredited because he is known for his unquestionable honesty, and he makes a case for Dmitri's innocence. Alyosha cites a conversation he had with his brother proving that Dmitri indeed was in possession of a large sum of money before the murder took place. Alyosha contends that needing Fyodor's 3,000 rubles could not have been Dmitri's motive for the murder. This testimony proves that Dmitri has not stolen the money that the police found on his person; he had it before the murder.

Katerina further strengthens Dmitri's case by recounting stories about Dmitri that show he is an honorable man at his core. She says that Dmitri did not blackmail or seduce her even though he had the chance. Katerina's testimony upsets Dmitri, for he believes this will besmirch her name, but she tells the story anyway to help the man she has sworn to support and cherish.

Ivan suddenly appears in the courtroom, and when cross-examined, he proves to be of little help to anyone. He is clearly not well, and he does not make sense. He gives no evidence against Smerdyakov; he barely gives any evidence at all. But as he is leaving the courtroom, he shows the court the 3,000 rubles that Smerdyakov gave him. He asserts that Smerdyakov murdered and robbed Fyodor and that the 3,000 rubles are his blood money. He adds that he has been visited by a devil—and people begin to murmur. Because of his apparent insanity, his knowledge of Smerdyakov's confession is discredited, and he is removed from the courtroom.

Katerina takes the stand again, inexplicably changing her position on Dmitri, showing the courtroom Dmitri's letter stating that he would kill Fyodor for money. The court asks her why she hid this evidence, and she answers that she had been trying to save her love at all costs, but his infidelity and lack of appreciation had finally gotten to her—she could take it no longer and felt she must tell the truth. Grushenka flies into a rage and insults Katerina for her duplicity, and the courtroom erupts into bedlam.

The prosecutor closes. He earnestly believes that Dmitri is guilty and that the crime is despicable. He talks about the declining morals of the Russian people, among many of whom honor has been replaced with sordid intellectualization. He attacks Fyodor for his rampant sensualism and selfish greed. He says that the old man's actions must have made a son bitter and angry. Nevertheless, he says, this awfulness does not excuse the horrible murder that he believes Dmitri committed. The prosecutor analyzes each Karamazov brother, concluding with the accused. He says that Dmitri has been both passionate and desperate, which are two telltale qualities of a murderer. He adds that Smerdyakov had neither of these qualities, putting to rest the theory of his guilt. Also, he points out that Smerdyakov had a seizure the night of the murder. The most damning piece of evidence against Dmitri is the letter that Katerina showed the court. He asks the jury to convict Dmitri of parricide.

Dmitri's lawyer is somewhat of a celebrity, and the courtroom is excited to hear his oration. He speaks precisely and warmly, charging the prosecution with "malice" and speaking with sensitive plaintiveness. He begins by setting out to prove why all the evidence against Dmitri is questionable. He makes subtle jibes at the prosecutor for his psychological inferences, pointing out how psychology is "a knife that cuts both ways." He explains how psychology could as easily prove that Dmitri is a sympathetic, impulsive man or a cold, calculating fiend. Hence, psychological evidence is questionable and undependable.

Besides, he adds, other pieces of evidence do not make sense. For instance, there is no proof that Fyodor had 3,000 rubles for Dmitri to steal. Dmitri's explanation of where the money came from is as good as the theory that he obtained it by robbing Fyodor. The defense sees great leaps of imagination, as if the events that have taken place are part of a great "novel."

The defense lawyer next explains how Fyodor was a horrible father, neglecting, abandoning, and generally abusing the boy. Dmitri was a misguided youth who essentially grew up without a father. In addition, Smerdyakov's guilt is called into question again. Finally, the lawyer argues that prisons are for reform, not punishment, but convicting Dmitri will actually ruin his chances for reform. When he finishes, the courtroom erupts into applause.

After a brief respite, the jurors return and pronounce that Dmitri has been found guilty. Over the din of the courtroom, Dmitri yells that he is innocent, that he forgives Katerina, and that he wishes his family will take care of Grushenka. He is led out of the courtroom.

Analysis

The final chapters of this novel take place in a courtroom, which is a fitting end to a novel centered around a murder. This is a novel about guilt, and though Dmitri is the one on trial, he is not the only one whose life is scrutinized during the legal proceedings. These final chapters are an allegory for the intense judgment every character faces, either internally or externally. Since religion is such a large part of the novel, this judgment calls to mind a spiritual reckoning. Whether it is with a court, with God, or with oneself, every character faces a trial. Father Zossima says that one's own conscience is the only meaningful means of punishment. Ivan's own struggle, for instance, is all in his own head (say, between him and his personal demons). Smerdyakov has carried out his own sentence on himself.

Though Dmitri's trial is public, suggesting that it is socially more important than the inner trials of the other characters, this is the least meaningful arena in which to assess moral guilt. In addition to the fact that public trial and punishment run counter to the ideas of Father Zossima (and perhaps of Dostoevsky, who experienced some of that himself), the reader knows from the beginning that Dmitri is innocent of the crime of which he is being accused. This trial is not about conscience, inner motives, or wickedness, which are all complicated and subject to interpretation. Despite the talk of psychology, this trial is about facts, and the state uses these facts to come to the false conclusion that Dmitri murdered his father. It is both sad and funny that the most explicit trial, with the most people analyzing it, is a failure of justice. This supports Father Zossima's posture that punishment by the state is a sham. One can only hope that self-analysis is more successful.

The trial is also a public spectacle because people are interested in the scandal and intrigue. The lawyer for the defense is known for his brilliant orations and his entertaining pleas, not for his strict attention to detail. In this trial, emotion has a starring role, and truth has just a supporting role. The fact that Dmitri may be innocent or guilty takes a back seat to what he represents for each member of the crowd and jury. Some spectators are sympathetic to Dmitri's good heart. They hope to see such a forthright soul acquitted. Others have moral problems with his seduction of Katerina and subsequent abandonment, not to mention his unpaid debt.

Indebtedness is an important concept in the novel. Partly because Russia has fallen under such difficult times, the presence or absence of money is tied into larger ideas of pride and honor. It is a very shameful thing not to pay one's debts, and characters such as Captain Snegiryov and Ivan go to great lengths to stay free from the burden of owing money. Their sense of integrity is based on their financial independence. It is a very disgraceful thing in the eyes of many townspeople that Dmitri has not paid back the generous loan from Katerina.

The facts of the case aside, the trial is a public performance centered around a licentious family drama. It is a battleground of morality and intrigue based on the deeply held beliefs and feelings of those watching the trial, not on details. Dmitri has become a celebrity. Others define themselves by their stance about the trial. A townsperson can know what kind of person someone else is by his or her opinion about Dmitri Karamazov. In this way the trial is more about the people watching than about Dmitri. The myriad spectators are reflecting aspects of their own identities.

The essence of each character becomes more clear as each one takes the stand. For instance, the testimonies of Grigory and Marfa are straightforward and condemning. These two are dedicated to their plain view of honesty, and if the truth puts a boy they helped to raise in prison, then so be it. This outcome is inevitable, for there is no other option for them. Alyosha is respectful, honest, warm, and insightful, and his testimony is not only beyond reproach but also, fortunately, helpful to Dmitri. Grushenka proves herself to be a good match for Dmitri, for her testimony is emotional and uncouth, but her devotion to Dmitri is clear.

Katerina, for her part, shows herself to be very deceptive. She gives a personally embarrassing testimonial about Dmitri's character, again humbling herself to help the man she ostensibly loves, yet before the trial is through, she gives evidence that seals Dmitri's fate, saying she is fed up with his mockery of her. It is unclear why she does this, but it is certain that she has a personal agenda and that her actions are not coming from her heart but from some plan of hers. Perhaps she wants to become a martyr or to win some kind of salvation or vindication with a devotion she does not feel. In any case, she is shady; her calm and loving exterior is covering up something more calculating and shadowy.

Ivan's "testimony" shows how deep his feelings of shame and guilt run. In this novel, as in Crime and Punishment, sickness has a direct correlation with conscience. The seriousness of Ivan's condition indicates his inner turmoil. Ivan, who seems so controlled and psychologically stable the rest of the time, has fallen apart. What at first seemed to be a cold and dispassionate manner is clearly a veneer. Under the light of a public inquisition, people like Ivan might reveal some hidden but true colors.

Dmitri's conviction for his father's murder has ramifications that range beyond family to the political and religious. Why would Dostoevsky end his novel with the wrong character being convicted of a crime? The wrongful conviction points out the injustice of the world—unless it is the justice of conscience after all, succeeding even though the state has been incorrect in this particular determination of right and wrong. Does Dmitri need to suffer for his life? Does Dmitri deserve to go to jail, even if he did not kill anyone? Insofar as Zossima's idea of punishment involves one's own conscience, true justice is personal or spiritual, not political.

Why, then, make a public trial so significant in the novel? Even though going to prison may not make a man change, it provides character-building hardships. As many characters in the novel explain, they long for suffering in order to purge their feelings of guilt and shame. Dmitri has been on the border between salvation and damnation the entire novel. This is Dmitri's chance to purge his guilt by enduring hardship, even if it is for the wrong crime. The conviction is thus a sort of blessing.

Smerdyakov, who escapes conviction, has fared much worse than Dmitri, according to Zossima's sense of justice. (Compare the view of Socrates in Plato's *Gorgias*: it is better for the guilty person to confess and pay a just penalty, rather than to go free and never be reformed.) The weight on Smerdyakov's conscience was apparently so great that he took his own life, alone and without the support of his society to help him. Ivan, who also feels guilt for the murder, is not put on trial either, but his feelings of guilt get the best of him, driving him insane.

The trial does not show, at least not to us, that Dmitri is guilty of any crime beyond what he already has determined about himself. Likewise, the other characters, more or less, show that they have met a kind of justice that does not depend at all on the jury. Rather, the press of public attention does help people come clean. The trial is thus not really about the penal system and its imperfections. Instead, it is a platform giving Dmitri, and to some degree others, a chance for absolution in a social and political context, with personal and spiritual ramifications. The trial is a public platform that tests the true character of all those involved.

Summary and Analysis of Epilogue

Alyosha visits Katerina, where he finds Ivan feverish and asleep. Katerina tells Alyosha that they are planning to break Dmitri out of prison so he can flee the country, and she needs Alyosha's help. Despite the fact that this will entail bribes and lies, Alyosha agrees with one condition, that Katerina will visit poor Dmitri in prison. When Alyosha visits Dmitri, Dmitri is consumed with a need to repent. He wants to be redeemed through suffering, but he says he needs Grushenka to help him through this difficult time in his life. Alyosha excitedly tells Dmitri of their plans for his escape. Dmitri says he will go along with the plan, but he says he feels a strong desire to return to Russia one day. Katerina visits Dmitri, and they make their peace. Grushenka visits Dmitri, too, and when Katerina sees her, she apologizes to her, too. Grushenka, however, does not forgive Katerina for her actions in the courtroom, which had led to Dmitri's conviction.

Ilusha dies. Alyosha goes to his funeral. He talks to all of Ilusha's friends and tells them to remember their friend. The boys all like him very much, and they cheer for their mentor and friend.

Analysis

This denouement is about redemption. It is not so much about Dmitri's redemption, though he explains how he plans to begin a new life. It is not so much about Ivan's redemption, even though he is being resuscitated in Katerina's arms. This epilogue shows that children are the redemption of Russia. When Alyosha talks to the children, they cheer his hopeful words and ideas, and one can assume that they will go out into the world and incorporate them into their lives. The search for redemption is larger than individuals such as Dmitri or Ivan. When Fyodor dies without redeeming his wicked, licentious life, the most lasting consequence is that the next generation inherits his burdens and debts. His sons, voluntarily or involuntarily, have all learned from him and have lived in his shadow all their lives. If they extricate themselves from this encumbrance in their lifetime, it is a small triumph. If they can pass down hope to the next generation, however, this is the greatest contribution they can make to their country and to their fellow man. When Alyosha passes words of love down to the young boys, he is doing his part to ensure the future of Russia. Dostoevsky felt very strongly about his country, and he had deep feelings for it. When Dmitri is talking to Alyosha about fleeing to another country, he expresses his determination to return to Russia one day, because even if it has forsaken him, it is his country and he loves it. This novel begins as a story about family and ends as a story about country, a place where individuals and families can be inspired to lead better lives.

Suggested Essay Questions

1. How are the three Karamazov brothers like or unlike their father?

   Possible Answer:

   Dmitri is very much like his father. He is ruled by his emotions and is hot-tempered. But his guilt and faith in God are unlike his father's shamelessness and atheism. Ivan's pessimism and atheism make him very much like his father. But his social conscience contrasts with his father's selfishness. Alyosha is not like his father. He is loving and sensitive, and he tries to do right by others. He has very little in common with his nihilistic father.
2. Who is the hero of the novel?

   Possible Answers:

   The obvious answer is Alyosha. He is the center of much of the action, and he participates in most of the discussions and intrigues throughout the novel. Dmitri is another possible answer, for he actually drives the action of the novel. He is very conflicted, so he embodies the collision of ideas, feelings, and morals in the novel. He does not simply personify one side of an argument; he reflects an argument's complexity.
3. Is the novel a love story?

   Possible Answer:

   There are many love triangles and romances in the novel, so a case could be made that romantic love is at the heart of the novel. But much in the novel suggests that it is more a philosophical work, since religion, morality, and suffering play such important roles. Also, the novel centers around a murder of a father, and though there are romantic relationships involved, one could argue that the intra-family dynamic is the focus of the novel. If the novel is a love story, it includes family love and spiritual love as much as romantic love.
4. Does the novel have a happy ending?

   Possible Answer:

   There is turmoil at the end of the novel. Fyodor, Smerdyakov, and Father Zossima are dead. Dmitri is in jail, and Ivan is very sick. Still, there is hope in the ending, for the children listen to Alyosha's teachings and applaud them. Also, Dmitri has a renewed faith in life. The world that is to come promises to be better than the present one.
5. Father Zossima asks Alyosha to go into the world to try to do good in it.

Does Alyosha succeed?

Possible Answer:

Alyosha is very loving and compassionate, and he gives of himself to everyone. He cannot prevent the murder of his father, the suicide of Smerdyakov, Dmitri's imprisonment, or Ivan's illness. Alyosha provides love despite hard times, but for them his love is not enough. With the children, however, he has found success.

6. Compare Fyodor with Father Zossima.

Possible Answer:

These two "fathers" differ greatly. Fyodor's neglect and acerbic nature contrast with Father Zossima's loving attentiveness. They both die, and their deaths create crises among the Karamazov sons. In the material world, their lives are at the moral extremes.

7. Ivan and Alyosha have the same mother. How are they similar?

Possible Answer:

Both brothers want to do good, and both brothers are burdened by the idea of responsibility. Alyosha goes into the world to embrace humanity, feeling that he has work to do that cannot be done in the monastery. Ivan is infuriated by the idea of suffering in the world, especially among children, and when Fyodor is murdered, he is tormented by the idea that he has shared in the responsibility of such an atrocious act.

8. Is Smerdyakov the villain of the novel?

Possible Answer:

At the outset of the novel, the reader expects the poor, pathetic, epileptic servant to be completely harmless. When he turns out to be the murderer, however, we see him as a manipulative, mean-spirited killer. Yet, maybe he is simply exacting a sort of roundabout justice upon a man who cruelly raped his mother and treated a son like a servant. Also, he could be seen as simply a suggestible pawn who responds to Ivan's ideas and acts on them because of his admiration and hero-worship of Ivan. Besides, Fyodor is rather villainous himself, and from a spiritual point of view, an athiest like Ivan, despite his good intentions in the world, could be seen as a villain.

9. Who is guilty of Fyodor's murder?

Possible Answer:

Though Smerdyakov actually murders Fyodor, the concept of shared responsibility leads the reader to consider everyone in the novel as a potential accomplice. This means that even loving, compassionate characters such as Father Zossima and Alyosha could share the guilt. In a sense, a murder is a failure of the family and the community. Indeed, many characters feel guilt over the murder, if only because of their inaction or their feelings, in addition to their actions and words.

10. Is it likely that Dmitri will change once he is free?

    Possible Answer:

    Dmitri is often governed by his emotions, so for him to change his nature and restrain these emotions will be difficult. But Dostoevsky implies that through suffering, one can gain knowledge and strength. Dmitri's suffering in prison should change his outlook on life, but we do not know how these changes will play out once he is free--still outside the circle of his family and Russian society.

Dostoevsky and Tchaikovsky

Dostoevsky was one of many important artists to emerge in Russia in the late 1800s. The tumultuous atmosphere in Russia at this time gave rise to a generation of artists who expressed suffering and internal conflict with poise and acuity. Dostoevsky often is grouped with Leo Tolstoy because the two authors created similarly dense, complex novels about the difficult Russian life around the same time. But another contemporary artist who echoed the soul of Dostoevsky's works, perhaps more closely, was Tchaikovsky. Dostoevsky's psychological drama and sweeping scope were expressed in Tchaikovsky's music; his complex symphonies have been called "Russia's music."

Critics have noted that the anguish and ecstasy in Tchaikovsky's works mimic the psychological dramatics of Dostoevsky. They were very different men with different ideas, but Tchaikovsky had a gift for being able to speak to the people of Russia. The two artists convey passion and tumult, and despite their differences, they hold a similar place in Russian cultural history as creators of epic works of art that express the heart of Russia.

Pyotr Ilich Tchaikovsky is an interesting counterpoint to Dostoevsky in reflecting the Russian mind with all its angst and suffering. The nationalism inherent in works such as the *1812 Overture* match Dostoevsky's love for his country. Dostoevsky's writing is expansive and ambitious; his characters struggle with dramatic issues such as murder and madness, and the stakes are very high. Tchaikovsky matched this emotional intensity with works such as his *Fourth Symphony*, which he began in 1877, the year before Dostoevsky began The Brothers Karamazov. This piece was heralded for its unusually evocative grandiosity.

Tchaikovsky was going through a very difficult time in his life, coming to terms with a bad marriage and his sexuality, and his *Fourth Symphony* reflects his inner turmoil. Tchaikovsky, like Dostoevsky, had the ability to convey grand themes as well as very personal emotional complexity. At the same time, both artists took their rightful places on the world stage, reflecting and developing some of the trends in Western music and literature at the time.

The two artists were grouped together for their many similarities, but they were not peers, and they did not hold all the same beliefs. Though many people compared the two artistic figures, Tchaikovsky met Dostoevsky only once. Tchaikovsky read Dostoevsky's works, and he was especially interested in The Brothers Karamazov. He came to the conclusion that the novelist was difficult, saying that the book was, on the whole, "intolerable." He said that every character was "crazy." Tchaikovsky favored a more conservative style. He was an avid Tsarist, and he was at odds with the nationalistic school of music started by Mily Balakirev. He disagreed with the Socialist movement, and when he included a Russian folk song in his *Fourth Symphony* with lyrics that translate roughly, "go to the people," it almost seemed ironic. He believed in his country, but he did not believe in the same grassroots populism that Dostoevsky believed in. Tchaikovsky's later works, however, such as *Romeo and Juliet*, are like reveries, verging on surrealism. He gave in to fancy and aloofness where Dostoevsky wrote about the difficult, gritty details of bleak Russian life. Dostoevsky and Tchaikovsky were influenced by the same aspects of Russian strife, but they were by no means ideological allies.

Author of ClassicNote and Sources

Kendrick Strauch, author of ClassicNote. Completed on August 15, 2007, copyright held by GradeSaver.

Updated and revised Adam Kissel December 01, 2007. Copyright held by GradeSaver.

Fyodor Dostoevsky, Trans. Konstantin Mochulsky. The Brothers Karamazov. New York: Random House, 1970.

Fritz Eichenberg, Malcolm Muggeridge, and J. I. Packer. The Gospel in Dostoyevsky: Selections from His Works. Maryknoll, New York: Orbis Books, 2003.

W. J. Leatherbarrow. The Cambridge Companion to Dostoyevsky. Cambridge: Cambridge University Press, 2002.

Essay: The Inquisition and the Quadrillion Miles

by Claudia Herr
July 25, 2002

> "You see, like you, I suffer from the fantastic and so I love the realism of earth. Here, with you, everything is circumscribed, here all is formulated and geometrical, while we have nothing but indeterminate questions!"(said to Ivan by "The Devil", 776)

Through Ivan, Dostoevsky sets up an impossible question that aims at the mystery of faith, the mystery of being able, paradoxically, to accept something that defies logic. Ivan desperately wants to believe; he has a strong mystical element to his character, but is tormented simultaneously by a bitterly imperative sense of rationality. This duality is his torment, his own personal paradoxical hell; his rational mind renders him unable to accept the God he so wants to believe in. The complex nature of his character is such that this emptiness is, for him, a torture. In his simplest sentiments, Ivan wants to believe in God with the same full-hearted faith as Alyosha. But in his fatal proclivity to measure his mysticism against his rationality, he stamps out the space for anything so enigmatic and incomprehensible, so "indeterminate" as faith.

Ivan's difficulty is not that he doesn't believe in God, (on the contrary, it is his belief in God that rends his soul), but that he can't bring himself to accept "God's world". What keeps Ivan from the perceived comfort of faith cannot accept the illogic of a world that, among other transgressions of reason, would allow children to suffer. Nor can he accept the idea of ultimate harmony in the Kingdom of God, if it is at a cost so detrimental as the suffering of even one innocent child. That God could allow such horror defies Ivan's stubborn, stringent sense of logic.

Ivan struggles, stuck "half-way" between faith and despair. He loves life, but he cannot reconcile the fact that he loves it "... regardless of logic..."(274). He cannot affirm, or even justify his love for the "... sticky little leaves as they open in spring..."(273) as it is without reason or rational "meaning".

Ivan reveals himself most often not through direct dialogue, (in conversation he is slippery and hidden), but through strange parables and visions. In his tale of `The Grand Inquisitor', Ivan reveals the true, torturous nature of his relationship with God.

In his fantastical "poem," Ivan recounts a meeting between the Grand Inquisitor and Christ at the height of the horrors of the Spanish Inquisition. Christ has come to earth again and is mysteriously recognized by all who see Him, including the Grand Inquisitor himself, who orders Him seized and imprisoned; there follows a "dialogue" between the two men.

The tale is a representation of the elements that are at war within Ivan. The Inquisitor is Ivan's relentless logical mind, and Christ represents Ivan's faith -- silent, and unable to answer any questions, but always undeniably, infuriatingly present.

Ivan's logic is bitterly furious with God, because it is God's existence that is the center of the paradox tormenting him. The Inquisitor berates God for having condemned man with the freedom that makes him so unhappy. The Inquisitor even sneers at God, mocking Him, boasting that he has made Him obsolete: "... and we shall have an answer for all. And they will be glad to believe our answer, for it will save them from the great anxiety and terrible agony they endure at present in making a free decision for themselves..."(308). Ivan is fatally caught between belief and reason, and he blames God.

"The heart has its reasons that reason cannot know."(Pascal) Ivan's dilemma is that he does not allow for his heart' -- his reason' must know' everything. Ivan's iron sense of reason has rendered him a man unable to justify even the most instinctive of his convictions; for Ivan as an intellectual, to exist without even faith in existence, is torture. Father Zossima discerns this torture in Ivan in the "unfortunate gathering" between the elder and the family Karamazov. In this revelatory scene, Zossima illuminates the paradox that wrenches Ivan's soul, the eternal paradox of the question of God's existence: "... the question is still fretting your heart... in your despair, you, too, divert yourself with magazine articles, and discussions in society, though you don't believe your own arguments, and with an aching heart mock them inwardly... That question you have not answered, and it is your great grief, for it clamors for an answer... If it can't be decided in the affirmative, it will never be decided in the negative."(79). By the same brutally rigid sense of logic that prevents Ivan from committing to the certainty of God's existence, he can never commit to the certainty of His non-existence.

It is not, however, Ivan's inability to commit to the existence of God that leads to his spiritual and mental collapse, rather it is his inability to commit to humanity. According to Dostoevsky, faith in God and faith in man are consecutive and inter-reliant, and for Ivan, lack of one has led to the lack of the other. Of the two, it is his lack of faith in humanity that proves to be the more fatal for Ivan.

When Smerdyakov confesses to the murder of Fyodor Pavlovitch Karamazov, Ivan is forced to a recognition of his criminal irresponsibility. Ivan's soul is shaken at the realization that all those nights around the dinner table when he was spouting empty philosophy and meaningless conclusions, as if life were nothing but a game of logic, there was someone taking every word for truth, as if it had come from "God Almighty"(737). "For every individual... who does not believe in God or immortality... crime must become, not only lawful but even recognized as the inevitable, the most rational, even honorable outcome of his position. There is no virtue if there is no immortality."(79) It is this absolutism that rends Ivan's soul. For Ivan there exist only two possibilities: either there is no God and everything is permissible, or God exists along with Absolute Virtue. There is no middle ground, because to relinquish the absolute is to throw oneself into the impossible paradox -- God exists, but there is no virtue, and everything is permissible. But Ivan cannot renounce his absolutist's logic, and it is out of this profound faith-lessness that Ivan speaks, and, unconsciously, "... puts [Smerdyakov] up to murder..."(751).

In visiting Smerdyakov therefore, Ivan is confronting the incarnation of the malicious fruits of his own reasoning mind. In his logical scheme of the world, Ivan has neglected to give validity to life and humanity, although he remains a part of life and humanity despite his self-imposed exile in the cold realm of intellect and reason. In hearing Smerdyakov's confession, Ivan must come to terms with the fact that he has not been isolated from man. He finally understands that "... we are all responsible to all for all..."(362), and that he has disgracefully shirked his responsibility. Ivan's wretched guilt goes beyond the murder of his father; he understands that he is guilty of invalidating humanity, and his only redemption is to confess his part in his father's murder, and so begin to accept his recognized responsibility. Symbolizing that he has resolved to accept his duty to humanity, on his way from his last interview with Smerdyakov, Ivan spends an hour helping the peasant whom he had previously knocked down in the snow find warmth and shelter.

At this point, Ivan has leaped from the rational extreme to the mystical, human extreme of his fatal absolutism. In a last strange parable, Ivan comes face to face with his devil, Logic.

In this surreal scene, it becomes clear that Ivan's fatal weakness is not merely his logic, but his absolutism. The reader understands that if only Ivan could exist between the paradox rather than deny it, if only he could affirm and embrace the contradiction and irrationality of life, he would be redeemed from insanity. "No, you must go and deny, without denial there's no criticism and what would a journal be without a column of criticism? Without criticism it would be nothing but one hosannah'. But nothing but hosannah is not enough for life, the hosannah must be tried in the crucible of doubt and so on...."(780) Ivan is willing to live only one extreme or the other; the distance between the two is a "quadrillion miles", and he is not willing to accept the arduous journey -- in his desperation, he still believes in the simple absolute of the "one hosannah".

But even this belief is shattered when Ivan learns of Smerdyakov's suicide. Ivan now recognizes that the impossible simplicity toward which he was desperately striving is truly impossible. He can no longer redeem himself from his damning logic by confessing and receiving punishment for his part in his father's murder. The paradox has multiplied and compounded itself until Ivan's spirit, in its weakness (for it has been weak all along), collapses of "brain fever": "... hesitation, suspense, conflict between belief and disbelief -- is sometimes such torture to a conscientious man..."(784).

Afflicted with a chronic faithless-ness, Ivan is truly a tragic figure. Condemned to allow himself to live only through the lens of his common sense, the "indeterminate questions" infuriate and exasperate Ivan's "three-dimensional mind". Through Ivan, Dostoesvky sounds the question of the value of intelligence and reason, if it is at the cost of compassion, humanity, and faith. Ivan undergoes a breakdown because his soul lacks the strength to travel the quadrillion miles. The paradox of Ivan's weakness is tragic -- because he cannot believe in the "two seconds of joy", he will never find even one moment of respite from the torture of his self-defeating logic.

Essay: Religiosity and Freedom in The Brothers Karamazov

by Sunny Hwang
September 02, 2002

The chapter entitled "The Grand Inquisitor" is unquestionably an integral part of The Brothers Karamazov. The poem allows Ivan to express many of the reasons that he cannot accept certain aspects of Christ's behavior, the existence of God, and mankind's intertwined freedom and suffering. Within the poem, the Grand Inquisitor represents one paradigm of belief, while Christ represents the antithesis. This is paralleled by Ivan's beliefs contrasting with Alyosha's in the frame of the novel itself. "The Grand Inquisitor" serves mainly to delineate the conflict between the two principal belief systems evident in The Brothers Karamazov - that of accepting mankind's freedom, and therefore his suffering, and that of rejecting it.

Those of unwavering faith are able to blindly accept the world and everything about it. They do not question mankind's suffering, instead attributing it to a larger, infallible plan of God's. They do not need to understand in order to accept. To them, earthly suffering is a small price to pay for the eternal rewards they will eventually reap. The suffering, whether supernal or otherwise, is viewed as ameliorative for both character and faith. They have accepted the burden of freedom placed on them by their God, and sought the strength and wisdom to control that freedom from their God. They do not view their freedom as a "burden," however, instead seeing the process whereby they master their freedom as a beneficial experience. Only in this manner are they able to accept the otherwise intolerable suffering of the innocent.

Alyosha strongly adheres to this belief system. He firmly believes that though it is indeed unpleasant, the suffering of the innocent is not in vain. God allows events to unfold according to a divine plan, which ultimately benefits all of mankind. The suffering of the innocent is akin to the sacrifice of the lamb, the crucifixion of Christ. The blood of the innocent has always been requisite to that which is most valuable - in this case, human freedom. Ivan challenges Alyosha as to whether or not he would found a world in which happiness would reign if that paradise were built upon the suffering of one innocent, and Alyosha responds that though he would not, that is indeed the action which Christ himself took. Alyosha responds to Ivan saying that he has forgotten the one who "...gave His innocent blood for everyone's sins and everyone's sakes" (296). Christ chose to give his life, in order that mankind would have the freedom to choose to come to him. Alyosha has, through the strength of his faith, accepted both the freedom and the suffering laid upon him. He has accepted God.

The Grand Inquisitor represents those who lack faith. They accept nothing freely, and instead question and challenge that which they do not comprehend, and reject that which cannot be answered. Their view of the suffering of the innocent and the freedom man possesses differs from that of those endowed with great faith. In place of faith, they have questions: Why must innocents suffer? Why must good come only through suffering? Why would a merciful, benevolent God cause anyone to suffer, much less the innocent? Why would Christ place so unbearable a burden as freedom on the shoulders of man, when he clearly cannot wield it? Until these questions can be answered, they simply can accept neither the suffering of the innocent nor the freedom of man. Until they can accept the suffering and the freedom, they cannot accept God.

Ivan, from the early stages of his life, questioned the circumstances around him and rejected that which he could not comprehend. He could not accept anything freely, including the charity on which he spent his childhood. The narrator says of Ivan, "I gather that by the time he was ten, he had become very aware that he... was living on other people's charity" (17). Because of this awareness, he began writing for journals as soon as he could, to support himself. This same fervent need for independence applied even when Ivan was in need of money. The narrator says, "It must be pointed out that...[Ivan] made no attempt whatsoever to ask his father for assistance" (17). Ivan's inability to accept munificence freely applied to all aspects of his life. This was the cause of Ivan's rejection of God. Ivan simply could not accept the salvation and mercy bought with Christ's innocent blood - the greatest act of charity. Likewise, he could not accept the freedom Christ bought for mankind when he refused Satan's temptations. Ivan found the suffering of innocents utterly repugnant, and in accepting the sacrifice of Christ, he would have been accepting the greatest instance of the unexpiated suffering of an innocent.

This chapter, "The Grand Inquisitor," personifies the ideological struggle that is prevalent throughout this novel by assigning each philosophy a tangible character to represent it. Through this book, Dostoevsky seeks to illustrate the tragic error in one's inability to accept Christ that will lead to one's ultimate demise. This poem of Ivan's, as well as Ivan's experiences throughout the entire novel, serve to more lucidly make this point. Within "The Grand Inquisitor" itself, the Grand Inquisitor and those he leads are also pictured as being spiritually dead as a result of having rejected Christ and having been deprived of the freedom for which he gave his innocent blood. Dostoevsky wishes the reader to realize the folly in not accepting Christ's sacrifice by contrasting Ivan's physical and spiritual emaciation with Alyosha's physical and spiritual salubrity. Acceptance of Christ is not only acceptance of mankind's freedom and suffering though; it is also the belief that with Christ, one has the strength to bear that freedom, and that the suffering of the innocent will in the end, bear more fruit.

Quiz 1

1. **How many mothers do Dmitri, Ivan, and Alyosha have between them?**
   A. Unknown
   B. One
   C. Two
   D. Three

2. **How many rubles does Dmitri have to return to Katerina?**
   A. Four thousand
   B. Three thousand
   C. One thousand
   D. Two thousand

3. **How is Smerdyakov related to the three Karamazov brothers?**
   A. He is their grandfather
   B. He is their half-brother
   C. He is their father-in-law
   D. He is their cousin

4. **What is Alyosha forbidden to consume during Lent (but consumes anyway)?**
   A. Wine and cheese
   B. Water and bread
   C. Vodka and sausage
   D. Beer and bread

5. **Who is Lise's mother?**
   A. Adelaida
   B. Madame Hohlakov
   C. Katerina
   D. Grushenka

6. **What illness does Smerdyakov have?**
   A. Hypochondria
   B. Dyslexia
   C. Epilepsy
   D. Colorblindness

7. **Who quarrels over Grushenka?**
   A. Smerdyakov and Fyodor
   B. Alyosha and Ivan
   C. Fyodor and Dmitri
   D. Ivan and Smerdyakov

8. **Who visits Ivan after his father's death?**
   A. Father Zossima
   B. The angel Gabriel
   C. Grushenka
   D. A devil

9. **Where does Father Zossima ask Alyosha to spend his time?**
   A. In France
   B. In the monastery
   C. In the world
   D. In the woods

10. **Who does Fyodor Karamazov NOT sleep with?**
   A. Adelaida
   B. Lizaveta
   C. Grushenka
   D. Sofia

11. **Who does "The Grand Inquisitor" visit in jail?**
   A. Ilusha
   B. Fyodor
   C. Katerina
   D. Jesus

12. **Who bites Alyosha's finger?**
   A. Ilusha
   B. Dmitri
   C. Grushenka
   D. Lise

13. **What happens when Father Zossima dies?**
   A. His body decomposes quickly
   B. Thunder crashes
   C. Birds appear in the room
   D. His body disappears

14. **When Dmitri visits his father's house when he is looking for Grushenka, what does he take with him?**
   A. A brass pestle
   B. An olive branch
   C. A hot poker
   D. A knife

15. **Who does NOT die in the course of the novel?**
   A. Ilusha
   B. Fyodor
   C. Ivan
   D. Smerdyakov

16. **Who is Smerdyakov's foster father?**
   A. Fyodor
   B. Grigory
   C. Ivan
   D. Kolya

17. **Which character is somewhat crippled?**
   A. Grushenka
   B. Lise
   C. Ivan
   D. Kolya

18. **What does Dmitri like to sing sometimes?**
   A. The Russian national anthem
   B. "Hymn to Joy"
   C. The chorus of "Hallelujah"
   D. Songs about women

19. **Who lends Dmitri money on the night of Fyodor's murder?**
A. Fyodor
B. Perhotin
C. Ivan
D. Captain Snegiryov

20. **Who is in love with Smerdyakov?**
A. Madame Hohlakov
B. Katerina
C. Lise
D. Marya

21. **Who is late to the meeting with Father Zossima?**
A. Dmitri
B. Fyodor
C. Alyosha
D. Ivan

22. **What is the name of the monk who opposes Father Zossima strongly?**
A. Father Ferapont
B. Father Snegyirov
C. Father Pavel
D. Father Josif

23. **Who is friends with Ilusha and listens to Alyosha's ideas?**
A. Andrey
B. Kalganov
C. Ivan
D. Kolya

24. **Who agrees with Ivan's ideas?**
A. Fyodor
B. Alyosha
C. Grushenka
D. Smerdyakov

25. **Who does NOT kiss someone during a conversation?**

A. Alyosha

B. Father Zossima

C. Lise

D. Jesus Christ on the cross

Quiz 1 Answer Key

1. **(C)** Two
2. **(B)** Three thousand
3. **(B)** He is their half-brother
4. **(C)** Vodka and sausage
5. **(B)** Madame Hohlakov
6. **(C)** Epilepsy
7. **(C)** Fyodor and Dmitri
8. **(D)** A devil
9. **(C)** In the world
10. **(C)** Grushenka
11. **(D)** Jesus
12. **(A)** Ilusha
13. **(A)** His body decomposes quickly
14. **(A)** A brass pestle
15. **(C)** Ivan
16. **(B)** Grigory
17. **(B)** Lise
18. **(B)** "Hymn to Joy"
19. **(B)** Perhotin
20. **(D)** Marya
21. **(A)** Dmitri
22. **(A)** Father Ferapont
23. **(D)** Kolya
24. **(D)** Smerdyakov
25. **(C)** Lise

Quiz 2

1. **Why doesn't Ivan agree that church and state should be separated?**
   A. He thinks separation is blasphemy
   B. He thinks if they were not separated, crime rates would decrease
   C. He thinks the church would run the government well
   D. He has studied Islam and Buddhism

2. **Who tells Dmitri she does not know where Fyodor has gone?**
   A. A drunken party-goer
   B. A groundskeeper
   C. A carpenter
   D. A maid

3. **Who defends Dmitri in court?**
   A. Fyodor
   B. Fetyukovitch
   C. Varvinsky
   D. Raskolnikov

4. **Which brother goes crazy?**
   A. Dmitri
   B. Alyosha
   C. Ivan
   D. Smerdyakov

5. **Which brother has been a monk?**
   A. Dmitri
   B. Alyosha
   C. Ivan
   D. Smerdyakov

6. **Which brother says he will kill him?**
   A. Dmitri
   B. Alyosha
   C. Ivan
   D. Smerdyakov

7. **Who does Father Zossima say is responsible for a sin?**
   A. The devil
   B. Everyone
   C. The family
   D. The sinner himself

8. **When Fyodor is speaking with Alyosha, whom does he insult?**
   A. His own mother
   B. Katerina
   C. Father Ferapont
   D. Alyosha's mother

9. **Who is NOT competing for Grushenka's affection?**
   A. Dmitri
   B. Fyodor
   C. Mussyalovitch
   D. Ivan

10. **To whom is Dmitri engaged?**
   A. Katerina
   B. Grushenka
   C. Lise
   D. Sofia

11. **Of whom does Father Zossima say Alyosha reminds him?**
   A. Ilusha
   B. Fyodor
   C. Himself
   D. His older brother

12. **Who has never been in the military?**
   A. Dmitri
   B. Alyosha
   C. Father Zossima
   D. Captain Snegiryov

13. **What happened to Lizaveta after Smerdyakov's birth?**
    A. She died
    B. She became Fyodor's maid
    C. She married Fyodor
    D. She ran away to China

14. **Who does NOT have a seizure?**
    A. Fyodor
    B. Alyosha
    C. Smerdyakov
    D. Captain Snegiryov

15. **Whom does Dmitri NOT strike?**
    A. Fyodor
    B. Grigory
    C. Katerina
    D. Captain Snegiryov

16. **What do Dmitri and Father Zossima have in common?**
    A. They look exactly alike
    B. They both participated in duels during their time in the military
    C. They both love veal
    D. The same middle name

17. **Why does "The Grand Inquisitor" tell Christ he needs to discontinue his actions?**
    A. He is interrupting the Church's hold on the people
    B. It is Lent
    C. He has not paid his taxes
    D. People are dying because of his actions

18. **What do Alyosha and Katerina do for Dmitri after his trial?**
    A. Plan his escape from prison
    B. Chastize the prosecution for using false evidence
    C. Bake him a cake
    D. Bake him bread

19. **Who shuts a door on her hand?**
   A. Adelaida
   B. Madame Hohlakov
   C. Grushenka
   D. Lise

20. **What is the name of the dog that Kolya trains?**
   A. Rasputin
   B. Perezvon
   C. Ivan
   D. Tsar

21. **What does Alyosha do after he wakes up from the dream he has after Father Zossima's death?**
   A. He embraces the earth
   B. He prays
   C. He denounces God
   D. He proposes to Lise

22. **How does Father Zossima mandate that a person treat servants?**
   A. Sternly
   B. As equals
   C. Lovingly
   D. Cordially

23. **What does Dmitri pawn to Perhotin for money?**
   A. A brass pestle
   B. His watch
   C. His mother's ring
   D. His pistols

24. **Which character is NOT involved in a love triangle?**
   A. Ilusha
   B. Dmitri
   C. Katerina
   D. Grushenka

25. **In what country do the Karamazovs live?**

A. Poland

B. Latvia

C. Russia

D. The Soviet Union

Quiz 2 Answer Key

1. **(B)** He thinks if they were not separated, crime rates would decrease
2. **(D)** A maid
3. **(B)** Fetyukovitch
4. **(C)** Ivan
5. **(B)** Alyosha
6. **(A)** Dmitri
7. **(B)** Everyone
8. **(D)** Alyosha's mother
9. **(D)** Ivan
10. **(A)** Katerina
11. **(D)** His older brother
12. **(B)** Alyosha
13. **(A)** She died
14. **(A)** Fyodor
15. **(C)** Katerina
16. **(B)** They both participated in duels during their time in the military
17. **(A)** He is interrupting the Church's hold on the people
18. **(A)** Plan his escape from prison
19. **(D)** Lise
20. **(B)** Perezvon
21. **(A)** He embraces the earth
22. **(B)** As equals
23. **(D)** His pistols
24. **(A)** Ilusha
25. **(C)** Russia

Quiz 3

1. **How many times was Fyodor Karamazov married?**
    A. Once
    B. Three times
    C. Twice
    D. Never

2. **Which brother does NOT dislike Fyodor?**
    A. Dmitri
    B. Alyosha
    C. Ivan
    D. Smerdyakov

3. **Which brother does Fyodor dislike?**
    A. Dmitri
    B. Alyosha
    C. Ivan
    D. Smerdyakov

4. **During their meeting, how does Father Zossima react to Fyodor?**
    A. He laughs at his jokes
    B. He is loving and understanding
    C. He silently fumes
    D. He ignores him completely

5. **What does Father Zossima think is the worst punishment for a criminal?**
    A. Starvation
    B. His own conscience
    C. Death
    D. Exile

6. **At whose feet does Father Zossima kneel?**
    A. Dmitri's
    B. Alyosha's
    C. Father Ferapont's
    D. Ivan's

7. **The child that Marya gave birth to had what type of deformity?**
   A. One leg
   B. No ears
   C. Six fingers
   D. Gills

8. **What is Lizaveta's nickname?**
   A. "Genius"
   B. "Darling"
   C. "Laocoon"
   D. "Stinking Lizaveta"

9. **To whom did Dmitri loan money?**
   A. Fyodor
   B. Alyosha
   C. Katerina's father
   D. Grushenka's former lover

10. **When Smerdyakov finds money that Fyodor lost, what does he do with it?**
   A. Saves it for his eventual departure
   B. Gives it to his foster parents
   C. Returns it
   D. Spends it on vodka

11. **Why does Katerina fawn over Grushenka?**
   A. Grushenka gives her a dress
   B. Grushenka says she is going back to a former lover
   C. Katerina finds out they are sisters
   D. Grushenka gives her money

12. **Who writes Alyosha a letter that he keeps?**
   A. Ilusha
   B. Father Zossima
   C. Lise
   D. Ivan

13. **How much of the 3,000 rubles from Katerina does Dmitri spend with Grushenka?**
    A. All of it
    B. None of it
    C. 1,500 rubles
    D. 2,500 rubles

14. **What does Father Ferapont advocate to live a holy life?**
    A. Unconditional love
    B. Fasting
    C. Evangelism
    D. Giving to charities

15. **What did Dmitri do to Ilusha's father?**
    A. Stole money from him
    B. Beat him at cards
    C. Slept with his wife
    D. Attacked him

16. **With whom is Ivan in love?**
    A. Katerina
    B. His mother
    C. Lise
    D. Marfa

17. **Of what does Madame Hohlakov disapprove?**
    A. Alyosha's engagement to Lise
    B. Ivan's theories
    C. Dmitri's dalliances
    D. Fyodor's debauchery

18. **When Alyosha is looking for Dmitri in a restaurant, whom does he find instead?**
    A. Grushenka
    B. Lise
    C. Ivan
    D. Smerdyakov

19. **What upsets Ivan about the lot of children in the world?**
   A. They are not educated enough
   B. They are brought up to be meek
   C. They are given too much freedom
   D. They suffer

20. **When does "The Grand Inquisitor" take place?**
   A. The Middle Ages
   B. The beginning of time
   C. The French Revolution
   D. The Spanish Inquisition

21. **What gift does the Inquisitor in "The Grand Inquisitor" think is too much for Man to handle?**
   A. Christianity
   B. Freedom
   C. God's love
   D. Companionship of his fellow man

22. **Who tells Dmitri about the signs Grushenka will use if she visits Fyodor?**
   A. Fyodor
   B. Grushenka
   C. Ivan
   D. Smerdyakov

23. **What happens that causes Alyosha to doubt his faith?**
   A. Ivan goes crazy
   B. His father is murdered
   C. Ilusha dies
   D. Father Zossima dies

24. **How did Father Zossima's older brother die?**
   A. Alcohol poisoning
   B. A duel
   C. Grief
   D. Consumption

25. **What does Dmitri plan to do when he sees Grushenka for the last time?**

A. Sail to America
B. Kill his father
C. Join the monastery
D. Kill himself

Quiz 3 Answer Key

1. **(C)** Twice
2. **(B)** Alyosha
3. **(A)** Dmitri
4. **(B)** He is loving and understanding
5. **(B)** His own conscience
6. **(A)** Dmitri's
7. **(C)** Six fingers
8. **(D)** "Stinking Lizaveta"
9. **(C)** Katerina's father
10. **(C)** Returns it
11. **(B)** Grushenka says she is going back to a former lover
12. **(C)** Lise
13. **(C)** 1,500 rubles
14. **(B)** Fasting
15. **(D)** Attacked him
16. **(A)** Katerina
17. **(A)** Alyosha's engagement to Lise
18. **(C)** Ivan
19. **(D)** They suffer
20. **(D)** The Spanish Inquisition
21. **(B)** Freedom
22. **(D)** Smerdyakov
23. **(D)** Father Zossima dies
24. **(D)** Consumption
25. **(D)** Kill himself

Quiz 4

1. **What happened at Father Zossima's duel?**
    A. He did not fire
    B. His opponent did not show up
    C. He killed his opponent
    D. He grazed his opponent

2. **Who hears Father Zossima's last words?**
    A. Ilusha
    B. Alyosha
    C. Madame Hohlakov
    D. No one

3. **Who tries to cheer up Alyosha after Father Zossima's death?**
    A. Fyodor
    B. Father Ferapont
    C. Grushenka
    D. Ivan

4. **What does Dmitri do to Grushenka's former lover?**
    A. He locks him in another room
    B. He kisses his feet
    C. He threatens his parents
    D. He kills him

5. **Where does Grushenka's maid tell Dmitri that Grushenka is when he asks her?**
    A. Moscow
    B. Fyodor's place
    C. Katerina's place
    D. She does not know

6. **Whose funeral does Alyosha attend at the end of the novel?**
    A. Ilusha's
    B. Fyodor's
    C. Father Zossima's
    D. Ivan's

7. **Who is NOT at the meeting with Father Zossima?**
   A. Miusov
   B. Alyosha
   C. Grigory
   D. Ivan

8. **What does Ivan do after the meeting with Father Zossima?**
   A. He curses at him
   B. He vomits
   C. He receives Father Zossima's blessing
   D. He leaves without a word

9. **What does Father Ferapont do after Father Zossima's death?**
   A. He cries
   B. He prays
   C. He grieves
   D. He mutters incoherently

10. **Which character is NOT religious?**
   A. Dmitri
   B. Fyodor
   C. Alyosha
   D. Father Zossima

11. **Which two characters die on the same day?**
   A. Ivan and Dmitri
   B. Adelaida and Sofya
   C. Father Zossima and Fyodor
   D. Ilusha and Lizaveta

12. **Which character shares his father's temper?**
   A. Dmitri
   B. Alyosha
   C. Father Zossima
   D. Ivan

13. **Who wants to marry Dmitri despite his loving another woman?**
   A. Katerina
   B. Lizaveta
   C. Grushenka
   D. Lise

14. **Who has tempted the prisoner in "The Great Inquisitor"?**
   A. Fyodor
   B. The Devil
   C. Grushenka
   D. Ivan

15. **Who is the youngest Karamazov?**
   A. Dmitri
   B. Fyodor
   C. Alyosha
   D. Ivan

16. **What profession did Father Zossima have before he became an elder?**
   A. Fireman
   B. Soldier
   C. Wedding planner
   D. Carpenter

17. **Who does NOT have a child?**
   A. Adelaida
   B. Katerina
   C. Lizaveta
   D. Sofya

18. **Who tells the courtroom Smerdyakov's damning confession?**
   A. Fyodor
   B. Alyosha
   C. Ivan
   D. Smerdyakov

19. **What does Ivan think of Alyosha at first?**
   A. He thinks he is very nice
   B. He thinks he is brilliant
   C. He hates him deeply
   D. He is skeptical of Alyosha's religious beliefs

20. **Who kills Smerdyakov?**
   A. Dmitri
   B. Fyodor
   C. Ivan
   D. Smerdyakov

21. **How did Dosteovsky's father die?**
   A. Murder
   B. Epilepsy
   C. Consumption
   D. Old age

22. **When did Dostoyevsky write "The Brothers Karamazov"?**
   A. Before he went to prison
   B. Right after his wife died
   C. After the birth of his son
   D. Right before his own death

23. **Who has a dog?**
   A. Ilusha
   B. Fyodor
   C. Grushenka
   D. Ivan

24. **Toward which character is Alyosha loving?**
   A. Dmitri
   B. Fyodor
   C. Ivan
   D. All of the above

25. **Where does Fyodor wait for Grushenka the night he is murdered?**

A. A hotel

B. Behind a shed

C. A restaurant

D. His own house

Quiz 4 Answer Key

1. **(A)** He did not fire
2. **(B)** Alyosha
3. **(C)** Grushenka
4. **(A)** He locks him in another room
5. **(D)** She does not know
6. **(A)** Ilusha's
7. **(C)** Grigory
8. **(C)** He receives Father Zossima's blessing
9. **(D)** He mutters incoherently
10. **(B)** Fyodor
11. **(C)** Father Zossima and Fyodor
12. **(A)** Dmitri
13. **(A)** Katerina
14. **(B)** The Devil
15. **(C)** Alyosha
16. **(B)** Soldier
17. **(B)** Katerina
18. **(C)** Ivan
19. **(D)** He is skeptical of Alyosha's religious beliefs
20. **(D)** Smerdyakov
21. **(A)** Murder
22. **(D)** Right before his own death
23. **(A)** Ilusha
24. **(D)** All of the above
25. **(D)** His own house

Other ClassicNotes from GradeSaver™

Utopia
A Very Old Man With Enormous Wings
Villette
The Visit
Volpone
Waiting for Godot
Waiting for Lefty
Walden
Washington Square
The Waste Land
Where the Red Fern Grows
White Fang
White Noise
White Teeth
Who's Afraid of Virginia Woolf
Wide Sargasso Sea
Winesburg, Ohio
The Winter's Tale
Woyzeck
Wuthering Heights
The Yellow Wallpaper
Yonnondio: From the Thirties

Printed in Great Britain
by Amazon

36976740R00076

DAVID HARTNELL'S

HOLLYWOOD TRIVIA

I'm not one to gossip but....

This is the book with all the OUTRAGEOUS answers

David Bateman

This book is for my best friend and life partner Somboon Khansuk, who, over many years, has taught me so much about myself and life. Without Somboon's unconditional love, trust and support my life would have been deadly dull. My only regret is that our paths didn't cross sooner.

This book is also for my wonderful mother, Gina Ward, for believing in me and supporting my career from day one.

The David Hartnell show broadcasts weekly on Triangle television.
For more David Hartnell trivia visit http://www.hartnells.ihug.co.nz

First published 2003 in New Zealand by David Bateman Ltd,
30 Tarndale Grove, Albany, Auckland, New Zealand

ISBN 1-86953-554-5

Design Carpé Diem Publications Ltd, Christchurch, New Zealand
Printed in China through Colorcraft Ltd

FOREWORD

My old friend, David Hartnell, is known as the 'Hollywood Scribe'. We first met in Sydney, Australia, many years ago, where he used to pop around with his celebrity radio show. He's informed the world of the machinations of the Tinseltown greats and semi-greats for decades. I see him often in La La Land, as he is a world-travelling jet-setter with bags packed, pen and laptop at the ready. He has the energy of a three-year-old. This man speaks one language—Hollywoodese Trash!

And it's all true!

Read him and weep … laughing!

Phyllis Diller

Phyllis Diller
Los Angeles, California, 2003

ACKNOWLEDGEMENTS

First of all, I'm indebted to and must thank those column readers, TV viewers, radio listeners and book buyers who have followed my career over many years. There are literally thousands of people who have made this book possible, sometimes unwittingly. I'm talking about the stars and celebrities who appear within these pages. Without their generosity in making news and being who they are this book would not have been possible—so thanks to you all.

Over some thirty years it's been a real privilege to have met and interviewed so many of Hollywood's illustrious people both in front of and behind the cameras. Also I would like to extend a big thanks to my friends who've helped when putting this book together. Darren Ruston my computer guru who's always extremely generous with his time, teaching me short cuts and updates on my computer. Michael S. Wilk and Eugene Buechele, for their valued Hollywood input over so many years. Clive Nelson, the Editor of the *Sunday News,* for believing in me, not only as a celebrity columnist, but also as a human being. Karine Thomas for her valuable marketing input. Tom Frank, for his generosity and for never being late with his weekly input into my column. My life long friend Robert Young, for the loyalty, encouragement, friendship and style he's shown me over more years than either of us will admit to. Dudley Raine, for his constant Hollywood input to my columns. Darling Phyllis Diller, for writing the foreword and the many many years of valued friendship we've shared. My endless gratitude to Brian Richards, for his friendship, sense of humor and always supporting my career in a positive way. Chris Windram, a gracious lady who put in endless helping me with promotional ideas. Max Cryer, for his years of unwavering friendship and his command of the English language, which I've had to call on from time to time. The late Alice May Williams who acted as my agent, special friend and confidant in Los Angeles for many years—what a lady. Darlene Backer-Russell, for so many excellent trivia tips. The Roosevelt Hotel's Sales Manager Ani Aghamalian, for giving me the green light to tell you so much about my favourite Hollywood hotel. Neville Tilsley, for his friendship and being the world's greatest housesitter, when my partner and I are away on promotional tours. Thanks to my brother-in-law Gordon Rushton for his help when putting together the TV commercial to promote my book. Jim Blackman the CEO and Founder of Triangle Television, for giving me the inspiration and the platform to do my first stand alone TV series. Aaron Beckett, for his hours of help in checking and adding to my Celebrity Birthday List. Miss Cele (our Australian Terrier), for sitting under my desk and keeping my bare feet warm during the winter months when writing this book. Designer Kim Dovey who's made my book look so fabulously Hollywood. To Lorraine Funk and Cara Torrance for their editorial work. A huge thanks to Tim Brown, for his valued input and for the hours he spent ruching my thoughts and words in place. To the entire team at David Bateman Ltd, for being such a delight to work with from day one and accepting this book on its first submission. Lastly but by no means least, a huge thank you to Yvonne Morgan who suggested to Tracey Borgfeldt that David Bateman Ltd publish my book.

CONTENTS

Marilyn Monroe said, 'Hollywood is a place where they'll pay thousands of dollars for your body and fifty cents for your soul … I've slept with producers for work. I'd be a liar if I said I didn't … All the girls did. It was like part of your job. They wanted to sample the merchandise. If you didn't go along, there were another twenty-five girls who would. It wasn't any big tragedy.'

Hollywood can be the cruellest city in the world when it comes to hopeful actors and actresses who move there willing to risk everything to realize their dream. Sure, a handful succeed, but thousands fail. Many times the pressures at the top of the Hollywood ladder can be the very same as the hardship and pain felt at the bottom. Cybill Shepherd once told me, 'Hollywood is the only city in the world where you can climb to the top of the success ladder, and still get stabbed in the back!' I think there's only one word that sums up Hollywood and that's 'survival'! Hollywood has always been a place of paradox. A place where it's best never to make close friends, because it makes it so much harder to stab them in the back.

While living and working in Hollywood I always lived by the three no-no's a Hollywood gossip columnist must never do. One, never answer the phone on the first ring, two, never say 'I'll be right over' and three, never let them see you sweat.

From the first day Hollywood came about, there was gossip, scandals and trivia about its stars. For many years I worked as a makeup artist in the industry and soon found the makeup room the best place to hear all the gossip. Years later I gave up my trade to become a full-time syndicated gossip columnist, something which I've never regretted. I hope you'll enjoy all the gossip and trivia in the following pages.

Now if I've got the occasional date wrong in the book, or the story 'seems' too far-fetched to be true, I'm not sorry. I'll tell you why… I believe in that Hollywood saying: 'Don't bother me with the facts — all I want is the GOSSIP!' I truly believe that there is no worse fate for a gossip columnist than to be taken seriously. After all, when you look up the word 'gossip' in the Collins English Dictionary it says: Gossip – idle talk about other persons, regardless of fact; idle talk or writing; one who talks thus; formerly, familiar friend. Engage in gossip; chatter.

David H.W. Hartnell.
Hollywood, California 2003

THE STARS ARE BORN — WHEN AND WHERE

Brendan Fraser and his wife Afton both share the same birthday—3 December. There is a year difference in their age—he's a year older.

Andy Garcia was born with a conjoined twin, which was no bigger than a tennis ball. Today Andy has a scar on his shoulder where his twin was surgically removed.

Here are some stars that have called Australia home, even though they were born elsewhere:
Olivia Newton-John was born in Cambridge, England, but grew up in Melbourne.
Hugo Weaving was born in Nigeria, Africa, and moved to Sydney when he was 16 years old.
Greta Scacchi was born in Italy and moved to Australia in 1975.
Russell Crowe was born in Wellington, New Zealand, and moved to Sydney at the age of four.
John Farnham was born in Essex, England, and moved to Melbourne at the age of ten.
Colin Friels lives in Australia but was born in Glasgow, Scotland.
Jimmy Barnes was born in Scotland and moved to Australia at the age of six.
Nicole Kidman was born in Hawaii and moved to Sydney at the age of three.
Mel Gibson moved from New York to Sydney at the age of 12 with his ten brothers and sisters.
Naomi Watts moved to Sydney from England when she was 14 years old.
Guy Pearce grew up in Geelong, Victoria, but was born in Cambridgeshire, England. He came to Australia at the age of four.

Minnie Driver was born in Barbados; she lived in the Caribbean until she was nine years old. Then her parents sent her to an English boarding school.

Andrew McCarthy was born the third son of four. His dad was a financier and his mum was an advertising executive.

Michael Douglas thinks being a Libra is a curse because it makes decision-making trickier.

Nicolas Coppola (he changed his surname to Cage) was the youngest of three sons. His mum, Joy Vogeslang, was a creative dancer and choreographer. His dad, August Coppola, taught comparative literature at California State University and later became the Dean of the School of Creative Arts at San Francisco State University. Movie director Francis Ford Coppola is his uncle, actress Talia Shire is his aunt and Sofia Coppola is a cousin. His mum and dad divorced when he was twelve.

Matthew Broderick was born in New York, the third child and only son of playwright/painter Patricia and actor dad James Broderick.

Andy Arturo Garcia Menendez (Andy Garcia) was born in Havana, Cuba, the youngest of three children. His dad was a lawyer who was known as 'The Mayor'; he owned quite a bit of property in Havana. His mum, Amelie, taught English. When the Americans invaded the Bay of Pigs, his mum took the children to Miami.

Madonna was born at Mercy Hospital in Michigan, which is now the Bradley House retirement home.

Laura Dern was the second of two daughters. Her older sister drowned as an infant.

Lara Flynn Boyle was an only child. At the age of six, her parents divorced.

Annette Bening was the daughter of an insurance salesman and was the youngest of four.

Robert Duvall was the second of three sons to be born. His dad was a rear admiral, and his mum was an amateur actress who encouraged his interest in acting.

Rebecca De Mornay was the daughter of American TV personality Wally George. Her parents divorced when she was two years old. Her mum remarried but unfortunately her stepdad died not long after she turned five.

Patricia Arquette was born the middle child of five.

Mickey Rourke is from Scots-Irish descent. His dad was an undertaker and bodybuilder who separated from his mum when Mickey was seven.

Michael Keaton is the youngest of seven children.

English actor Bob Hoskin's dad was a bookkeeper and his mum was a school cook.

Matthew Modine was the youngest of seven children; his father was the manager of a drive-in theatre.

American TV talk-show host Jay Leno's mum Catherine was born in Scotland. His dad, Angelo, is Italian.

Pamela Anderson was the first Canadian baby born on Canada's Centennial Day in 1967.

Many times it's been said and printed that Mel Gibson was born in Australia—not true—he was born in Peekskill, New York. His family moved to Australia when Mel was 12; he attended acting school in Sydney at the State Theatre of New South Wales and the rest is history.

Jack Nicholson was born to an unwed mother who was abandoned by an alcoholic husband. His 'mum' Ethel May, supported daughters June and Lorraine and son Jack by running an at-home beauty parlour. In the early seventies, Jack learned Ethel May was really his grandmother; Lorraine, his aunt; and June, his mother.

Elizabeth Taylor's parents were American, but she was born in London on 27 February 1932. On her 16th birthday, her parents presented her with a baby blue Cadillac, but they wouldn't let her take driving lessons. Elizabeth didn't learn to drive until 1989, when she was well into her fifties. In 1944, after she'd completed the movie *National Velvet*, MGM studios gave her a small birthday party and gifted the 12-year-old with her co-star, the horse called The Pi (short for Pirate), whose real name was King Charles. Many years later when Elizabeth Taylor celebrated her 60th birthday at Disneyland on 27 February 1992, she gave the biggest private birthday party the theme park had ever seen by inviting 1,000 of her closest friends.

Bianca Jagger, ex-wife of Rolling Stone Mick, was born in Nicaragua.

Donald Duck was born in 1934 in Los Angeles, at the end of Walt Disney's pencil.

Kings of the horror movies Christopher Lee, Peter Cushing and Vincent Price all share the same birthday, 27th May.

Johnny Cash, Cher, James Garner and Burt Reynolds are all part Cherokee.

Audrey Hepburn was born in Belgium.

Julie Christie was born in India.

In *Indiana Jones and the Last Crusade*, Sean Connery played Harrison Ford's father. Since Sean was born in 1930 and Harrison in 1942, that means Sean would have been 12 when Harrison was born.

It's often stated that actor Sam Neill was born in New Zealand. In fact he was born in Ireland and immigrated to New Zealand with his parents at the age of seven. His real name is Nigel Neill, but his parents nicknamed him Sam as a baby and the name stuck.

American actress Victoria Principal was born in Japan.

Patrick McGoohan, star of the 1960s cult TV series *The Prisoner*, was not English; he was born in New York.

Robin Williams was born in Edinburgh. His dad was a top executive with the Lincoln car firm, which was based in Scotland. When Robin was one they moved back to America.

WHAT'S IN A NAME?

LL Cool J's first real name is James.

Hugh Grant is listed in the English edition of *Who's Who* as Hugh John Mungo Grant.

In 1996, ex-Beatle Ringo Starr appeared in a Japanese advert for apple sauce, which, just coincidentally, is what his name means in Japanese.

Hulk Hogan's real name is Terry Bollea.

Sir Elton John has a nickname for Billy Connolly—Maureen. Sir Elton's nickname is Sharon.

Originally the movie *Close Encounters* was going to be titled *Watch the Skies*.

Liza Minnelli's middle name is May.

Vin Diesel was born Vincent but he's never revealed his true last name.

It's rumoured that the Beatles were originally going to be called the Meatles. Legend has it they picked the name because John Lennon once worked in a meat market.

The smash hit Austin Powers movie *The Spy Who Shagged Me* didn't easily translate into other languages. Here are a few examples:
Iceland: *The Spy Who Nailed Me*
Japan: *Austin Powers Deluxe*
Spain: *The Spy Who Serviced Me*
France: *The Spy Who Shot Me*
Singapore: *The Spy Who Was Good To Me*
Germany: *The Spy in the Secret Missionary Position*
Latin America: *The Seductive Spy*
Then the movie was nearly called *Austinpussy*.

He started his professional wrestling career as Flex Kavana, then he took on the name, Rocky Maivia. Today we know him as movie star, The Rock. Mind you, his parents still call him by his real name, Duane Johnson.

In 1997, Madonna provoked condemnation from the Catholic Church after naming her baby daughter Lourdes.

Kate Hudson's middle name is Garry. Because of the space between her eyes, her brother Oliver nicknamed her Hammerhead Shark.

An agent once suggested to Leonardo DiCaprio that he should change his name to Lenny William, which was easier to pronounce.

In November 2002, Courteney Cox dropped her actor husband David Arquette's last name from her moniker. Speaking to *In Style* magazine, the TV actress revealed she had reverted to her maiden name out of respect for her father Richard Cox, who had died of cancer in 2001. 'When I was a kid, I wanted to change my name so badly because I didn't like it,' she said. 'Now that my dad's gone, I don't want to lose it. It's not an issue for David ... I am an Arquette, but I'm also a Cox ... And when we have children they will not be Cox-Arquettes, they will be Arquettes.'

Richard Gere and actress Carey Lowell named their son Jigme—which is 'fearless' in Tibetan—in honour of Richard's Buddhist faith.

Country super-singing-star Shania Twain was originally named Eileen Edwards. When she signed with Mercury Records, she was urged to change her first name and selected Shania because it honours her stepfather's Ojibwa Indian ancestry and means 'I'm on my way' in Ojibwa.

R2D2, the little robot hero of the 1977 movie *Star Wars*, was named after a piece of film editors' jargon—it means 'Reel 2, Dialogue 2'.

Harrison Ford's dad was an Irish Catholic who worked as an advertising executive. His mum was a Russian Jew.

Nicolas Cage was born Nicholas Coppola. He changed it and assumed the name Cage in admiration of composer John Cage and comic-book character Luke Cage.

Debra Winger was born into a Hungarian-Jewish orthodox family in Ohio. Her family were the owners of the Winger Brothers Meat Company.

Kiefer Sutherland's first name was taken from the writer Warren David Kiefer, who scripted his dad Donald's debut movie, *Castle of the Living Dead*. He was christened Kiefer William Frederick Dempsey George Rufus Sutherland in London, where he was born in 1966.

Lou Diamond Phillips was named after the World War II hero, Leland 'Lou' Diamond. His dad was a navy aircraft mechanic.

Laura Dern was born with theatre and show business in her blood; both her mum, Diane Ladd, and her dad, Bruce Dern, are Oscar nominees. They parted when Laura was just two years old. Her great-uncle was the poet and playwright Archibald MacLeish; Tennessee Williams was a cousin and her great-grandfather was a governor of Utah. She says that one of her earliest memories of her dad was in the movie *Hush Hush, Sweet Charlotte*.

At an early age William Dafoe rebelled against his name, because he hated the nickname Billy, so he changed it to Willem.

Best-selling author Anne Rice was born Howard Allen O'Brien.

Michael Douglas changed his name to Michael Keaton, because there was already a Michael Douglas in show business. He named himself Keaton after seeing a newspaper picture of Diane Keaton.

Courtney Thorne Smith's name is a combination of her dad's name, Smith, and her mum's maiden name, which was Thorne.

It's rumoured that John Travolta named his son, Jett, because of his passion for planes. After all, John has eight different jet licences.

Bruce Springsteen never liked his nickname 'The Boss', which he got back in the 1970s while he was working small nightclubs in Asbury Park, New York.

Sir Elton John has used the names Bobo Latrine, Sir Brian Bigbum and Sir Humphrey Handbag when he's booked into hotels around the world. He did it as an 'in' joke and so the press and fans don't know what hotel he's staying in.

The 'L' in Samuel L Jackson stands for Leroy.

Christina Claire Ciminella changed her name to Wynonna after the town of Wynonna, when she heard it mentioned in the song *Route 66*.

Catherine Zeta-Jones adopted the name Zeta from her grandmother's Christian name.

Gordon Matthew got the nickname 'Sting' because his favourite shirt had black-and-yellow stripes just like a bee.

Sean Penn and his wife Robin named their son (born in 1993) Hopper Jack after Dennis Hopper and Jack Nicholson.

Rob Lowe's middle name is Helper.

Lucy Liu's middle name is Alexis.

At 22, Nathan Lane took the name Nathan (his real name is Joseph) after playing Nathan Detroit in a dinner-theatre production of the musical *Guys and Dolls*. Also, there was another Joe Lane already registered with the American Actors Equity.

Joseph Fiennes's middle name is Alberic.

Robert Downey Jr's middle name is John.

Benjamin Bratt was so thin at high school he got the nickname 'Scarecrow'.

Kevin Spacey's real surname is Fowler. Spacey is a contraction of Spencer Tracy, his favourite actor.

Jamie Lee is married to Christopher Guest, who is an English Lord. He became the fifth Lord Haden-Guest when his father died in 1966. So by rights you should always address Jamie as Lady Haden-Guest.

Jennifer Aniston only uses her maiden name for film and TV credits. Her family name used to be Anastassakis.

Actor Jude Law was named after the Beatles song *Hey Jude*.

Avid painter and long-time singer Tony Bennett signs his paintings under his family name, Anthony Domenick Benedetto.

Whoopi Goldberg's real name is Caryn Johnson. School classmates nicknamed her Whoopi Cushion; her mum suggested switching cushion to Goldberg so she'd be taken seriously as an actress.

When *Frasier* star David Hyde Pierce moved to Hollywood and joined the Screen Actors Guild, he discovered there was another David Pierce, and began using his middle name as well.

Amanda Rogers changed her name to Portia De Rossi at the age of fourteen.

The two English actors Colin Firth and Peter Firth are not related.

Marie Osmond's first name is really Olive. Somehow Olive Osmond doesn't have the same ring as Marie Osmond.

Some cartoon characters started life with a different name. Mickey Mouse was born Mortimer Mouse; Goofy was first known as Dippy Dawg; Happy Rabbit changed his name to Bugs Bunny and Tom, of *Tom and Jerry* fame, was first named Jasper.

Shock rocker Marilyn Manson's real name is Brian Warner.

Paul was the real name of the original Lassie, and every Lassie since has been given the nickname Paul.

Sir Elton John, born Reg Dwight, took his stage name from two of his friends, Elton Dean and Long John Baldry, whom he played with in a band in grammar school. He was the very first superstar to admit to being bisexual.

Dustin Hoffman's mother was a great fan of the silent cowboy movie star Dustin Farnum, who starred in the first full-length movie ever made in Hollywood. That's where Dustin gets his name.

Have you ever wondered how River Phoenix, the young Hollywood actor, got his name? His parents were hippies in the 1960s and named him after the River of Life in Hermann Hesse's book *Siddhartha*. They took their surname, Phoenix, from the mythical bird which burnt itself but rose from the ashes to live again. Incidentally, River's brothers and sisters also have names reminiscent of flower-power days; Leaf, Rainbow, Summer and Liberty.

When they were making the first *Jaws* movie, the cast and crew nicknamed the shark Bruce, which was a name that stuck through all the sequels.

Doris von Kappellhof was named Doris Day by bandleader Barney Rapp, whose favourite song was *Day After Day*, which Doris had sung many times with the band.

Maurice Joseph Micklewhite got his stage name from the movie *The Caine Mutiny*. We know him as Sir Michael Caine.

Marilyn Monroe got her Christian name from her 20th Century-Fox agent Ben Lyon, because of his admiration for the actress Marilyn Miller. Monroe was her mother's maiden name.

Here are a few more celebs that tried to improve on the names they were given at birth:

IS	WAS
Andy Garcia	Andres Garcia-Menendez
Axl Rose	William Bailey
Bono	Paul Hewson
Bo Derek	Mary Cathleen Collins
Ben Kingsley	Krishna Bhanji
Brad Pitt	William Bradley Pitt
Cher	Cherilyn Sarkisian
Courtney Love	Love Michelle Harrison
Christian Slater	Christian Hawkins
David Bowie	David Jones
Demi Moore	Demitria Guynes
Doris Day	Doris von Kappellhaf
Elle Macpherson	Eleanor Gow
Eric Clapton	Eric Clapp
George Michael	Georgios Kyriacos Panayiotou
Geena Davis	Viginia Davis
Goldie Hawn	Goldie Studlendgehawn
Julie Andrews	Julia Elizabeth Wells
Jane Seymour	Joyce Penelope Frankenberg
Jason Alexander	Jay Scott Greenspan
Jackie Chan	Chan Kwong-Sang
Jonathan Taylor Thomas	Jonathan Weiss
Jodie Foster	Alicia Christian Foster
Jennifer Jason Leigh	Jennifer Morrow
Kate Capshaw	Kathy Sue Nail
Kathy Bates	Kathleen Doyal Bates
Kirk Douglas	Issur Danielovitch
Meg Ryan	Margaret Hyra
Mel Gibson	Columcille Gerard Gibson

Michael Keaton	Michael Douglas
Ricky Martin	Enrique Martin Morales
Rita Hayworth	Margarita Cansino
Stevie Wonder	Steveland Morris Hardaway
Susan Sarandon	Susan Abigail Tomalin
Sting	Gordon Sumner
Tim Allen	Tim Allen Dick
Tom Cruise	Thomas Cruise Mapother IV
Woody Harrelson	Woodrow Tracy Harrelson
Woody Allen	Allen Stewart Konigsberg
Whoopi Goldberg	Caryn Johnson
Winona Ryder	Winona Horowitz

Jim Carrey's middle name is Eugene.

Nicole Kidman's nickname in school was 'Stalky'.

Mickey Mouse is known as 'Topolion' in Italy.

Sesame Street characters Bert and Ernie were named after Bert the cop and Ernie the taxi driver in Frank Capra's 1946 movie *It's a Wonderful Life*.

Billy Joel's nickname is 'The Piano Man', but years ago he played piano in a Los Angeles hotel lounge bar under the name of William Martin.

The sorcerer's name in the Disney movie *Fantasia* is Yensid, which is Disney spelt backwards.

Muppet Show creator Jim Henson named Kermit the Frog after Kermit Scott, a childhood friend who became a Professor of Philosophy at Purdue University.

Robbie Williams' middle name is Maximillian.

It is rumoured that *Nightmare on Elm Street* director Wes Craven named the nasty Freddy Krueger after a grade school bully who always tormented him.

Jennifer Love Hewitt's older brother Todd picked Jennifer's name when she was born.

Cybill Shepherd was named after her grandfather Cy and her father Bill.

LOVE, MARRIAGE AND DIVORCE, HOLLYWOOD STYLE

In late 2002, Liz Hurley refused an offer of $313,000 a year from American millionaire Steve Bing, the father of her baby son, towards the child's upbringing. Steve said he would pay the money into a trust for his son Damian, until he was 18. Liz replied by saying that the money was 'not wanted or welcome'.

The *New York Post* reported that Russell Crowe demanded that the waiters at a Sydney restaurant hand over photos they took of his engagement party. Crowe had let staffers snap away as he asked Danielle Spencer to marry him and celebrated with family and friends. Russell swore the waiters to secrecy until the engagement was officially announced on Sunday 15 December 2002. The next day he ordered the restaurant to turn over the film. There was a fear that they would be published; so the restaurant gave them up.

In 2002, Billy Crystal and his wife Janice celebrated 25 years of married life together; a record for a Hollywood couple these days.

Janet Jackson married video director Rene Elizondo in secret, a secret they kept from the public for nine years. Only family and very close friends knew of their marriage. They split up in June 2000, after 15 years together. In the divorce papers, Rene claimed the marriage was not announced, as Janet 'wanted me out of the limelight'. He also stated that he'd co-written some 37 of her songs, but never once received a credit for them in order to protect their secret.

For David Arquette's 31st birthday bash in 2002, his wife Courtney Cox-Arquette hired his favourite hamburger fast-food truck, which she placed in the car park of the trendy nightclub Forty Deuce on Melrose Avenue. Among the who's who celebrity guest list were: Jon Lovitz, David Spade, Brad Pitt, Jennifer Aniston and Tobey Maguire. To top off the birthday celebrations David's drag-queen brother, Alexis, sang *Happy Birthday* a la Marilyn Monroe!

In July 2002, at the age of 84, the debonair actor John Forsyth secretly married 62-year-old Beverly Hills businesswoman Nicole Carter. John was widowed in 1994 when Julie, his beloved second wife of 51 years, died.

In November 2002, American magician David Blaine broke up with actress Daryl Hannah because he claims she was too good for him.

Jennifer Aniston and Brad Pitt paid $100,000 to ensure their fans, paparazzi and any uninvited guests didn't gate-crash their wedding.

In 1998, David Arquette did things the old-fashioned way when he asked Courteney Cox's dad for permission to marry her.

In 1994 twenty-six-year-old Anna Nicole Smith married 87-year-old J. Howard Marshall. He died 14 months later at the age of 90 and a court awarded Anna nearly $90 million of his fortune in 2002.

On Madonna's 27th birthday, 16 August 1985, and the day before Sean Penn's 25th birthday, they were married at the seaside Malibu home of a Penn family friend. One Italian journalist in total camouflage gear camped out in the bushes from 1.30 a.m., only to be caught and removed from the property. Another very enterprising photographer rented a helicopter, which hovered over the wedding site, completely drowning out the couple's wedding vows. A guest had written an obscene message in the sand for the helicopter pilot and photographer to read. One tabloid reported that Sean had actually fired a pistol at the chopper. It was said that Sean later declared, 'I would have been very excited to see one of those helicopters burn and the bodies inside melt.' On 5 January 1989 Madonna filed for divorce.

Susan Sarandon went out with David Bowie for three years in the 1980s.

When Julie Andrews was 13, she met a 13-year-old boy called Tony Walton who later in life became a stage designer and Julie's first husband. In 1967 Julie filed for divorce on the grounds of mental cruelty. From that day to this she has refused to discuss exactly what this entailed.

Don Johnson bought Bamboo Island in Vietnam as a first wedding anniversary present for his wife, Kelly Phleger.

Marilyn Monroe converted to Judaism when she married Arthur Miller.

In December 1985, Sylvester Stallone dismayed his mother by marrying Brigitte Nielsen, 22, in Beverly Hills. Both returned to the set of *Cobra* the next day. A couple of weeks before the wedding Sylvester's mum came out swinging at the bride in a US tabloid saying 'My son Sly has fallen for a gold digger.'

A FEW SHORT MARRIAGES IN HOLLYWOOD HISTORY ARE:

Actor Colin Farrell and English actress Amelia Warner split in November 2001 after just four months of marriage.

Courtney Thorne-Smith said goodbye to her scientist hubby Andrew Conrad in June 2001 after seven months of marriage.

Shannen Doherty and Ashley Hamilton tied the knot in September 1993, but approximately four months later they parted.

Baywatch star Carmen Electra and basketball's wild man Dennis Rodman filed for annulment after only nine days. They tied the knot in November 1998. They untied it five months later.

Cher and Greg Allman were married for five days.

Dennis Hopper and Michelle Phillips tied the knot for eight days.

Patty Duke and rock promoter Michael Tell lived in wedded bliss for 13 days.

Lisa Marie Presley and Nicolas Cage lasted 170 days; Nic filed for divorce in December 2002.

In September 1995, Charlie Sheen walked down the aisle with model Donna Peele. He walked out on the marriage five months later.

Alyssa Milano was married to musician Cinjun Tate on 1 January 1999. Both called it quits 10 months later.

Oscar-winner Helen Hunt was married to Hank Azaria. The couple called it quits in June 2000 after a scant 11 months.

Jennifer Lopez's marriage to Cris Judd lasted just nine months.

In 1986, it was rumoured that Arnold Schwarzenegger invited the Pope to his wedding to Maria Shriver. He didn't show up.

Demi Moore was once engaged to Emilio Estevez. She married Bruce Willis in 1987; they were married by singer Little Richard.

Christie Brinkley was married to Ricky Taubman in December 1994; seven months later they called it quits.

Following Joan Collins' celebrated divorce from Peter Holm in December 1986 (11 months after their wedding), Joan was noticed wowing London in a low-cut gown; flashing a cleavage that appeared more pneumatic than usual. An English tabloid newspaper speculated that Joan had augmented her already imposing bustline; she threatened to sue the paper, but never got around to taking the case to court.

In 1998, Catherine Oxenberg said, 'I do' to movie producer Robert Evans; 10 days later the marriage was over.

Paula Abdul and Emilio Estevez's 1992 marriage lasted two years — even longer than Paula's 17-month second marriage to Brad Beckerman in 1996.

Julia Roberts and country star Lyle Lovett parted in March 1995 after 21 months of marriage. The couple had spent only seven weeks together during their first eight months of marriage.

Drew Barrymore's marriage to Jeremy Thomas (a bar owner) in 1994 lasted just short of five months. Her second marriage to Tom Green in 2001 lasted 165 days.

Lisa Marie Presley slapped Michael Jackson with divorce papers in January 1996 after a marriage of 20 months.

Janet Jackson and James Debarge married in September 1984; they called it quits in January 1985.

Robin Givens and Svetozar Marinkovic were married for a day on 22 August 1982 and called it quits on 23 August 1982.

Liza Minnelli turned down an invitation to mum Judy Garland's fifth marriage, saying: 'I can't make it, Mama, but I promise to come to your next one.'

In 1995, on the set of *Seven*, Gwyneth Paltrow and her co-star Brad Pitt fell in love. Later that year when Brad won a Golden Globe Award for *Twelve Monkeys*, he called her, 'My angel, the love of my life'. They got engaged the following year, and then called it off the next.

Jada Pinkett Smith's parents divorced not long after she was born. She was brought up by her mum and grandmother in a rough Baltimore neighbourhood.

Celine Dion married Rene Angelil in 1994. In 2000 they renewed their vows at Caesars Palace in Las Vegas.

Keanu Reeves once played singer Paula Abdul's love interest in a music video.

Sarah Jessica Parker lived with Robert Downey Jr for seven years during the 1980s.

Danny Moder bought Julia Roberts two first edition D H Lawrence books as a wedding gift.

Angelina Jolie demanded that her estranged husband Billy Bob Thornton return five phials of her blood, fearing that he would use them to put a curse on her. Angelina demanded that he gave them back as part of her 2002 divorce proceedings. Billy, the son of a psychic mother, allegedly once told her: 'As long as I have your blood, I'll always have control of you.'

Exactly nine months after Elvis Presley married Priscilla on 1 May 1967, Lisa Marie Presley was born.

1990 saw a number of movie stars fall in love with each other on the set: Tom Cruise and Nicole Kidman, *Days Of Thunder*; Kiefer Sutherland and Julia Roberts, *Flatliners*; Warren Beatty and Madonna, *Dick Tracy;* and Nicolas Cage and Laura Dern, *Wild At Heart*.

When Elizabeth Taylor married Larry Fortensky in 1992 (a construction worker whom she'd met while at the Betty Ford Clinic), Mrs Nancy

Reagan gave them a silver cake server as a wedding gift. One observer was overheard to say, 'Considering Liz has continually battled an eating problem, that really takes the cake.' After her wedding she threw her wedding bouquet over her shoulder and songwriter Carol Bayer Sager caught it. Elizabeth snatched it right back and sent it the next day to be permanently preserved by a special chemical process. While married to Larry Fortensky, the 200-rose bouquet was displayed behind glass at her home. In 1995, Elizabeth agreed to give Larry $4 million and an apartment to make him 'go quietly'.

Cher once said being married to Greg Allman was 'like going to Disneyland on acid. You knew you had a good time, but you can't remember what you did.'

After a broken romance, a 21-year-old Elton John tried to commit suicide but it was, in his words, 'a Woody Allen-type suicide'—he turned on the gas and 'left all the windows open'.

When former *Partridge Family* TV teen idol David Cassidy (41 at the time) married his songwriter girlfriend Sue Shifrin (42 at the time), at a private ceremony in Los Angeles, their two-month-old son Beau was their best man.

Tommy Lee and Pamela Anderson were married 20 days after they first met.

Warren Beatty has held the title of Hollywood Sex Symbol for more than 25 years. His romantic involvements have been well publicised in every gossip column, with just about every eligible woman in Tinseltown. Here are some of his better-known celebrity dates over the years: Mary Tyler Moore, Jackie Onassis, Jane Fonda, Goldie Hawn, Faye Dunaway, Joan Collins, Catherine Deneuve, Britt Ekland, Diane Keaton, Kate Jackson, Joni Mitchell, Vivien Leigh, Vanessa Redgrave, Diana Ross, Jean Seberg, Madonna, Barbra Streisand, Elizabeth Taylor, Natalie Wood, Cher, Candice Bergen, Julie Christie and Brigitte Bardot. When Warren dumped singer/songwriter Carly Simon, she wrote the smash-hit song *You're So Vain* and dedicated it to him. He married Annette Bening in 1992.

Robert Redford proposed to his wife from a pay phone in New York.

In October 1977, actor John Ritter married actress Nancy Morgan. The morning after their wedding night John had an early start on his TV sitcom *Three's Company.* As a protest at having to work while on honeymoon he turned up on the set in his pajamas.

Mel Gibson is very much a married man; he and his wife Robyn celebrated their 20th year of marriage in 2000. Mel calls home an 800-acre cattle farm in Australia. Mel is well known for his zany impressions of Hollywood stars; Sylvester Stallone, Marlon Brando and James Cagney are among his favourites. Mel doesn't think much of his worldwide sex-symbol image. 'If my wife thinks I'm sexy, it means a lot more to me.'

To date only two Hollywood actresses have married royalty; Rita Hayworth married Prince Aly Khan in 1949 and Grace Kelly married Prince Rainier in 1956.

In 1974, Liza Minnelli married Jack Haley Jr. Jack Haley Sr played the Tin Man in *The Wizard of Oz* and escorted Liza's mum, Judy Garland, down the yellow brick road. They divorced in 1978.

Composer Lord Lloyd-Webber's first two wives were both called Sarah. His second wife, Sarah Brightman, was a dancer in his London production of *Cats*; he later fell in love with her when he heard her sing Rachmaninov in Russian. He then cast her in the lead role of Christine in the original stage production of *The Phantom of the Opera*.

Danny DeVito and Rhea Perlman married at their home during a lunch break from their TV series *Taxi* in 1982.

After a huge celebrity wedding on the 17th March 2002—with 15 bridesmaids, Michael Jackson as best man and Elizabeth Taylor as matron of honour—Liza Minnelli and David Gest called it quits, 16 months later.

BRIEF BIOGRAPHIES

The only alien footprints outside Mann's Chinese Theatre on Hollywood Blvd, belong to the aliens from *Star Wars*: C3PO, Darth Vader and R2D2.

Brad Pitt went to Springfield, Missouri's Kickapoo High School.

In 1954, *The Guinness Book of World Records* voted actress Greta Garbo the most beautiful woman who ever lived.

Marilyn Monroe sang *Happy Birthday* to President John F. Kennedy in 1962, but it was Audrey Hepburn who sang *Happy Birthday, Mr President* to him for his last birthday in 1963.

A few stars that are vegetarian:
Bryan Adams, Rosanna Arquette, Tobey Maguire, Alec Baldwin, Kim Basinger, Danny DeVito, Woody Harrelson, Michael Jackson, Madonna, Steve Martin, Matthew Modine, Meatloaf, John Corbett, Kelly Osbourne, Sir Ian McKellan, Russell Simmons, Natalie Portman, Jerry Seinfeld and Lindsay Wagner. Jennie Garth, a vegetarian who doesn't mind devouring the odd ugly living creature said: 'It's very hard for me to eat anything with a face. Shrimp is about it for me. They're not very cute.' Josh Hartnett's decision to go meat-free came several years ago and happened in an instant. He says, 'One day I was cutting up a chicken for my mom, and I hit a tumour with the knife. There was pus and blood all over the place. That was enough for me.'

Oscar winner Halle Berry lost 85 per cent of the hearing in her left ear—this was caused by a one-time boyfriend she's always refused to name, only ever saying that he was well known in Hollywood and had bashed her.

It's rumoured that Puff Daddy owns five mobile phones and makes some 150 calls a day. 'The secret to success in business is making and returning calls,' he says. Puff also owns no less than 30 pairs of designer sunglasses.

Matthew McConaughey and Renée Zellweger were friends at college; they appeared together in a number of school productions.

Britney Spears once admitted to stalking Brad Pitt when she was younger. She used to stand outside his house for days hoping to get a look at her dream man.

Jerry Hall was the leg-wrestling champion at her Texas high school.

When actor Ed Norton graduated from Yale University he had a degree in history.

James Van Der Beek was an honours student, but while at kindergarten he was found to be dyslexic. He learned to read in a special class.

Gene Simmons of the shock-rock group Kiss, was born in Israel. He speaks four different languages and holds a BA in Education.

Do you know what Marilyn Monroe and Albert Einstein had in common? Their intelligence quotients (according to some sources). As amazing as this sounds, both Marilyn and Albert had IQs of 160 plus, making them intelligence equals.

Sean Connery has made over 50 movies. In 1988, he won his first Oscar for Best Supporting Actor as cop Jim Malone in *The Untouchables*. He was 32 when he became James Bond for the first time; he went on to play 007 in seven movies. In 1969 he made his first James Bond comeback, receiving 1 million dollars plus 12.5 per cent of the profits. Sean hated every minute he had to wear his James Bond toupée, and got rid of it the second he gave up his licence to kill.

The gaudy Graceland mansion that was once the home of Elvis Presley is still one of America's biggest tourist attractions. On an average day 1,700 people visit there; four people call asking to speak to Elvis and three people are ejected from the grounds for trying to take away chunks of earth from his grave. The mansion receives around four to five letters a day addressed to Elvis.

At the age of 11, Sigourney Weaver was 6 feet tall. She changed her name from Susan to Sigourney, which she got from a character in F Scott Fitzgerald's novel *The Great Gatsby*. The character was called Mrs Sigourney Howard.

In November 2002, Barbie finally joined the ranks of her on-screen peers when her prints were set in cement at Mann's Chinese Theatre on Hollywood Blvd. Doing the honours at the ceremony to mark the release of *Barbie as Rapunzel* was Barbara Handler, the daughter of the curvaceous doll's late originator Ruth Handler.

In an Internet UK poll in mid 2002, Kate Winslet was voted the number-one celebrity that most English people wanted to see performing on the London stage.

Olivia Newton-John was born in Cambridge, England. When she was five, her father moved the family to Australia, where he took up a job as headmaster of a Melbourne grammar school. At the age of 15, Olivia went back to live in England, and a couple of years later toured with Cliff Richard. She still calls Australia home.

When Steven Spielberg applied to the University of Southern California Cinema School he was turned down. He applied a second time and the same thing happened.

Julie Roberts joined the American Screen Actors Guild; she found another Julie Roberts already listed, so she became Julia.

Harrison Ford struggled before reaching the top. After bit parts in such TV shows as *Gunsmoke*, *Ironside* and *The Virginian*, and a role in the 1970 flop *Zabriskie Point*, he became a carpenter. George Lucas cast Ford in *American Graffiti* in 1972, but Ford didn't hang up his carpenter's tools until the 1976 blockbuster *Star Wars*.

At the age of 14 Jerry Hall announced to her father, a long-distance lorry driver, and her mother, a medical-records clerk, 'Ah'm goin' to be real famous and real rich some day.' The 5 ft 11 in model has lived up to her prediction. She was 'discovered' by a model agent scout on a St Tropez nudist beach in 1972.

Raquel Welch was once crowned Miss San Diego. Her first TV appearance was as a weather girl on a San Diego TV station; a job she took up a few weeks after leaving high school.

Coming up to 40 with five children to bring up, Phyllis Diller was a copywriter for a California radio station before she found fame and fortune as a stand-up comic at the Purple Onion nightclub in San Francisco in 1955. In the 1960s she was named one of the world's most outrageous stars for remarks like, 'When I go to the beach wearing a bikini, even the tide won't come in!' Her idol and good friend was Bob Hope.

In the 1960s, Bette Midler, still a struggling actress, worked her way up from the chorus to a leading role as Tevye's eldest daughter in the Broadway show *Fiddler on the Roof.*

Joan Collins's first job in theatre was assistant stage manager in Maidstone, Kent. She swept the stage, helped prompt the actors and was the dresser for the leading lady. At 19 she signed up with the J. Arthur Rank Organization for $120 a week. Not until the age of 40, however, when she played Blake Carrington's wife in *Dynasty* did she suddenly become a superstar. In 1983, at the age of 50, she posed semi-nude for *Playboy* magazine, which made the issue a complete sellout. In 1985, America's *TV Guide* magazine named her the most beautiful woman on TV.

When rock queen Tina Turner turned the big five-0 in 1989, she hired London's ultra-exclusive Reform Club and had it decorated with hundreds of white lilies and over 1,000 white candles. Her birthday cake stood three feet high, was topped with a life-size royal crown, and cost a whopping $8,000. Tina arrived in a Dior one-off designer gown at a cost of $40,000. Her guests included Shirley Bassey, Dire Straits, Duran Duran, Jerry Hall, Mick Jagger and Eric Clapton. In her birthday speech Tina said she did not worry about turning 50; in fact she hasn't worried about age since she became a Buddhist.

Michael Caine had to redub 127 lines in the movie *Alfie*, to make his accent intelligible for American audiences.

Tom Cruise suffered from dyslexia, as did both his mother and sister. As a child he was put on a special reading course.

Steve Martin was a cheerleader at high school in Texas where he was born.

Before he became a full-time singer Art Garfunkel majored in architecture at Columbia University in New York.

Kim Basinger was once an agoraphobic who didn't want to leave her house for months at a time.

At the age of 12, singer/actress Olivia Newton-John won an English Hayley Mills look-alike contest.

Superstar Mel Gibson almost became a Catholic priest instead of a box-office idol. His staunchly religious dad, Hutton, pounded the faith into all his 11 children. Mel is even named after an Irish saint. When he was an altar boy 'I used to trip over my cassock or set myself on fire,' he said. At the age of 12 he entered a strict all-boys Catholic school and began to think about becoming a priest.

Robert Redford refuses to give autographs, and hates being stopped or pointed out by people in the streets.

Actress and one-time Revlon model Lauren Hutton used to raise earthworms as a child and sell them.

On 18 May 1989, actor Rob Lowe was caught in a compromising position by Fulton County officials who announced they had a home video of night games starring Rob and an underage girl.

Comedian and TV star Bill Cosby has a PhD in Education from the University of Massachusetts.

When Courtney Love was in her early teens, she stole a *Kiss* T-shirt from a department store. She was sent to a juvenile detention centre for the theft.

As a child Orlando Bloom faced the challenge of being dyslexic head on, at school he ended up with eight O-levels and three A-levels. These days dyslexia hardly affects him.

SPORTS, GAMES AND HOBBIES OF THE STARS

Justin Timberlake collects cars for a hobby. At last count he had nine including a Dodge Viper and a Porsche to name but a few. He also has five motorbikes.

For years, Pierce Brosnan has enjoyed painting as a hobby; he's become an accomplished abstract and impressionist painter.

Kylie Minogue has a pocket Scrabble set which she takes wherever she goes; she loves board games and plays them at every opportunity.

Mick Jagger makes home-made jam and gives it to all his friends.

William Shatner and his fourth wife Elizabeth Martin have a love of horses; he's a horse breeder and she's a horse trainer.

David Arquette's hobby is painting clowns; he's received rave reviews for them.

In 2002, Justin Timberlake became addicted to yoga; he now does it every day.

Sylvester Stallone paints in oils and has had a number of exhibitions in the US.

Minnie Driver has written a number of songs and some day she hopes to start a pop career.

Neve Campbell was a member of the National Ballet of Canada until she was sixteen.

In late July 2002, John Travolta was not allowed to land at Hong Kong airport because his old plane is too noisy. At the time he was on a world tour promoting QANTAS airlines. Planes have been his hobby for years.

Sarah Michelle Gellar was a champion figure skater and toyed with the idea of becoming a professional. She also has a brown belt in tae kwon do.

Geena Davis is among the top 30 women archers in the US. She is also a very talented cartoonist and can play the drums, flute, organ and piano.

Lisa Kudrow is a dab hand at pool.

George Clooney owns a model-train set and keeps a pot-bellied pig called Max.

Gerard Depardieu owns a very successful wine business in France, producing Bordeaux wine.

One of Leonardo DiCaprio's hobbies is impersonations; he does a very good Jack Nicholson.

Robert Duval has a huge passion for the tango; he practises every day.

One of Denzel Washington's hobbies is writing poetry.

Orlando Bloom is a wonderful sculptor.

John Stamos collects Sammy Davis Jr memorabilia.

Jennifer Tilly collects hats from the 1920s.

Freddy Prinze Jr has a huge collection of old comic books.

Salma Hayek collects religious symbols.

Sarah Michelle Gellar collects antique books.

Matt LeBlanc has a passion for photography; landscapes are his speciality. It's a hobby that has taken him all around the world, both photographing and showing his work.

Edward Norton speaks fluent Japanese, which started as a hobby.

Pink collects stuffed frogs.

Josh Hartnett's hobby is oil painting.

As a teenager Hillary Swank competed in the Junior US Olympics and the Washington State Championships in swimming.

Matthew Broderick has a collection of 76 trombones.

Did you know that Paula Abdul got her showbiz start as a cheerleader for the Los Angeles Lakers basketball team? After a few months she took over as the group's choreographer and later became Janet Jackson's dance instructor.

Funny lady Phyllis Diller is an excellent painter of stylised heads; her work sells for big bucks in art galleries all around the world. This is something she started to do as a hobby for relaxation. She also collects vintage cars. Her prized car is a three quarter scale model of a 1927 shiny black Mercedes Benz hotrod which has a bright leather interior. She bought the car new in 1968 for $30,000.

Steven Spielberg used to breed chickens as a hobby.

When Ted Danson landed the role of bartender Sam Malone on *Cheers*, he went to the American Bartender School and graduated second in his class. Originally his character was meant to be an ex-football player, but at the last minute the show's creators made him an ex-baseball player because they didn't think Ted looked athletic enough to have played football.

In the 1990s, Academy Award winner Robert Duvall was voted by *Tennis* magazine as the best celebrity tennis player.

Kenny Rogers has a 1,200-acre farm in Georgia, where he breeds Arab horses and cattle.

Jade Jagger collects greyhounds.

Arnold Schwarzenegger's favourite hobby is chess.

FAMILY TIES

Leonardo DiCaprio's mother was born in a bomb shelter during an air raid in the UK. She travelled to America after World War II.

Tom Hanks is a descendant of Nancy Hanks, US President Abraham Lincoln's mother.

What do Hans Christian Anderson, Carol Burnett, Frank Sinatra, Jack Nicholson, Barry Manilow, Eric Clapton, Louis Gossett Jr, Charlton Heston, Al Pacino, Lisa Marie Presley and Robin Williams have in common? They are all only children.

Pierce Brosnan's parents split up when he was a child; he didn't see his dad until he was 33 years old.

Bill Murray told the Columbia University School of the Arts class of 2000, 'I just sort of got into acting to get out of the house. My mother was driving me nuts.'

In the 1960s, Sally Field's stepfather actor Jock Mahoney played Tarzan three times in the movies.

Just about every day on the movie set of *Catch Me If You Can* (2002), Leonardo DiCaprio's parents along with his grandmother visited to see their favourite star in action.

Mariska Hargitay is the daughter of 60s screen siren, the late Jayne Mansfield. Her dad was American bodybuilding champ and actor Mickey Hargitay.

Actor Vin Diesel has a twin brother called Paul who's a film editor.

Oscar winner Adrien Brody grew up in New York an only child, his mum was a photojournalist and dad was a schoolteacher.

In December 2002, Leonardo DiCaprio took his much-loved grandmother as his partner to the *Gangs of New York* premiere in New York.

David Arquette's dad, Lewis Arquette, got his acting break in the hit 1970s TV series *The Waltons*.

Linda Hamilton's sister stood in as her double in the movie *Terminator 2*.

Ben Stiller is the son of comedy couple Jerry Stiller and Anne Meara.

Marie Osmond has eight children, five of whom are adopted.

Freddie Prinze Jr's dad committed suicide in 1977 when Freddie was 10 years old. He was the star of the 1970s TV series *Chico and the Man*; he was high on prescription drugs and very low over the recent divorce of his wife.

Dustin Hoffman's brother Ronald briefly had a career as a child actor. He had a very small role in the 1939 Frank Capra movie *Mr Smith Goes to Washington*.

Cher's mum Jackie Jean Crouch (later Georgina Holt) was a country-and-western singer and her dad was a farmer; they married when Jackie was 18.

Cameron Diaz says that when she was about nine years old, she and her family went to visit her Cuban grandmother in Florida. She wasn't allowed to play outside the house 'in case I broke my arm or was kidnapped.'

Marilyn Monroe once claimed to be a descendent of James Monroe, US President 1817–25. She claimed it was through her maternal grandmother Della Hogan Monroe Grainger.

Marlon Brando has fathered a son by both the actresses who played Fletcher Christian's Tahitian lover in the 1935 and 1962 versions of *Mutiny on the Bounty*. Morita Castenda, who starred in the 1935 version, was his second wife; Tarita, who played opposite him in the 1962 version, was his lover both on and off screen.

Christian Slater was born with show business running through his veins. His dad was actor Michael Hawkins and his mum was Mary Jo Slater.

Neve Campbell's mum once owned a dinner-theatre, and her dad taught drama in a high school. They divorced when she was a toddler.

Jimmy Smit's mum is Puerto Rican; his dad is from the former Dutch colony of Surinam.

Leslie Nielsen's dad was a Royal Canadian Mountie.

English actress Helena Bonham Carter lived with her mum and dad until she was 30; she helped care for her dad who was paralysed.

Jason Priestley's grandfather was a circus acrobat.

Robin Wright and her brother were raised by their mum who was a cosmetics salesperson.

John Cusack's dad is the Emmy Award-winning documentary film maker Richard Cusack. His older sister is actress Joan Cusack, who was nominated for an Oscar for her role in the movie *Working Girl.*

Jean-Claude Van Damme's dad was an accountant, who ran a flower shop in Brussels with his wife. It was his dad who first introduced him to karate classes when he was nine years old.

Uma Thurman's dad was a college professor; he was also the Dalai Lama's first American Buddhist Monk. Her mum is a psychotherapist

Tim Robbins' dad was a magazine distributor and his mum Gil was a Greenwich folk singer. At one time his dad was a member of *The Highwaymen*, the group that had a number one hit with *Michael, Row the Boat Ashore*.

Barry White's original birth certificate read 'Barry Eugene Carter'. When his unmarried father saw it he changed his son's birth certificate to his surname, which was White.

Luke Perry's father was an itinerant, violent type. When Luke was six, his mum divorced his dad.

In August 2002, actor Jon Voight went on American television and pleaded for his estranged daughter Angelina Jolie to seek help for 'serious mental problems'. Within a day she'd contacted her dad.

[illegible] INSTANCES WHERE RELATIVES HAVE PLAYED THE SAME RELATIONSHIP ON SCREEN

Diane Cilento and Jason Connery as mother and son in *The Boy Who Had Everything* (1985).

Lillian and Dorothy Gish as sisters in *Orphans of the Storm* (1921).

Joe and Buster Keaton as father and son in *Neighbors* (1920).

Mervyn and Glynis Johns as father and daughter in *The Halfway House* (1943).

Richard and Constance Bennett as father and daughter in *Bought* (1931).

Margaux and Mariel Hemingway as sisters in *Lipstick* (1976).

Christopher and Nicholas Guest as the Ford brothers in *The Long Riders* (1980).

Ryan O'Neal and Tatum O'Neal were probably father and daughter on screen, although it was never revealed whether he is her father in *Paper Moon* (1973).

Priscilla Pointer and Amy Irving as mother and daughter in *Carrie* (1976).

Anthony and Duncan Quinn as father and son in *The Children of Sanchez* (1978).

Mario and Megan Van Peebles as brother and sister in *South Bronx Heroes* (1985).

Sir Michael and Vanessa Redgrave as father and daughter in *Behind the Mask* (1958).

John and Hayley Mills as father and daughter in *The Truth About Spring* (1965). He also played father to his other real-life daughter Juliet Mills in *In Which We Serve* (1941) and again in *History of Mr Polly* (1949).

Dan Aykroyd's dad was an assistant deputy Minister of Transport in Ottawa. His grandfather was a Canadian Mountie.

Roger Moore's daughter Deborah had a cameo in the Bond movie *Die Another Day*.

Matt LeBlanc is always being taken for an Italian. In fact, he has a mixed heritage of Italian, English, Irish, French and Dutch.

It's rumoured that Elvis Presley slept in the same bed with his mum, Gladys, until he reached puberty. She also walked him to and from school every day, and packed his own silverware in his lunch box so he wouldn't catch germs from the other kids.

Matthew Broderick's dad James played the father in the TV series *Family*. He died of cancer in 1982.

Rene Russo was just two years old when her sculptor father Nino walked out on her mother Shirley, Rene and her sister Toni. She saw her father again, when she was working as a model; she was 19 years old. He spotted her on the cover of *Vogue* magazine, contacted her and asked if they could meet, which they did.

Tea Leoni made a guest appearance in an episode of *The X-Files*, which was directed by her husband David Duchovny.

In September 2000, Tom Jones's supposed illegitimate son, who is rumoured to have been the result of a one-night stand, made his stage debut. He performed in the USA under the stage name 'Blond Jon'.

In 1989, Chris Rock's truck-driving dad Julius died of an ulcer at the age of 55; it hit Rock very hard. The tragedy forced him to re-evaluate his life and become more ambitious. Two years later Chris made his movie debut in the streetwise *New Jack City*.

In mid 2002, the 94-year-old stepmother of Liza Minnelli dropped her legal action against her stepdaughter. Lee Anderson Minnelli, who was married to Liza's father Vincent, accused Liza of selling her long-time Beverly Hills home out from under her. According to reports Lee was persuaded to drop her action after a phone call from Liza, who planned to move her stepmother into a rented apartment.

Glenn Close's dad was a brilliant physician, who spent 16 years in Zaire trying to find a treatment for the deadly ebola virus.

Elvis Presley was very close to his parents, and in *Loving You* (1957) he had them appear as extras. It was their first and last movie.

Sting is father to six children.

Macaulay Culkin is godfather to Michael Jackson's son Prince.

Heather Graham's dad was an FBI agent and her mum is an author of children's books.

Athena Cansino is the great-niece of the golden-age Hollywood star Rita Hayworth.

TV actor Ed Asner is the son of a Kansas City scrap-iron dealer.

Oscar winner Holly Hunter is the youngest of seven children; she grew up on a farm in Georgia.

Mel Gibson's father moved the entire family to Australia from New York in the 1960s, so his son wouldn't be drafted.

Christopher Lee is cousin to James Bond author Ian Fleming.

Charles Bronson said in an interview that his family was so poor that he started school in dresses, which were hand-me-downs from his older sister.

Kirk Douglas, born Issur Danielovitch Demsky, grew up the only boy among six girls. His parents were impoverished Russian immigrants in Amsterdam, New York.

In August 1998, Jerry Hall and Mick Jagger's 14-year-old daughter Elizabeth Scarlet Jagger took to the catwalk with her mum to show the latest fashion collection from Thierry Mugler.

Denzel Washington is the son of a minister, a fact that may account for his clean-cut family image.

Edward Norton's grandfather invented the concept of shopping malls.

Hollywood loves royalty, and has tried to cash in on Diana Princess of Wales by raking up some of her long-lost relations. Humphrey Bogart was her seventh cousin twice removed, Olivia de Havilland is her fifth cousin three times removed, Orson Welles was her eighth cousin twice removed, Lee Remick was her tenth cousin and Lillian Gish was her double seventh cousin three times removed.

Burt Reynolds's father was once the Chief of Police in Rivera Beach, Florida.

Goldie Hawn's father was Presbyterian, her mother was Jewish and Goldie is Buddhist.

A few days after she turned one, Brooke Shields was a professional model. At 12 she played a child prostitute in the controversial *Pretty Baby*, which attracted international attention. Brooke's mother Teri is the driving force behind the scenes. Brooke was born four months after Teri's marriage to Frank Shields, who was vice-president of the cosmetic empire, Helena Rubinstein. Their marriage lasted only a matter of weeks.

Pamela Stevenson was born in Auckland, New Zealand. Both her parents are doctors who are involved in cancer research. She is a teetotaller, non-smoker and a vegetarian.

In 1950, Marilyn Monroe starred in *The Asphalt Jungle*. Also up for the lead was Georgia Holt, better known today as Cher's mother.

Actor Billy Dee Williams has a twin sister.

Oliver Reed was the nephew of movie director Sir Carol Reed. Whenever there is a royal birthday, he flew two large Union Jacks from the roof of his Sussex farmhouse.

Margaux and Mariel Hemingway are the granddaughters of Ernest Hemingway.

Bill Cosby's children are named Erika, Erinn, Ensa, Camille, Evin and Ennis.

Sylvester Stallone's father played the timekeeper in the first *Rocky* movie.

Jaclyn Smith's grandfather lived to be 102 years old. She says one of her ambitions is to do the same.

When Tatum O'Neal was three years old her father Ryan, then starring in the TV soap *Peyton Place,* divorced her mother Joanna Moore. On the same day he married *Peyton Place* co-star Leigh Taylor-Young. Ryan lost custody of Tatum to her mother. At the age of eight she ran away to her father. The resulting custody battle featured high courtroom dramas of drug addiction and child abuse, which were supposed to have occurred while Tatum and her younger brother Griffin lived with their mother in a wild hippie commune.

Actress Sally Field's stepfather, Jock Mahoney, played Tarzan in the early 1960s.

Warren Beatty is the real-life brother of Shirley MacLaine.

Country-and-western singer Loretta Lynn was married at the age of 15, and became a grandmother at twenty-nine. Her sister is singer Crystal Gayle, whose real name is Brenda. The nickname comes from the Krystal hamburger chain in Kentucky where she was born.

Cher's mother Georgia Holt has been married eight times, thrice to the same man. Cher still feels very bitter towards her father who abandoned her in 1945 when she was only one.

The sons of Marlon Brando and Frank Sinatra have both been kidnapped and later returned to their fathers—Christian Brando in 1972 and Frank Sinatra Jr in 1964.

Sylvester Stallone's son is named Sage Moonblood.

Matthew Perry's parents divorced when he was a year old. He went with his mother to live in Ottawa, Canada, where she later married NBC TV broadcaster Keith Morrison. Perry lost the tip of his middle finger of his right hand in an accident when he was a child.

Orlando Bloom grew up thinking the renowned civil rights campaigner Harry Bloom was his father, but when he turned 12 his mum Sonia revealed her boyfriend Colin Stone was in fact his biological parent. 'Orlando has a very has a very happy background. Orlando is not sad. It was marvellous when he learned that Colin was his father. He was brought up surrounded by a loving family.' Says his mother Sonia Copeland Bloom.

HOME SWEET HOME

Jim Carrey has a chocolate Labrador dog called Hazel. She's such a pampered pooch Jim had a $20,000 three-room doghouse, complete with sofa, specially designed.

Before Barbra Streisand stayed at London's Dorchester Hotel, it's rumoured that she had her American interior designer re-decorate her suite, making it a home away from home.

Sandra Bullock did a painting she called *Elephant in a Fire* when she was four years old. It still hangs in her Texas home.

When Jermaine Jackson (one of Michael's brothers) bought his 1.9-acre mansion estate (once the home of Johnny Wiessmuller), he decided to have gates built to give him and his family more privacy. These became the most expensive gates ever to adorn a private home in Beverly Hills, costing a quarter of a million dollars and personalised with initialled crests. Jermaine's wealthy neighbours, who instantly demanded he take them down, considered the 16-feet-high gates an eyesore. Only weeks after they were installed, he was ordered to have them cut in half to conform with local zoning.

Mae West, 1930s sex siren, still holds the record for a Hollywood star living the longest in the same apartment. She lived in the Ravenswood apartment block from 1932 until she died in 1980. Her apartment was totally white-on-white. Even today her penthouse is pointed out on just about every Hollywood tour. For many years it was thought that she owned the whole block of apartments, but after her death it was found that she only owned her own.

In 1976, singer Engelbert Humperdinck bought the Holmby Hills Los Angeles home of the late Jayne Mansfield, which was painted shocking pink and known as The Pink Palace. The house was three storeyed, Spanish style, with an elevator and seven fireplaces. Engelbert bought it from a spinster who lived mainly in a back room of the nearly 10,000 square feet house. It was built in the 1930s for a Texan oilman who sold it to Hollywood star Rudy Vallee, but it only became famous when Jayne bought it and painted it shocking pink. She lived there until she was killed in a car accident in 1967. Jayne and her husband, muscleman Mickey Hargitay, designed and built a heart-shaped swimming pool for their back garden. Mickey wrote 'I love you Jaynie' on the bottom of the pool, which is there to this day. Jayne's initials remain in the wrought-iron gates, which face on to Sunset Blvd. Somewhere in the house there is supposed to be a hidden wall with Jayne's magazine covers, which had all been framed, but nobody has ever found that secret wall. These are not the only reminders of Jayne to remain in the house. Both Engelbert and his wife have seen her ghost on several occasions.

Comedian Phyllis Diller lives in a multi million dollar mansion in the exclusive Brentwood area of Los Angeles. Her 90-year-old house is packed with priceless antiques, set on an acre of lush surroundings. This two storey elegant mansion has 22 rooms, 6 fireplaces, an art studio, a room devoted to over 3,000 wigs and stage costumes, a king size kitchen, a card room and a parlour dedicated to her long time friend the late Bob Hope. 'I enjoy my home greatly,' says Phyllis. 'It's a home of comfort, happiness and creativity.'

DEBUTS

Camryn Manheim got her first big acting debut next to Clint Eastwood in an elevator in the movie *Sudden Impact*.

In the ninth grade, Michael Chiklis landed his first role in a stage production of *M*A*S*H*, playing Hawkeye.

October 2002 saw the dolls Ken and Barbie make their debuts in the roles of super sleuth 007 and his latest Bond girl. They were given their movie-star makeup and costume image to mark the 40th anniversary of the secret agent's screen debut. 'The James Bond 007 Ken doll and Barbie doll gift set pays tribute to the many memorable James Bond films and their famous characters over the last 40 years,' said a spokesman for Mattel, the company producing the dolls. They were launched as the latest James Bond flick, *Die Another Day*, starring Pierce Brosnan and Halle Berry went on general release in both the UK and the US.

Kellie Martin made her movie debut in Whoopi Goldberg's *Jumpin' Jack Flash*.

Kevin Spacey's first ever-acting role was on the stage playing Captain Von Trapp in *The Sound of Music*.

Tom Hanks's movie debut was in the 1984 hit comedy *Splash*. His son Colin appeared in his debut-starring role in the 2002 movie *Orange County*; he was 24 years old.

Robert De Niro made his film debut in *Hi Mom* (1970).

Sally Field played a modest supporting role in her movie debut, *The Way West* (1967). She didn't appear in another movie for nine years.

Charlie Sheen made his professional acting debut in the TV movie *The Execution of Private Slovik*, which starred his dad. One year later Charlie starred as an extra in the movie *Apocalypse Now*, which again starred his dad, Martin Sheen.

Sean Connery made his movie debut in 1956; the movie was called *No Road Back*.

Mel Brooks's first movie was a cartoon he created and narrated in 1964 called *The Critic*. He won an Oscar for Best Animated Short Subject.

Steve Martin's first venture into the movies was in 1970 starring in a short film he wrote called *The Absent-minded Waiter.* The movie was nominated for an Academy Award.

Wesley Snipes made his movie debut in the Goldie Hawn comedy movie *Wildcats*, where he played a high-school football player.

Oliver Stone made his acting debut in the 1981 movie *The Hand*, which he wrote and directed.

Robert De Niro's first acting role was playing the Cowardly Lion in his school production of *The Wizard Of Oz*.

Elizabeth Perkins made her movie debut as Demi Moore's roommate in the movie *About Last Night*.

Timothy Hutton made his movie debut at the age of five, in a domestic comedy called *Never Too Late*, starring his dad Jim Hutton and Connie Stevens.

Brendan Fraser made his debut in a very small role in Nancy Savoca's *Dogfight* starring River Phoenix.

At the age of five Bridget Fonda made her cameo debut in 1969 in the movie *Easy Rider,* which starred her dad.

At the age of 15, Lara Flynn Boyle landed her first professional role, playing Robert Urich's daughter in the TV mini series *Amerika*. The series took nine months to shoot and was shot on location in Nebraska and Toronto. In 1988 she made her movie debut in *Poltergeist III*.

On 4 March 1986, President Ronald Reagan's son Michael made his TV acting debut as a politician on the daytime US soap opera *Capitol.* Months later he debuted again on TV, hosting his own game show called *Lingo*, which was only screened in Canada.

Drew Barrymore made her first professional debut at 11 months, appearing in a dogfood commercial. Some months later, she appeared in her first TV movie *Suddenly, Love* with Joan Bennett and Cindy Williams.

Sarah Jessica Parker was eight when she appeared in her first TV special; it was called *The Little Match Girl*. She went on to study with both the Cincinnati Ballet and American Ballet Theatre companies.

Jennifer Jason Leigh left high school six weeks before graduation. She did this to act in her debut movie, which was *Eyes of a Stranger* in 1980.

Kirstie Alley was six years old when she made her acting debut as a sun in a class play.

Cameron Douglas made his big screen debut in the movie *It Runs in the Family* alongside his dad Michael, grandad Kirk and grandmother Diana.

Leonard Nimoy debuted on the stage at the age of eight in a community theatre production.

Madonna's TV debut was on the 1982 American TV series *Dancin' On Air*. She was 24 years old.

In 1987, Adam Sandler made his first TV appearance as a comic, on a US TV show called *Showtime*.

Jim Carrey debuted on US TV in 1983, on a show called *An Evening at the Improv*.

Jennifer Love Hewitt made her singing TV debut with a song called *Lollipop, Lollipop*; it was on a show called *Kids Incorporated* back in 1991.

A five-year-old Sarah Michelle Gellar made her TV debut extolling the virtues of red meat, in a series of TV commercials for Burger King.

Jay Leno's debut on a TV sitcom was playing Mackenzie Phillips's biker boyfriend in the series *One Day at a Time*.

The first American actor to make his own movies for TV was William Boyd, alias Hopalong Cassidy, who during 1952 and 1953 made 26 half-hour *Hopalong Cassidy* movies for TV.

Ryan Phillippe played the first openly gay character on daytime TV in the soap *One Life to Live*.

Gwyneth Paltrow's movie debut was a small part in the 1991 movie *Shout*.

Lucy Liu's big TV debut came when she landed a role on the teen hit TV show *Beverly Hills 90210*. It was later followed by walk-on parts in *The X-Files*, *ER* and *NYPD Blue*. Her big break came with the TV series *Ally McBeal*. She originally auditioned for the role of Nell Porter, which went to Portia de Rossi. Lucy really impressed producer David E Kelly, so much so that he created the ill-tempered character of Ling Woo especially for her.

Lisa Kudrow's movie debut was in the 1990 movie *Impulse*, but unfortunately her scenes were left on the cutting-room floor.

Ron Howard's directing debut movie was *Grand Theft Auto* (1977). It was shot over 20 days and cost $602,000; it grossed $15 million.

Christian Slater made his stage debut at the age of nine in the US stage revival of *The Music Man*.

Marie Osmond made her TV debut at the age of three; by 12 she had recorded her first number-one hit on the country charts, *Paper Roses*. She made her debut on Broadway playing Maria in *The Sound of Music* in 1988.

At 13, Jennifer Love Hewitt released her debut CD, *Love Songs*; it was released in Japan but not the US.

In 1971, Christina Applegate made her TV debut at the age of three months in the arms of her mum Nancy Priddy, in the US soap *Days of Our Lives*.

The first movie from the big screen to premiere on network TV in America was *The Constant Husband* with Rex Harrison and Kay Kendall, transmitted by NBC on 6 November 1955.

The first feature-length movie made for TV was *High Tor* starring Bing Crosby, which aired on 10 March 1956.

I Believe in You (1952) was the first of nine movies Joan Collins would do for the English Rank Organisation before being brought to America to become Twentieth Century-Fox's 'answer' to Elizabeth Taylor.

I Love Lucy, starring Lucille Ball, was the first American sitcom import for UK TV; it aired in Britain on the ATV network in 1955.

The first British coronation to be televised was that of King George VI on 12 May 1937. The first live appearance of British Royalty on American TV was on 10 June 1939 when King George VI and Queen Elizabeth visited the New York World's Fair. The first Trooping of the Colour ceremony to be televised was by the BBC on 9 June 1938. The first funeral of a sovereign to be televised was that of King George VI on 15 February 1952. The first member of the English Royal family to appear on TV was HRH the Duchess of Kent (formerly Princess Marina), who was seen buying a hat from a London store during a Baird experimental high-definition transmission in 1953. The exact date was never recorded. The first visit of a reigning sovereign to a TV studio took place on 28 October 1953 when HM Queen Elizabeth II and HRH the Duke of Edinburgh visited the BBC's Lime Grove studios for a special programme. The first Royal broadcast from an English TV studio was on 17 May 1957 when Prince Philip, Duke of Edinburgh, presented a programme called *Round the World in Forty Minutes* for the BBC. The first time HM Queen Elizabeth II delivered a major speech on television was at 6 p.m. on 14 October 1975 from Ottawa. The speech lasted nine minutes. The first Royal Variety Performance to be televised was on 16 May 1960 on the UK ATV network. On 21 February 1969 the BBC took their cameras inside Buckingham Palace for the first time to shoot the interior. The first Royal wedding to be televised was that of HRH Princess Elizabeth (later HM Queen Elizabeth II) to Lieutenant Philip Mountbatten RN (later Prince Philip, Duke of Edinburgh) in Westminster Abbey on Thursday, 20 November 1947. The first full British Royal wedding to be shot in colour for TV was that of HRH Princess Anne to Captain Mark Phillips at Westminster Abbey on 14 November 1973. The first Royal occasion presented by women on both British and American Television was *Barbara Walters in America* for the ABC network and Angela Rippon in Britain for the BBC's worldwide live transmission. The first Royal drama series made with Royal approval was *Edward the Seventh,* produced by ATV. Scripts were submitted to HM the Queen and she gave her full permission for Royal residences to be used throughout its 13 hour-long episodes. The first went to air in the UK on 1 April 1975; that year the series was sold to 44 countries worldwide. The first solo film appearance of a Royal on television was when HRH Princess Anne appeared on the *Blue Peter Royal Safari,* which was shown on the BBC on 11 April 1971.

Woody Allen made his movie debut in *What's New, Pussycat* (1965).

Sesame Street's *Big Bird in China* was the first Chinese–American television co-production; it was first shown on ITV UK as a special on 1 January 1983.

Christina Aguilera made her TV singing debut on America's *Star Search*; she was runner up singing *The Greatest Love of All*.

Elijah Wood's debut into the world of acting came at the age of seven; he played a pint-sized executive in Paula Abdul's *Forever Your Girl* video.

The 1933 movie, *King Kong*, was the first movie to have its sequel, *Son of Kong*, released in the same year.

Billy Crystal played Jodie Dallas, the first openly gay character on the ABC's TV comedy series *Soap*, which aired in the US from 1977 to 1981.

Carrie Fisher made her movie acting debut in 1975 as a 15-year-old who tried to seduce hairdresser Warren Beatty in the movie *Shampoo* by saying: 'You wanna f**k?' She went on to play Princess Leia in the 1977 *Star Wars* movie.

Kevin Costner gave small cameo roles to his wife who he met at Disneyland when she was playing Snow White in the theme park. He gave cameo roles to his two children in his 1991 movie *Dances with Wolves*.

Pamela Anderson made her TV debut on the hit US TV series *Home Improvement* in 1991.

Angelina Jolie made her acting debut at just 6 years of age in the movie *Lookin' To Get Out*, which also starred her dad Jon Voight.

The first recording that Barbra Streisand ever made was in 1955 at the age of 13 with her mum; it was called *One Kiss*.

Queen Elizabeth a movie star? In 1975, movie producer Sam Arkoff who made *I Was a Teenage Werewolf*, shot *Hennessy*, a thriller all about a man who was plotting to blow up Queen Elizabeth. Sam spent all his money hiring Hollywood stars Rod Steiger and Lee Remick, and didn't have a cent to hire a queen look-alike. Never one to be beaten, Sam located some newsreel footage of Queen Elizabeth speaking before Parliament and spliced it into the movie to look as if the Queen was reacting to Rod Steiger. Buckingham Palace aides had a fit, and Her Majesty was not amused either. The Palace applied pressure and the movie had to have a disclaimer saying the Queen had not been a willing participant in the movie.

Teen superstar Britney Spears made her stage debut at the age of five; she sung *What Child Is This?* at her kindergarten graduation.

Grace Kelly, the late Princess Grace of Monaco, was the first Hollywood movie star to appear on a postage stamp.

James Dean's first professional acting job was for a Pepsi commercial. He was only paid $30, but got noticed by Hollywood.

At the 1935 Royal Command Performance, a little 3-year-old stepped on to the stage to entertain King George V and Queen Mary, dancing with her ballet class. Her name was Elizabeth Taylor.

Alfred Hitchcock directed Shirley MacLaine in her first movie *The Trouble with Harry* in 1955.

Marilyn Monroe made her film debut as an extra in *Scudda Hoo! Scudda Hay!* (1948).

Jon Voight made his Broadway debut in *The Sound of Music*.

Alyssa Milano, the young star of TV's *Who's the Boss*, got her first big break as Annie in the American stage show. She won the role at an open audition of more than 1,000 hopeful little girls.

The multi-talented daughter of Judy Garland and Vincent Minnelli, Liza Minnelli, was still an infant when she made her movie debut. She was carried in her mother's arms into the happy ending of the musical, *In the Good Old Summer Time* (1946).

Monaco's Prince Albert completed his first movie role in October 1997. It was a tiny role as an Irish soldier in the 1840s in a movie called *One Man's Hero*, and starred Tom Berenger and Patrick Bergin. Albert's screen credit read Albert Grimaldi.

Jim Carrey made his debut as a stand-up comic at the age of fifteen. Among the stars he could impersonate were James Dean, Jimmy

Stewart, Elvis Presley and Clint Eastwood. He was discovered by comic Rodney Dangerfield. Jim arrived in Hollywood from Canada at the age of 19; however, it would be another 13 years before he hit the big time.

Tom Selleck first came to the notice of the Hollywood talent scouts as the model in the billboard adverts for Salem cigarettes. As a teenager he won a four-year basketball scholarship to USC. He also had a lead speaking role with Mae West in *Myra Breckinridge* (1970), a role he would like to forget.

Sylvester Stallone made his debut as a subway mugger in the 1971 Woody Allen movie *Bananas*.

TV star Henry Winkler made his Broadway debut in *42 Seconds from Broadway*, which closed the night it opened.

In his teens, actor James Garner modelled bathing suits for a swimwear catalogue.

In 1961 Phyllis Diller made her movie debut in *Splendor in the Grass* along with Warren Beatty.

Jodie Foster's mother (a former Hollywood press agent) took her and her brother to audition for a TV commercial in the mid 1960s. Jodie's brother missed out, but she got the job. At the age of three she became the Coppertone girl, with a dog pulling at her knickers. Later Jodie switched to TV drama roles and at 10 landed the lead role in the Peter Bogdanovich TV series *Paper Moon*, which was adapted from the movie starring Tatum O'Neal.

Elizabeth Taylor's movie debut was not *Lassie Come Home* (1943), but *There's One Born Every Minute* (1942).

Linda Evans, who played John Forsyth's wife in the huge TV hit series, *Dynasty*, was given her first big acting break by him in 1957. When she was just 15, John cast her in his smash-hit TV series *Bachelor Father*, never dreaming that some 30 years later they would play husband and wife in a world-renowned soap.

Barbra Streisand's son Jason Gould never played the violin in his mum's 1992 movie *The Prince of Tides*. He did learn to play for the role, but the piece, *Praeludium and Allegro*, was played by virtuoso Pinchas Zukerman.

In 1950, Sean Connery was a contestant in the Mr Universe Contest. During the competition he met the director of *South Pacific* (1951), and was offered the role of Lieutenant Buzz Adams in the stage show. He accepted, and a star was born.

Jane Fonda made her movie debut in *Tall Story* (1960).

John Travolta made his movie debut in *The Devil's Rain* (1975).

Goldie Hawn worked as a can-can dancer at the 1964 New York World Fair, then as a caged go-go dancer in New Jersey. She moved on to Las Vegas and danced in several reviews as a showgirl. It was while in Las Vegas in the late 1960s that she got her first big TV break in the series *Laugh-In*.

Bette Midler's first movie was *Hawaii* (1965), in which she played a missionary's wife who suffered from seasickness.

At the tender age of 23, Warren Beatty had a contract with MGM Studios, and went to Broadway to star in his first stage show. The show was a complete flop, but director Elia Kazan saw Warren in it and signed him on the spot to star in *Splendor in the Grass*, which was the start of his career.

Bruce Springsteen's *Born in the USA* was the first CD pressed in the US.

The first black American musician to have his own US TV network variety series was Nat King Cole in 1957.

The first cast member of *Coronation Street* to be honoured was Violet Carson who played Ena Sharples. She was awarded the OBE on 12 June 1965.

Ralph Fiennes was the first English actor to win a Tony award for playing Hamlet on Broadway.

MUSIC, MUSIC, MUSIC – AND MUSICIANS

In mid 2000, Craig David's breakthrough single *Fill Me*, went to number one on the UK charts. This made him the youngest male solo artist to reach number one in the UK at just nineteen.

In December 2002, it was rumoured that Shania Twain had her new CD banned from being played in Tour-de-Peilz in Switzerland where she lives, because she doesn't want to be famous there.

Mariah Carey says she can't sing unless she's had 12 hours' sleep.

Actor Stephen Dorff's father composed music for the hit TV show *Columbo*.

The theme song for the Austin Powers movie is *Soul Bossa Nova*, which was composed by Quincy Jones for the movie *The Pawnbroker.*

The Spice Girls album, *Spice*, hit number one in 1997 in 14 countries and sales rocketed to 12 million in just six months. This made it the fastest-selling album ever by a British group.

In 1982, Michael Jackson's *Thriller* was voted the most popular album of all time; it sold 47 million copies worldwide.

October 2002 saw Robbie Williams sign the biggest record deal in British history. EMI paid him 80 million English pounds for his next six albums. 'My mum said it would be really uncouth of me to talk about money,' he chirped to the press. 'I'm going back now to count it all.'

Actor Jon Voight's brother wrote the song *Wild Thing*, which became a huge hit for the *Troggs*. He wrote it under the alias of Chip Taylor.

In September 2002, hell-raising rocker Ozzy Osbourne said he was going to sell his LA mansion so he could move closer to the Beverly Hills Hotel, which he said made the best cuppa in LA.

According to reports, Eminem once caused quite a ruckus at Buckingham Palace. It's rumoured that HM the Queen was not at all amused—in fact, she was disgusted—to hear one of Eminem's infamous four-letter outbursts blasting out of HRH Prince William's car stereo so she immediately introduced a royal ban on the rap star.

Sir Paul McCartney wrote the lyrics to *Wings'* songs on the back of supermarket receipts. In September 2002 one of the receipts was auctioned in London for £30,000.

At the age of seven, after seeing Elvis Presley on the *Ed Sullivan* TV show, Bruce Springsteen told his mum he wanted to be a singer like him. The next day his mum went out and bought him a guitar, even though his hands were too small to play it.

Leonardo DiCaprio said that two of his favourite bands are *Pink Floyd* and *the Beatles*.

Kevin Bacon (who starred in the 1984 movie *Footloose*) said, 'Every time I went to a wedding, a bar mitzvah, a club, or a disco, the disc jockey would play *Footloose*, at which point people would form a circle around me and start to clap in unison, expecting me to start flipping and performing like a trained monkey.'

At 16, movie actor Jeff Bridges wrote a song which appeared on the soundtrack of the 1969 movie *John and Mary*. Jeff is a prolific songwriter, and to date has written over 200 songs.

In World War II Australian troops in North Africa adopted *We're Off to See the Wizard* as their marching song as they went into battle with Italy.

5 February 1992 marked Michael Jackson's first onscreen kiss in his video, *Remember the Time*—or was it? The scene occurs when Michael, fleeing from the Pharaoh, played by Eddie Murphy, and stumbling upon the boudoir of Princess Iman finds himself in the somewhat towering clutches of the willowy supermodel. She gracefully sinks to Michael's height where he proceeds to kiss her. But shock horror, at this very point a shaft of bright light appears out of the blue between their lips. So still the big question is: was this Michael's first ever onscreen fully consummated kiss? It's still one of Hollywood's best-kept secrets.

The English *Daily Mirror* reported in August 1998 that Prince Charles wrote to Spice Girl Geri Halliwell when she quit the *Spice Girls*, saying he would miss her 'wonderfully friendly manner'. Ginger Spice, who quit the group in May 1998, made a habit of always giving Charles a big kiss and even a couple of times pinched his bottom when they met at charity events. 'Dear Geri, I want to drop you a line to say how sorry I was to discover you had decided to leave the rest of the *Spice Girls*. I suspect I am not the only one to feel sad either! The group certainly will not be the same without your wonderfully friendly greeting in the future,' wrote Charles. A few months before Geri left the group Charles had invited the girls to tea with his younger son Prince Harry.

On 2 October 1975, a Bruce Springsteen concert in Milwaukee was interrupted by a bomb scare. After a few hours the fans were let back into the theatre at midnight. A shaken Bruce arrived back at the theatre on the roof of his car where he finished the concert in the early hours of the morning.

In 1988, singer Boy George was slung out of Britain's most famous showbiz nightspot, the Café de Paris, for being far too scruffy.

Billy Idol once issued a press release to dispel a rumour that he had become a Christian after the motorcycle accident that damaged his leg. In an interview he clarified a point that he had made in an earlier radio interview by saying that he was 'into porn again' and not 'born again'.

Madonna's four-letter outburst in 1990 prompted toothpaste makers MacLeans to send her a box of their new Active Mouth Guard to her London suite. The message read, 'We hope this might help you clean up your act!' MacLeans, whose motto is 'Cleans Even the Foulest of Mouths', never got a reply from Madonna.

In 1990, singer Janet Jackson gave a press statement to say that she wouldn't use a black leopard in her act because her fans have expressed concern about its welfare. Some audience members worried the animal could be harmed being carted from location to location on Janet's world tour.

In 1985, terrorists hijacked an American civil airline and flew to Beirut where a number of passengers were held hostage. Among the prisoner passengers were Greek singer Demis Roussos and the elder brother of *Cheap Trick* drummer, Bun E Carlos.

Rap singer Vanilla Ice was arrested in June of 1991 after allegedly pulling a gun on a man in a Studio City car park; he was 23 at the time.

Country-singing star Garth Brooks holds a degree in advertising from the Oklahoma State University.

In 1991, rapper L L Cool J gave away some 350 pairs of athletic shoes to inner-city youngsters in a programme to discourage them from dropping out.

By the time Michael Jackson was five, he had been voted in as lead singer of the *Jackson Five*. He recorded four hit singles before he was a teenager.

Dolly Parton's hit song, *Coat of Many Colours*, is about a real patchwork coat she once owned that her classmates ridiculed as a coat of rags.

Patrick Swayze was a successful singer. His single *She's Like the Wind* made the American Top Ten and landed at number 17 on the British charts.

Dennis Quaid wrote songs for three of his movies: *The Night the Light Went Out in Georgia*, 1981, *Tough Enough*, 1983 and *The Big Easy* in 1987.

In 1998, Will Smith starred in *Men in Black* and produced the movie's soundtrack; the title track was a worldwide number-one hit.

In June of 1988, *The National Enquirer* reported that Michael Jackson, who owns the *Beatles* song catalogue, only sold *Revolution* to Nike after John Lennon's ghost came to him and said, 'Let my music live'. Says Michael, 'I'd been thinking about the Nike ad all day. I immediately understood what he was telling me.'

On 24 July 2002, *WHO* magazine reported that a judge in San Francisco upheld a lower court's 1998 ruling that MCA artists *Aqua*'s 1997 hit *Barbie Girl* (during the song Barbie is referred to as a 'blonde bimbo') is fair and legal freedom of speech and not a trademark violation as Mattel, who manufacture the doll, argued. The judge also ruled against a counter suit in which MCA accused Mattel of defamation. The judge said, 'The parties are advised to chill'.

The name of the plane that crashed, killing Buddy Holly, Ritchie Valens and The Big Bopper was named *American Pie*. I wonder if that's where Don McLean got the title of his famous tune?

In June 1984, Bruce Springsteen's *Born in the USA* began an 84-week run in the US Top Ten.

The Rolling Stones played on a water tank full of trained seals at the 1964 San Antonio State Fair, during their first tour of America.

Queen Elizabeth II was the first Royal to ever receive a gold disc after the 2001 Party at the Palace. The CD sold 1 million copies in its first week.

Elvis Presley failed music at school.

When the *Beatles* were looking for a corporate symbol for their Apple Records label, they used a Granny Smith apple.

The *Beatles* partnership was legally dissolved on the 24 December 1974.

Guns N' Roses made music history in September 1991, by selling an estimated 500,000 albums in just two hours. Thousands of fans lined up across America to buy the two *Use Your Illusion* albums.

In 1973, singer Stevie Wonder was in a bad car smash. He suffered a contusion of the brain and the doctors thought he was a goner.

In June 1998, Sir Elton John gave his full support to the Northern Ireland peace process by playing a concert in the grounds of Belfast's Stormont Castle. It was the very first time that a rock concert had ever been played at the venue. Over 15,000 fans comprising both Catholics and Protestants enjoyed the event.

In June 1998, rock star Liam Gallagher was given a lifetime ban by the Hong Kong airline Cathay Pacific. The ban was also extended to other members of the *Oasis* group; this was all because of their unruly behaviour on a flight to Australia in February 1998. The captain even left the cockpit to intervene, at one point threatening to handcuff Liam to his seat and divert the plane to throw him and his entourage off.

Barbra Streisand and Neil Diamond both went to Erasmus High School in Brooklyn, New York. They even sang as kids in the same school choir.

Sherwood Schwartz composed the theme songs for the TV shows *Gilligan's Island* and *The Brady Bunch*. He once said that he earns around $60,000 annually in royalties from those two tunes alone.

The British rock star Billy Idol changed his name to 'Billy Idol' when he remembered that one of his high school teachers had written on his report card, 'Billy is idle'.

In June 1998, singing star Michael Bolton had the big snip. The singer renowned for his flowing blonde locks had them cut off.

In the mid 1970s, Don Johnson co-wrote several songs for the Allman Brothers. Back in the 1980s he released his own solo album.

Michael Jackson was to make a surprise guest appearance at James Brown's comeback concert in Los Angeles on 9 July, his first since leaving prison. James's producers wanted Michael to come on stage and put a king's robe on James's shoulders. But rumour has it that when Michael saw thousands of people at the theatre, he panicked, refused to leave the sanctuary of his deluxe limo and went home without ever appearing at the concert.

Singing star Julio Iglesias speaks seven languages: his native Spanish, Portuguese, Italian, French, German, English and Japanese. He can sing in all but Japanese.

When Audrey Hepburn sang in the 1964 movie, *My Fair Lady*, her songs were dubbed by Marni Nixon.

A promoter has booked a showroom on permanent hold in Las Vegas, just in case Elvis Presley is still alive and wants a room to stage his comeback. What's even more amazing is that some people have already paid for ringside tickets. Mind you, Elvis still has well over 500 fan clubs worldwide; I don't think another celebrity alive could say that.

In the early 1960s, Chuck Berry spent two years in prison for income-tax evasion, and was convicted of further tax evasion in the late 1970s.

If you have a copy of *Meatloaf*'s *Bat out of Hell* and your plants are dying, try playing the song over and over again to them. A British scientist claims that this will make them perk up and grow faster.

Within four weeks of Al Jolson's record *Sonny Boy* hitting the American market in 1928, it had sold 12 million copies.

In 1971, Vincent Damon Furnier, at the age of 23, suddenly transformed himself into Alice Cooper, aptly designated by *Time* magazine as the 'King, Queen, Unicorn and Godzilla of schlock rock'.

Kenny Rogers was once a member of the *New Christy Minstrels* singing group.

Singer Al Martino played the Italian singer in *The Godfather* (1972).

Singer Johnny Mathis admitted that he had eaten monkey brains during a trip to the Philippines.

In May 1984, President Ronald Reagan presented Michael Jackson with an award for allowing *Beat It* to be used in anti-drink-driving ads across America.

Carol King's 1971 Grammy-Award-winning album *Tapestry* was the largest-selling LP in history, selling 13 million copies, until *Fleetwood Mac*'s *Rumours* and the score for *Saturday Night Fever* came along.

Phyllis Diller's comedy act is just that, an act. In real life she's a very accomplished classical pianist who's performed with some one hundred symphony orchestras. Between 1972 and 1982, Phyllis appeared as a piano soloist, playing Bach and Beethoven at symphony concerts in Canada, Mexico, Hawaii and all over America.

Barry Manilow had the fastest ticket sell-out in Broadway history for his concert series.

On 21 January 1990, superstar Michael Jackson unveiled a painting of himself bought by a Japanese businessman for $2.1 million. At the time it was said to be the most valuable portrait of a living person. The painting depicted Michael as a modern Renaissance man, dressed in a red jacket and blue tights sitting on a stool and clasping a book, which did not have a title on its cover.

Miss World 1963 was Miss Holland, Catherina Lodders, who on 12 December 1963 married Ernest Evans, better known as Chubby Checker.

Every cent earned from the song *God Bless America* goes to the Boy's and Girl's Scouts of America. Irving Berlin, who wrote the song, insisted on this many years ago.

When, in the summer of 1967, John Lennon remarked that the *Beatles* were more popular than Jesus, it started off a string of *Beatles* burnings, which began in Georgia where listeners to WAYX gathered to burn *Beatles* records. Many radio stations around the world banned the playing of *Beatles* records.

Ex-Beatle, Paul McCartney, is the proud owner of the rights to all the late Buddy Holly's songs.

White Christmas is the biggest-selling song from a movie. Bing Crosby sang it in *Holiday Inn* (1942). To date it's sold well over 30 million copies.

Art Garfunkel met Paul Simon when he played the Cheshire Cat, and Paul played the White Rabbit, in a grammar-school production of *Alice in Wonderland*. They later found out that they grew up just three blocks away from each other in Queens. A few years later they teamed up and recorded under the name of *Tom and Jerry*, scraping into the charts with a song called *Hey—Schoolgirl*.

It's rumoured that Elvis Presley once fired a gun at his TV set when singer Robert Goulet appeared on the screen.

Glen Campbell was the seventh son of a seventh son. His family was so poor that Glen had to share a bed with three of his brothers. As a young boy he sang in the Church of Christ in his hometown in Arkansas, where his grandfather was the preacher. He left school at 14, bought a guitar and taught himself to play. From time to time he would accompany the local gospel church service. In the mid 1950s he hit the road with his own band called *Uncle Boo's*.

At first, the song *Over the Rainbow* was dropped from *The Wizard of Oz* (1939), because the producer thought it slowed down the pace. Months later, the song was put back, and the rest is history.

At one point in 1978, the *Bee Gees* tied with the *Beatles'* record for having five singles in the same top ten; they were all from the soundtrack for *Saturday Night Fever*.

Elvis Presley changed to fancier lamé costumes after he saw the flamboyant Liberace's stage wardrobe for his Las Vegas act.

Pianist Ray Charles became blind at the age of five.

Barry Manilow has taken a cue from the late Joan Crawford. He has it written into his concert contract that the auditorium temperature must be in the low 60s, the same demand Joan Crawford had put into her contracts for studio filming.

CBS records honoured Michael Jackson as their label's biggest moneymaker of the 1980s; his fans bought more than 110 million of his records in that decade.

Tom Jones's famous sexy gyrations incite hundreds of female fans to toss their lacy panties and room keys on stage at every show. One night at his Caesars Palace concert in Las Vegas, they collected 5,000 keys from the stage. When Tom bought his beautiful brick Tudor mansion in Bel Air, California, he had all his furniture shipped from his homeland, Wales. His most sentimental piece is a phonebox from his village of Pontypridd, that he once used to ring a local sweetheart from, now his long-time wife Linda.

Singer Chuck Berry has a degree in Cosmetology from an American beauty school.

Bandleader Lawrence Welk has a licence plate, which reads Al AND A2, which was how he always started his music.

Woody Allen was once the lead member of the New Orleans Funeral and Rag Time Orchestra, which played in New York's Greenwich Village.

For her outspoken views on politics, the CIA labelled singer Eartha Kitt a 'sadistic nymphomaniac with a vile tongue'. She once made a necklace of dead crickets for her baby daughter to cure teething pains, and always carries a clove of fresh garlic with her to ward off evil spirits.

RCA put Elvis Presley under contract in 1955 and within 12 months he had sold 10 million singles. In the same year he was a guest on the *Ed Sullivan* TV Show. Though billed as 'Elvis the Pelvis', he was only shown from the waist up; his sexy gyrations were considered totally unsuitable for Sunday night family viewing.

Singer Bruce Springsteen went to a strict Catholic school in Asbury Park, New Jersey, where he was asked to draw a picture of Jesus and hand it to the nun taking the class. When Bruce handed in his personally prophetic drawing of Christ crucified on a guitar, the nuns were not amused.

In 1989, Elton John backed top piano makers Steinway and Sons' bid to save the endangered African elephant by not using real ivory piano keys any more.

Bill Howard, son of Dorothy Lamour, once managed a pop band called *Dino, Desi and Billy.* Desi Arnaz Jr and Dean Martin's son Dino were the other two members of the 1960s rock group.

Gene Simmons, lead singer in the rock group *Kiss*, has a tongue 7 inches long.

Stevie Wonder, born Steveland Morris Haraway, has been blind since birth. By the time he was 10 years old he was a virtuoso on the piano, bongos, harmonica and guitar, and at the age of 12 he cut his first record, *Fingertips*.

Elvis Presley's favourite movie of all time was *King Solomon's Mines* (1950), which starred Stewart Granger. Elvis had an original copy of the movie, which he would play over and over again. There was some talk of him starring in a remake in the late 1960s.

Rock star Billy Joel once worked as a piano player in a Los Angeles bar under the name of William Martin. His first solo album was recorded at the wrong speed, which gave him a higher-sounding voice.

Richard Rogers took only five minutes to write the music to *Bali Hai* for the musical South Pacific.

THE SMALL SCREEN

The first US TV series bought for screening in the Soviet Union was *Fraggle Rock*.

The smash-hit teen TV series *Beverly Hills 90210* was called *The Sensation of Living* in Spain.

George Clooney appeared in 13 TV pilots that went nowhere; his first big TV break came as a regular on *The Facts of Life*.

Agent 99's name was never revealed on the hit 1960s–70s TV comedy series *Get Smart*.

A young mum who lives in California loves the TV show *Friends* so much she named her triplets Joey, Chandler and Ross.

In November 2002, at the age of 69, Joan Collins did a TV advert for the British store Marks and Spencer's Christmas push. She appeared naked, wearing only jewellery and covered in fur.

Condom commercials were shown on American TV for the first time in 1987. It was an attempt to reverse an increase in AIDS cases.

In 1995, some 5.6 million viewers tuned in every day to watch the real life trial of O J Simpson for the murder of his wife Nicole.

In 2002, the American *TV Guide* magazine named *The Jerry Springer Show* the worst show in the 50-year history of TV. Jerry's reply was: 'The show has no redeeming social value. But I'm just hired to be the host.'

More than 150 American babies born during the same 30 minutes as Pebbles in the TV cartoon series *The Flintstones*, were sent by the production company a $25 savings bond along with a Pebbles doll. The babies' mums received a bunch of a dozen roses.

In 1954, Elvis Presley made his first and only TV commercial; it was for 'Southern Maid Doughnuts'.

In the 1980s, the American TV soapie *Dynasty* screened in 80 different countries in 20 different languages.

In September 2002, Susan Sarandon saved an African girl from poverty by giving her a goat. The girl thanked her on the *Oprah Winfrey Show.*

In Saudi Arabia, *The Muppet Show* was banned, because one of its stars was Miss Piggy and pigs are considered taboo in Islamic culture.

The American TV drama, *Law and Order,* was re-named *New York District* when it screened in France.

In 2002, *Sesame Street* muppets Bert and Ernie said hi to the first HIV-positive muppet in their TV cast. The female character joined *Takalani Sesame*, made for TV in South Africa, where the HIV virus is found in one in nine people. There was no mention of sex in the show's script. But there were questions like: what do I do if I cut my finger?

The four-letter word 'love' appears in more movie and TV titles than any other word.

Hawaii has been the backdrop for many TV shows and movies over the years: *Island Sun*, *Magnum PI*, *The Thorn Birds* and *Jake and the Fat Man* were all shot there for TV. Hawaii stood in for Mexico in the movie *10*, the Australian cane-fields in *The Thorn Birds*, Okinawa in *Karate Kid II*, the jungles of South America in *The Raiders of the Lost Ark*, the Caribbean in *Islands in the Stream*, and the Adriatic in the 1933 submarine movie *Hell Below.* Burt Lancaster and Deborah Kerr's classic beach love scene in *From Here to Eternity* was shot on the shores of Hawaii. The 50th state also provided a backdrop for *The Caine Mutiny* with Humphrey Bogart, *Mr Roberts* with Henry Fonda, *Tora Tora Tora* and *Midway,* and the mammoth war series *Winds of War* and *War and Remembrance*. Elvis Presley loved Hawaii and shot three of his movies there: *Blue Hawaii, Paradise Hawaiian Style* and *Girls Girls Girls!* The 1950 TV detective series *Hawaiian Eye* was all shot inside a Hollywood studio, but the *Hawaii Five O* series was shot on location in Hawaii, using the Breakers Hotel on Beachwalk, Waikiki, for many of the scenes. The hotel is still there and is a great place to stay.

Samuel L Jackson played second fiddle to Bill Cosby; he was his stand-in for three years on the show.

At the age of 16, Ralph Macchio beat out over 2,000 other young actors for the role of Jeremy, a troubled nephew in the hit TV series *Eight is Enough*.

Patrick Stewart said he was so sure that his role in the initial season of *Star Trek: the Next Generation* wouldn't last, that he didn't unpack his bags after arriving in LA from England until he was six weeks into the season.

Both Rhea Perlman and Shelly Long were pregnant in real life while appearing on the hit TV series *Cheers*. Rhea's pregnancy was written into the show's script, but Shelly had to spend the whole time behind the bar, hiding an ever-largening waistline.

On 20 November 1995, 22 million viewers tuned in to TV to watch Diana, Princess of Wales, return to public life after a two-year withdrawal. The show was the English *Panorama* TV series.

There have been many unsolved TV sitcom mysteries; loose ends which have been left untied. Here are a few that have never been solved during the opening credits for *All in the Family*, you can clearly see Archie Bunker's house has a screened-in front verandah. But every time the Bunker's front door was opened the verandah was never there. The hit series ran in the US from 1971–79. When the series *Family Matters* debuted in the US in 1989, Urkel's neighbours, Carl and Harriette Winslow, had three children, Laura, Judy and Eddie. But when the 1993 season started Judy Winslow had vanished with no explanation. When *Happy Days* first aired in the US in 1974, Richie and Joanie had an older brother called Chuck. But after the second series he was never mentioned again. There was always a mystery about how Oscar and Felix originally met on the hit sitcom *The Odd Couple*. The show's writers provided three totally different versions during the show's five-year run: (1) they first met when they were kids; (2) they met each other while they were in the Army; (3) they met when they were both serving on a jury and became firm friends.

The hit TV series *Seinfeld* appeared on one of just 15 stamp designs depicting 1990s pop culture that were printed in 2000.

One of the titles high on the consideration list as a name for the hit TV series *Friends* was Insomnia Café.

In 1991, the American magazine *Entertainment Weekly* published a list of items and prices based on a 1991 *Star Trek* convention in Arlington. Today some of these items would be priceless to a collector:

Star Fleet Academy sweatpants: $20

Star Trek insignia button: $6

Star Trek collector's plate: $75

Star Trek collector's plate with autographs: $100

Star Trek glow-in-the-dark yo-yo: $3

Star Trek 'beam me up, Scotty' pen: $1

Star Trek 10" high Captain Kirk doll: $50

Star Trek 10" Mr Spock doll: $60

Star Trek phaser: $35

Star Trek phaser with working lights and sound effects: $225

Star Trek stuffed Tribble: $3

Star Trek Enterprise charm necklace: $15

Star Trek chess set with gold-and-silver-plate pieces: $944

Star Trek plastic lunch box: $20

Star Trek communicator: $60

Star Trek communicator with working lights and sound effects: $225

Star Trek rubber stamp: $14

Star Trek transporter mug (add cold water and Spock disappears): $12

Star Trek sound-effect cassette: $10

Star Trek feet surgical scrubs: $15

Star Trek 25th anniversary silver medallions: $125

Star Trek pewter mug: $195

Star Trek quartz watch: $195

Star Trek T-shirt: $10

Star Trek tricorder with working lights and sound effects: $225

Star Trek trading cards: $1 per pack

Jamie Farr, who played Klinger on the long-running hit TV series *M*A*S*H*, was the only member of the cast who actually served as a soldier in the Korean War.

How did Mr Ed, the talking horse, mouth those lines in his hit TV series? Seconds before a take they would slip a teaspoon of peanut butter-like substance between his cheek and gum. As the cameras rolled, Mr Ed (whose real name was Bamboo Harvester) wanted to get rid of it, which he did by working his lips. This movement was then put in sync with a voice-over by actor Allan Lane.

Mr Spock's blood type is T-negative. Did you know that the TV series *Star Trek* originally had lyrics? They went like this, 'Beyond the rim of the starlight, my love is wandering in star-flight. I know he'll find in star-clustered reaches, love. Strange love a star woman teaches. I know his journey ends never; his star trek will go on forever. But tell him while he wanders his starry sea to remember, remember me.'

In June 2002, Jennifer Lopez said 'Y' know' 56 times in her short appearance on the British TV chat show *Parkinson*.

It's rumoured that the studio that made *The X-Files* sent the real life feuding stars Gillian Anderson and David Duchovny to relationship counselling.

Jamie Farr, from the *M*A*S*H* TV series, starred as Santini in *The Blackboard Jungle* (1955).

The only Hollywood movie ever to be shown on Soviet TV was *They Shoot Horses, Don't They?* (1969), which starred Jane Fonda and Susannah York.

In September 1997, a roving-camera segment on the *Late Show with David Letterman* led to a bitter custody dispute played out on American national TV. The show placed a camera crew outside the New York studio and spotted a woman identified as Rene Nelson and her son, Gaston, eating pizza outside Joe G's pizzeria, which is right next door to the studio. 'Apparently, the boy's father, in Minneapolis, was watching the show and saw his wife and son,' said a *Late Show* spokeswoman. Neil Peterson alleged his ex-wife moved away four years earlier, and had been denying him court-ordered visitation rights.

In 1974, the BBC bosses said that actor Richard Burton would never work for them again, and he never did. He was blacklisted for calling Winston Churchill 'power corrupted', and a 'coward' after portraying Winston Churchill in the BBC TV play, *A Walk With Destiny*.

In the 1990s, ex-*Charlie's Angel* star Jaclyn Smith's clothing line for women was the fourth best-selling fashion line in the US.

TV talk-show queen Oprah Winfrey was the first woman ever to own and produce her own TV talk-show anywhere in the world.

Oprah Winfrey was born out of wedlock. She went public on her own chat show about being raped at the age of nine by a teenage cousin who was babysitting her. Over the next five years she was abused by three other men, who were all friends of the family.

Actress Marlee Matlin gave birth to a 3.4 kg baby girl, Sarah Rose, on 19 January 1996, the same day as a pre-recorded episode of *Picket Fences* aired with her character, Mayor Laurie Bey, giving birth to a son. The same thing happened to Lucille Ball with her real-life son Desi Jr and her TV character on the same day, 19 January, 43 years before.

The X-files star David Duchovny is blind in his right eye, due to an injury he suffered playing basketball back in high school.

In January 1964, the most watched TV show in America was *The Beverley Hillbillies*.

In June 1998, *Friends* star Matthew Perry found out on the Internet that he was supposedly engaged to a woman called Amy. Matthew's sense of humour went into overdrive. He recorded a new message on his answerphone, 'Hi, you've reached Matthew and Amy. We're not in right now, but as you can imagine we have a lot of planning to do, so leave a message.' Matthew didn't even know anyone called Amy, but it sure got the Hollywood gossip network going.

TV star Richard Dean Anderson wanted to be a professional ice-hockey player, but after breaking both his arms in two separate hockey games on the ice, he took up acting.

TV talk-show host Sally Jessy Raphael admitted to having been fired 18 times in her 36 years as a broadcaster.

TV's Roseanne spent a night in jail when she was 15, after she 'stole' the family car and was involved in an accident. The next year, Roseanne got caught stealing a can of baby food at a supermarket. The same year at the age of 16, she was hit by a car and was in a coma for four days. She spent eight months in a Utah mental institution when she was seventeen. At 18 she gave birth to a daughter out of wedlock. She was on welfare at the time. Like her or loathe her, you've got to take your hat off to Roseanne.

American TV and stage comedic actress Carol Burnett's parents both died of alcoholism. Her grandmother who was a devout Christian Scientist raised her.

American TV chat show host Leeza Gibbons says her most memorable moment was when Sir Paul McCartney sang to her first baby Lexi, before she was born. 'I was very pregnant when I interviewed him and he put his hand on my stomach and sang, *She Loves You*. I will never forget the day Sir Paul McCartney sang to my swollen stomach.'

To celebrate Jay Leno's fifth anniversary on *The Tonight Show* in May 1997, Mel Gibson presented Jay with a huge birthday cake. Moments after giving Jay the cake, Mel started a cake fight, which Jay happily entered into.

TV star Calista Flockhart was engaged back in her college days, but she broke off the relationship in 1988.

Star Trek's Scotty played by James Doohan was once a captain of artillery in the Royal Canadian Army.

Alec Baldwin began his career on the stage, before appearing on television in the soapie *The Doctors*, and also in *Knots Landing*.

In August 1998, the Duchess of York announced that she would host her own TV chat show, *Surviving Live,* on Britain's Sky TV, with her fee going to charity.

While the TV soapie *Dynasty* was in its heyday, Rudolph Hess was reported to be a keen fan and never missed an episode.

In 1964, CBS TV rejected the *Star Trek* concept. They said they had their own science-fiction brainchild, *Lost in Space*.

In 1991, Dana Plato, the 26-year-old former star of the TV series *Different Strokes*, pleaded guilty to robbery charges after her arrest for holding up a video store in the US.

In May 1988, Johnny Depp landed himself on the wrong side of the law, and was hauled off to a jail cell for a few hours, for jaywalking. At the time, Johnny was 24 and playing Tom Hanson in the TV hit *21 Jump Street*. It all took place around midnight, when Johnny and some of his pals were grabbed after crossing a Hollywood intersection. At the time they were all off to a trendy Hollywood nightspot.

In 1991, American actor Macdonald Carey who played patriarch Dr Tom Horton for 26 years on the NBC soap *Days of Our Lives* died at the age of seventy-eight.

The first televised US presidential debate was on 26 August 1960, Richard M Nixon vs John F Kennedy.

On 18 October 1990, the American TV soapie *All My Children* had a very important guest, noneother than First Lady Barbara Bush. In the storyline she played herself delivering a public service announcement; encouraging viewers to be medically tested to see if they were potential bone-marrow donors. The soap's ratings went through the roof. Mrs Bush is the first First Lady 'in office' to appear on a daytime soap. Betty Ford guest-starred on night-time's *Dynasty* back in 1986 in a party sequence with former President Gerald Ford and former Secretary of State Henry Kissinger.

In 1990, the movie *Total Recall* was the first movie to be released on video with an onscreen warning that it was protected by macrovision, a process that makes it virtually impossible to make a good copy of the tape.

In 1983, Joan Collins told England's *Sun* newspaper to stop calling her a bitch. She said she finds the word extremely insulting and offensive. She landed the title while playing the bitchy TV role of Alexis on *Dynasty*.

Demi Moore played newspaper reporter Jackie Templeton on *General Hospital* during the 1982–83 season.

In 1979, American actor Clayton Moore who made his name as TV's Lone Ranger, was told he could never again wear his character's famous black mask in public as the Lone Ranger. The company, which owned the rights to the character, was planning to relaunch the TV show with a younger star.

When Candice Bergen starred in the hit TV series *Murphy Brown*, her contract guaranteed her the free services of a babysitter whenever her daughter Chloe visited her on the set.

In 1988, when the hit TV series *Fawlty Towers* was sold to Spain, there were worries about what the Spanish TV audiences would make of Manuel, the put-upon Spanish waiter. The problem was solved when they made Manuel Italian.

Tori Spelling auditioned for a part on TV's *Beverley Hills 90210* using the name Tori Mitchell, because she didn't want her dad, Aaron, who owned the show, to know that she was auditioning. The show's director says he didn't know until a week after he had cast her that she was really Tori Spelling.

In February 1992, as a tribute to outgoing TV *Tonight Show* host Johnny Carson, Elizabeth Taylor made her first appearance on the long-running show. The show had been trying to book Elizabeth since it started back in 1962; Johnny left the show in March 1992 after 30 years.

It's rumoured that when Farrah Fawcett was married to TV's *Six Million Dollar Man*, Lee Majors, there was a clause in her *Charlie's Angels* contract 'demanding' she get home in time to put his dinner on the table.

It's said that the 1963 movie *Spencer Mountain* was the inspiration for the hit TV series *The Waltons*.

In 1989, the American *TV Guide* magazine admitted that it had put the head of TV talk-show queen Oprah Winfrey onto the silkily clad, lithe body of Ann-Margaret for their August issue. I'm sure Oprah was very flattered.

In 1991, Angela Lansbury struck a blow for animal rights. She banned any real fur from her hit TV show *Murder She Wrote*. She also made the show's producers dump thousands of dollars worth of makeup and skincare products because they were tested on animals.

Miss Piggy, the star of TV's *Muppet Show*, was removed from Turkish TV during religious festivals so the sight of an 'unclean' animal wouldn't offend the viewers.

One of the regulars who sipped real beer at the *Cheers* TV bar during its 1987 series, was Phil Perlman, the real-life dad of Rhea Perlman, one of the stars of the show.

In August 1991, the first American TV soap was screened in Japan; it was *Santa Barbara*, which was billed as a daytime drama for the Japanese audience.

On 20 July 1968, English actress Jane Asher broke off her engagement to Paul McCartney in a BBC television interview. This meant Paul learnt the news the same time as the millions watching.

In April 1990, Walter Lantz, creator of the Woody Woodpecker cartoon character, received the first star on Universal Studios Florida's Walk of Fame as part of his 90th-birthday celebrations. Walter had been affiliated with Universal Studios since the 1930s; he's drawn cartoon characters for more than 800 animated movies in 72 nations for TV and the big screen.

In 1983, Joan Collins called off a dinner date with her estranged husband Ron Kass after reading in a paper his revelations about their marriage, in which he says living with Joan 'was as bad as living with her character Alexis from the hit TV series *Dynasty*'.

In 1991, the Californian Burbank Unified School District expelled the TV series *The Wonder Years* from its John Burroughs High School. District officials said the filming of the hit TV series had become far too disruptive during school hours. The school gave up thousands of dollars in location fees.

Adam West, the original Batman from the hit 1960s TV series, was on a plane, which was hit by extremely bad turbulence. As the plane was being buffeted around an elderly woman turned to Adam in the seat next to her and said, 'You're Batman—do something!'

Hollywood mega-rich TV producer Aaron Spelling will not fly. The story is that years ago when he was flying in the American military, he missed a flight that crashed. It's rumoured that Aaron's parents were so distraught that they made him promise he'd never fly again if he could possibly avoid it.

In 1975, Sylvester Stallone appeared in one episode on TV's *Police Woman*, starring Angie Dickinson. He played a cop called Elmore Quincy Caddo. In one scene he asks his cop partner to call him Rocky, which is his nickname. A year later Sylvester starred in his first *Rocky* movie.

In the 1987 hit TV series, *LA Law*, the names on the firm's door read MacKenzie, Brackman, Chaney, Kuzak and Becker. The partner Chaney never appeared in the series because he died in the pilot episode face down in a bowl of soup.

In 1991, a woman reported in the prestigious *New England Journal of Medicine* that she suffered an epileptic seizure every time she heard Mary Hart's voice on the TV show *Entertainment Tonight*.

In September 1991, Burt Reynolds was taping his TV show *Evening Shades* in front of a live audience. One scene called for Burt to heat a baby's bottle in a microwave; the bottle was to explode, and be doused by another actor. Without warning the powder that spewed from the prop fire extinguisher ignited, engulfing Burt in a ball of fire. Instantly Burt fell to the studio floor; cast and crew rushed to his side, fearing that his eyesight could have been damaged, or he'd inhaled deadly fumes. The flames burnt his toupee and eyebrows, but after chest X-rays and blood tests, Burt was back on the set the next day.

On Christmas Day 1991, the blockbuster movie *Batman* was shown on British TV for the first time, but it was heavily censored. The BBC cut several gruesome scenes for its family time screening at 6 p.m. The major cut was the blood-curdling moment when the Joker, played by Jack Nicholson, plunges into a vat of acid. The acid-scarred face of the Joker's girlfriend, played by Jerry Hall, was also cut.

In July 1991, 25 years after the debut of *Star Trek* on TV, Paramount Studio honoured the show's producer, Gene Roddenberry, by naming a new building on its Hollywood lot after him.

Jeanne Cooper, as Kay Chancellor on the American soapie *The Young and the Restless* had a 'real' facelift on the show in 1984. The footage of her facelift was for real, filmed in the operating room, and then edited into the storyline. The hands doing the actual operation were those of the real doctor, but the doctor on screen was an actor.

On 14 February 1962, First Lady Jacqueline Bouvier Kennedy invited America into her home, the White House. An estimated 80 million Americans fell under the spell of the 32-year-old Jacqueline. All three American networks broadcast the 60-minute tour. She received a special Emmy Award, and the show was exported to 106 foreign countries, even the Soviet Union.

On 14 March 1991, around 4.30 a.m., the *Fawlty Towers* hotel, used for filming external shots of the classic English comedy, was gutted in a mystery fire. The 40-bedroom hotel, almost 100 years old at the time of the fire, had been empty since 1989.

On 23 September 1991, Neil Armstrong, the first man on the moon, became a TV host by fronting a new cable-TV documentary series on aviation called *First Flights*.

In January 1992, the soundtrack from a hard-core pornographic movie popped up on a repeat episode of the TV comedy *Gilligan's Island* telecast in Toledo, Ohio.

TV talk-show host, Sally Jessy Raphael, took the Jessy part from her father and added the Raphael; she was living in Puerto Rico at the time where most people have three names. Rumour has it that in 1983 she had trouble reading the studio tele-prompter. She walked into a five-and-dime store, bought the only pair of reading glasses left in the store, which just happened to be red. The studio execs hated them, but Sally didn't give in; she loved them and today they've become her trademark.

In 1968, a scene from Petula Clark's TV special *Petula* had to be re-shot because she'd had the temerity to hold guest star Harry Belafonte's arm while they did a song together. Both the network and show's sponsor feared that this mere touch might suggest the idea of a sexual attraction between the two.

In August 1988, 29-year-old Will Smith, the star of the hit TV series *The Fresh Prince of Bel Air* said, 'I believe if I set my mind to do it, within the next 15 years, I could be the President of the United States.' Guess we'll just have to wait to see if another Mr Smith goes to Washington.

In Evansville, Indiana, on 26 September 1991, actors Tom Hanks and Geena Davis went on local TV to recruit 5,000 extras to watch them play baseball in a movie they were filming. The movie was *A League of Their Own* starring Tom, Geena and Madonna, and was about an all-woman professional baseball league set in the 1940s and 1950s.

25 July 1990 saw American comedian Roseanne rendering the American National Anthem at a San Diego baseball stadium including spitting and

grabbing her crotch after the anthem. She stunned the crowd of some 25,000 by plugging her ears with her fingers and screeching out the words. The item made the TV news all around the world. Her rendition of the *Star-Spangled Banner* struck out with fans who booed and shouted obscenities at her as she left the stadium. She defended her performance by saying, 'I was not paid to sing the anthem. They didn't hire me because I am Beverley Sills.' She was referring to one of America's most famous opera singers. Roseanne said she was pleased with her performance.

Steven Spielberg's movie, *E.T.*, first aired on American TV on Thanksgiving night, 1991. Years later when the movie went onto home video, it sold more than 12 million copies.

At the age of three, American actor Peter Falk developed a tumour in his right eye, and, tragically, lost his sight in that eye. But that never stopped him becoming an internationally popular TV star as the shabby and modest, but deviously clever, detective Columbo in the long running series of the same name.

American TV interviewer Leeza Gibbons still cringes when she remembers her TV interview with screen legend Bette Davis. Leeza was trying to make small talk with her when the elderly star asked, 'Is the tape on yet?' When Leeza replied no, Bette bellowed, 'Then why the hell should I talk to you!'

In 1965, Dustin Hoffman supplemented his acting income by hawking the Volkswagen Beetle in a TV commercial.

The breakfast TV show *Wake Up America* failed to feature special guest Tony Randall who was to have discussed National Sleep Disorder Month. He'd overslept.

The number-one TV soap *Dallas* started because David Jacobs, a New York writer of children's books, moved to Los Angeles to be near his 12-year-old daughter, who was living with his ex-wife. He decided to write something for TV to get money while he worked on another children's book. Two years later, *Dallas* was on the TV screen, the first evening soap series to succeed in America since *Peyton Place* in the 1960s.

Kelsey Grammer originally signed to play Frasier for only six episodes in *Cheers*; the rest is TV history.

When they were casting for Tony Danza's role in the hit TV series *Taxi* they were looking for an Irish heavyweight fighter, who was to be called Phil Ryan. After Tony auditioned for the role they changed his name to Tony Banta.

The TV series, *Cagney & Lacey*, has a history arguably more amazing than the show. The series was based on the 1981 TV movie starring Loretta Swit and Tyne Daly. Because Loretta was a regular on the *M*A*S*H* TV series, she did not want to do *Cagney & Lacey*, which is why Meg Foster played opposite Tyne in the 1982 episodes. When the show came up for another series, Meg was fired and her replacement was Sharon Gless. The series was cancelled in 1983, but the network brought it back because of its popularity. Behind closed doors at CBS the show was nicknamed 'Dykes'.

Alan Alda, who played Hawkeye, and Loretta Swit, who played Margaret Houlihan, were the only stars to be in the series *M*A*S*H* from beginning to end; there were 255 episodes. *M*A*S*H* ran for 11 annual seasons on American TV, starting in September 1972 and ending in January 1983. It was a touch of Hollywood, since the real Korean War lasted for only three years, from June 1950 to July 1953. Gary Burghoff, who played Radar, was the only member of the original movie cast to be carried over into the TV series. The Koreans did not like the series; the director of the Korean Cultural Service in New York said in an interview with *The New York Times* that he was glad the show was ending, because 'It has been building a wrong image of Korea and its people in the minds of the American public.' Over its years on the air, the series received 99 Emmy nominations and won 14 Emmys, a selection of Golden Globes, a People's Choice Award and a number of others. The final episode was watched by 100 million-plus people in America, which beat the *Dallas* episode of *Who Shot JR*? American TV advertisers paid big bucks for a 30-second commercial spot in the final episode.

American TV talk-show host Oprah Winfrey has her own TV production company called Harpo—which is Oprah spelt backwards.

On the soap *The Young and the Restless* there was so much backstage hysteria about AIDS infection from kissing that in 1985 the producers brought in a medical expert to talk to the cast.

Before Tom Selleck became a superstar he appeared on the American TV show *The Dating Game* as a bachelor, and came in as second choice.

The American ABC is the only TV network ever to employ a psychic to help select shows that would rate well. From 1978 to 1980, Beverlee Dean was on the payroll with a contract of $24,000 for the first year, and $30,000 for the second. Over those two years the ABC network was number one, with shows like *Mork & Mindy*, *Benson* and *Taxi*, which Beverlee picked to be smash-hit comedies. At the end of her contract in 1980 the studio did not renew it.

Marie Osmond turned down the starring lead role in the movie *Grease* on moral grounds.

The most popular movie shown on American TV is *Casablanca*; it is also the movie which has had the most reruns on TV.

Stephen King made his TV acting debut as a cantankerous bus driver in August 1991 in the CBS show *Golden Years*, which he created and wrote.

The role of superbitch Alexis in *Dynasty* was originally intended for Sophia Loren. Joan Collins was second choice … but what a second choice!

Robin Williams once picked up $150 a day miming on the steps of the Metropolitan Museum of Art in New York at weekends. This was in the 1960s, long before he burst onto TV screens as Mork in *Mork & Mindy*, which became the biggest TV comedy hit of 1978 and 1979.

Lorenzo Lamas, who plays the sexy playboy Lance Cumson in *Falcon Crest*, has a weakness for fast cars. In 1977 he was in a bad crash where he cracked his skull; he was partially paralysed and couldn't speak for three days. Then in 1985 a 100-mile-per-hour racing car smash left him with a broken collarbone and a badly dislocated shoulder.

In the 1950s, Louis Armstrong made a TV commercial, singing and dancing with toddlers to promote a range of dolls called *Suzy Cute*.

The Commerce Bank of Beverly Hills was made famous by the TV series *The Beverly Hillbillies* in the 1960s. Mr Milburn Drysdale ran the bank, and it was the bank which housed the $50 million of the Clampits. People started to think the bank was real, and quite a few very wealthy Beverly Hills residents inquired about depositing their fortunes with it. The power of television!

As a teenager, Kate Jackson, ex-*Charlie's Angels*, set her sights on becoming a professional tennis player. She got an appetite for acting after a short run in a summer stock show. Years later she came up with the idea for a TV series about three karate-chopping women detectives; the studio liked it, and *Charlie's Angels* was born.

When the network was putting together the *Mary Tyler Moore Show*, the producers sent out word that they wanted a Betty White type to play the double-edged Sue Ann Nivens, but the producers never offered the role to Betty herself. One day she sashayed in and offered herself for the role. They couldn't believe their luck.

I Love Lucy TV star Vivian Vance's contract stipulated that she stay 20 pounds overweight for her role as Ethel Mertz. The show's producers and directors wanted her to look older and frumpier than Lucille Ball, even though in real life there was only 13 days difference in age between them.

Larry Hagman, who plays J R Ewing in *Dallas*, got his first taste of TV soap operas in 1961 in the afternoon show *The Edge of the Night* in which he played a lawyer. He was with the show for three years, then left New York for Hollywood, where he played Major Tony Nelson in the smash-hit comedy series *I Dream of Jeannie*.

The Desilu TV studio contracted New York columnist Walter Winchell to narrate the series *The Untouchables* for $25,000 per episode.

Emma Samms had a dream of following in her mother's footsteps as a ballerina. But at the age of 16 her dreams were dashed by a hip injury that threatened to cripple her for life if she didn't give up dancing. At 26, she landed the role of Holly Sutton on the TV soap *General Hospital*, and then went on to superstardom as Fallon in *Dynasty*.

The licence plate 'LA LAW', seen in the opening segments of the hit 1980s TV series, belongs to a lawyer named Richard Niederberg, who received a very modest fee for its use.

Because of the very strict laws which protect child actors, twins are often used. In the TV series *Bewitched*, twins Erin and Diane Murphy played Tabitha Stevens.

Carroll O'Connor played in 27 movies and over 120 TV shows before he landed the role of the bigot Archie Bunker in the superhit, *All in the Family*, which grossed him around 3 million dollars annually in the mid 1970s.

In 1981, Elizabeth Taylor was the first movie superstar to guest on an American soap opera. The soap was *General Hospital*, where she played a widow called Helena Cassidine. She thus made soap operas respectable and many big movie stars have followed in her footsteps with guest roles.

Jackie Coogan, one of Hollywood's first child stars, played Uncle Fester in TV's send-up horror series *The Addams Family*. In the early 1970s he won Emmy Awards for directing episodes of *M*A*S*H* and the TV series *The White Shadow*.

Mary Tyler Moore's face was never seen on the TV series *Richard Diamond*, even though she played the switchboard operator.

The original Hollywood police station in Wilcox Avenue became the Metropolis police station on the old *Superman* TV series.

During the shooting of the *Carol Burnett* TV shows the cast and crew would run a sweepstake to see how long it would take Harvey Korman to crack up in a sketch. These sweepstakes went on for years before Harvey found out, and when he did, he cracked up again!

Roger Moore, best remembered for his James Bond roles, once played Beau Maverick in the TV series *Maverick*.

It's rumoured that Joan Collins and Linda Evans are not exactly bosom buddies. Whenever the two stars had to make joint personal appearances for *Dynasty*, the situation got a little tense. The show's publicity director always requested that the two never be given plane seats together, and never have their hotel suites on the same floor.

Before Mary Tyler Moore got the TV role of Laura Petrie in the *Dick Van Dyke Show* in 1961, she played a 3-inch-high Happy Hotpoint in a TV appliance commercial. Some 20 years later she emerged as a multimillionaire television tycoon.

During a love-scene take on *Dynasty*, Michael Nader, who plays Dex, grabbed Joan Collins, who plays Alexis, and planted an exuberant kiss on her lips. The powerfully built actor didn't know his own strength in the kissing department; he badly bruised Joan's lips and she had to take the rest of the day off kissing an ice pack.

When NBC cancelled its TV series *The Monkees* it received more letters protesting the cancellation than for any other series it ever produced, including *Star Trek*.

In 1985, Jamie Farr, who played Corporal Clinger in *M*A*S*H,* fronted a TV commercial, selling stick-on notepaper called Clingers. It's reported that he was paid 4 million dollars for doing the commercial.

In 1977, Danny DeVito's on-the-spot thinking and quick wit got him the role as Louie, the smart mouthed cab dispatcher in *Taxi*. As soon as he entered the audition room he saw the producer's face freeze, and instantly knew he had to do something to break the ice and tension. He climbed onto the stage and growled in his deepest voice, 'Now before I start, I just gotta know one thing; who wrote this s---?' Everyone fell about and Danny was on the road to TV stardom.

Lucille Ball loved to give Christmas presents to the entire cast and crew on her TV series; it's said that she gave presents which were monogrammed so that if you didn't like it you could never return the gift. Bob Carroll, head writer on the series, remembers that Lucy didn't like kudos for her good work. 'She was embarrassed by any compliments,' he says. 'We used to give her a silver dollar after a particularly good episode. She liked that tradition, because it didn't involve talking about it.'

William Shatner was not the first choice to play *Star Trek*'s Captain James T Kirk. The original choice, Geoffrey Hunter, turned the role down. He died in 1969.

William Moulton Marston, a lawyer, invented the polygraph (known as the lie detector) in 1915. He also created *Wonder Woman*, which he introduced in comic-book form in 1941, and on which the 1970s Universal TV series was based.

Joan Collins received between 11,500–12,000 love/ hate letters per week when she was playing the bitch on TV's *Dynasty.*

In the 1940s, the top American TV show was *The Ed Sullivan Show.* Just about every star clamoured to be on it; some would even appear for nothing. Not so when it came to Dean Martin and his partner Jerry Lewis—they took half the talent budget of $400 as their fee when they appeared on the show in 1948, quite a fee in those days.

When they were looking for a Lou Grant type for the *Mary Tyler Moore Show,* they wanted comedian Shelly Berman for the role. But Shelly wanted to continue with his comedy TV and stage performances, so the role went to Ed Asner.

When the *Cosby* series was rating number one week after week on American TV, the price of a 30-second commercial slot during the show was around $605,075. Even so, there was a long waiting list of clients.

At the age of 52, Ronald Reagan made his last movie, *The Killers* (1964). The movie was made for TV, but was later considered too violent for the small screen, and was only shown in cinemas.

According to *American Variety* magazine, Loretta Lynn's film biography, *A Coal Miner's Daughter,* is now ranked among the All Time Film Rental Champs on the American market. In 1989, the total number of rentals reached a staggering 35 million-plus, not counting the number of videotapes sold.

On 16 November 1989, hundreds of *Batman* fans fluttered around a spotlight outside Tower Records in Hollywood, which was casting the Bat sign high in the LA night sky above Sunset Blvd. Around 9 p.m., the Batmobile rolled up and the Joker jumped out, bearing bags filled with the coveted Bat videos. The show sold 100 videos of the movie in the first 40 minutes, while the movie was still playing at more than 500 theatres in North America.

Larry David, who created the hit TV series *Seinfeld*, modeled the George character after himself.

Singer/dancer Ann Miller was the first tap dancer to appear on American TV.

Larry Hagman's chair on the set of *Dallas* read 'Lawrence of Malibu'.

THE ONES THAT GOT AWAY: ROLES THEY TURNED DOWN

Jodie Foster was a strong contender for the role of Princess Leia in the 1977 *Star Wars* movie. Also high on the list were Amy Irving and Cindy Williams, but it was Carrie Fisher who landed the role.

Tina Turner was first choice to play a lead role in the movie *The Colour Purple*, but she was not available at the time. The role then went to Margaret Avery who won a Best Supporting Oscar nomination.

Burt Lancaster was originally offered the lead in the movie *Kiss of the Spider Woman*. After he turned it down it went to William Hurt, who won for himself a Best Actor Oscar in 1985.

Debra Winger was cast in the leading role of the movie *Peggy Sue Got Married*, but unfortunately she badly injured her back and the role went to Kathleen Turner.

James Woods turned down the leading role in the movie *Platoon*.

Goldie Hawn, Cher and Shelly Long were all offered the lead role in the movie *Working Girl*. Melanie Griffith was selected, and in 1988 was nominated for the Best Actress Oscar.

Holly Hunter's role in *Broadcast News* was first offered to Debra Winger.

Both Nancy Reagan and Esther Williams were offered the lead role in the 1996 movie, *Mother.* The role finally went to Debbie Reynolds, who was so good in the role it launched her into a huge comeback career.

Holly Hunter turned down the lead role in the 1997 movie, *As Good As It Gets*. Helen Hunt got the role and took home the Best Actress Oscar.

Originally the lead roles for the 1998 movie *Shakespeare in Love* were going to be a vehicle for Daniel Day-Lewis and Julia Roberts.

It's rumoured that Mel Gibson was first offered the role of Maximus in the movie *Gladiator.* The role went to Russell Crowe who won for himself his first Oscar.

Director John Huston really wanted Charlie Chaplin to play the role of Noah in the movie *The Bible*. Charlie said a very firm no on several occasions, so John stepped into the role himself. The movie was a smash hit at the box office making it the biggest grosser for 1966, but it didn't receive one Academy Award nomination.

Hollywood director Billy Wilder's first choices for the leading male role in *Ben-Hur* were Marlon Brando and Rock Hudson. Charlton Heston got the role and took home the Best Actor Oscar in 1959.

It's said that Bette Davis turned down the role of Scarlett in the movie *Gone with the Wind*. Her reason was she didn't want to work with Errol Flynn who was number one on the list to play Rhett Butler. The role finally went to a man she would have killed for to be his leading lady—Clark Gable.

Movie director Louis Malle originally wanted to cast Robert Mitchum in his 1980s movie *Atlantic City.* Finally he went with Burt Lancaster who got himself a Best Actor Oscar nomination, but lost out to Henry Fonda for the movie *On Golden Pond*.

Richard Burton initially turned down the role of George starring next to his wife Elizabeth Taylor in the 1966 movie, *Who's Afraid of Virginia Woolf?* He changed his mind after she persuaded him. It turned out she won Best Actress for her role as Martha and he received a nomination for Best Actor, but lost to Paul Scofield who starred in *A Man for All Seasons*.

At the last minute Billy Baldwin dropped out of a small role in the 1991 movie, *Thelma & Louise*, and the role went to Brad Pitt. He wasn't even screen-tested for the role; he read for one of the movie's production assistants who then recommended him to both the movie's director and producer.

In early December 2002, Jude Law turned down a starring role in *White Powder,* a movie about the drug trade. Earlier the same year he and wife Sadie Frost went through a nightmare when a tab of ecstasy left lying around somewhere in a restaurant was ingested by their baby.

Steven Spielberg considered directing the 1988 movie *Big*. He also considered Harrison Ford for the leading role. Both ideas were canned and in the end Penny Marshall directed and Tom Hanks landed the starring role.

The role of Luke in the 1967 movie *Cool Hand Luke* was originally offered to Telly Savalas, best know as Kojak in the TV series. At the time he was in Europe working. Telly wanted the role, but was afraid of flying and wanted to take the boat back; the producers couldn't wait that long and cast Paul Newman instead.

The studio wanted Princess Grace Kelly to come out of retirement for the leading role in the movie *Turning Point*; she was delighted, but her husband Prince Rainier said no.

Carrie Fisher was originally cast as *Carrie* in the 1976 movie of the same name. Rumour is she turned the role down because she wouldn't do nudity.

Keanu Reeves was not the first choice to play Thomas 'Neo' Anderson in the hit movie *The Matrix*. It was offered to Ewan McGregor and Will Smith; both turned it down.

Rachel Weisz turned down the role of Richard Gere's daughter in the 1985 movie *King David*. At the time her father didn't think it would be a good career move.

Thandie Newton said thanks, but no thanks to a starring role in the movie version of *Charlie's Angels*. Instead, she opted for a role in a low-budget thriller called *It was an Accident*, which just happened to be written by her husband.

Robert Duvall, Gene Hackman, Jeremy Irons and Brian Cox were all offered, and turned down, the role of Hannibal Lecter in *Silence of the Lambs*. Anthony Hopkins took it and the rest is history. Meg Ryan and Michelle Pfeiffer were both offered the role of FBI agent Clarice Starling, which finally went to Jodie Foster.

Winona Ryder turned down the role opposite Harrison Ford in the comedy movie *Sabrina*.

Oscar-winning director James Cameron wanted O J Simpson to play the lead role of the killer humanoid in the first *Terminator* movie. But the role went to a then little-known Arnold Schwarzenegger.

Frank Sinatra was offered the leading male role in the movie *Funny Girl* starring Barbra Streisand. He turned the offer down because he was offered second billing to Barbra, even though it was her debut movie. It was then offered to David Janssen, but he also turned it down and the part went to Omar Shariff, after his success in the movie *Doctor Zhivago*.

Nicole Kidman was originally going to star in the movie *Panic Room*. But during the filming of *Moulin Rouge* she was injured, and the role went to Jodie Foster.

Guy Ritchie turned down directing *Oceans Eleven*.

Paul Newman and Robert Redford turned down 4 million dollars to play Superman in the movie. Christopher Reeve, who was a lesser-known star at the time, landed the role and was paid $250,000.

Paul Newman and Steve McQueen were first choice to play the cold-blooded murderers in the 1967 movie *In Cold Blood*. Instead the roles went to Scott Wilson and Robert Blake. Paul Newman chose to star in *Cool Hand Luke* and Steve McQueen starred in *The Thomas Crown Affair*.

Leonardo DiCaprio and Freddie Prinze Jr were considered for the role of Peter Parker in the 2002 *Spider-Man* movie.

Movie star Mickey Rooney said thanks, but no thanks to the role of Archie Bunker in *All in the Family*. It's said that Mickey believed the show to be far too rough for TV audiences.

Martin Landau turned down the role of Mr Spock in *Star Trek* to play a lead in the hit TV series *Mission Impossible*.

William Shatner said no to the TV role of *Dr Kildare,* which made Richard Chamberlain an overnight TV star.

Fred MacMurray turned down the role of Perry Mason; he said he didn't want the workload that came with doing an hour-long weekly TV series. Raymond Burr landed the role and the rest is TV history.

Michael Richards auditioned for the role of Al Bundy in the TV series *Married with Children*. A rejection gave him the role of Kramer in the smash-hit TV series *Seinfeld*.

Penny Marshall was up for the role of Gloria in the 1970s TV mega-smash-hit series *All in the Family*. In the end the role went to Sally Struthers.

In a long line of acting roles, Charlton Heston has played three American presidents, three saints and two geniuses.

When Johnny Weissmuller was given the part of Tarzan, he was under contract to model BVD underwear and swimming trunks. MGM wanted Johnny so badly that they had to agree to let their top stars like Jean Harlow, Joan Crawford, Greta Garbo and Marie Dressler model BVD swimwear for advertisements in order to get Johnny for the role.

At one time there was talk about making the movie *The African Queen* into a musical starring Doris Day and Lee Marvin. Bette Davis and John Mills were up to star in a British production a couple of years before the 1951 version with Humphrey Bogart and Katharine Hepburn.

In 1964, auditions were held right across America and Europe for seven young actors to play the Von Trapp children in the movie version of Rogers and Hammerstein's Broadway hit, *The Sound of Music*. Some 300 child actors auditioned, including an 18-year-old called Mia Farrow, who was rejected. For the movie's 25th anniversary, all the children turned up in America, except for Nicholas Hammond-Friedrich, who was working on a movie in Australia.

Timothy Dalton appeared as James Bond in two movies, *The Living Daylights* (1987) and *Licence to Kill*, (1989). He never appeared in another James Bond movie. The producers of the James Bond movies did say they were satisfied with his performance.

Jack Nicholson rejected the plum role of Michael Corleone in the *Godfather*. He felt that a real Italian should play the role, so Al Pacino was offered it. Instead, Jack made a forgettable movie called *King of Marvin Gardens*.

For his first American movie in 1979, director Franco Zeffirelli chose to remake *The Champ*, and he wanted Ryan O'Neal for his leading man. Ryan suggested his son, Griffin, to play his son in the movie. Franco wasn't too enthusiastic about the idea, but he did do a screen test with Griffin. Franco refused to cast Griffin in the role, so Ryan quit the movie. The role went to Jon Voight.

When Michael Douglas was having trouble casting his leading lady in *Fatal Attraction*, it was his younger brother Eric who introduced him to Glenn Close who got the role.

Prior to Roger Moore landing the role of James Bond in the movie *Live and Let Die*, Burt Reynolds, Paul Newman and Robert Redford were all considered.

Neve Campbell once auditioned for the hit TV series *Baywatch*, but was turned down for the part. They said she was too pale.

Chris O'Donnell was originally cast as Barbra Streisand's son in the movie *Prince of Tides*. But nepotism reared its head and she cast her only child Jason Gould in the role.

The role of Bob Fosse in his autobiographical movie musical *All That Jazz* was to star Paul Newman, but he turned the role down because he wasn't a particularly good dancer. Next up was Richard Dreyfuss who was hot Hollywood property after just winning an Academy Award for his role in the 1977 movie *Goodbye Girl*. He was all set to play the role when suddenly a week out from shooting he quit the production. The role finally went to Roy Scheider, who was nominated for an Oscar.

Macaulay Culkin was in the 1989 Tom cruise movie, *Born on the 4th of July*, but you'll never see him because his scenes were left on the cutting-room floor.

Both Sylvester Stallone and Jack Nicholson turned down the part of the paraplegic Vietnam veteran in the 1978 movie *Coming Home*. Jon Voight snapped up the role along with the Academy Award for Best Actor.

In 1965, Kirk Douglas said no to the dual role in the western comedy movie *Cat Ballou*. The role went to Lee Marvin who won the Oscar for Best Actor.

American Gigolo (1980) and *An Officer and a Gentleman* (1982) starred Richard Gere, but both movies were tailored for John Travolta. It seems that John pulled out at the last minute on both movies.

Jane Fonda said thanks, but no thanks to the role of Bonnie in the 1967 movie *Bonnie and Clyde*. Warren Beatty originally wanted his former girlfriend Natalie Wood as his co-star, but she wasn't keen on working with her ex. The role eventually went to Faye Dunaway, who landed herself an Oscar nomination.

Patricia Neal was all signed to play Mrs Robinson in the 1960s movie *The Graduate*, but she suffered a severe stroke before shooting started. Candice Bergen was on the shortlist but the role went to Anne Bancroft who landed herself an Oscar nomination for Best Actress.

In the 1961 movie *West Side Story*, George Chakiris played the leader of the Puerto Rican gang, the Sharks. But when the show opened in London's West End, George played the leader of the opposing gang, the Jets.

Marlon Brando was director David Lean's first choice to play *Lawrence of Arabia* in the 1962 movie.

Yasmine Bleeth turned down a regular role in the hit TV series *Beverly Hills 90210*.

Diane Keaton replaced Mia Farrow in Woody Allen's 1993 movie *Manhattan Murder Mystery* when the press published horrific details of Mia's breakup with Woody. Diane was a former girlfriend of Woody.

Paul Newman replaced Robert Redford in the 1982 movie *The Verdict* because Robert felt the role of the down-and-out attorney was too seedy for his image. Paul was nominated for a Best Actor Oscar; some say that this was Paul's best performance on the screen.

For his directorial debut in the 1980 movie *Ordinary People*, Robert Redford wanted Ann-Margaret to play the part of the ice-cold mother. She was very interested in the role but passed on the offer. Mary Tyler Moore stepped in and got herself nominated for an Oscar.

Dustin Hoffman really wanted Goldie Hawn to be his leading lady in the 1982 classic comedy movie *Tootsie*, but she felt that the movie was too much Dustin's vehicle. So Jessica Lange was cast and won the Best Supporting Actress Oscar.

Shirley MacLaine was first choice to play Sally Bowles in the 1970s movie *Cabaret*. But seeing that her 1969 movie *Sweet Charity* didn't do too well at the box office, the studio went with Liza Minnelli instead. Liza was pleased they did; she took home the Oscar for Best Actress in 1972.

The original director of the 1989 movie *Dead Poets Society* was Jeff Kanew, who wanted Liam Neeson for the role of the teacher. Later, Kanew was replaced by Peter Weir, who sought out Dustin Hoffman for the role, but he passed on the offer. Robin Williams was cast and received his second Best Actor Oscar nomination for his performance.

Steven Spielberg had an older man in mind to take the leading role in his 1977 movie *Close Encounters of the Third Kind*. He thought that Jack Nicholson would be perfect for the role. However, Jack turned his offer down to direct his own movie, *Goin' South*. The role went to Richard Dreyfuss.

The casting director for the 1974 movie *Murder on the Orient Express* wanted Marlene Dietrich for the role of the grand duchess, but instead it went to actress Wendy Hiller.

The 1974 hit comedy movie *Moonstruck* was developed by Sally Field's own production company; she was to play the lead role. After reading through the script she became unhappy and decided against accepting the role. The part went to Cher, who won an Academy Award for her performance.

Burt Reynolds turned down the role of the 'astronaut next door' in the 1983 movie *Terms of Endearment*; he felt it was too much of a supporting role for him. Jack Nicholson replaced him and won for himself his second Oscar for Best Supporting Actor.

American character actor Paul Douglas was cast in Billy Wilder's 1960s comedy movie *The Apartment*, but unfortunately he died two weeks before shooting began. Fred MacMurray replaced him.

Kate Jackson was to play the role of Dustin Hoffman's estranged wife, Joanna, in the movie *Kramer vs Kramer*. She ran headlong into conflicting availability problems and was unable to be released from her TV series *Charlie's Angels*. Meryl Streep replaced her and won for herself an Oscar.

Eric Stoltz was fired 14 days into the making of the 1985 movie *Back to the Future*. He was replaced by Michael J Fox.

Burt Lancaster was signed to play the part of Molina, the gay cellmate in the movie *Kiss of the Spider Woman*, but he suffered a heart attack before production started. The 1985 movie role went to William Hurt, who won that year's Academy Award for Best Actor.

Daryl Hannah was offered the Julia Roberts role in the movie *Steel Magnolias*; she turned down the offer to play the somewhat mousy and awkward beauty shop assistant. Julia landed herself an Oscar nomination for her role.

Annette Bening was cast as Catwoman in the movie *Batman Returns.* She fell pregnant before filming started and lost the role to Michelle Pfeiffer.

Meryl Streep and Goldie Hawn were considered for the roles Geena Davis and Susan Sarandon played in the movie *Thelma & Louise*.

In the late 1940s, Bob Hope had an opportunity to replace Curley and join *The Three Stooges*, but he turned the offer down.

Mick Jagger once auditioned for the role of Frank-N-Furter in the movie *Rocky Horror Picture Show.*

Lara Flynn Boyle landed her role in *Men in Black II* after Famke Janssen was forced to drop out.

Matthew Modine was supposedly the first choice to play Maverick in *Top Gun*. Tom Cruise ended up making the role all his own.

Billy Zane failed his screen test for the 1986 movie *The Night Before*.

Julia Roberts turned down the role in *Shakespeare in Love* that ended up winning Gwyneth Paltrow an Oscar.

Sting turned down the role of the villain in the James Bond movie *A View to a Kill.*

Both Nicolas Cage and John Malkovich turned down the role of the Green Goblin in the 2002 *Spider Man* movie. Willem Dafoe took it and made it his own.

Kevin Sorbo auditioned several times for the TV role of Superman in *Lois and Clark: the New Adventures of Superman.* He lost the role but later landed the role of Hercules in the TV series and received international fame.

Kim Cattrall originally said no to the TV role of Samantha in *Sex and the City* because she thought it might interfere with her movie career.

After Demi Moore's salary demands were turned down, Sandra Bullock landed the lead role in the movie *While You Were Sleeping*.

Charlize Theron turned down the lead female role in the 2001 movie *Pearl Harbor*; the role went to Kate Beckinsale.

Calista Flockhart said no to an audition for the role of Ally McBeal in the TV series because she was too busy in live theatre, besides, she was rather reluctant to do TV. The show's producers kept on at her and in the end she flew to LA for an audition between the Sunday-matinee and Monday-evening performances. Calista was offered the leading role on the spot and the rest is TV history.

Pierce Brosnan's late wife Cassandra, who played a countess in the Bond movie *For Your Eyes Only* (1981), introduced Pierce to Albert Broccoli who was the producer of the 007 series. There was lots of talk about Pierce replacing Roger Moore as James Bond, but at the last minute Pierce couldn't get out of his contract with the NBC network which was producing his TV series *Remington Steele*. It wasn't until 1995 that he finally stepped into James Bond's shoes for the big screen in *Goldeneye*.

The lead role in the 1971 movie *Dirty Harry* was originally intended for Frank Sinatra. After he turned it down it was offered to both Paul Newman and John Wayne who said no; finally, Clint Eastwood accepted the role and the rest is history.

Heath Ledger passed on the leading role in the *Spider-Man* movie, leaving it open for Tobey Maguire.

Johnny Depp turned down the lead in *Speed* and Keanu Reeves stepped in.

John Travolta turned down *As Good As It Gets*; Jack Nicholson stepped in and won himself an Oscar.

Robert De Niro just couldn't imagine himself starring in *Die Hard*, so he turned it down. Enter Bruce Willis.

Gisele Bunchen turned down a role in the movie *Charlie's Angels*.

Daniel Day-Lewis turned down the role of Aragorn in *Lord of the Rings*.

Matthew McConaughey was first choice for the role of leading man Jack in *Titanic*.

Lara Flynn Boyle auditioned for the role of Ally McBeal.

Sixth Sense director M Knight Shyamalan turned down the job on *Harry Potter and the Philosopher's Stone*.

Hilary Swank cried on set because she thought her showbiz career was over when she was cut from *Beverly Hills 90210*.

The movie *Jerry Maguire* was originally written with Tom Hanks in mind for the lead role.

Jennifer Aniston originally auditioned for Courtney Cox's part in the TV series *Friends*.

Molly Ringwald turned down the female lead in *Pretty Woman* before it was offered to Julia Roberts.

Kelly McGillis first turned down the leading female role in the 1986 movie *Top Gun* because the producers wanted her to play a bimbo gymnast. She only said yes when the part was rewritten as an astrophysicist.

Ron Howard offered Tom Cruise a role in his 1991 movie *Backdraft*, but Tom turned the offer down flat because it was too similar to the one he'd just played in *Days of Thunder*.

It's rumoured that Marilyn Monroe was offered the leading role in the 1961 movie *Breakfast at Tiffanys*, but turned it down; it then went to Audrey Hepburn.

Warren Beatty claims he was offered the Superman role before Christopher Reeve, but decided wearing tights on screen would not suit his image.

Both Robert Redford and Beau Bridges turned down the leading man role in the 1970 movie *Love Story*. Ryan O'Neal jumped at the chance.

Judy Garland landed the role of Dorothy in MGM's *The Wizard of Oz* when Fox Studios refused to loan Shirley Temple for the role.

Judge Reinhold lost out to Matthew Modine in the 1987 movie *Married To the Mob*.

Rick Moranis, Judd Nelson and even Whoopi Goldberg all rejected the role of *Ace Ventura: Pet Detective* before Jim Carrey signed up.

Fred MacMurray was all set to play TV's best-loved defence lawyer, Perry Mason, but the heavy workload made him pass on the role. The role went to Raymond Burr.

William Shatner was offered the role of television's Dr Kildare, long before taking the helm of the *Starship Enterprise*. The role went to Richard Chamberlain.

Barbra Streisand asked Elvis Presley to play opposite her as her leading man in her 1976 remake of *A Star Is Born* (which Kris Kristopherson got), but his lifetime manager, Colonel Tom Parker, told him not to do it.

James Dean turned down the lead in *The Silver Chalice* (1954), which went to Paul Newman. Later Dean beat Newman for the lead role in *East of Eden* (1955). Then came *Somebody Up There Likes Me*, and Dean got the lead role, but on 30 September 1955 he was killed in a car accident. His replacement was Paul Newman.

Actress/dancer Cyd Charisse had to turn down *Easter Parade* (1948) because she broke her leg a matter of weeks before shooting was to start. Then in 1951 she had to give up the starring role in *An American in Paris* because she found out she was pregnant; the role went to a newcomer, Leslie Caron.

The first choice to play the title role in *Scrooge* was Richard Harris, but he turned it down. The next choice was Rex Harrison, but the deal fell through at the last minute, and the part went to Albert Finney.

In 1961, Laurence Olivier decided not to accept the leading role in *Judgement at Nuremburg*, so it went to Burt Lancaster.

In 1940, Van Johnson was a matinee idol. In the 1950s he was offered the role of Elliot Ness in a new TV series called *The Untouchables*, but turned the role down. Next in line was Robert Stack, who starred in the show from 1959–1963.

Anthony Newley, James Booth, Terence Stamp and Laurence Harvey all turned down the lead in *Alfie* (1966). Michael Caine was fifth choice. Cilla Black sang *Alfie*, the song in the movie, but it was Dionne Warwick who made it a number-one hit.

First choice to play Miss Ellie in *Dallas* was Doris Day, and first choice to play J R was Robert Kulp.

At the last minute, Betty Hutton stepped in and took over the starring role from an ailing Judy Garland in *Annie Get Your Gun* (1950).

Albert Finney was first offered the title role in *Lawrence of Arabia* (1962). He turned the role down and it went to Peter O'Toole.

Christopher Reeve turned down a million dollars to star in *American Gigolo*. When the role was offered to Richard Gere, he didn't think twice.

James Mason and Bette Davis were Edward Albee's first choices to star in the movie version of the play *Who's Afraid of Virginia Woolf?*, but the roles went to Richard Burton and Elizabeth Taylor, who won the Oscar for Best Actress in 1966. This was the movie that broke all the Hollywood taboos for adult material with its four-letter words.

George Peppard accepted the role of Blake Carrington in *Dynasty*, but walked off the set in a huff during the filming of the pilot. The role was handed to second choice John Forsythe.

Warren Beatty turned down both of the lead roles in *Butch Cassidy and the Sundance Kid* (1969).

Both the studio and the producers of *Lolita* (1962) desperately wanted Hayley Mills to play the lead, but at the time she was under contract to Disney Studios and they would not release her.

The original casting for *The Wizard of Oz* (1939) was Shirley Temple as Dorothy, Buddy Epsen as the Tin Man and W C Fields as the Wizard. In the movie, Frank Morgan got to play five roles: a guard at the door of the Emerald City, a guard at the doorway to the Wizard's Chamber, a coachman, Professor Marvel and the Wizard of Oz.

In 1967, Shirley MacLaine turned down a million-dollar contract to appear in *Casino Royale*; just as well, the movie was a flop at the box office.

Alan Ladd turned down the role of Jeff Rink in *Giant* (1956), thereby giving James Dean the movie role he's best remembered for.

Noel Coward, Michael Redgrave and George Sanders all turned down the stage role of Professor Higgins in *My Fair Lady*.

Anne Bancroft was up for the role of Joan Crawford in the movie version of Christina Crawford's controversial bestseller *Mommie Dearest,* but at the last minute Faye Dunaway replaced her.

In 1981, Tom Selleck was into his new TV role as *Magnum PI*, so he turned down the lead in *Raiders of the Lost Ark*.

When the movie *The Jazz Singer* was offered to Eddie Cantor, he turned it down, and suggested another actor called Al Jolson for the role.

Susan Dey, from TV's *LA Law,* and Henry Winkler, 'The Fonz', turned down the lead roles in *Grease*.

Bette Davis turned down the starring role in *Come Back Little Sheba* (1952), and it went to Shirley Booth, who won an Academy Award for her movie debut as Lola. In her Oscar acceptance speech she thanked Bette for turning the role down.

Both Mary Martin and Elizabeth Taylor were considered for the part of Nellie Forbush in the 1958 movie *South Pacific*. Mary Martin played the role on both the West End and Broadway stages, but the movie role went to Mitzi Gaynor.

Trevor Howard, Richard Burton, James Mason and Peter Finch were all considered for the part of James Bond in the first Bond movie.

Robert Redford has turned down the following roles: Nick in *Who's Afraid of Virginia Woolf?* (1966); Benjamin Braddock in *The Graduate* (1967); Guy Woodhouse in *Rosemary's Baby* (1968); Oliver Barrett IV in *Love Story* (1970); the Jackal in *The Day of the Jackal* (1973). He thought none of these roles were right for him!

Gene Kelly's broken ankle forced him to give the lead role in *Easter Parade* (1948) over to his friend Fred Astaire.

Jackie Onassis turned down a 1 million dollar deal to portray herself in *The Greek Tycoon*. The role went to Jacqueline Bisset, who received $500,000.

In the 1963 movie *Cleopatra*, Laurence Olivier, Peter Finch and Trevor Howard all turned down the role of Julius Caesar, which was eventually played by Rex Harrison.

Singer/actress Grace Jones is rumoured to have turned down $50,000 an episode to star in the TV series *The A-Team*.

Cary Grant was first choice to play in the following movies, but turned them all down: *The Third Man* (1949) went to William Holden; *Sabrina Fair* (1954) went to Humphrey Bogart; *A Star Is Born* (1954) went to James Mason; and *My Fair Lady* (1964) went to Rex Harrison.

Angie Dickinson was first offered the role of Krystal Carrington in *Dynasty*, but didn't want to act in a soap opera. Today, Angie says it was one of the biggest mistakes in her career. The role went to second choice Linda Evans.

In 1952, Gregory Peck turned down the lead role in *High Noon*. Gary Cooper accepted, and won the Academy Award for Best Actor. Gregory said he thought he could never do justice to the part.

In the 1931 classic *Frankenstein*, the role of Elizabeth was first offered to Bette Davis. She turned it down and it went to Mae Clarke.

In 1954, Jennifer Jones found out she was pregnant, Greta Garbo turned it down flat, so the starring role in *The Country Girl* went to Grace Kelly. In 1954, she won the Best Actress Award for her performance.

In 1946, producer Darryl F Zanuck was looking for a strong male lead to play the king in *The King and I*. His first choices were James Mason and Robert Montgomery, but Yul Brynner got the role—his first in an American movie.

Alan Alda said no to the *M*A*S*H* role when it was first offered to him—'If it was going to be just hijinks on the battlefield, I wanted no part of it.' Little did he know the show would be his ticket to stardom. In 1974, Alan got an Emmy Award as the most outstanding actor in a TV series.

David Niven and Bette Davis were first choices to play the leading roles in *The African Queen* (1951). The roles went to Katharine Hepburn and Humphrey Bogart.

Deanna Durbin was on the first list to play Dorothy in *The Wizard of Oz*, but her voice was not up to standard and she was rejected. Walt Disney personally tested Deanna for *Snow White and the Seven Dwarfs* (1937), but again she was rejected because of her voice. Walt thought it had the wrong feel to it for his Snow White.

Richard Dreyfuss walked out of the starring role in the movie *All That Jazz* after 10 days. Roy Scheider replaced him.

Rock Hudson was considered for the lead in *Ben-Hur* (1959). Charlton Heston was going to play Messala, but a matter of weeks before shooting started he was cast in the leading role. Messala was played by Stephen Boyd, who had to wear dark contact lenses over his blue eyes. Only Charlton was allowed to have sparkling blue eyes in the movie; the director thought it gave him more sex appeal and masculinity.

The original *Road To* movies were written for Fred MacMurray and George Burns. Bob Hope and Bing Crosby, who made the movies so popular, were second choice.

In *Harlow* (1965), Ginger Rogers replaced Eleanor Parker, who replaced Rita Hayworth, who replaced Judy Garland as Jean Harlow's mother.

Matthew Broderick was first choice to play Alex Keaton in the TV series *Family Ties*, but turned it down because his father James was gravely ill in New York and Matthew did not want to leave him. The role went to an unknown called Michael J Fox, and the rest is TV history.

Bing Crosby was asked to play the lead in the *Columbo* TV series, but he turned it down and it went to Peter Falk.

Audrey Hepburn said no to the leading roles in *The Diary of Anne Frank* (1959) and *The Inn of the Sixth Happiness* (1958).

Steve McQueen, Warren Beatty and Marlon Brando were all very high on the consideration list for the role as the Sundance Kid in *Butch Cassidy and the Sundance Kid* (1969). But director George Roy Hill always wanted Robert Redford, and of course got his way.

Kirk Douglas was among the first choices to play Blake Carrington in *Dynasty*.

As you probably know, it was because of Laurence Olivier, indirectly, that Vivien Leigh was cast in *Gone with the Wind*. William Wyler went to England to try to entice Olivier to Hollywood to make *Wuthering Heights*, not an easy task because the English star wasn't particularly interested in making American movies. Wyler said he found Olivier living with a very pretty girl whom the actor repeatedly identified as an actress. 'I knew he was hinting that I should cast her in Wuthering Heights,' Wyler said, 'so I offered her the part of Isabel, a supporting role. She said she didn't want to play Isabel; she wanted to play Kathy, the lead. I told her that was impossible for at least two reasons. In the first place, Merle Oberon had been cast; and in the second place, if Merle didn't play the lead, there'd be no picture. But Vivien kept insisting that she wanted to play Kathy, until I finally lost patience and said, "The role of Isabel is the best you'll ever be offered in your first American picture."' Leigh still refused to play Isabel, but did accompany Olivier to California, where, in her first American picture, she played the lead in *Gone with the Wind*.

The role of Nurse Ratchet in *One Flew Over the Cuckoo's Nest* (1975) was turned down by Geraldine Page, Angela Lansbury, Anne Bancroft and Colleen Dewhurst. The role went to Louise Fletcher, who won an Oscar for Best Actress.

Gary Cooper was the first star considered for the leading role in the 1950s movie *Wagon Train*.

Because of his very thick West Indian accent, Sidney Poitier was turned down by the American Negro Theatre.

George Segal walked away from the movie *10* saying he was unhappy with the way it was being handled. The producers cast again and came up with Dudley Moore.

Julie Harris was director Fred Zinnemann's first choice for the part of Alma in *From Here to Eternity* (1953), but the role went to Donna Reed who won the Best Supporting Actress Oscar.

Patty Duke stepped into the role of Neely O'Hara in *Valley of the Dolls* (1967) after Petula Clark turned it down.

Dark Victory (1939) was originally planned for Greta Garbo, but she saw herself more as Anna Karenina. The role went to Bette Davis—very much a second choice.

Henry Fonda turned down the leading role in the movie *Network*, saying it was too hysterical for him. Just as well for Peter Finch; it was Peter's last movie, for which he was given a posthumous Oscar in 1976.

Billie Burke got the role of the good witch, Glinda, in *The Wizard of Oz* (1939) after the studio's first choice, MGM starlet Helen Gilbert, chose to run off with Howard Hughes instead.

In 1955, MGM bought the movie rights to Tennessee William's Pulitzer Prize-winning play, *Cat On a Hot Tin Roof*. They wanted to star Grace Kelly and James Dean in the leading roles. Unfortunately, it was not to be. In 1956, Grace retired from acting to become the Princess of Monaco, and six months after MGM bought the rights, James Dean was killed in a car accident. The 1958 movie starred Elizabeth Taylor and Paul Newman, which earned both of them Academy Award nominations.

Billy Crystal was the first choice to do the voice of Buzz Lightyear in the movie *Toy Story*. He said no to the offer and Tim Allen scored the role.

UNEXPECTED APPEARANCES

The originator of the *Batman* comic strip, Bob Cane, was signed up to appear in the 1989 movie *Batman*. But because of last-minute scheduling conflicts, he unfortunately had to pull out. In the movie, Bob did the drawing that the newspaper reporter shows of Batman.

Trumpet player Herb Alpert appeared as an extra in *The Ten Commandments* (1956).

John Travolta's mother appeared with him in the 1977 movie *Saturday Night Fever*. She was the woman he gets the paint from. His sister also appears briefly as the pizza lady.

In the 1995 movie *Apollo 13*, US astronaut Jim Lovell appeared briefly playing the captain of the *USS Iwo Jima*. His wife Marilyn appears as an extra watching from the grandstand during the launch.

Security guard Frank Wills, who discovered the break-in at the Watergate building, played himself in the 1976 movie *All the President's Men*.

Josh Hartnett appeared in the 1997 Tommy Hilfiger campaign.

Watch out for Ted Turner in a cameo role as a Confederate Colonel in the 1993 Civil War epic *Gettysburg*. He gets shot as he climbs over a split-rail fence. Ted helped bankroll the movie.

Because Elizabeth Taylor was a Jewish convert, her 1963 movie *Cleopatra* was banned in Egypt.

Speaking at a landmine clearance centre in October 2002 near Manchester in England, American actress Angelina Jolie hinted that she might give up her career in order to devote herself full-time to solving the worldwide problem of landmines, which kill and maim thousands every year. Angelina first became aware of the problem while filming in Cambodia. 'Wherever I was working, you would see a lot of people with missing limbs,' she said. 'It was more shocking than anything I had ever seen and I soon became all too familiar with the agony and suffering landmines were causing innocent civilians, one third of them children.'

In 1983, Zsa Zsa Gabor was starring in the stage production of *40 Carats* in Philadelphia. During the first half she stormed off stage in a rage, because she felt the handicapped people in the audience were making too much noise.

In the 1993 movie *Sleepless in Seattle*, the silhouettes of the couple on the chocolates that Tom Hanks and Meg Ryan spot in the New York shop window are in fact them.

Anthony Hopkins said that after starring as Hannibal in *The Silence of the Lambs* he could hardly stop at traffic lights without somebody rolling down their window and singing out, 'Had your dinner yet, Hannibal?'

In 1985, Bette Davis donated 59 of her personal scrapbooks to the Boston University library. The University was delighted, but was amazed to find that every picture of Joan Crawford in Bette's scrapbooks had her teeth blacked out. Nobody was ever game enough to ask Bette about this.

In September 1990, a British journalist who worked for the *Daily Mail* newspaper very quickly found out that the British Police failed to see any humour in his attempt to play a prank on Hollywood actress Zsa Zsa Gabor as she arrived at London's Heathrow Airport. The reporter dressed up as an American policeman to meet Zsa Zsa; he hoped to pose for pictures with Zsa Zsa in a joke reference to her run-in earlier that year when she slapped a Beverley Hills cop. The journalist completely failed to take into account the action of Heathrow security officers, who were already keyed up because of fears of attacks by Iraqi terrorists. As soon as the airport security spotted the fake American cop, they pushed him up against a wall, his imitation Magnum pistol was seized and he was taken to the cells for questioning. Zsa Zsa arrived off her LA flight totally unaware of the prank.

In 1990, Joan Collins was twice thrown out of the Royal enclosure at the Ascot race meeting. The ageless star managed to get inside the enclosure 'without' an admission badge, but was stopped by an eagle-eyed official. A few hours later, Joan made her second attempt to get in, but was turned away by a policeman.

As a stand-up comic, Roseanne Barr was once the opening act for Julio Iglesias.

In 1981, Robert De Niro went to Rome on a private visit. He went to a huge amount of trouble to remain incognito, which led to his arrest as a suspected terrorist. He was kept under lock and key for over an hour while his real identity was checked out.

Kurt Russell did the voice of Elvis Presley in the 1994 movie *Forrest Gump*. His name did not appear in the movie's credits.

Both Kirstie Alley and Rhea Perlman's dads, and George Wendt's parents, have all played extras in the hit TV series *Cheers*.

While on a concert tour of Japan in 1987, Michael Jackson visited the Mayor of Osaka, and turned up with his pet chimp Bubbles. 'We were surprised to see the chimpanzee,' said a city official, 'but we understand he is his good friend.'

In 1983, to celebrate the 50th movie anniversary of the premiere of *King Kong*, a 50-foot gorilla balloon was attached to the tower of New York's Empire State Building.

A bullet certainly made an unexpected appearance in the 1970 movie *Little Big Man*. During filming Dustin Hoffman shot himself in the leg while drawing a loaded gun.

Watch out for *The Lord of the Rings: the Fellowship of the Ring* director, Peter Jackson, who appears as a bystander when the hobbits come into Bree.

At the age of five, Robert Downey Jr played a puppy in his dad's movie *Pound*.

In *Quo Vadis* (1951) you can see a very scantily dressed Sophia Loren appearing as an extra.

Elizabeth Taylor appeared in a close-up crowd scene in *Quo Vadis* (1951). She was also an extra (as a reveller) in *Anne of a Thousand Days* (1969), which starred Richard Burton. For neither brief appearance did she receive a billing.

Koo Stark can be spotted making appearances in such movies as *Star Wars* and *The Rocky Horror Show*. She was born in America, daughter of TV actress Kathi Norris and B-movie producer Wilbur Stark.

Bela Lugosi left his Dracula cape behind to play the monster in *Frankenstein Meets the Wolf Man*. This was the only time Bela played Frankenstein's monster.

In 1939, actor/dancer Donald O'Connor played Beau Geste as a 12-year-old in the movie of the same name.

In *The Blackboard Jungle* (1955), Sidney Poitier played the delinquent high-school student, Gregory W Miller; he was 31 at the time. Twelve years later he played the high-school teacher, Mr Braithwaite, in *To Sir with Love*.

In 1965, Peter Sellers produced and directed a movie which featured Lord Snowdon and Princess Margaret along with actress Britt Ekland. Peter sent it as a gift to Her Majesty Queen Elizabeth II on her 39th birthday.

Before Raymond Burr became famous in *Perry Mason* (1957–1966), and later in *Ironside* (1967–1975), he was the narrator in *Godzilla* (1954).

John Larroquette, star of TV's *Night Court*, was an extra in *Star Trek 2: the Wrath of Khan*. Another extra on the same movie was *Cheers* star Kirstie Alley; she wore pointed ears and John wore a crab on his head.

Babe Ruth played himself in the movie *Pride of the Yankees*.

As a young man, Fidel Castro appeared in *Holiday in Mexico* (1946), talked into it by the producer, and Xavier Cugat.

Alfred Hitchcock's daughter appeared in *Stage Fright* and *Psycho* as well as *Strangers On a Train*.

Helen Keller, who was deaf, dumb and blind, appeared as a pilot in *Deliverance* (1918).

In the 1960s, Davey Jones, one of the original *Monkees*, played the Artful Dodger in both the Broadway and London stage productions of the musical *Oliver*.

Walter Huston played Captain Jacoby in *The Maltese Falcon* (1942).

Mickey Rooney played a Japanese eccentric in *Breakfast at Tiffanys* (1961).

1976 American Olympic Decathlon gold medallist, Bruce Jenner, starred in the 1980s movie *Can't Stop the Music* (1980).

Director Steven Spielberg played a clerk in an assessor's office in his movie *Close Encounters of the Third Kind.*

Jacqueline Susann, who wrote the highly successful novel *Valley of the Dolls*, appeared in a cameo role as a reporter in the 1967 movie of the same name, the only time she ever appeared in a movie.

Jean Harlow played an unbilled extra in Charlie Chaplin's classic *City Lights* (1931).

In *The Return of Dr X* (1939), Humphrey Bogart made an appearance as a vampire.

Playing himself in *The Greatest Show on Earth* (1952) was circus owner John Ringling North.

Here is a list of stars and the movies they appeared in without receiving any credit: Lauren Bacall, *Two Guys from Milwaukee*; Humphrey Bogart, *Two Guys from Milwaukee* and *Love Lottery*; Yul Brynner, *The Magic Christian*; Joseph Cotton, *Touch of Evil*; Richard Burton, *What's New, Pussycat?;* Vincent Price, *Beach Party*; David Niven, *Road to Hong Kong*; and Boris Karloff, *Bikini Beach.*

GOOD LUCK CHARMS

As a 20-year-old, Oscar winner Denzel Washington had a reading from a fortune teller/prophet who foretold his stardom.

Melanie Griffith requested an east-facing hotel room for her healing crystals during a stay in London.

Violinist Vannessa-Mae always has to spill some water on stage before performing. After doing it once by accident, now it's become her lucky charm.

Arnold Swarzenegger deliberately destroys a pair of sunglasses on every film set for luck.

Steven Spielberg's lucky charm is a gold charm of *E.T.*, which he keeps in the glove compartment of his car.

Cameron Diaz wears a necklace given to her by a friend to ward off ageing, and as a lucky charm.

Enrique Inglesias has become so attached to his lucky leather trousers he patches them up rather than throw them away.

Sigourney Weaver says that she believes the spirit of anthropologist Dian Fossey protected her during the shoot in Africa of *Gorillas in the Mist*.

There are a great number of Hollywood celebrities that believe crystals provide energy and have healing powers: Bianca Jagger, Phyllis Diller, Richard Gere, George Hamilton, Cybill Shepherd, Tina Turner, Joan Collins, Betty White, Elizabeth Taylor, Sharon Stone and Jane Fonda to name a few.

Opera superstar Luciano Pavarotti won't sing or act a word until he finds a bent nail on stage. He always carries a large handkerchief to recitals, because he was given one at his very first recital.

Bob Hope never wore a watch in a movie; he thought it would bring him bad luck.

Burt Reynolds once purchased a pair of small white gloves embroidered M M, which belonged to Marilyn Monroe, at a Hollywood auction for an undisclosed amount. These could be his lucky charm.

Cate Blanchett keeps the pointed elf ears she wore in *Lord of the Rings* as a good luck charm; she keeps them on her mantelpiece.

Robin Williams always carries a good luck charm; it's a carved ivory trinket that once belonged to his late father.

Legendary singer Lena Horne is afraid peanut shells in her dressing room will bring her bad luck.

Bob Hope never goes on stage without a pair of old gold cufflinks, which were presented to him by Paramount Studios 30 years ago. He believes they bring good luck because they carry the face of Saint Genesius, the patron saint of actors and comedians.

When Barbra Streisand was younger, she believed the colour lavender had special significance. She redid the interior of her house in lavender and began to wear clothes in the colour. It's rumoured she believed that lavender was a protection against death.

Jennifer Lopez always brings her own sheets with her when she stays in hotels.

Tori Spelling always boards a plane right foot first. Also, before she drives into a tunnel she always honks twice.

Watch out for Superman, who will appear somewhere in every episode of *Seinfeld*. Maybe he was the show's lucky charm.

Joan Collins's three acting superstitions that she always goes by are:

1. Don't put red and white flowers together in a dressing-room vase; they must be all white or all red.
2. Never whistle anywhere near the theatre.
3. Don't wear real jewellery on stage and never have real flowers on stage at any time.

Jimmy Stewart collected every hat he'd ever worn in a movie. He was also very proud of a pair of shoes he'd worn in more than 20 of his movies; they were his good luck charm.

Every night while Michael Crawford is in a stage production, he has a good luck superstition ritual. He asks his dresser and makeup artist to stand in the same place before each show. He goes to the stage at exactly the same time every night, passing the same people and shaking or touching their hands in exactly the same way.

Rocker-turned-actress Courtney Cox won't step on stage without wearing her 'lucky' old shoes.

Leonard Nimoy always wears an old wool hat whenever he tries out for a new part; it's the very same hat he wore when he auditioned for the role of Dr Spock in the original TV series of *Star Trek*.

Elizabeth Taylor has a passion for the colour purple, and insists that her dressing rooms are painted violet and that any flowers sent to her dressing room must be lavender coloured.

There didn't seem to be any good luck charms on the set of the remake of the 1956 movie *The King and I*, renamed *Anna and the* King, and starring Jodie Foster and Chow Yun Fat. Some joked it should have been named *The Jinx and I*. Here's a list of things that happened: Jodie Foster fell ill and then bruised her ribs; less than a week later she twisted her ankle. A young boy on the set was very nearly crushed by an elephant. A worker fell off a hotel balcony, splitting his head open. A metal object fell on the movie's director Andy Tennant's hand and broke several bones. Co-star Bai Ling broke her nose when she fell during a boat ride. An assistant crew member was very nearly strangled to death when he mistook a large boa constrictor for a speed bump in the road and rode over it on his bike. If it wasn't for a local villager killing the boa the crew member would have died. It's also rumoured that three horses fell off a cliff during the making of the movie.

Liza Minnelli never travels without her pair of lucky old ruby-red slippers.

Mr T always wears non-matching socks.

Bo Derek always lets the phone ring four times before picking it up.

Barry Manilow has a clause written into all his contracts that says, 'Nobody may cross his path from the time he leaves his dressing room until the second he steps on stage.'

Robert Morley has a good luck charm in the shape of a teddy bear, which he takes everywhere. He's had the same bear since he entered show business.

Lynn Redgrave will not appear in any movie, stage show or TV series unless her teddy bear is in her dressing room.

Orchestra conductor Leonard Bernstein kissed his cufflinks before every performance.

When Susan Hayward placed her handprints in the forecourt of Grauman's Chinese Theatre (in 1978 it was renamed Mann's), she sprinkled a handful of gold dust over her prints. She did this as a good luck charm, giving back some of the gold Hollywood had given her over the years.

For a touch of personal good luck, Sophia Loren wears something red every day.

Peter O'Toole almost always wears emerald-green socks; he considers this his good luck charm.

William Sanderson, who plays Larry in the *Newhart* TV show, won't make an entrance without having a quarter coin stuck in his left ear for luck.

When a jet-black cat crosses Zsa Zsa Gabor's path, she will walk backwards three steps, or back her car up a couple of feet if she's driving at the time.

Richard Chamberlain will never allow anyone to whistle in his dressing room. If they do, he gets them to go outside, close the door, turn round three times and then come in.

TINSELTOWN—FOR BETTER OR FOR WORSE

In December 1990, actor/comedian Robin Williams won the last prime spot in front of Hollywood's landmark Mann's Chinese Theatre with the unveiling of his star, number 1926, on the Walk of Fame.

'Stardom is a blessing and a burden, and no movie luminary wears the mantle more gracefully than Tom Hanks,' said *People* magazine in their special collector's edition, *The 100 Greatest Movie Stars of Our Time.*

As a surprise for the cast and crew of their 2002 movie *Cold Mountain*, Nicole Kidman and Renée Zellweger prepared a Thanksgiving feast. Renée made her special home-made biscuits and Nicole did the stuffing for the turkey.

The movie *Bad Company*, starring Chris Rock and Sir Anthony Hopkins, was the last movie to be shot at the World Trade Center before the September 11 disaster. Most of the subway scenes were shot there.

To get into shape for his starring role in the movie *Platoon*, Charlie Sheen spent several gruelling weeks in boot camp.

On 15 December 1939, *Gone with the Wind* premiered in Atlanta, Georgia. The State's governor was so happy to have the world premiere in his state that he declared the day an official State holiday.

At the opening of the movie *Ben Hur* (1959), MGM's Leo the Lion symbol did not roar for the first time ever, due to the movie's religious theme.

The studio had a clause written into Shirley Temple's contract that her hair must always have 56 little curls in it when she appeared in front of the cameras. Her curly-top trademark was checked three or four times a day during filming by the studio hairdresser, to see that none of the 56 had fallen out.

Originally, the climax for *King Kong* (1933) was to take place in the Yankee Stadium, but at the last minute the writers changed it to the top of the Empire State Building in New York. The movie had a working title of *The Eighth Wonder* because they wanted to keep the name King Kong under wraps until a few weeks before the launch. Fay Wray was not the first choice to play Ann Darrow; producer Merian C Cooper wanted Jean Harlow, or second choice Ginger Rogers, for the role.

Adolf Hitler's all-time favourite movie was *King Kong*.

In 1921, Hollywood made and released 854 full-length feature movies. This record has never been broken.

At 33, Dustin Hoffman played the greatest age span by a single actor in a movie. In the title role of *Little Big Man* he aged from 17–121.

When Clark Gable removed his shirt and revealed that he wasn't wearing anything underneath, T-shirt sales plummeted in America. The movie was *It Happened One Night* back in 1934.

Shooting had to shut down on the set of the 1990 movie *Three Men and a Baby* when Tom Selleck got a badly inflamed eye from a misdirected shot from an aerosol spray. For several days, Tom wore an eye patch and did his lines off camera so that they could do other actors' close-ups. After seeing a doctor, Tom was forced to take a break from the production for a few extra days.

Heather Menzies, who played the tomboy Louisa in the 1965 movie *The Sound of Music*, married American actor Robert Urich.

Adolf Hitler owned a copy of every movie Greta Garbo ever made; he was totally besotted with her.

When Nikita Khrushchev visited Hollywood in 1960 he was not allowed to visit Disneyland for security reasons. Instead, he had a private visit to 20th Century-Fox studios to see the making of their latest movie, *Can Can*. He thought the movie was disgusting.

There is a larger movie industry in India than in Hollywood.

Nick Nolte ate dogfood in the movie *Down and Out in Beverley Hills* in a scene where he shows the dog how to use a dog bowl.

In 1915, pioneer moviemaker D W Griffith produced his masterpiece *The Birth of a Nation*. From that moment on, he turned movie making into an art form, introducing such techniques as the close-up, the fade out, the long shot, the fade in and cross-cutting. These techniques are still used today in the world of movie making.

The historical character most portrayed in the movies is Napoleon Bonaparte. Between 1897 and 1988 he appeared in 177 movies.

There was never any love lost between Bette Davis and Joan Crawford. During the movie *What Ever Happened to Baby Jane?* the two were often at each other's throats. While filming a fight scene, Joan was so afraid that Bette would really hit her that she demanded they use a dummy. Joan later said that Bette managed to kick her in the head just before the dummy took over for her character. Later in the shooting, Joan got her revenge when Bette had to carry her after a death scene; she wanted Bette to suffer at every step, so she wore heavy weights strapped to her body.

In *You're in the Army Now*, Jane Wyman and Regis Toomey engaged in a kiss that lasted three minutes and five seconds, still an onscreen kiss record today.

The largest outdoor movie set in Hollywood history was in the silent movie *Intolerance* (1916), directed by D W Griffith.

The snow-peaked mountain top, which has become the trademark of Paramount Studios, is a picture of a real mountain in Wasatch, Utah.

Zsa Zsa Gabor always calls everybody darling, because she can never remember people's names. Tallulah Bankhead was the first to use the same line, making it her trademark.

The surfside embrace of Deborah Kerr and Burt Lancaster in *From Here to Eternity* (1953) has gone down in movie history as one of the most passionate love scenes ever shot.

In the 1937 movie *A Star Is Born*, two extras in the scene at the bar at Santa Anita were Carole Landis and Lana Turner.

With a total of 176 movies played by 76 different actors, Sherlock Holmes remains the most often depicted fictional character on film.

Talk about self-promotion. One of the books used as a prop in the 1941 movie *Ball of Fire* had the title *The Life and Times of Irving Sindler.* This just happened to be the prop master's name on the movie.

It's often assumed that James Dean only made three movies. In fact, he made six movie appearances: *Fixed Bayonets*, 1951; *Sailor Beware*, 1951; *Has Anyone Seen My Gal?* 1952; *East Of Eden*, 1955; *Rebel Without a Cause*, 1955; and *Giant*, 1956. He also made some television appearances along the way.

In June 1990, the 75-minute movie called *The Fast Forward*, starring Jenny Seagrove, Jerry Hall and Fiona Fullerton, earned a place in the *Guinness Book of Records* after being completed in just 13 days from start to finish.

In June 1990, the Judy Garland Festival in Grand Rapids, Minnesota, saw the largest gathering of Munchkins since the making of *The Wizard of Oz* in 1939.

In 1990, the biggest and most successful movie-making studio in the world celebrated its 75th anniversary. It all started with a pipe dream—literally. It is said that pioneer moviemaker, Carl Laemmle arrived in California and spotted a truck going by with its company name on the side, which said 'Universal Piping Company', and he appropriated the name, his dream being to become the 'biggest film-manufacturing company in the universe'. On 15 March 1915, he opened the gates to his studio on the site of a former chicken farm. On that day some 20,000 visitors turned up and Universal Studios was born.

Rodney Grant played Wind in His Hair in *Dances with Wolves* (1991). After the movie, he was named Indian of the Year by the American Indian Exposition.

Emilio Estevez, son of actor Martin Sheen, says that he's seen the movie *Jaws* (1975) more than 70 times.

Tom Cruise books all his hotel reservations in the name of the last character he played. That way he always remembers his pseudonym.

Before *The Colour of Money*, Tom Cruise spent eight weeks playing pool in seedy clubs to get into character. He worked as a barman before making *Cocktail*, and sat in a wheelchair for six weeks before playing a Vietnam vet in the movie *Born On the Fourth of July*.

The greatest number of costume changes in a movie is credited to Elizabeth Taylor in the 1963 movie *Cleopatra*.

While Julia Roberts was playing Tinkerbell in the 1991 movie *Hook*, she preferred to go without shoes between takes. But whenever they strapped Julia into the flying harness to film, her feet were filthy dirty on the bottom. So Steven Spielberg hired a man solely to clean her feet before shooting scenes.

In June 1990, both Anthony Perkins and Janet Leigh, stars of the original *Psycho*, placed memorabilia from the movie in a time capsule on the grounds of Universal Studios in Florida.

On 9 October 1990, 51 years after it had its premiere in the US, *Gone with the Wind* had its premiere in the Soviet Union. The charity premiere was to raise funds to fight AIDS. The movie was shown in English with Russian subtitles, but on its general release in Russia in January 1991, it was dubbed into Russian.

The following actors have also directed films: Leslie Howard, *Pygmalion* (1938); John Wayne, *The Green Berets* (1968); Charlton Heston, *Antony and Cleopatra* (1971); and Dennis Hopper, *Easy Rider* (1969).

Butterfly McQueen, who played Prissy in *Gone with the Wind* (1939), was barred from the whites-only premiere. Fifty years later she was the guest of honour celebrating the movie's 50th birthday in December 1989. Her real name was Thelma McQueen; she received her nickname, 'Butterfly', when she appeared in Harlem Theatre Group's production of *Midsummer Night's Dream* in the butterfly ballet sequence.

In 1989, Hollywood funny man Chevy Chase nearly died when filming went horribly wrong on the set of the movie *National Lampoon's Christmas Vacation*. Chevy was electrocuted in a scene where he is trapped in Christmas-tree lights; his screams on the set were ignored as the crew all thought he was ad-libbing. They only switched off the power when he fell in a heap on the studio floor.

While making the movie *Colours*, Sean Penn received over a dozen death threats. After the first couple of calls he insisted on wearing a bullet-proof vest during the entire making of the movie.

The Doctor and the Devils (1985) took 31 years to get to the screen after completion of the script. This is still a record.

Lily Tomlin wanted sell-out ticket sales for her movie *The Search for Signs of Intelligent Life in the Universe*, which opened for an 'exclusive engagement' on Friday, 27 September 1991 at a Manhattan theatre. So she sold tickets in the theatre's box-office for all six showings; the movie was a complete sell-out.

In the mid 1950s, Universal Studios would not renew the contracts of Clint Eastwood and Burt Reynolds because they thought neither actor showed any promise.

Like clockwork every day on an Alfred Hitchcock movie, at 4 p.m. tea would be served, no matter what. It was something Alfred insisted on with all his movies.

Eccentric billionaire Howard Hughes was a fan of Sean Connery, and felt that Sean was his look-alike. He once said if they made a movie about his life he wanted Sean to play him.

Between 1931 and 1937, Edward G Robinson was shot and killed in six movies.

Sharon Stone refused to appear with Clint Eastwood in the hit movie *In the Line of Fire*, simply because he wasn't a big enough star any more.

In *The Cannonball Run* (1981), Roger Moore plays an Englishman called Seymour Goldfarb who suffers from a delusion that he is Roger Moore the actor.

Michelle Pfeiffer hated being stared at as she was driven around the studio lot in her curve-hugging Catwoman costume for the *Batman 2* movie. So she had the studio fit a curtain to her golf cart so nobody could see her until she arrived at the set.

Hollywood star Harrison Ford bans any of his co-stars from wearing either perfume or aftershave; he claims it makes him feel sick.

In 1979, a scene was cut out of *The Muppet Movie* on the grounds of gratuitous violence. The scene which gave them trouble showed Fozzie Bear being menaced by a drunken sailor with a broken bottle.

In December 1991, Richard Gere broke a rib when a violent scene in the movie *Mr Jones* went dreadfully wrong. He ended up in a chest brace for quite a few days.

The London *Sun* newspaper said that Martin Scorsese's Mafia movie *Good Fellas* was the foulest movie of 1990. The F-word was said an incredible 246 times.

In the first *Terminator* movie, Arnold Schwarzenegger only spoke 17 lines, which works out to 65 words.

Johnny Weissmuller never said 'Me Tarzan, You Jane' in *Tarzan the Ape Man* (1932). Actually he said, 'Tarzan ... Jane.' And in *Casablanca* (1943), Humphrey Bogart never said 'Play it again, Sam.' He said, 'You played it for her; you can play it for me. If she can stand it, I can play it!'

When the movie *The Sound of Music* was screened in Germany, the studio had to edit out most of the Nazi scenes, otherwise the movie would have been banned.

Comic movie stars Bud Abbott and Lou Costello once took out insurance with Lloyds of London in case any member of their audience should die laughing.

James Cagney was always being quoted as saying 'All right, you guys' and 'You dirty rat'. In fact he never said either in any of his movies.

In George Cukor's *The Women* (1939) he cast 135 actresses. There were no males in the movie.

In 1967, when *Hawaii*, with Julie Andrews, was shown at the Center Theater at High Point in America, the theatre manager was arrested for showing a movie, which the police thought obscene. It contained scenes of chaste but bare-bosomed native girls. Under a local ordinance, which had been in force since the mid 19th century, any depiction of unclad breasts was an indictable offence.

In 1952, veteran groups picketed Columbia's film version of Arthur Miller's *Death of a Salesman* because Miller had refused to issue an anti-communist statement. The feeling was that the play's protagonist, Willy Loman, was a rotten salesman, not the victim of a hard-hearted system.

No movie made in Japan before World War II was permitted to have any kissing scenes.

Joan Collins says the worst movie she ever appeared in was *Empire of the Ants* (1977), in which she played a Florida real-estate developer threatened by giant ants.

A few weeks before filming was to start on the Bond movie *A View to a Kill*, the entire 007 sound stage burnt to the ground. The stage was totally rebuilt in less than four months. In honour of Cubby Broccoli's efforts in having the stage rebuilt, the English studio Pinewood renamed it *The Albert R Broccoli 007 Stage*.

The only movie musical with an all-child-star cast was Alan Parker's 1976 gangster spoof movie *Bugsy Malone*. It starred a very young Jodie Foster and Scott Baio.

Jamie Bell auditioned seven times for the role of Billy Elliott; he was selected over 2,000 other young boys.

During their 29 years together as Hollywood's most successful comedy duo, Stan Laurel and Oliver Hardy made 104 movies. They spanned the silent and sound eras, two-reelers, three-reelers and hour-plus movies.

When the Pope came to Los Angeles in 1987, they covered the letter 'L' from the big white HOLLYWOOD sign on Mt Lee so that it read Holywood.

Hollywood says that Shirley Temple was probably the biggest child star in movie history. She was number one at the American box office for three years in a row, from 1935–1937 and at one time had 4 million members in her fan club.

English graphic designer Sian Thurkettle has seen the movie *E.T.* an astounding 773 times. Well, that is up to the time of this book going to print.

In 2002, an American Film Institute poll of producers, actors, writers and directors voted the most romantic movie ever made as *Casablanca*, starring Humphrey Bogart and Ingrid Bergman. No movies produced or released in the past 40 years were in the top five. *Citizen Kane* beat *Casablanca* to the number-one spot as greatest American film of all time.

Speed, the 1994 box-office hit movie starring Sandra Bullock and Keanu Reeves, used 12 buses during the movie. Two of them were blown up, and they used a specially rigged one for the now famous freeway jump.

The Three Stooges made a total of 207 movies, which is more than any other comedy team in US movie history.

Ninety per cent of the extras in the 1995 movie *Braveheart*, starring Mel Gibson, were reserves in the Irish army.

In 1943, Bette Davis and John Garfield founded the Hollywood Canteen to entertain World War II servicemen.

The Wizard of Oz was first a Broadway musical; it had 293 performances and then went on a US tour that lasted nine years. Then 37 years later, the MGM studios turned it into a movie.

Hollywood California was founded in 1886 when Harvey Wilcox of Kansas bought 120 acres in the Cahuenga Valley area. It was really Mrs Wilcox who gave the movie capital its name. While travelling on a train, a woman told her about her summer home in Illinois, which she had named 'Hollywood'. Mrs Wilcox liked the name so much that she chose it for her husband's newly bought land. On 1 February 1887, Mr Wilcox officially filed a map for subdivision selling purposes, and a city was born.

Hollywood was a totally independent city from 1903–1910. In early 1910, Hollywood had 5,000 settlers, and became a district of Los Angeles. By 1930, there were over 160,000 people permanently living in Hollywood, mainly due to the quick growth of the movie industry. Hollywood boasted '350 days of sunshine' to lure film makers to build their studios there.

An oil explorer, Barton Green, named Beverly Hills. After buying up some unnamed acreage in Los Angeles and finding no oil there, he subdivided the area for homesites, built himself a huge house, and named the area after his hometown, Beverly Farm, in Massachusetts.

Renowned British artist David Hockney painted the inside of the Hollywood Roosevelt's hotel swimming pool, making it Hockney's largest painting to date and the only public pool in the world where you can swim inside a work of art. The underwater mural of blue parentheses, valued at $1 million, was a gift to the hotel by the artist.

Author Rex Reed: 'Beverly Hills is the only place in the world where the police have an unlisted telephone number.'

Hollywood's 20th Century-Fox Studio cut all the scenes showing any physical contact between the young curly-haired darling Shirley Temple and the black dancer and actor Bill 'Bojangles' Robinson in the 1934 movie musical *The Little Colonel*. These cuts were the only way the movie was assured to get US wide distribution particularly in the south. The audiences were still shocked when Shirley's fingers touched Bills during their now famous staircase dance sequence.

The oldest movie studio in Hollywood was built in 1917–18, and was known as the Peralta Studios. Today, the studio is called Paramount Studios. This studio lot has had many different names over the years. In 1920, it was the Brunton Studios, then it was called the United States Studio from 1921–1926, when Paramount bought it. Although most Hollywood historians claim that Rudolph Valentino made many of his movies there for Paramount, he in fact died before Paramount bought it in 1926. He made his Paramount pictures at the old Lasky Studio on Sunset and Vine Streets.

The Lorimar Studios in Hollywood changed the name of the Robert Taylor Building after producers and tenants complained in a petition that the late actor testified before the Un-American Activities Committee against the so-called Hollywood Ten; he was considered a supporter of the Hollywood blacklist. The building has now been renamed the George Cukor Building.

Musso and Frank Grill on Hollywood Blvd is the oldest restaurant in Hollywood. It opened in 1919 and was a favourite of writers like F Scott Fitzerald and stars like Gloria Swanson, Mary Pickford, Douglas Fairbanks and Cecil B De Mille.

Bill 'Bojangles' Robinson taught little Shirley Temple the famous staircase dance on the stairway leading from the lobby to the mezzanine in the Roosevelt Hotel, Hollywood.

The oldest house in Hollywood is hidden by trees and heavy shrubbery in the middle of Farmer's Market. It is one of Hollywood's best-kept secrets. The house, built in 1852, was the birthplace of Earl Gilmore, founder of Farmer's Market. Earl died in the house in 1964, in the same bed he was born in. Today, his bedroom is kept exactly as it was at the time of his death.

Marlon Brando said, 'Hollywood is a frontier town ruled by fear and love of money. People around here are trapped by success and wealth. Hollywood is one big cash register.'

In the 1930s, Universal Studios built grandstands where tourists could watch movie making for just 25 cents. Because the movies were silent, the tourists used to join in, cheering their favourite hero, but this was dropped when the talkies came in.

The Hollywood Roosevelt has always been a very popular location for movie and TV crews. *Highway to Heaven*, *Simon and Simon*, *Hunter*, *Moonlighting*, *MacGyver*, *Beverly Hills Cop 2*, *Knots Landing*, *Sunset* and *Sledge Hammer* are just a few of the productions which have used the hotel lobby and ballroom.

Walter Winchell once said about Hollywood, 'It's a place where they shoot too many pictures and not enough actors.'

The largest advertising sign in Los Angeles, perhaps even the world, is the HOLLYWOOD sign, on Mt Lee, in the hills above Hollywood. Each letter stands approximately 50 feet high and 30 feet wide. The sign was first built in 1923, at a cost of $21,000, and was originally lit by 4,000 light bulbs. It was erected to advertise a subdivision called HOLLYWOODLAND; maintenance was discontinued in 1939, and in 1949 the 'land' letters were in extremely bad repair and were removed. In 1960, the Hollywood Chamber of Commerce started to restore the sign. In the mid 1960s it was declared a Historic/Cultural Monument of America. It was so rundown that during 1978, a large campaign headed by the LA Chamber of Commerce began to save the sign. Hugh Hefner was first to help by holding a fundraising party at his Playboy mansion, which raised $45,000 to sponsor the letter 'Y'. Soon, other stars joined in. Alice Cooper sponsored one 'O', in memory of Groucho Marx. Gene Autry sponsored an 'L'; Andy Williams the 'W' and Warner Brother's Records sponsored another 'O'. Each letter cost $27,700. Today, the sign stands 45 feet high and is 450 feet long, made from baked snow-white enamel weighing some 480,000 lbs. The brand new sign was formally unveiled to the public on 14 November 1978, which was the Hollywood Diamond Jubilee year. In early 1999, an anonymous bidder on the American Home Shopping TV Network paid $100,000 for sponsorship rights to the sign.

Metro-Goldwyn-Mayer stands for Metro (Marcus Loew's early film company), Goldwyn (Samuel Goldwyn), Mayer (Louis B Mayer). The MGM lion is called Leo and the studio motto is *Ars Gratia Artis* 'Art for Art's Sake'.

In 1960, two of Hollywood High's graduates were actresses Linda Evans and Stephanie Powers.

When asked for her thoughts on Hollywood, Grace Kelly said, 'I hated Hollywood. It's a town without pity. Only success counts. Anyone who doesn't have the key that opens the doors is treated like a leper. I know of no other place in the world where so many people suffer nervous breakdowns, where there are so many alcoholics.'

The world-famous Vine Street in Hollywood was so named because it once ran through Senator Cornelius Cole's vineyard.

United Artists was established in 1919. The artists who 'united' were Charlie Chaplin, D W Griffith, Mary Pickford and Douglas Fairbanks.

Capitol Records Tower at 1750 Vine Street in Hollywood was the world's first circular office building when Nat King Cole and Johnny Mercer built it in 1956.

In its heyday, there were four big movie studios in Hollywood: Columbia, Paramount, 20th Century-Fox and MGM. Today only Paramount is left in Hollywood; most of the other studios are in nearby Culver City.

With the AIDS scare hitting Hollywood, many stars sought legal advice. Top Beverly Hills attorney Marvin Mitchelson had a number of actresses who wanted to know if they should refuse to do love scenes or kissing scenes with a leading man known to be bisexual or gay. One actress wanted the right to have her leading men take a blood test written into her contract, but the studio said no way. The AIDS fear rocketed through Hollywood after Rock Hudson, knowing he had AIDS, kissed Linda Evans in *Dynasty*.

The Bel Air Hotel, which was built in the 1920s and is one of Los Angeles's most deluxe old-world hotels, was the home of Grace Kelly during her Hollywood career.

The movies: *How Green Was My Valley*, *Planet of the Apes* and *The Sand Pebbles* were all shot in the vicinity of the Malibu Creek State Park in Los Angeles.

Today, very few stars live in Hollywood; most live in Beverly Hills, Pacific Palisades, Malibu, Bel Air or Brentwood.

The four Warner brothers were Harry, Jack, Sam and Albert. The Warners started out on an investment of $1,000. In 1966, Jack, the last surviving brother, sold his share in Warner Bros for $32 million.

Burt Reynolds once said of Hollywood, 'In order to make it in this town and be really popular, you have to kind of go into the dumper every other year.'

In 1998, the Hollywood Memorial Park Cemetery, which is located right behind Paramount Studios, was renamed Hollywood Forever. The cemetery is where most of the famous names in Hollywood are buried. Today it's one of the most visited cemeteries in the world; they even give out free maps so you can find where your favourite star is buried.

MONEY, MONEY, MONEY

A white grand piano once owned by Elvis Presley was sold at an auction in London for a whopping £430,000.

The Union Jack mini-dress, originally worn by Geri 'Ginger Spice' Halliwell during a 1997 TV performance, sold at Sotheby's London auction house for $66,112.

In 2002, the US box-office saw its best year ever with a record 22 films breaking the $100 million dollar mark with the long-awaited instalments of *Men in Black II, The Lord of the Rings: the Two Towers, Star Wars: Episode II* and *Harry Potter.* Their magical powers bought a total of $9.37 billion dollars. Topping the 2002 blockbusters for that year was *Spider-Man* with a whopping $406 million in ticket sales.

In late December 2002, a black and white publicity photograph of the legendary star Marilyn Monroe sold at Christie's London auction house for £14,000 at an auction of movie memorabilia. It was taken in 1949, and signed to Hollywood agent Johnny Hyde inscribed, 'To John, I love you, my dearest, Marilyn.' The buyer was a former employer of the agent.

Kelsey Grammar inked a deal back in 2001 for his starring role in *Frasier,* which now makes him the best-paid TV actor ever. His take-home pay packet is $2.7 million an episode.

During World War II, the most popular pin-up girl was movie star Betty Grable, whose nickname was 'Legs'. She had her legs insured with Lloyds of London for $250,000.

One of the most extensive collections of movie-star autographs in the world can be seen at the Max Factor Beauty Museum in Hollywood. The Scroll of Fame has been signed by the hundreds of stars that once endorsed Max Factor products; it's been valued as priceless.

The courtyard in front of Mann's Chinese Theater on Hollywood Blvd, which immortalises many stars' hand and footprints in cement, was built in the 1920s at a cost of $1 million. It seats 2,200 people. The first movie to be shown there was Cecil B De Mille's *King of Kings*, on 18 May 1927. On the opening gala night, they charged $2.00 per seat, a high price in those days.

Paramount Studios paid Ringling Brother's Circus, $250,000 for the use of their name in the 1952 movie, *The Greatest Show On Earth*. Some of their performers and equipment appear in the movie.

The movie *Rocky* was written by Sylvester Stallone in just four days; it was shot on a budget of $975,000 in just under four weeks. In 1976, it won both Best Picture and Best Director Oscars.

In 1982, the movie *E.T.* became the highest-grossing movie to date, taking in around $187 million.

Novelist and screenwriter Michael Blake, who wrote the movie *Dances with Wolves*, often slept in his car while writing the script because he was so broke. In 1990, the movie won Best Picture and Best Actor for Kevin Costner.

The jewellery designer to the stars, Harry Winston of Beverly Hills, lent more than $12 million worth of jewellery to presenters and nominees to wear at the 1994 Academy Awards TV presentation.

In 1994, the American magazine *Entertainment Weekly* said that Tom Hanks was the only actor worthy of $20 million.

The Empire Strikes Back (1980) cost $30 million, which was a staggering amount for the time, but within 13 weeks of its release it had completely covered its production costs. The movie went on to gross around $300 million worldwide, not to mention the spin-off dollars from the merchandising.

In 1999, Michael Jackson paid $1.5 million for David O Selznick's Oscar, which he won for Best Picture *Gone with The Wind*. This was three years before movie producer/director Steven Spielberg shelled out $550,000 for Clark Gable's Best Actor Oscar for the same movie. He then donated it back to the Academy.

When TV's *Sex and the City* episode aired in the US featuring Carrie's 'good' engagement ring (not the flashy one her fiancé wanted to give her), Beverly Hills jeweller Harry Winston sold over 30 of the 3-carat emerald cut rings at $50,000–$78,000 each.

For the 1998 Academy Awards TV presentation, Gwyneth Paltrow's hair and makeup came to $10,000, not to mention the cost of her jewellery, shoes and gown. But that night, she did take home the Best Actress Oscar for the movie *Shakespeare in Love*.

The producers of the 1976 movie *Rocky* offered its creator Sylvester Stallone an extra $150,000 if he would stand down and let Ryan O'Neal play Rocky. He said no way, because he'd only sold the story rights on the condition that he would play Rocky and the rest is history as they say.

The train wreck in the 1927 movie *The General* cost around $42,000, making it the most expensive single shot in the silent-movie era.

In December 2002, a US judge in LA awarded Pamela Anderson and her ex-husband Tommy Lee $1.5 million in damages after what has now become a notorious video of them having sex on their honeymoon. The tape was only ever sold over the Internet. The video recording of the couple having sex first appeared on a website in 1997, and became the biggest-selling porn of all time. They both insisted that a construction worker working on their Malibu home stole the videotape in 1995. The company that was selling the video has conveniently gone bust. Both Pam and Tommy shared in the $1.5 million payout ending a five-year battle.

When American TV celebrity Caroline Rheas took over from Rosie O'Donnell to host her hit TV show, the first thing she went out and bought was dishes! She said, 'Reason being who knew if I'd ever earn big later on again down the line. And who knew if I'd have a husband that made a major salary. So I had to strike while I had it. I don't want to be old and gray with an old and gray husband and no cups or saucers. So I bought the whole lot of china with my first paycheck.'

An American biscuit company put a picture of the late Fred Astaire on the tin of its new range of biscuits. The star's widow teamed up with his surviving dance partner, Ginger Rogers, and jointly sued the biscuit company for millions for using Fred's image. In the end, the company settled out of court and removed all the picture tins from the market.

Marilyn Monroe licensed her image while she was alive, which would continue after her death. Today the millions made in royalties since her death in August 1962 are shared between New York's Lee Strasberg Drama School where she learned to act, and the Anna Freud Centre in London.

Julia Roberts was paid $20 million for the title role in the movie *Erin Brockovich*, which won her her first Academy Award for Best Actress (2001). Julia also holds the record for making the most movies to gross over $100 million at the box-office.

It's rumoured that Arnold Schwarzenegger was paid $30 million for his role in the 2003 movie, *Terminator 3*.

It's said that Britney Spears insists on having a telephone installed in her dressing rooms with only an outgoing line on it. If the singer receives any calls, the promoter is fined $5,000.

In 1994, at an auction at Sothebys in London, Bono paid $56,000 for the Hitler-like suit worn by Charlie Chaplin in the 1940s movie *The Great Dictator*.

The necklace worn by Nicole Kidman in the movie *Moulin Rouge* was made of platinum and real diamonds. It was the most expensive piece of jewellery ever made for a movie. The Stefano Canturi-designed necklace contained 1,309 diamonds, weighing a total of 134 carats; it's worth an estimated $1 million.

In November 2002, Matt Damon went to his college reunion and bought each of his 36 classmates a Rolex watch.

In 1994, Sophia Loren signed a multi-million-dollar deal to allow her name to be used to promote a line of furs. Both the animal-rights activists and former French movie star Brigitte Bardot lambasted her, for her endorsement. Brigitte attacked Sophia in a public letter. It stated, 'Even if your financial situation motivates such a gesture, it is degrading, repugnant, lamentable and unworthy to accept bloody money derived from animal hides.'

Russell Crowe shelled out around $30,000 to have the 2002 Aussie Bathurst 1,000 V8 Supercar race beamed live to his hotel suite in Mexico, where he was filming *The Far Side of the World*.

In August 2002, an auction in England of Marilyn Monroe memorabilia that marked the 40th anniversary of her death raised over £16,000. Among the items were a silk Gucci dress worn by Marilyn, which went under the hammer for £3,500, and a ring with the letter 'M' studded in diamante stones for £5,000.

In 1979, Sid Luft, the third husband of Judy Garland, sold a pair of her used false eyelashes for $125.

The vintage Christian Dior gown worn by Jennifer Aniston at the 2002 TV Emmy Awards was later auctioned on the net for $51,000.

Donna Douglas, who played Elly May Clampett in the hit 1960s/70s TV series *The Beverly Hillbillies*, was only paid $500 per show in the first series.

It's rumoured that fashion designer Donatella Versace moisturises her toes with $300 Crème De La Mer and never leaves home wearing less than $100,000 worth of jewellery.

In October 2002, Nicolas Cage sold his collection of comic books for a cool $1.6 million. His 1938 copy of Action Comics #1, the first to feature Superman, sold for $86,250. Detective #38, which debuted Batman's sidekick Robin in 1940, sold for close to $121,000. All-Star Comics #3, which introduced us to the Justice Society—the Green Lantern, Hawkman and the Flash—sold for $45,000.

Some of the world's most glamorous women contributed autographed bras for an auction to benefit the 2002 English Breast Cancer Society. It was pop singer Kylie Minogue's skimpy little bra, which got the top bid of the night at £2,400. The event raised about £12,000 for the cause.

In October 2002, Ben Affleck surprised his girlfriend Jennifer Lopez with a $450,000 custom-built Mercedes Sedan car. Among the added extras were bullet-proof tyres and a computerised tracking system.

The volleyball that kept Tom Hanks's character company in the 2000 movie *Castaway*, sold for $18,000 in an online auction of Hollywood movie props in September 2001.

Forty years after he left Dartford Grammar School with seven O-levels and two A-levels, rock icon Sir Mick Jagger donated £100,000 to the academic institution, which helps youngsters get a start in the music world. Sir Mick has named the music programme the 'Red Rooster Project', after the Rolling Stones' 1964 hit *Little Red Rooster.* While he was a pupil there in the late 1950s, Sir Mick organised a rebellion over the school dinners, leading to staff being fired and new kitchens being built.

Pamela Anderson Lee (at the time she was still married to Tommy), was slapped with a $5 million lawsuit by the producers of the movie *Hello, She Lied*. Pamela apparently committed to the movie, and then backed out a matter of days before the principal photography was to start.

In 1982, Scott Thorson said, 'We lived together as man and wife'; that's why he sued Liberace for $113 million. He said, 'He promised me half of everything he owns, he even wanted to adopt me as his son. Then, without warning he cut me off. That's why I'm suing him.' In 1987, Scott settled for $95,000.

Faye Dunaway was cast as Norma Desmond, the faded star in Sir Andrew Lloyd Webber's stage production of *Sunset Boulevard*. 'She could not satisfactorily sing the part,' said Sir Andrew, who then abruptly closed down the LA production before its opening run. In August 1994, Fay retaliated by suing for $6 million for breach of contract, defamation and fraud. The case was settled out of court in January 1995; it's rumoured that the settlement to Fay was for $1.5 million. The role went to Glenn Close.

Sharon Stone sued Beverly Hills jewellery store Harry Winston for $12 million after the store demanded that she return the $400,000 necklace they say they loaned her. Sharon claims it was given to her outright in exchange for publicity.

Always the perfectionist, Barbra Streisand refused to give in on her movie *The Mirror Has Two Faces* until absolutely everything was just the way the diva wanted it. Several people fell to the wayside, including actor Dudley Moore, who was released from his contract. In 1996, when the movie shot its last few frames, about a dozen crew members had either walked out or been fired, and the budget had rocketed to around $46 million.

Joan Collins's first husband, actor Maxwell Reed, wanted to accept an offer of £10,000 if she'd sleep with a certain wealthy Arab. Joan said a firm no and the offer was off; not long after, so was the marriage.

In the 1990s, Arnold Schwarzenegger bought himself a $57,000 Hummer (Humvee), the wide all-terrain vehicle that taxied soldiers about during the Gulf War. It's rumoured that he once owned seven of them.

Raquel Welch won a breach-of-contract/defamation suit against MGM, which fired her during the shoot of their 1982 movie *Cannery Row*. Eventually, the studio paid her a $10 million settlement.

The first thing Matt Damon and Ben Affleck did when they got paid for their movie *Good Will Hunting* was to lease a huge house in Beverly Hills and invite two of their friends to move in rentfree.

In early October 2002, Eminem blew $25,000 on a shopping spree in a California mall, on clothes and records for him and his mates.

Matt Damon once lost $10,000 in a poker game in Las Vegas.

Dan Aykroyd co-scripted the 1980 movie *The Blues Brothers*. At the time it was classed as Hollywood's first truly big-budget comedy, costing $30 million to make.

The large billboard poster for *Casablanca* is still the most dollar-worth and collectable best-selling movie poster of all time.

In April 1990, James Bond star Timothy Dalton accepted undisclosed libel damages at London's High Court for a magazine article which suggested he was to be replaced to save any future 007 movies from financial disaster. The magazine had to undertake not to repeat the article, which had appeared on 15 August 1989.

In 2001, London's *Sunday Times* newspaper estimated Mick Jagger's fortune to stand at around $216 million.

In 1992, Mariah Carey's stepdad sued her for failing to share the profits from her 1990 hit album. In 2001, she signed a multi-album deal with Virgin Records, which was estimated to be around $80 million.

According to the *New York Post*, in September 2002, three minutes with Jon Bon Jovi costs a cool $64,000. That's how much the rocker's performance of *You Give Love a Bad Name* at the 2002 NFL kick-off live event in Times Square cost the show's producer. A source close to the company said the season-opening extravaganza, which featured performances by Enrique Inglesias and Eve, cost Clear Channel $4 million altogether, or $19,000 per minute.

Charlie Sheen has his very own $1.5 million custom-designed bus with a full-size master bedroom, which he uses on location when he is working.

Dustin Hoffman won a $3 million verdict in 1999 against an LA magazine for running a computer-altered picture of him in an evening dress and high heels. It was thrown out on appeal.

In 1957, Elvis Presley purchased Graceland, which became his home for the last 20 years of his life. He paid $100,000 for the building, which started out its life as a church. Elvis painted the two-storey mansion blue and gold, so it would glow in the dark.

Robert Redford has invested the millions he's made from the movies by buying hundreds of acres in the Utah Mountains. He's ecologically minded and has built a beautiful cedar house, equipped with the latest solar-energy devices, along with his own personal ski-slopes.

A commercial during the final episode of *Friends* in the US cost an all-time high, $3 million for a 30-second commercial.

The island in the 1960s hit TV series *Gilligan's Island* was an artificial island in the middle of an artificial lake at the CBS studios in LA, which cost $75,000. The pilot episode was shot on the Hawaiian island of Kauai, where the movie *South Pacific* was filmed.

Jack Nicholson's over-the-top performance as The Joker in Tim Burton's *Batman* reportedly earned him $50 million.

On the day of Judy Garland's death, 23 June 1969, a tornado touched down in Kansas. The next year, on 3 May, MGM auctioned off Judy Garland's size 4½ ruby slippers from *The Wizard of Oz*. They went for $15,000 (US).

Kiefer Sutherland was 17 when he landed a very lucrative jeans advertisement in Canada; it paid $3,500. With the money, he bought a car and drove to California. He slept in the car to save money before landing a role in the TV series *Amazing Stories*, which was directed by Steven Spielberg. The episode was called *The Mission*.

THREE OF THE BIGGEST MOVIE FLOPS TO START OFF THE MILLENIUM WERE:

Battlefield Earth (2000) starred: John Travolta. Cost: US $73 million. Made: US $21.5 million.

Town and Country (2001) starred: Warren Beatty, Goldie Hawn. Cost: US $90 million. Made: US $6.7 million.

3000 Miles to Graceland (2001) starred: Kevin Costner, Kurt Russell. Cost: US $62 million. Made: US $15.7 million.

The Majestic (2002) starred: Jim Carrey. Cost: US $80 million. Made: US $27.7 million.

Pluto Nash (2002) starred: Eddie Murphy. Cost US $100 million. Made: US $2.2 million at the box-office on its first weekend in North American theatres.

When both the *Matrix* movies finished shooting, the star Keanu Reeves, treated all the cast and crew to drinks. The bill came to nearly $81,000.

After the 2002 movie *Men in Black 2*, and the appearance of Frank the Pug Dog, sales of the breed skyrocketed in the US and Europe. The designer dinner suit Frank wore to the US movie premieres was modelled after the ones Will Smith and Tommy Lee-Jones wore in the movie, and was made by Mr O, the same man who designed the stars' black suits. Frank's suit cost $2,000.

In July 2002, a fan paid $14,450 for an 18-carat gold watch that Elizabeth Taylor gifted Richard Burton. Taylor gave him the Patek Phillippe watch when they were newly romancing on the set of *Cleopatra* in 1963. The watch has an inscription on the back 'W'i'n' Dy Garu Di'—I love you in Welsh, Richard's native tongue.

When Pope John Paul I died after only 34 days as Pontiff in 1978, Clint Eastwood bought his Mercedes-Benz car.

Tobey Maguire received $4 million for starring in the 2002 movie *Spider-Man.* Not at all a bad fee for a then relatively unknown leading man.

In the 1930s, Marlene Dietrich was signed by Paramount at the astronomical depression-era price of $125,000 per picture.

In 1988, Julia Roberts was paid $50,000 for appearing in one of the lead roles in the movie *Mystic Pizza*. In 1992, she'd won the title of the highest-paid actress in the history of Hollywood, reportedly commanding $12 million a movie.

In 1998, a shirt Leonardo DiCaprio wore in the 1997 movie *Titanic* sold for $10,000 at a Hollywood memorabilia auction. At the same auction, a cane used by Charlie Chaplin went for $32,000.

When Celine Dion's shoe collection reached 1,000 pairs, her husband had a 300-square-foot shoe wardrobe built, which cost $200,000.

In 1997, fans of the flamboyant Sir Elton John snapped up some 4,000 articles of his used clothing during a fundraiser dubbed 'Elton's Closet'. The event raised $500,000 for his AIDS foundation.

Band of Brothers, a 10-part TV miniseries made in 2002, and directed by Steven Spielberg and Tom Hanks, was the most expensive ever made for TV. The $120 million production was drawn from historian Stephen E Ambrose's true-life novel, *Band of Brothers*, which is based on letters and journals of an elite World War II US Army airborne unit known as Easy Company.

In October 1998, movie star husband and wife team Natasha Richardson and Liam Neeson won big bucks in libel damages and a public apology after a newspaper claimed their four-year marriage had collapsed. At their request, the payout was donated to the fund for victims of the Omagh bombing in Northern Ireland, which killed 29 people.

MGM offered W C Fields $75,000 to star in the *Wizard of Oz* as the wizard. He demanded $100,000; the studio said no way and gave the role to one of their contract players, Frank Morgan.

One specially-created cell from the hit TV series *The Simpsons* brought $24,000 at a Christie's auction of Simpsons material in 1991.

In January 1982, Coca-Cola announced an agreement with Columbia Pictures for $750 million. It wasn't long before objects bearing the Coke logo started appearing in their movies, like playing out roles right in front of coke machines or dialogue such as 'Would you like a Diet Coke?' popping up in their scripts.

The London Hospital Medical College rejected a $500,000 offer from Michael Jackson to buy the remains of John Merrick, the Elephant Man. When the offer was turned down, it's rumoured that Michael doubled the first offer. That was also turned down, with a strong message from the hospital saying they are not for sale.

Lucille Ball and her then husband Desi Arnaz became immensely wealthy after Desi took the gamble of their lives and took a weekly $1,000 cut in salary if CBS would give up its 50 per cent stake in the sitcom. This made Lucy and Desi sole owners of their hit TV sitcom *I Love Lucy.*

In late 2000, Steven Spielberg was rumoured to have obtained the movie rights to *The Bible* for $1.32 million.

It's rumoured that Sean Connery's toupee cost $52,000 for his role as James Bond in the 1983 movie *Never Say Never Again*.

Author J R R Tolkien sold the movie rights to *The Lord of the Rings* back in 1968 for £10,000. The book was first published in 1954, and sold more than 100 million copies; to date it's been translated into over 40 languages.

The huge appeal of Elvis shows no sign of flagging, topping the 2002 *Forbes* 'Top-Earning Dead Celebrity' list for the second year running. Elvis raked in a whopping $37 million in the last year, including $4 million from the 2002 remix of his 1968 hit, *A Little Less Conversation.*

When Geri Halliwell left the *Spice Girls* she auctioned off her performance wardrobe. It earned her $246,000, which she donated to charity.

Jim Carrey's $20 million pay cheque for his 1996 movie *The Cable Guy* was the highest salary ever paid to a comedian up to that time.

In June 1995, Hugh Grant was arrested on Hawthorne Avenue in Hollywood for performing a 'lewd act' with 'other woman' Divine Brown, aka Estella Thompson. They were in Hugh's 1995 BMW 325i; LA vice-squad officers had seen Hugh picking up Divine about 1.30 a.m. on Sunset Blvd then driving to a residential area. After the officers observed the goings on between the two in the BMW, they hauled them in. Hugh was sentenced to two years' probation, fined $1,180, which included court costs, and ordered to complete an AIDS education programme. Divine was sentenced to six months in jail, fined $1,350 and ordered to do five days of community service.

In September 1994, Johnny Depp was charged with trashing a $1,200 a night hotel room in New York. He ended up paying out $9,767.12 in damages.

When Drew Carey appeared as a contestant on the TV show, *Who Wants to Be a Millionaire*, he raised $500,000 for the Ohio Library Foundation.

Three days after his wedding to Danielle Spencer on his 39th birthday, Russell Crowe bought Sydney's most expensive apartment. The penthouse apartment cost a cool $15 million Australian dollars, $5 million Australian more than Sydney's previously most expensive apartment, which sold in 2002. It has views of Sydney harbour and floor-to-ceiling windows, and is in the exclusive Woolloomooloo Finger Wharf complex in Sydney.

British Airways misplaced four of Victoria Beckham's matching Louis Vuitton bags; the airline awarded her £100,000 for the loss.

May of 2003 saw 30-year-old Ben Affleck sign a lucrative million-dollar contract as the new face of L'Oreal, five years after his movie star fiancée Jennifer Lopez was the international spokesperson for the company's cosmetics. Ben will promote men's grooming products for the firm. 'Ben embodies a new generation of men who show their strength in their personality but are not afraid to care for their appearance', said a L'Oreal spokesperson.

In June 2001, Sir Elton John netted himself US$2.75 million dollars from a Christies auction for 20 of his luxury classic cars.

In 1998, Nicole Kidman won $580,000 in libel damages from the British Newspaper *Express On Sunday.* They published a story which claimed both she and her then husband Tom Cruise might be closet gays in a sham marriage.

In October 1998, Calista Flockhart, who played lawyer Ally McBeal on the hit TV series, was sued by a law firm for 5 per cent of her total earnings. The law firm claimed that they negotiated the contracts which landed her the role with the Fox TV studio.

In 1988, Penelope Cruz donated her entire salary from her movie *The Hi-Lo Country* to Mother Teresa's children's sanctuary in Calcutta.

Ben Affleck and Matt Damon became friends at elementary school; by the time they got to high school they were both talking about a career in the movies. They wrote the script for *Good Will Hunting* out of total frustration when no acting jobs were coming their way. They eventually sold the script to Miramax for $800,000 and the rest is Hollywood history.

Jayne Mansfield, the busty 1950s and 1960s bombshell Hollywood movie star, once sold bottles of her used bath water for $10.

In mid 2002, it was confirmed that Jennifer Lopez was the highest-paid Latin actress in movie history. At that time she was earning US$12 million per movie.

The Italian screen goddess Sophia Loren spent a month in prison back in 1982 for income tax irregularities.

Americans went wild over the movies in 1933; a total of 80 million people went to the movies each week, paying 25 cents for adults, and 10 cents for children. For this, you got a double feature and the chance to win a door prize.

It's been reported that Dolly Parton has her famous trademark bust insured for $600,000.

For his first screen role in the 1969 movie *The Wedding Party* Robert De Niro received a mere $50.

When Ronald Reagan was earning $200,000 a year as President of the US, his ex-wife, actress Jane Wyman, raked in $1.6 million for her role in TV's 1980s *Falcon Crest*.

In May 1986, Michael Jackson signed a $15 million deal with Pepsi. The *Guinness Book of World Records* declared it was the biggest commercial sponsorship deal ever.

Elvis's first guitar cost just $12.95. His mum bought it for him; he really wanted a bike but they couldn't afford one.

The most expensive TV production up to 1980 was the British TV drama serial *Brideshead Revisited,* an 11-part Granada adaptation of Evelyn Waugh's novel. The cost of £3 million in 1980 rose to £5 million in 1981. The serialisation first aired in the UK on 12 October 1981; it was later sold to 14 countries worldwide.

In November 1994, the auction house of Christies in London set a new world record for any Ian Fleming book when a bidder paid $14,000 for a first edition of the James Bond yarn *The Spy Who Loved Me*.

Titanic's original budget was $170 million; the movie's final cost was $307 million. The 1997 movie cost more to create than the original ship. That works out to around $1.5 million per minute on screen. The running time of *Titanic*, the movie, was three hours, 14 minutes, while the sinking time of *Titanic*, the real ship, was 2 hours, 40 minutes. The length of time it took to build the real *Titanic* was 26 months. The length of time it took to film *Titanic* was nine months. In January 2000, one of Leonardo DiCaprio's costumes went up for sale in a US catalogue for $14,800.

Kim Basinger was offered $5 million to star in the sequel to *9½ Weeks*; she said thanks, but no thanks. In 1989, she bought a town in Georgia called Braselton for $20 million, with plans to develop it into a tourist attraction. Not long after, she was declared bankrupt, leaving residents very angry and wondering what their future held for them. In 1993, she was asked to pay almost $9 million to the makers of the movie *Boxing Helena*, because after giving a verbal contact to appear in it she dropped out.

Back in 1940, a then astronomical salary of $125,000 was paid to Cary Grant for his starring role in *The Philadelphia Story*; he donated his entire fee to the British War Relief Fund.

For playing Anna in the 1999 movie *Anna and the King*, Jodie Foster received $15 million.

Sigourney Weaver's $18 million pay cheque for the upcoming *Alien 5* will set a brand new record for women's salaries in the movie business.

At the end of filming the 1982 epic movie *Gandhi,* actor Martin Sheen donated his entire pay packet to charity.

In June 1991, TV's favourite barrister, Horace Rumpole, toasted a £300,000 sponsorship deal. This made him the first network television character to be sponsored in the UK.

In 1967, actor Donald Sutherland was finding things tough getting acting jobs, and his cash was at rock bottom. In desperation, he phoned his old mate Christopher Plummer and told him he wanted to go to America to look for roles to play, but unfortunately didn't have enough money. The following day, Christopher's lawyer rang Donald and told him Christopher had put $1,500 into his account. Later that year, Donald's career picked up and so did his bank account; he repaid every cent to Christopher.

Tim Allen received US $5 million, for doing the voice of Buzz Lightyear in *Toy Story 2*.

A wealthy Australian socialite once returned a very expensive designer gown to a Sydney boutique and demanded her money back. She said she had seen Dame Edna Everage wearing an identical dress on her TV show.

$13 million is rumoured to be the fee Sharon Stone was offered for the sequel to *Basic Instinct*.

In August 1992, the tiny island nation of St Vincent released a set of nine Elvis Presley postage stamps, beating the United States Postal Service by nearly a year. Each of the St Vincent stamps were four times the size of an American postal stamp and had a face value of $1.

In October 1991, a pair of rubber ears worn by Mr Spock in the cult TV series *Star Trek* was sold at a London charity auction for £700, to an anonymous bidder. Leonard Nimoy, who played Spock, donated them; the auction was to raise money for the city's boys' clubs.

When Walt Disney released the movie *101 Dalmatians*, the price of Dalmatian puppies in America increased by 400 per cent.

An autographed bra worn by Madonna in her movie *Truth or Dare* sold for $11,000 at a Rotary Club fundraiser in September 1991.

In the 1992 $70 million-dollar movie about the life and times of Charlie Chaplin, Geraldine Chaplin, who was his real-life eldest daughter, played Charlie's mother Hannah.

US army sergeant Harold Russell (who lost both his hands in a D-day accident), went on to win an Academy Award as Best Supporting Actor in the 1946 movie *The Best Years of Our Lives*. In 1992, Harold, then 78, was the first Oscar winner to put his gold statuette up for auction—it sold for $55,000. He sold it to raise cash because his wife Betty needed an eye operation.

Columbo, the TV detective played by Peter Falk, walked onto the set on 15 September 1970, wearing a rumpled raincoat. Twenty years later he was still wearing the very same rumpled trademark raincoat in a TV special called *Death Hits the Jackpot* to mark Columbo's 20 years on the TV beat. He bought the raincoat in 1967 for $30 from a store in New York.

The only James Bond movie to ever lose money at the box office was the 1967 movie *Casino Royale* in which David Niven played 007.

In 1963, Elizabeth Taylor starred in a one-hour TV special for CBS, called *Elizabeth Taylor in London*. She was paid $500,000 for her work, which at the time made her the highest-paid television entertainer for a single special.

In 1990, *New Kids On the Block* grossed $74.1 million from concerts during that year; Billy Joel ran second at $43 million.

Towards the end of Ronald Reagan's last term in the White House, the producers of *Dynasty* (at the time America's number-one soap) approached him with a $1 million offer to join the show in the role of one of Alexis's (Joan Collins) ex-husbands.

In New York in August 1998, James Parker, 48, a golf caddie, filed a $155 million lawsuit against Michael Douglas. He alleged that in October 1997, Michael hit a golf ball that hit him in the groin. James said that he required surgery to remove a testicle. In a statement, Michael called the claims 'false and slanderous'.

In July 1995, LaToya Jackson filed for bankruptcy, claiming she could pay only half her debts of nearly $1.5 million.

On 14 December 1995, the bowler hat and cane that helped make Charlie Chaplin the star of many a silent comedy movie fetched £44,750 at a British auction of movie memorabilia at Christies. Chaplin's belongings, which were offered by a descendant of his half-brother Wheeler Dryden, were bought by a private Swiss museum. The Arab robes worn by Peter O'Toole in the movie *Lawrence of Arabia* went for £12,375, which was well above the estimate.

The first Oscar ever to be auctioned in Europe, which was awarded to Ethel Barrymore in 1944 for her performance in *None But the Lonely Heart* failed to sell and was withdrawn. The gold-plated Oscar statuette, billed as the sale centrepiece of the auction, only drew bids of £8,000, which was half the estimated price.

The budget for the original 1931 *Frankenstein* movie was $262,000. The budget for the 1994 remake was $40 million.

In 1990, Whitney Houston underwrote the cost of two lion cubs at the Bronx Zoo for the first year of their lives.

In February 1996, Joan Collins, who was 62 at the time, sued the New York publishing giant Random House for the return of a $1.8 million advance paid to her for manuscripts it claims were unfinished and unpublished. Joan won the case.

In April 1996, Tina Turner gave a hush-hush performance for the family of the Sultan of Brunei. She sang for 300 at the birthday party of the niece of Sultan Hassanal Bilkiah, the world's richest person. So how much did she get paid? Nobody is quite sure.

Hollywood loves to give out awards for just about anything. In 1999 alone, the entertainment industry bestowed a whopping 3,182 trophies on itself at 332 separate ceremonies. That means that up to nine awards were handed out every single day of the year. Only in Hollywood!

On 12 December 1995, Lady Penelope, star of the British TV puppet series *Thunderbirds* was parted from her pink Rolls Royce, and Parker, her once devoted chauffeur and butler. A British collector at an auction in London bought the upper-crust Lady puppet for £13,000. Parker went for £19,500 and Lady Penelope's 2.74 metre-long pink Rolls Royce went for £23,000.

In 1982 when Michael J Fox landed the role in TV's *Family Ties* it's rumoured he was down to his last few dollars.

In August 1998, Mimi Rogers filed a $10 million libel suit in the LA Federal Court against the American TV Home Shopping Network. Mimi claimed the cable station planted an article in the tabloid *National Enquirer*, which said that she wrecked the network's waiting room after they cancelled her appearance. She was there to front two promotional commercials for her exercise machine.

A number of dead artists and celebrities have stayed in demand. The following list was compiled by *Forbes* magazine and shows earnings for the period from June 2001 through to June 2002:

Elvis Presley $37 million

Charles Shulz $28 million

John Lennon $20 million

Dale Earnhardt (NASCAR driver) $20 million

Theodore Geisel (Dr Seuss books) $19 million

George Harrison $17 million

JRR Tolkien $12 million

Bob Marley $10 million

Jimi Hendrix $8 million

Tupac Shakur $7 million

Marilyn Monroe $7 million

Jerry Garcia $5 million

Jane Seymour, who was born Joyce Penelope Wilma Frankenberg, posed for Playboy's centrefold—with her clothes on! She first posed in 1973 and then again in 1986. It's rumoured that when she moved to Hollywood in 1976, all she had with her was 'one suitcase, 280 English pounds and a return ticket'.

The movie *She Done Him Wrong,* starring Mae West, was made for $260,000 and grossed $3 million. It was the biggest box-office attraction in 1933.

In 1989, when Sammy Davis Jr was rushed into hospital for weeks of painful radiotherapy for throat cancer and had to cancel a very profitable tour, Frank Sinatra paid all the hospital bills for his lifelong friend. When Sammy died on 16 May 1990, he also paid for his funeral. It's also said that he gave Sammy's widow, who had financial difficulties at the time of Sammy's death, a cheque for $50,000.

In 1964, Richard Burton was offered more than £75,000 to become the new James Bond. 'He's just the rugged, debonair type of actor ideal for the hard-drinking, fast-living James Bond role', said movie producer Kevin McClory.

When Frank Sinatra's will was read after his death in 1998, it was found that Frank left a clause that would disinherit any beneficiary who challenged it. The bulk of his will's bequest went to his wife Barbara.

In 1988, talk-show queen Oprah Winfrey purchased a television production complex for an undisclosed amount. This purchase made Oprah the first black person and the third woman in American history, behind Mary Pickford and Lucille Ball, to own such a studio.

The first James Bond film, *Dr. No* (1962), earned Sean Connery only £15,000. Nine years later, he was offered £1 million for *Diamonds Are Forever.*

A 14-carat gold pendant given to Marlene Dietrich by one of her lovers, French actor Jean Gabin, was rumoured to be bought in November 1997 by American TV star Ellen DeGeneres and her partner, actress Anne Heche. The pendant sold for $4.64 million at Sothebys of Beverly Hills. It had the word 'Toujours' (French for always) inscribed on one face and 'Jamais' (never) on the other.

The 'diamond' hair ornament worn by Audrey Hepburn in *Breakfast at Tiffanys* sold in 1996 for $26,605.

Kate Winslet's *Titanic* chiffon evening gown with satin sash, antique lace and faux pearl bodice sold for $17,165.

In 1995 Sylvester Stallone's Everlast boxing shorts from the first *Rocky* movie, sold for $16,305.

The military outfit Tom Hanks wore in *Forrest Gump* (his pants, tie and belt) sold in 1995 for $25,747.

Elvis Presley's income dropped from $400,000 a month to $78 a month after he was drafted into the US Army on 19 December 1957.

By the year 2000, Celine Dion had sold 110 million CDs worldwide. In her homeland of Canada, she'd sold 9 million more CDs than any other Canadian performer.

Nine times out of 10 Ricky Martin wears Armani at public appearances, this is because Giorgio Armani paid him $50,000 in modelling fees when he was starting out on his musical career.

In *Steel Magnolias*, the Olympia Dukakis character conducts interviews in a high-school football locker room while young men walk around her naked. The guys who wore jockstraps received $100 a day; the ones who didn't got $150 per day.

Paula Jones, the woman who accused President Bill Clinton of exposing himself to her, revealed all in *Penthouse* magazine for a rumoured $180,000.

Shirley Temple was a millionairess before she had her 10th birthday.

In May 2000, the Godfather of Soul, James Brown, offered a $40,000 reward to catch the arsonist who set fire to his offices.

When the American TV series *Happy Days* went on air in the 1970s, its star Henry Winkler, who played The Fonz, was paid about $750 per episode. The series was an overnight success, and the next season he signed a contract which gave him an estimated $80,000 per episode plus a cut of the profits.

It's rumoured that actor Oliver Reed wanted his mates to have a fantastic wake when he died. He once said 'That's why I've left £10,000 out of my estate to be spent in my local pub.'

When Madonna was asked what Warren Beatty had that other men didn't, she said, 'About a billion dollars.'

Jack Nicholson's first movie, *Cry Baby Killer* (1958), was completed in 10 days; it came in on budget at just $7,000 and ran for 59 minutes.

Sean Connery did a cameo appearance of just 45 seconds as Richard the Lionheart in *Robin Hood: Prince of Thieves;* his fee was $500,000.

The day after Elvis Presley died, pirated copies of his post-mortem were rumoured to have been selling for $5,000 a copy.

The first scene ever shot for *Gone with the Wind* was the burning of Atlanta. The movie started shooting on 10 December 1938, and was completed a year and a day later. Author Margaret Mitchell originally wanted to call her book (which she took 10 years to write) *Tomorrow Is Another Day.* Producer David O Selznick paid $50,000 for the movie rights, which at the time was a record. Fourteen screenwriters were employed on the screenplay, and seven Technicolour cameras were used to get the effects for the three-hour-40-minute movie.

In December 1995, at Christie's auction, London, the jumpsuit worn by Roger Moore in the 1979 James Bond movie *Moonraker* fetched £6,750. An anonymous buyer splashed out £15,750 on the military uniform Charlie Chaplin had worn in his 1940 movie *The Great Dictator.*

On 19 August 1998, Priscilla Presley, 53, won a $75,000 defamation action against Lavern Currie Grant, a former army buddy of Elvis Presley, who said he had an affair with her before she married the King. His false statements were used as the source for Suzanne Finstad's book, *Child Bride: The Untold Story of Priscilla Beaulieu Presley.*

On 24 October 1989, TV preacher Jim Baker was given a 45-year jail sentence and fined $500,000 for swindling his followers out of millions.

When Frank Sinatra's pet dog was killed by a hit-and-run driver, he offered $5,000 to anyone who could identify the driver.

Marlon Brando received $4 million for just three days work in the 1978 movie *Superman*, which makes him the highest-paid actor in the history of Hollywood for less than 10 minutes onscreen work.

Al Pacino was paid $35,000 for *Godfather 1.* But two years later, he was paid $600,000 for the sequel plus a percentage of the gross profit.

Singer/actress Bette Midler once got paid in solid gold bars for a concert tour; half a million dollar's worth.

The cost in Hollywood of insuring a film against production delays is 1–3 per cent of the budget. The amount paid to insurance companies for such coverages in 1988 was $300 million. The amount paid by insurance companies to irrigate the farm used in *Field of Dreams* during the 1988 drought was $200,000, and to replace Sean Young who broke her collarbone in a riding accident with Kim Basinger in the first *Batman* movie was $500,000.

Tarzan of the Apes was the first Hollywood movie to gross over 1 million dollars. It starred the first Tarzan, Elmo Lincoln.

When Dustin Hoffman arrived in New York in the 1950s to study at the Lee Strasberg Actors Studio, he was so broke he slept on Gene Hackman's kitchen floor. He took work waiting on tables, and on his days off he typed up entries for the *New York Yellow Pages* to get money for his acting classes.

As a struggling actress, Lindsay Wagner used to babysit Glen Campbell's children to make extra money. Later she struck gold with the TV series *The Bionic Woman*.

The double bed used by Marilyn Monroe and Joe DiMaggio during their brief marriage fetched $25,000 at an auction in New Jersey in 1989.

In 1925, Hollywood made its most expensive silent movie, Fred Niblo's *Ben Hur*, which ended up costing $3.9 million, a fortune in those days.

When Sylvester Stallone sold the screenplay for *Rocky*, he was working as a lion's cage cleaner with only $160 in his bank account.

Hollywood costume designer Edith Head designed the most expensive movie costume, in mink and sequins, for Ginger Rogers in *Lady in the Dark* (1944). The gown cost Paramount Studios $35,000. Nineteen years later, Elizabeth Taylor's gown in *Cleopatra*, made from 24-carat gold cloth, cost $65,000. Her wardrobe budget for the movie was $194,000, the highest ever spent for a single performer in any one movie.

A shop on Melrose Avenue, LA, called *A Star Is Worn*, sells used clothing of the stars. Every garment has a tag with the owner's name on it along with the price. For example: Marlon Brando's breeches for *Mutiny On the Bounty*—$1,000; John Travolta's autographed suit for *Saturday Night Fever* and the cover shot on *Time* magazine—$2,500. Sometimes the store accepts clothing from the stars on consignment. Most of them give their share of the sale to charity.

After the San Francisco earthquake in 1989, Paul Newman donated $250,000 to the victims. He also ordered his company, Newman's Own, to provide about 10,000 pounds of spaghetti to the thousands of homeless in Watsonville, California, which was very near the epicentre of the quake. Since Paul started his company in 1982, he's donated more than $22 million to various charities.

On 14 May 2000, the stars of the smash hit TV series *Friends*, Jennifer Aniston, Courteney Cox-Arquette, Lisa Kudrow, Matt LeBlanc, Matthew Perry and David Schwimmer, renewed their contacts for a further two years on the show. They will each receive US$750,000 an episode, which is $40 million each, making it the largest TV payout in history for a sitcom. At the time, Matthew Perry was hospitalised in LA where he was recuperating from a severe case of the flu—he was the only cast member not at the negotiations.

In 1985, Bill Cosby and Joan Rivers battled in a New York auction house for a set of Tiffany silverware, bidding against each other for quite a few minutes. Bill came out on top with $95,000.

Producer David O Selznick was fined $5,000 for allowing the word 'damn' (in Clark Gable's famous line) to be used in *Gone with the Wind* (1939).

In 1999 a top price was paid in the US for Madonna's sneakers, which, believe it or not, went for $4,500. Probably by the time you read this they will have doubled in value.

The voice of *E.T.* was done by 82-year-old American housewife Pat Welsh, who received just $750 for her work.

In August 1989, at a Christie's auction in London, Australian restaurateur Janette Wilkins bought a dress worn by Marilyn Monroe for $12,000. The dress was worn by Marilyn while touring US bases in Korea. The two-piece, skin-tight, silk-crêpe cocktail dress went on show at her Melbourne restaurant.

Michael Keaton, who starred in the 1989 *Batman* movie, wore out 28 rubber bat suits during the filming, at a cost of $600,000. He ruined them doing most of his own stunts.

In 1989, a selection of Marilyn Monroe's personal items was placed under the auction block. This is what they fetched: a sterling silver jewellery box given to her by Jack Benny, and engraved 'Thanks Marilyn. Jack Benny'—$5,000; a plain cigarette case gifted to Marilyn by Clark Gable while they were filming *The Misfits*, engraved 'To Marilyn, Love Clark'—$10,000; a brass charm bracelet from her Aunt Lowry, with two small hearts hanging from it, engraved 'To Marilyn, Love Aunty Lowry'—$3,500; a small mother-of-pearl hair comb given to Marilyn by the producer of *Bus Stop*, engraved 'Marilyn, use at any bus stop, John Logan'—$5,000; a sundial from her Brentwood home (the one she died in), which Marilyn bought on a visit to Japan in 1954—bought by a major Japanese company for $20,000; a large embroidered black and white scarf with Marilyn's name worked into the design—$2,500.

MGM once held a huge garage-type sale, which lasted three weeks. The studio sold off tons of movie props, costumes and so on, and made $4 million simply by selling cast-offs.

To date $3.5 million was the highest ever paid by Hollywood for the rights to make a movie. It was paid to William P Blatty for *The Exorcist*.

Cleopatra (1963), starring Elizabeth Taylor and Richard Burton, cost $12 million to make.

The two lowest-paid stars in the movie *The Wizard of Oz* were Judy Garland and the dog Toto.

As a child star, Shirley Temple reportedly earned more than $20 million for 20th Century-Fox, to whom she was under contract.

At a 1989 Hollywood auction, fans bought the following items of memorabilia: George Reeves's Superman costume from the 1950s TV series for $12,000; Clark Gable's white suit worn in *Gone with the Wind* for $24,000; a signed postcard from Marilyn Monroe for $18,000.

The fee paid for the use of a private home in Bedford, New York, for the filming of *Fatal Attraction* was $500 per day.

In December 1989, Christies in New York auctioned the dress that Judy Garland wore for publicity shots in *The Wizard of Oz*. It went to a collector for $19,800, $4,000 more than the previous record for a Judy Garland movie costume. The gallery's pre-sale estimate of the dress's value was $10,000–$15,000. At the same auction a collector paid $275,000 for a pair of Italian 18th-century rococo walnut commodes used in the 1950s MGM movies, *Susan Slept Here* and *Slightly Scarlet*.

Goldfinger, the third James Bond movie, made $10 million in its first 14 weeks. At the time, it was the fastest moneymaker in the history of the movies.

The famous nude picture of Marilyn Monroe (in her days as an unknown in Hollywood) was taken by a photographer called Tom Kelly, who was paid $500 for the print by a calendar company; Marilyn was paid $50, and the calendar company netted $750,000. Today, the original print and negative are worth a small fortune.

The witch's hat worn by Margaret Hamilton in *The Wizard of Oz* (1939) sold at a Hollywood auction for $33,000. In the late 1980s, a pair of Dorothy's ruby slippers worn by Judy Garland were sold to a collector for $165,000. Clark Gable's personal script from *Gone with the Wind* sold for $77,000.

Elvis Presley always kept $1 million in his personal cheque account.

Warner Brothers paid $52,000 for Sean Connery's hairpiece in *Never Say Die*. To date, this is the most expensive toupee ever made for a Hollywood star, and paid for by a studio.

The world record for the most money lost on the making of a movie goes to *Heaven's Gate* directed by Michael Cimino, which lost $34.5 million.

In February 1990, model Jerry Hall turned auctioneer in London and put Marilyn Monroe's skimpiest swimsuit under the hammer. The jet black, hand-sequinned suit, along with its white bathing cap, sold for $9,812. The buyer was a record company promoting the career of 22-year-old Marilyn look-alike, Pauline Bailey. Jerry Hall was selected as auctioneer because she had just opened in London's West End production of *Bus Stop;* the role Marilyn made famous in the 1956 Hollywood movie of the same name.

When Dustin Hoffman starred as Benjamin Braddock in the smash hit *The Graduate* (1967), he received $17,000 for his role. After the movie, Dustin couldn't find acting work and collected unemployment insurance. The movie went on to gross over $50 million.

The most sought-after item of Elvis Presley memorabilia from the 1980s is a 45-rpm record given away to people who toured his home in Tupelo, Missouri, in August 1982. Only 7,500 copies were handed out, and the record was never released commercially. They're now worth around $300 each.

The movie *The Longest Day* ended up costing a lot more than the real war on which it was based.

Early posters for the *Star Wars* sequel used the original title *Revenge of the Jedi.* By the time it was re-titled *Return of the Jedi*, some posters had already been printed, and they're now worth around $400 to avid collectors.

Sylvester Stallone was offered $360,000 for his first *Rocky* script, however, they would only pay him $75,000 if he came with the script to star in the movie as he was unknown at the time. He went with the script and the rest is history.

In 1934, a then unknown actor called Robert Taylor signed with MGM for just $35 a week.

In 1989, the pinafore Judy Garland wore in *The Wizard of Oz* was auctioned at Christies for $20,000.

Jaws was the first Hollywood movie to top $100 million in ticket sales.

Hollywood's first child star, Jackie Coogan (who played the title role in Charlie Chaplin's *The Kid* in 1921), was a millionaire by the age of six and was broke by 23, after his mother squandered his fortune. This inspired the first laws to protect child actors and their earnings.

Jack Nicholson is rumoured to have been paid a cool $11 million for his role as the Joker in *Batman* (1989).

In 1988, a script copy of *Gone with the Wind*, autographed by 32 people connected with the movie, fetched $22,000 at auction.

James Dean's first fully paid acting job was a Pepsi TV commercial; he received $30.

In 1980, Larry Hagman became the highest-paid star on any prime-time soap. The Lorimar production company gave in to Larry's financial demands and agreed to pay him a whopping $75,000 per episode.

CBS paid $15 million for the TV rights to the movie *Star Wars*. To date this is still the highest price ever paid for movie rights by a television network.

Elizabeth Taylor was the first movie star to demand $1 million, for her role in *Cleopatra* (1963).

When George Clooney made a cameo appearance on the 11 May 2000 episode of *ER*, he worked for union scale—just $596,000.

In the early 1950s, Clint Eastwood signed a contract at Universal Studios for $75 a week to do walk-ons in low-budget horror movies. The studio fired him when an executive decided his Adam's apple protruded too far for him to ever become star material!

John Travolta is totally passionate about flying and planes, so much so that he once bought a house in Florida with a private runway.

To date Whoopi Goldberg holds the record for wearing the most expensive jewellery at the Academy Awards. When she hosted the 1999 cermony she wore an estimated $71 million of diamonds onstage, including a $10 million diamond ring by Beverly Hills jeweller to the stars Harry Winston.

While shopping in a West Hollywood supermarket, Renée Zellweger was a lucky winner of a $1,500 shopping spree. She gave her prize away to a homeless man who was sitting outside the store.

In July 2003 the original Superman costume worn by actor George Reeves sold for $226,000 at auction in the USA.

A single mum in the UK forked out £1,610 at a charity auction for a pair of light blue autographed Yves St Laurent boxers worn by former Boyzone singer Ronan Keating.

Jackie Collins once said she expects to live to her mid-eighties. At that age she intends to ask all her relatives around to her house, secretly videotape them and study the tapes. At this time she will figure out which ones want her money. 'Then I'll give it to the ones who don't want anything.'

STARS IN PRINT

Blockbuster authors Jackie Collins and Shirley Conran write all their first draft books in longhand.

Lucille Ball holds the record for appearing on the cover of America's *TV Guide;* 24 times in all, including the very first issue in 1952, on which she was pictured with her newborn son, Desi Arnaz IV.

After the 1968 assassination of Senator Robert F Kennedy, Elizabeth Taylor took out a full-page advertisement in *The New York Times* in support of gun control in the US.

In September 1998, an American movie magazine named the top five cheesiest lines in movie history. Demi Moore topped the list with her 'Suck my d**k' line in *GI Jane*. The next award went to action man himself, Arnold Schwarzenegger, who said, 'You want to be a farmer? Here's a couple of ache-ers!' while delivering a kick to his rival's nether regions in *The Last Action Hero*. In third place was Leonardo DiCaprio's *Titanic* shout, 'I'm king of the world!' Fourth place went to Charlie Sheen with, 'I'm much more than a walking penis. I'm a flying penis!' in *Terminal Velocity*. Last place went to Sean Connery, 'If that's a confession, my arse is a banjo', from the movie *Just Cause*.

At the tender age of 12, Ally Sheedy published her first book titled, *She Was Nice to Mice*, a story about Queen Elizabeth's civility to mice. The book rocketed to the best-seller list; later she used the title again when she set up her very own company, *Nice to Mice Productions*.

Mike Myers wrote the script for the original *Austin Powers* movie in just three weeks.

In 1980, Elvis Presley's stepmother Dee Presley shocked the world with her book, *Elvis: We Love You Tender.*

Ethan Hawke wrote his first novel titled *The Hottest State*; he received from the publishing company a much higher advance than any other first-time author. His second novel *Ash Wednesday* was inspired by the changes he went through when he became a husband and father.

William Shatner wrote a series of books; his first was called *TekWar*. They were all turned into movies in which he starred.

International model Naomi Campbell wrote a novel called *Swan.* She did it to extend her talents beyond the catwalk.

In May 1982, Jane Fonda put pen to paper and wrote an exercise book, which became a best-seller.

John Travolta holds the record for having the most *Rolling Stone* covers for an actor; he has four.

Bruce Springsteen's breakthrough *Born to Run* album of 1975 landed him on the cover of both *Time* and *Newsweek* magazines on the same day, a feat that had never been accomplished by any other singer, not even the *Beatles* or Elvis Presley.

When Burt Reynolds posed nude as *Cosmopolitan* magazine's first celebrity centrefold in 1972, a Chicago woman bought 500 copies of the magazine, which cost her $700, to wallpaper her bedroom. Burt said, 'For $700 I would have gone over and seen her myself!'

Publisher Hugh Heffner first wanted to call his new magazine Stag Party, but a magazine called *Stag* objected, so Hugh settled for his second choice, *Playboy*. Hugh once worked in the subscription department of *Esquire* magazine, but walked out to start up his own magazine when they refused to raise his salary from $60 to $85 per week.

'Mae West' was the name given by the British RAF to their inflatable life jackets during World War II. Even today, it's recognised by compilers of dictionaries. This makes Mae West the only movie star ever to be listed in a dictionary, something she was always very proud of.

In 1991, Rupert Everett published his first novel, *Hello Darling, Are You Working?*

In 1954, a novel by Ian Fleming called *Casino Royale*, about a British agent known as James Bond, sold only 7000 copies in its first printing.

Peter Sellers was the first male to appear on the cover of *Playboy* magazine in America.

Grace Kelly was the first movie star to appear on a postage stamp.

The first American actress to appear on the cover of *Life* magazine was Jean Harlow on 3 May 1937.

Eva Gabor was the first Gabor sister to go to America in the 1930s, and she quickly launched herself as a minor star. She speaks English, French, German and Hungarian, plays the piano extremely well and entitled her biography *Orchids and Salamis* (1951). When asked to explain the title, she said, 'Simple, dahling, because all I ever seemed to have in my fridge were orchids and salamis.' In her major TV role as Lisa Douglas, the socialite wife who finds herself down on the farm in *Green Acres* (1965–1971), she wore all her own gowns.

In 1978, at the age of 60, singer/actress Lena Horne was ranked alongside Elizabeth Taylor and Farrah Fawcett as one of the 10 most beautiful women in the world by the magazine *Harper's Bazaar.*

At the age of 19, novelist Dame Barbara Cartland was the gossip columnist on the *Daily Express* newspaper in England. She wrote her first book at 21 and in her lifetime wrote 723 books. She dictated 7,000 words per day, and had a daily intake of honey along with 70 vitamin pills. She wrote right up to the day she died, 23 May 2000, which was two months away from her 99th birthday.

John Lennon was on the first cover of *Rolling Stone* magazine in November 1967.

Marilyn Monroe appeared on the first cover of *Playboy* magazine.

Richard Chamberlain, who played Dr Kildare on TV, was erroneously listed twice in the 40th edition of *Who's Who in America*.

Tony Curtis has been billed as James Curtis, Anthony Curtis and Tony Curtis in different movies. In 1977, he wrote a best-selling novel called *Kid Andrew Cody and Julie Sparrow.*

Charlie Chaplin was on the first cover of *Time* magazine dated 6 July 1925.

In December 1989, Sean Connery was voted 'the sexiest man alive' by *People* magazine. The vote for sexiest second-generation actor went to Jeff Bridges.

Actress Drew Barrymore was paid a $250,000 advance to write her life story. At 14 she holds the record for the youngest autobiographer of all time.

Fabian, the 1960s pop singer, posed nude for the centrefold of an early 1970s *Playgirl* magazine.

When *Blood Feast* (1963) was previewed, the movie publicist issued every member of the press with a paper bag to be sick into.

In 1983, E.T. the extra-terrestrial was runner-up for *Time* magazine's Man of the Year award.

In mid 1967, Jacqueline Susann's novel *Valley of the Dolls* set a record by selling 6.8 million copies of the paperback edition in just six months.

During 1965 and 1966, actress Raquel Welch was nicknamed the 'Cover Girl'. In that time, she appeared on the covers of 108 magazines.

Actress Cate Blanchett was the first guest celebrity editor on the June 2000 issue of *Vanity Fair* magazine.

In November 2002, Tom Arnold said he was disappointed that the American store Wal-Mart refused to sell his latest book, *How I Lost 5 lbs in 6 Years* (St. Martin's). The problem came from a blurb from Steve Tisch on the back cover, 'You've heard Arnold talk about his small penis. Now you can read about it.' Tom told the *New York Post*, 'You'd think a big corporation like Wal-Mart would be more sensitive to a fellow's handicap.'

Marilyn Monroe has had more books and articles written about her than any other actress or actor. Most were written after her death in 1962.

Elizabeth Taylor became the favourite cover girl of *Life* magazine. Over 25 years, she appeared on its cover 11 times, still a record for a movie star.

The original name for the comic strip *Dick Tracy* was to have been Plain Clothes Tracy.

In July 1978, John Travolta became the first male to have his picture on the cover of *McCalls* magazine in 100 years.

Joan Collins was voted Miss Press Clippings in 1982, and wore a dress to the press conference made from all the newspaper stories which had been written about her that year.

In the 1970s, Julie Andrews wrote two children's books, *Mandy* and *The Last of the Really Great Whangdoodles*, under her married name Julie Edwards.

Actor Sean Penn weighed in on the international debate over a possible war with Iraq. In October 2002, he paid $56,000 for an advert in the *Washington Post* accusing US President George W Bush of stifling debate and threatening civil liberties. In the open full-page letter to the President, he urged the President to stop a cycle where 'Bombing is answered by bombing, mutilation by mutilation, killing by killing. I beg you, help save America before yours is a legacy of shame and horror.' The letter was signed, 'Sincerely, Sean Penn, San Francisco, California.' A spokesman for the *Washington Post* confirmed that it was placed by the Hollywood celebrity who has starred in more than 40 movies.

Actress Diane Lane is one of a selected group of women to have appeared on the cover of *Time* magazine. The reason she held the cover shot in 1979 was for her profile on rising child stars in the industry.

In Cybill Shepherd's autobiography, *Cybill Disobedience*, she says that in 1988 when she got her star on the Hollywood Walk of Fame, Bruce Willis sent her a telegram saying, 'Sorry I can't be there, one of us has to work.'

In 1978 Joan Collins wrote her autobiography 'Past Imperfect' then in 1996 she updated her autobiography in a book called 'Second Act'.

WHAT THEY DID BEFORE, AND AFTER

Between the ages of 13 and 16, Bette Midler worked part-time in a pineapple cannery in Hawaii.

Alex Dimitriades landed the lead role in the 1993 movie *The Heartbreak Kid*, after his high-school drama teacher recommended him to the movie's director.

While waiting for fame and stardom, Madonna worked as a coat-check girl at New York's Russian Tea Room. She was fired for dressing provocatively.

Singer Craig David's first job was as a telemarketer, selling windows.

Long before he became a singer with *Guns'n'Roses*, Axl Rose was paid $8 an hour to smoke cigarettes for a science experiment at UCLA.

Daniela Bianchi, who played the Bond Girl in the 1963 movie *From Russia with Love*, was 1960's Miss Universe.

Ashton Kutcher once modelled for Calvin Klein jeans, and did modelling fashion shows in both Paris and Milan before looking towards a career as an actor. He also appeared in an *Abercrombie & Fitch* catalogue.

Before making her mark as an actress, Mariska Hargitay was crowned Miss Beverly Hills in 1982.

In 1967, Arnold Schwarzenegger became Mr Universe, a title he won five times. He became Mr Olympia seven times, before he gave it all away and started his movie career.

French actress Catherine Deneuve once modelled for a French banknote.

Vin Diesel worked for nine years as a bouncer at a New York club, his movie script *Doorman* is based on that time. As a teenager he was a breakdancer on the streets of New York.

Before English TV hypnotist Paul McKenna entered show business, he was a Cardinal in the Church of England.

Long before she became famous, actress Beverly D'Angelo sold vacuum cleaners by phone.

While at drama school at Australia's Victoria College, Rachel Griffiths supported herself by posing naked for aspiring painters.

Jenny McCarthy once worked in a grocery store as a meat slicer.

As a tiny tot, Cameron Diaz won first prize at a school fancy-dress competition. She went as Kermit the Frog.

Joely Fisher was once an ice-cream vendor.

Denzel Washington loves ballet and in his youth trained to be a dancer.

American actor John Corbett is a qualified hairdresser.

Chuck Berry was once a licensed hairdresser, then he gave it away to further his career as a rock 'n' roll singer. The rest is history.

Luke Perry once worked in a doorknob factory.

Ryan Reynolds failed his drama class, but that didn't hinder his career in the movies.

American actor Peter Boyle is a former monk.

While taking dance lessons at night, Jennifer Lopez worked at a law firm during the day. She got her big TV break when she appeared as a 'Fly Girl' on TV's *In Living Colour.*

Ronald Reagan's last role in a movie before entering politics was in the 1964 movie *The Killers*.

Long before stardom, Jennifer Anniston used to work in telemarketing.

Val Kilmer and Kevin Spacey went to the same drama school. Kevin was discharged from military college for hitting someone over the head with a tyre.

Before being discovered by George Lucas (he spotted her in a high-school play), Kathleen Quinlan was set on becoming a gymnastic teacher.

In 1981, Ted Danson did a number of Aramis TV adverts for their men's toiletry products.

As a teenager, Matt Damon occasionally did breakdancing in Harvard Square at Harvard University to raise a little cash.

Meryl Streep once called cheeky Dustin Hoffman 'an obnoxious pig', when he grabbed her breast during her audition for a Broadway play he was producing. At the time Meryl was a struggling young actress. Years later, the couple went on to star together in *Kramer vs Kramer.*

During the lean years, when there was no acting work coming in, Harrison Ford built a sun porch for actress Sally Kellerman. Today, she has a sign on her sundeck saying 'This is the deck HF built'.

During her teenage years Holly Hunter raised chickens, one year her chicken was placed eighth nationaly in a poultry-judging contest in the US.

The florist's assistant in the 1935 movie *Top Hat* was played by an aspiring young actress named Lucille Ball.

In the 1962 movie *State Fair,* Kurt Russell was the nine-year-old boy who kicked Elvis Presley in the leg. Elvis was 27 years old at the time. Years later, Kurt played Elvis Presley in a TV movie; he was 27 years old.

American comedienne Sandra Bernhard once worked as a manicurist and pedicurist at a Beverley Hills beauty salon. During this time, she polished the nails of many Hollywood stars, including Jaclyn Smith and Dyan Cannon.

Hollywood movie star Ronald Reagan became the 40th President of the United States. He was the son of an alcoholic shoe salesman, the first divorced man to be elected President and the oldest at the time of his election. He was considered for the leading role in the 1964 movie *The Best Man*, which was about a presidential candidate, but United Artists executives turned him down; the reason: 'Ronald Reagan did not have the presidential look.'

On 8 April 1986, Clint Eastwood, who was then 55, trounced incumbent Charlotte Townsend by a vote of 2,166 to 799 to become mayor of the small, rich seaside town in Carmel, California. He retired from public office when his term was over in 1988.

As a young fashion model in her teens, songbird Whitney Houston graced the covers of both *Glamour* and *Seventeen* magazines.

In her hometown of Consort, Canadian singer k.d. lang, is also remembered as Kathryn Dawn Lang—an outstanding athlete. She excelled at volleyball, basketball and badminton. At high school, she was voted 'Athlete of the Year' three years in a row for her Olympic-level performance in javelin throwing.

Patrick Swayze had a brief career as a professional ice skater.

Arriving in LA in 1986 from his birthplace Oklahoma, Brad Pitt took a variety of part-time jobs to make money to pay for his acting classes. He once dressed in a giant chicken outfit plugging a fast-food chain and played chauffeur limo driver to several Strip-O-Gram artists.

As a teenager, Billy Joel was New York's Long Island welterweight boxing champion.

As a teenager, Pierce Brosnan ran away and joined a circus where he did fire eating.

Billy Connolly was once a welder.

In 1960, Christopher Walken spent the summer months working as an assistant lion tamer.

Oliver Stone worked as a teacher in the Free Pacific Institute in South Vietnam, and drove taxis in New York before the movie bug bit him.

At the age of 16, Mark Wahlberg was convicted and served 45 days in jail. It came about because of his involvement in the beating of two Vietnamese men during a robbery.

Movie and TV mogul Ted Turner once sold space on billboards for the family business.

Quentin Tarantino worked for four years in an LA video store.

Christian Slater made his stage debut at the age of nine in a revival production of *The Music Man*.

Ozzy Osbourne's first couple of jobs were a car-horn assembly line worker and a slaughterhouse worker.

Darryl Zanuck started his show business career as a scriptwriter of *Rin-Tin-Tin* stories. Later he became the head of the powerful 20th Century-Fox studios.

Dermot Mulroney was an award-winning cellist before becoming an actor.

At 14, Matt Dillon was spotted in the corridor of his junior high school by a talent scout.

English actor Bob Hoskins left school at 16 and had a series of jobs, including window washer, truck driver and porter at Covent Garden.

At 16, Rene Russo dropped out of high school. She had a series of jobs, including working in an eyewear factory. In 1989, she won a role as Tom Berenger's girlfriend in the movie *Major League*, but her big break came three years later starring opposite Mel Gibson in *Lethal Weapon 3*.

Before playing her Academy Award-winning role in the 1993 movie *The Piano*, Anna Paquin's only acting experience had been playing a skunk in her primary school play. Rumour has it she only attended the auditions for *The Piano* as a day out with her friends. Despite her lack of acting experience, the movie's director Jane Campion was in no doubt, 'Anna was impassioned—you totally believed her.'

As a kid, Sarah Jessica Parker played *Annie* in the Broadway stage production of the same name.

Patrick Stewart's first job was as a journalist.

One of the breakdancers in the closing ceremony at the 1984 Olympic Games in LA was none other than Oscar winner Cuba Gooding Jr.

Before she started high school, Jennifer Aniston had one of her paintings shown at the Metropolitan Museum of Art in New York.

Natalie Portman was discovered in a New York pizza parlour by a talent scout.

Singer Lenny Kravitz says being a choirboy taught him a lot.

Jay Leno got fired from a job washing Ford cars at an Andover, Mass., dealership, but he was re-hired after writing to Henry Ford II.

Lucy Liu moved out to LA from New York, and took a job as a waitress to support herself while she attended auditions.

Ashley Judd once worked cleaning out the tour buses of her mum and sister, country singers Naomi and Wynonna Judd. For her cleaning efforts she received $10.

When she was eight, Whitney Houston got her start in singing in the New Hope Baptist Junior Choir.

Marilyn Monroe once modelled in an advert for Idaho potatoes.

Ethan Hawke wanted to be a TV newsreader when he was a boy.

Renée Zellweger worked as a bartender's assistant.

Kate Winslet worked at a delicatessen in England.

Barbra Streisand was a switchboard operator and theatre usher.

At nine, Britney Spears was rejected by the Mickey Mouse Club because she was too young. Two years later she was welcomed to the club.

Wesley Snipes acted in a street puppet troupe; he also worked as a telephone installer and parking attendant.

When Arnold Schwarzenegger moved to the US in the 1960s, he started a bricklaying business. The money from this helped him finance his bodybuilding career.

Steven Seagal taught English and wrote articles for Japanese magazines and newspapers when he lived there in 1968.

Ray Romano was a gas-station attendant.

At the age of 18, Eddie Murphy discovered Chris Rock. It all happened one night when Chris did his comedy act at an open-mike night at a New York Comedy Club.

Tim Robbins was kicked off his high-school hockey team for fighting.

As a young man, Burt Reynolds was signed to play football with the Baltimore Colts; however, a car accident put a stop to his sporting career and he turned to acting instead.

David Hyde Pierce worked in a menswear store and played the church organ.

As a kid, Steve Martin lived not far from Disneyland. This is where he got his start; performing magic tricks and playing his banjo.

Actor Nathan Lane worked as a police-bail interviewer.

Josh Hartnett worked in a San Francisco video store.

Sally Field was a cheerleader in high school.

Robert Duvall worked as a postal clerk and dishwasher.

Johnny Depp sold ballpoint pens over the phone.

Ellen Degeneres sold vacuum cleaners.

Willem Dafoe worked as a carpenter, electrician and a part-time model. He also worked as a magazine binder for *Penthouse*.

Mariah Carey worked as a hat-check girl, a restaurant hostess and a waitress.

Movie director/producer/writer and editor, James Cameron, worked as a machinist, school bus driver and part-time truck driver.

Country singing star Garth Brooks worked as a bouncer in a nightclub.

Kathy Bates worked as a cashier in the gift shop of the Museum of Modern Art in New York.

Keanu Reeves once worked in an ice-skating rink sharpening skates.

A young George Lucas had planned to become a racing-car driver. However, a near-fatal crash just two days before his high-school graduation totally altered his plans. Days later, he decided to take a career in film production.

Aussie actor Paul Hogan once worked in a morgue.

Before he got his big break as an actor in 1961, funny man Gene Wilder was working as a toy salesman, chauffeur and even taught fencing to make ends meet.

For many years, the voice of Julie Andrews could be heard in all British Airways planes instructing your in-flight procedure.

Jon Voight once sold encyclopaedias door to door, to make a little extra cash between acting jobs.

Jim Carrey left school at 16; his first full-time job was working in a fibreglass factory in Canada.

TV star and stand-up comedian Jerry Seinfeld once sold light bulbs by phone to get money to help his comedy career.

When he was 16, Tom Cruise worked as a caretaker in the block of flats in New York where he lived.

Before their showbiz careers, *Star Trek* mastermind Gene Roddenberry and singer/actor Kris Kristofferson earned their livings as aeroplane pilots.

Because David Schwimmer's mum and dad are both attorneys, he thought he might take that track before settling on acting.

Antonio Banderas worked as a waiter and modelled clothes for both Ralph Lauren and Gucci.

Alec Baldwin was a doorman at the famous Studio 54.

David Duchovny was a bartender.

Wesley Snipes installed telephones in people's homes.

Bruce Willis was a bartender in Philadelphia.

Jon Bon Jovi was once into a very different type of heavy metal; he worked in a junkyard. In those days, he went under his real name of Jon Bongiovi.

Chow Yun-Fat left school when he was 17 and got a job as a hotel bellboy; he started acting in 1972.

In the early 1940s, Charlton Heston was a nude model for the Art Student League in New York. He earned a mere $1.25 per hour.

Sean Connery, the Scottish-born actor, was a male model, a coffin polisher, a bricklayer and a milkman before he got into acting.

SOME OF THE BIGGEST HOLLYWOOD STARS GOT THEIR START ON THE SMALL SCREEN IN SOAP OPERAS:

Patty Duke played Ellen Dennis on *The Brighter Day* when she was a child.

Kevin Bacon played Tod Adamson on *Search for Tomorrow.*

Kevin Kline played Woody Reed on *Search for Tomorrow.*

Susan Sarandon played Patrice Kahlman on *Search for Tomorrow.*

Billy Dee Williams played Dr Jim Frazier on *Guiding Light*.

Judith Light played Karen Wolek on *One Life to Live*.

Tom Selleck played Jed Andrews on *The Young and the Restless.*

Larry Hagman played Ed Gibson on *The Edge of Night*.

David Hasselhoff played Snapper Foster on *The Young and the Restless.*

Sigourney Weaver played Avis Ryan on *Somerset*.

Ted Danson played Tom Conway on *Somerset*.

Tom Berenger played Tim Siegel on *One Life to Live*.

Robert Redford once served as sewer commissioner for the Provo Canyon in Utah.

Carol Burnett was once an usherette at Graumans Theatre in Hollywood, until she got the sack!

In 1926, Ronald Reagan served as a lifeguard. He claimed to have saved 77 people from drowning that year.

Before Steve Martin got his big break in show business, he spent eight years selling Davy Crocket coonskin hats and Mouseketeer ears at Disneyland. He started earning $1,500 a week as a scriptwriter for TV personalities like Sonny and Cher, Glen Campbell, John Denver, Dick Van Dyke and the Smothers Brothers before he got into acting.

Jobeth Williams played Carrie Wheeler on *Somerset.*

Kathleen Turner played Nola Aldrich on *The Doctors*, and Alec Baldwin played her husband.

Christopher Reeve played Ben Harper on *Love of Life*.

Rue McClanahan played Caroline Johnson on *Another World.*

Charles Durning played Gil McGowan on *Another World.*

Demi Moore played Jackie Templeton on *General Hospital.*

John Stamos played Blackie on *General Hospital.*

Richard Dean Anderson played Dr Jeff Webber on *General Hospital.*

Ray Liotta played Joey Perrini on *Another World.*

Meg Ryan played Betsy Androupolous on *As the World Turns.*

Robin Wright played Kelly Capwell on *Santa Barbara*.

Kyra Sedgewick played Julia Shearer on *Another World.*

Before Gregory Peck became an actor, he worked as a carnival barker at the 1939 World's Fair, then as a tour guide at New York's Rockefeller Centre, giving him extra money for acting classes.

Clayton Moore, who played the Lone Ranger on television for several seasons, was noticed and signed up by a Hollywood talent scout while working as a circus trapeze artist.

Jean-Claude Van Damme worked as a bouncer, model, pizza deliveryman and carpet installer before he hit the big time in the movies.

Oscar winning actor, Dustin Hoffman, once worked at a psychiatric hospital on his way up the ladder to stardom.

Kevin Costner once worked as a deck hand on a deep-sea fishing boat.

Dennis Franz worked as a postman.

Bob Crane, who played the lead in TV's *Hogan's Heroes*, was once a drummer with the Connecticut Symphony Orchestra.

Danny DeVito was a hairdresser working in his sister's beauty salon; he specialised in beehive hairdos.

Jaclyn Smith started ballet at the age of three. Her love for ballet inspired her to set up a ballet school for underprivileged children in New York's Upper West Side slums.

Kiss singer Gene Simmons once taught English at a Spanish Harlem grammar school in New York City.

King of the horror movies, Vincent Price was once the art buyer for the Sears Roebuck Company in Los Angeles.

Before he hit the big time in Hollywood, Alan Alda worked as a clown, a cabdriver and a doorman. At one point he even coloured baby photographs for a living.

Actor Ben Kingsley's first job after leaving school was as a penicillin tester for ICI. He quit the job in the early 1960s to start acting. He then went to a theatre school and earned $20 per week.

Singer/actress Debbie Harry, from the pop group *Blondie*, once worked as a *Playboy* bunny.

Sylvester Stallone was once a trainee beautician, but got thrown out of a New York beauty school when he was nineteen. Later, he became a gym instructor at a Swiss boarding school for girls, and then studied acting at the University of Miami. His first Broadway show was *Score*, a nudie musical review.

Farrah Fawcett dropped out of art school in 1969; 22-year-old Farrah then became the face of Wella Balsam shampoo and moved to Hollywood. Four years later she married Lee Majors, star of *The Six Million Dollar Man*. Six years later they separated when she fell for Lee's best friend Ryan O'Neal.

Besides being in the movies what else do the following stars have in common: Warren Beatty, Uma Thurman, Burt Reynolds, Michael Caine and Sidney Poitier. They all worked as dishwashers long before they became household names in the entertainment business.

In his youth, Patrick Swayze, was a struggling New York ballet dancer, and to make ends meet he did some fashion menswear modelling. In 1974, he posed for a shot advertising men's briefs, which later appeared in the gay magazine *After Dark*. Today, the picture is a collector's item.

INTIMATE DETAILS

Tom Cruise is allergic to cats.

Actor John Corbett says he doesn't wear underwear, 'I've never owned a pair of underpants in my life.'

Tobey Maguire's Spider-Man costume for the second *Spider-Man* movie has an inbuilt escape hatch so he can go to the toilet without having to remove the entire costume, unlike the costume he had to wear in the first *Spider-Man* movie.

A gerbil attacked Christina Ricci when she was three years old; since then she's developed a phobia of the little critters.

In an interview in November 2002, Christina Aguilera revealed the reason behind her prolific piercing. At the time, she had 11 piercings ranging from the usual common places, to some not so public places on her body, 'If I was having a bad day, or if something was really getting me down—boy troubles, whatever—I wanted to go out and get a new piercing', she said in the interview. 'It was definitely a release for me, something that made me feel a little more strong or empowered. Because it was something that had to do with me and no one else.'

David Arquette loves stilettos; he says he has a high-heel fetish.

Puff Daddy only wears his trainers once; after their first wearing into the rubbish they go.

Christian Slater's Hollywood home has six bathrooms.

In 1987, Joan Collins banned her Beverly Hill's dustman from collecting her rubbish after he sold it to fans. Joan thought it a gross invasion of her privacy, so she bought a paper shredder and hired a private company to remove all her rubbish.

Sheryl Crowe's two front teeth are false. She lost them years ago when she tripped and fell on stage.

To stop her highlights from fading, Jennifer Aniston adds two crushed aspirin pills to her shampoo every wash.

As a young child, Catherine Zeta-Jones caught a virus and nearly died. She had to have a tracheotomy to open her windpipe.

Angela Bassett says she tends to stay in character the whole time she's doing a movie, which can be very draining.

Angelina Jolie is left-handed.

In 1990, royal photographer Lord Lichfield listed 22-year-old Nicole Kidman as one of the 10 most beautiful women in the world.

Priscilla Presley says she was never allowed to eat caviar in all the years she was married to Elvis. He hated any kind of fish food, and told her he would have her thrown out of the house if he caught her eating any.

Hans Christian Andersen, the Danish storyteller, had no trouble at all in telling stories, but he did have trouble in reading them. It's rumoured that he was dyslexic.

Phyllis Diller stayed in her beautiful air-conditioned Brentwood home during most of the 1990 Californian summer heatwave. She was worried that her plastic surgery would melt in the 38-degree heat, and her face would literally start to slide downwards.

Pat Morita, the Japanese-American movie actor, was confined to bed at the age of two because of spinal tuberculosis. He spent the next nine years in bed.

Madonna dropped out of the University of Michigan after only three semesters.

The Australian actor, Paul Hogan, suffered a cerebral haemorrhage back in 1986 when he tried to press 250 pounds of weights on a Nautilus machine.

When Prince stayed at London's Mayfair Hotel in November 1990, he asked the hotel to fill his baths with whipped cream and honey during his stay. It's rumoured that Prince said it gave him 'creative inspiration'.

New Zealand-born Russell Crowe lost one of his front teeth during a rugby game in Wellington when he was just 10 years old.

Sandra Bullock claimed that her former boyfriend, Matthew McConaughey, often stunk. He is on record as saying, 'I don't like to use soap.'

Comic actor Damon Wayans was born with a clubfoot.

In September 2002, Geri Halliwell admitted to an English newspaper that she spends £1,000 a week on lingerie.

While working on the US TV series *Living Dolls*, Halle Berry went into a coma during filming. After tests, she found out she was diabetic.

In 1999, Sir Elton John had a pacemaker installed.

Melanie Griffith was 14 years old when she moved in with Don Johnson, who was then twenty two. They married when she was 18, and they divorced a year later.

Brad Pitt chipped his tooth while making *Fight Club*, but didn't get it mended as he thought it 'added character'. As soon as the movie was completed he had the tooth capped.

HERE ARE SIX SCARS OF THE STARS:

Joaquin Phoenix has a scar on his upper lip; this is the result of repairing a cleft lip. At 14, a horse Sharon Stone was riding galloped under a clothesline, slashing her neck from ear to ear. Harrison Ford has a scar on his chin; this happened when he was 21—his car smashed into a telephone pole cutting his chin on the steering wheel. Catherine Zeta-Jones has a scar on her neck, which was the result of a life-saving tracheotomy; it kept her breathing when her windpipe swelled shut at 18-months-old. A stuntman crashed into Pierce Brosnan while he was shooting the 007 movie, *Tomorrow Never Dies*, leaving a nasty scar above his upper lip. Sandra Bullock has a small scar over her left eye; this was caused when she dived into a lake and sliced the skin on a rock.

Sarah Michelle Gellar has a navel ring and five holes in each of her ear lobes.

In September 2002, Aussie fans of Kylie Minogue stole hundreds of giant billboards posters of her in her underwear, which were erected to promote her new CD.

European belt maker Giuseppe Acacia sent Madonna a chastity belt for her 44th birthday, which was inscribed with the words, 'Like a Virgin'.

It's rumoured that James Bond star Pierce Brosnan was so shaken by how thin his legs looked in the stockings he wore in a fencing scene in the 2002 movie *Die Another Day*, that he used padding to make his calves appear more muscular.

Mark Hamill, aka Luke Skywalker, did his own stunts in *The Empire Strikes Back* and *Return of the Jedi*.

There were 30 lifeguards on patrol watching the 17 million-gallon tank where most of the filming of *Titanic* (1997) took place.

Hollywood holds the title of the plastic surgery capital of the world. It's rumoured that more than 200,000 faces are lifted and over 800,000 breasts enhanced each year. At least half the plastic surgeons in America live in LA.

Debra Messing is allergic to the perfume from flowers and cosmetic perfume.

In 2002, Tom Cruise wore braces on his teeth for six months, metal on the bottom and clear on the top. At 40, Tom's front teeth were pushing hard on his lower teeth, so he needed to change his bite.

David Bowie's left pupil was badly damaged when he was hit in the eye during a fight when he was a teenager. This resulted in its permanent dilation and the appearance of mismatched eyes.

Rumour has it that Brad Pitt prefers to wear boxer shorts with cow-print, stripes or polka-dot designs.

From the age of 10–14, Rene Russo wore a body cast to correct a curved spine.

Shirley MacLaine says she wants Renée Zellweger to play her if they make a movie on her life.

Billy Joel uses only dark towels to wipe his brow while performing on stage.

Some say that *Friends* star David Schwimmer has had electrolysis on his hairline.

George Hamilton, who played the vampire in the movie *Love at First Bite*, keeps a supply of his own blood at home, just in case he has an accident and needs a transfusion.

It's said that Mel Gibson makes sure that every movie contract he signs has a clause in it guaranteeing him a personal chiropractor to be available every day of shooting. The Oscar-winning actor has scoliosis—curvature of the spine.

Blind singer Stevie Wonder signs all his legal documents using his fingerprint, which replaces his signature.

In August 2002, veteran American actor Charlton Heston revealed on TV that he has Alzheimer's disease. He said he was going public with his illness after having 'lived my whole life on the stage and screen before you. For an actor there is no greater loss than the loss of his audience', the 78-year-old said. 'I can part the Red Sea but not with you. That's why I won't exclude you from this stage of my life. If you see a little less spring in my step, if your name fails to leap to my lips, you'll know why. And if I tell you a funny story for the second time, please laugh anyway.'

Jennifer Aniston has suffered from sleep-walking since she was a child.

Kate Winslet has large feet. She wears a size 9½ shoe, and was teased about it by Leonardo DiCaprio during the filming of *Titanic*.

Actor Rob Lowe is deaf in his right ear.

Melanie Griffith was clawed in the face by a lioness during the filming of the 1981 movie *Roar*.

Gossip is that Marilyn Monroe had her first facelift before Christmas in

1950. She supposedly had the tip of her nose lifted to make her top lip seem more sensuous, and cartilage inserted into her jaw to give her a stronger chin line. It's said that Marilyn wiggled her rear because she was slightly bow-legged. This made her hips sway, so she emphasised her gait by sawing ¼ inch off the heel of her right shoe. Later the movies cashed in on her wiggle, and every young woman in the 1950s was trying to walk like Marilyn.

Sylvester Stallone had a nerve on the left side of his face severed as he was being born. His left side is still slightly paralysed.

Elizabeth Taylor has seen her way through some 30-odd serious illnesses since she was a child star.

For the role of Michael Corleone in *Godfather III*, Al Pacino had his dentist file down his teeth and apply a yellowish stain to them, to give more credibility to his role as an elderly man. After shooting was completed, Al had his teeth capped.

Singer Johnny Cash always wears jet-black when he performs; he even has it written into his contract.

When singer Julio Iglesias first visited LA, he was convinced the water was ruining his hair, so he had five gallons of pure filtered water flown in from his Miami home for shampooing only.

In *The Wizard of Oz*, Judy Garland wore extra dark makeup on the bridge of her nose to improve the appearance of her snub nose.

Buddy Epsen was originally selected to play the Tin Man in *The Wizard of Oz*, but the silver makeup gave him a skin complaint.

Producer/director Howard Hughes would never allow himself to be X-rayed.

It's reported that John Travolta spends about $50 a day on lotions and restorers to combat his receding hairline.

Stacy Keach, star of TV's *Hammer* detective series, wears a moustache to hide a scarred upper lip, the result of four operations to repair a harelip.

CELEBRITY TATTOOS:

Justin Timberlake has a tat of an angel with the word 'Guardian' over the top along with his mum's initial between his shoulder blades.

Glen Campbell has a dagger on his arm.

Cher gave her then 15-year-old son, Elijah Blue Allman, a gift of a tattoo on his arm. She took Elijah to Hollywood's Red Devil tattoo parlour, where they pored over imprint possibilities before settling on a heart with a dagger through it.

Angelina Jolie had a dragon on her left upper arm with Billy Bob written over the top, when they separated she had his name removed. In April 2003 she had an ancient Khmer script etched on her left shoulder blade.

Pearl Bailey had a heart on her leg.

Ringo Starr has a half moon and a shooting star on his arm.

Melanie Griffith has a pear on the left cheek of her rear end.

Alyssa Milano has five tattoos: rosary beads on her back, a heart on her bum, a fairy that's kneeling on the grass on her hip, an angel on her left ankle and a garland of little flowers around her right ankle.

Ben Affleck has a Native American Indian on his shoulder.

Ozzy Osbourne has smiley faces tattooed on each knee, which 'cheer him up each morning'.

Ricky Martin has a small tattoo of a rose surrounding a heart with an arrow through it; it's situated just above his groin.

When Winona Ryder and Johnny Depp were engaged, he had 'Winona Forever' tattooed on his arm. When their relationship broke up he had a few of the letters removed; today it reads, 'Wino Forever'.

Pamela Anderson's upper arm has a circlet of barbed wire and her left ring finger says, 'Tommy's', and is in the shape of a wedding ring.

Whoopi Goldberg has the Charles Schultz's bird, Woodstock, on her left breast.

Traci Lords has a crucifix on her left ankle.

Drew Barrymore has a collection of butterflies, daisies and angels on her back. Her ankle has a large ornate cross and on her lower stomach there are flowers.

Portia de Rossi has a tattoo of a ring on her right middle finger.

Jon Bon Jovi has a cow skull with hanging feathers on his right arm.

Geena Davis's right ankle has 'Renny' under a cherub, which is her husband's name.

Sean Connery has a tattoo on his right arm, which reads 'Mum & Dad Scotland Forever'.

Lorenzo Lamas has a Harley Davidson on his right shoulder.

David Bowie has a Japanese love ode on his left ankle, in honour of his wife Iman.

Julia Roberts's left shoulder has a red heart ringed by a Chinese word-picture, which means 'strength'. Two months before she married Danny Moder in mid 2002, they had their respective initials tattooed on their lower backs.

Cher has a chrysanthemum flower on her left ankle; on her upper left arm a necklace and on her lower abdomen another flower.

Antonio Sabato Jr has a tattoo on his lower back that depicts a yellow moon overlaid with a black Batman symbol.

Gregg Allman has a coyote on his forearm.

Peter Fonda has dolphins on one of his shoulders and three stars on his inner forearm.

Joan Baez has a flower on the small of her back.

Daryl Hall has a seven-pointed star on his shoulder.

Gene Simmons has a rose on his arm.

Charlie Sheen has an assortment of 12 tattoos.

Charlize Theron and her mum have matching tattoos.

Britney Spears has the word 'strange' tattooed on her hip in Chinese.

Kelly Osborne has a tiny pink wig tattooed on the upper left-hand side of her back.

In 2002 Robbie Williams had the opening bars of the *Beatles* hit classic, *All You Need Is Love* added to the tattoos on his lower back. In early 2003 he was sporting a new tattoo behind his left ear, a 'B', which apparently is in memory of his late grandmother who was called Betty. In May 2003 he added the French phrase 'Chacun à son gout' ('Each to hi s own') in large letters around his neck.

Bhupat Giri, an Indian movie producer, is different from any other producer in the world because he is blind.

Lynn Redgrave was confined to a wheelchair until she was six, due to an acute case of anaemia.

It was rumoured that Marilyn Monroe was born with six toes on her right foot, and the extra digit was surgically removed. A photograph taken of her on the beach in 1946 appears to prove this was fact and not a rumour.

In the 1980s, Patrick Swayze had a complete knee-reconstruction operation to repair a high-school football injury. His leg became badly infected with staphylococcus and at one point there was talk of amputation. Patrick Swayze hates his smile; he says it's lopsided. Over the years, as an actor and a champion dancer, he has broken his ribs, his left knee (five times), ankle, foot and all his fingers. He says he'd like to be remembered as a perfect Southern gentleman.

Robbie Williams has a personal masseuse backstage to de-stress him after every performance.

Movie star Angelina Jolie was angry when she saw a poster for her second *Tomb Raider* movie had been retouched to remove her nipples. Her protruding nipples were removed after the producers feared they could be offensive and start an avalanche of complaints.

Ewan McGregor's wife Eve admitted that his on screen love scenes make her feel uncomfortable. *OK* magazine quoted her as saying the scene in *Trainspotting* upset her the most. Eve, who was pregnant at the time said: 'Maybe it was my hormones, but it took me until after the birth not to tremble when I saw Kelly.'

Steven Spielberg does not like flying and avoids it whenever possible.

In August 2003 a number of male bidders at an LA AIDS charity auction offered thousands of dollars for a kiss with actress Sharon Stone. The top bidder was Ms Joni Rimm, whose top bid was $75,000 for the once-in-a-lifetime opportunity. Sharon, who's always a great sport, puckered up for a passionate kiss that went on for 45 seconds. Proceeds from the charity event went to Project Angel Foods, an organisation that delivers free meals to people with aids.

HOLLYWOOD WIT

Robin Williams: 'God gave men one brain and one penis but not enough blood to run the two at the same time.'

Elizabeth Taylor: 'Some of my best leading men have been horses and dogs.'

In October 2002, Calista Flockhart said of her hubby-to-be, actor Harrison Ford, 'He was my action-man hero—now he's my real-life hero. I can't believe my luck.'

In late 2002, a reporter called Dame Elizabeth Taylor 'an icon', to which she replied, 'Don't call me an icon, honey. An icon is something you hang in a Russian church. Call me Dame Elizabeth or call me an ageing movie star, but I am not an icon.'

Phyllis Diller says that Hollywood women want men, careers, money, children, friends, luxury, comfort, independence, freedom, respect, love and a $3 pair of pantyhose that won't run.

Liza Minnelli on her life: 'Listen, I came out of the womb and somebody slapped me on the ass and I've been in the public ever since.'

Sharon Stone: 'Women might be able to fake orgasm, but men can fake whole relationships.'

Joan Collins said: 'Women who are strong and dominant are often called bitches for the want of a better word. But a strong, dominant man is never called a bastard.'

Joan Rivers said about gender-bender Boy George, 'That's all England needs—another queen who can't dress.'

Cher, when asked what she thought made her sexy: 'I don't know how to make sex appeal. If anybody asks me how I do it, I tell him I don't know how I do it, I just do it.'

Jane Fonda: 'Working in Hollywood does give you a certain expertise in the field of prostitution.'

Leading Hollywood divorce lawyer Marvin Mitchelson once said, 'If you think it's expensive supporting your wife, try not supporting her.'

Groucho Marx once joked about Doris Day, saying that her arse was so firm you could play a game of bridge on it. He also said that he'd known her before she was a virgin. Doris never spoke to Groucho again.

Joan Rivers made lots of cruel remarks about Elizabeth Taylor's weight problems in her nightclub act. When asked about these remarks, she said, 'Liz Taylor should be very grateful to me; my jokes are one of the reasons she went on a diet. Besides, it was very embarrassing when I took her to Sea World. Shamu the whale jumped out of the water and she asked in a loud voice if it came with vegetables.'

American TV talk-show host Oprah Winfrey, on how wealth and fame had changed her: 'My feet are still planted firmly on the ground; they are just in more expensive shoes.'

When Michael J Fox was asked if being short had hindered his acting career, he said, 'You know what the difference between a short actor and a short star is? The short actor stands on an applecart, and the short star has them dig ditches for everybody else!'

Comedienne Lily Tomlin once prophesied: 'There will be sex after death—we just won't be able to feel it.'

When Marlene Dietrich was approached to endorse a product on TV, she said, 'I would never do a TV commercial, it totally destroys a star's image. The most ludicrous thing I ever saw was John Wayne dressed as a cowboy sitting on a horse, praising the effectiveness of a headache powder.'

Dorothy Parker: 'Scratch an actor and you'll find an actress.'

Bette Davis once said of Joan Crawford: 'The best time I ever had with Joan Crawford was when I pushed her down the stairs in *Whatever Happened to Baby Jane*?'

Barry Humphries, the master of Dame Edna Everage, was once banned by an airline after he pretended to throw up in flight into a sick bag. He then asked the hostess for a spoon and fork, and proceeded to eat the contents of the bag. The other passengers were horrified; they didn't know that Barry had secretly emptied a Russian salad into the bag before take-off.

In *Crimes and Misdemeanors*, Woody Allen claimed that 'The last time I was inside a woman was when I visited the Statue of Liberty.'

Comedian Rodney Dangerfield: 'If it weren't for pickpockets, I'd have no sex life at all.'

The outspoken actress Tallulah Bankhead once said, 'It's the good girls who keep diaries, the bad girls never have the time.'

Woody Allen: 'I'm a practising heterosexual, but bisexuality immediately doubles your chances for a date on a Saturday night.'

Phyllis Diller said she was once so wrinkled that she could screw her hat on.

When gender-bender Boy George was asked by a reporter what he would like to be reincarnated as, he replied, 'Matt Dillon's underwear.'

Zsa Zsa Gabor is a genius of the one-line quip. Here are a few of her memorable views on marriage and sex:
'Divorce? I've always been a housewife—I always kept the house.'
'What do I think of condoms? It depends what's in it for me!'
'Darlink, I always give back the ring after a divorce, but I keep the stone.'
'I know nothing about sex because I was always married!'
'I never hated a man enough to give him his diamonds back.'
'I've always said, don't marry a man for his money. Darling, you can borrow it cheaper.'
'I vant a man who only has to be kind and understanding. Is zat too much to ask of a multi-millionaire?'

After Bette Davis and Joan Crawford finished filming, *Whatever Happened to Baby Jane?* (1961), the studio wanted them to do a promotional tour across America. They were to split up for personal appearances, covering 150 cinemas, but Joan protested that Bette had been given the best cinemas and dropped out of the tour. Bette jumped in and did the entire tour by herself. During it, she told a TV interviewer how hard it had been for the producers to raise the money for the film, as no one in the industry wanted to back a movie starring 'two old broads'. A few days later, Bette received a very stiff handwritten note from Joan, telling her in no uncertain terms not to refer to her as an 'old broad'. From that day on, their relationship was never the same. Bette said that Joan wore three sets of breasts—small, medium and large—during the filming of *Whatever Happened to Baby Jane?* (1961), in which they starred together. For the final scene on the beach, Joan wore her large set. 'I had terrible trouble dragging her along the sand; it was like I was climbing over mountains. Nobody, no matter how well endowed they are, has breasts which stick up in the air when they are lying flat on their back.'

Seeing your father as a daddy one moment, then in a frock to play superstar Dame Edna Everage the next can be a bit confusing for young children. When Barry Humphries's son Oscar was asked what his father did, he replied very proudly, 'He's an actress.'

Marilyn Monroe on Hollywood: 'It's a place where they'll pay you $50,000 for a kiss and 50 cents for your soul.'

Hollywood sex siren Mae West (the Madonna of yesteryear) had the best one liners in the business, she accrued for herself a kind of negative, self trivialising allure. The following are some of her most memorable one liners:

When she signed a contract with Paramount studios she told the Hollywood press: 'I'm the girl that works at Paramount all day and Fox all night.'

'Good sex is like playing a good game of bridge. If you don't have a good partner you had better have a good hand.'

'Give a man a free hand and he will run it all over you.'

'I used to be Snow White, but I drifted.'

'I feel like a million tonight—but one at a time please.'

'It's better to be looked over than overlooked.'

'When a girl goes wrong, men go right after her.'

'Is that a gun in your pocket or are you just glad to see me?'

'Between two evils, I always pick the one I haven't tried before.'

'It's not the men in my life that counts; it's the life in my men.'

'I always say, keep a diary and one day it will keep you.'
'When I'm good I'm very very good, and when I'm bad I'm never better.'
'A little hush money can do a lot of talking.'
'I've been on more laps than a table napkin.'
'I don't know a lot about politics but I'd recognise a good party man when I see one.'
'A curve is the loveliest distance between two points.'
'You must get out of those wet clothes and into a dry martini.'
'Too much of a good thing can be wonderful.'

Al Pacino says the F word 183 times in *Scarface.* Joan Collins quipped: 'That's more than most people get in a lifetime.'

Judy Garland said of her daughter Liza Minelli: 'I think she decided to go into show business when she was an embryo.'

FIRSTS

Kim Basinger's first TV appearance was a guest role on *Charlie's Angels*. A few months later, she landed a guest role on *The Six Million Dollar Man*. The year was 1976.

Jennifer Lopez set herself firmly in entertainment history when she became the first female artist to have both a number-one album and a movie in the same week. The movie was *The Wedding Planner* and her album was *J.Lo*.

The first bronze star to be placed in Hollywood's famous Walk of Fame on Hollywood Blvd was dedicated to Joanne Woodward in 1958.

After winning the 1975 Best Actress Oscar for her role as nurse Ratched in the movie *One Flew over the Cuckoo's Nest*, Louise Fletcher was the first Oscar winner to speak in sign language from the podium.

The 1969 movie *Midnight Cowboy*, starring John Voight and Dustin Hoffman, was the first, and so far the only, X-rated movie to win an Oscar. It took home the Best Picture and Best Director Oscars.

The first mystery detective movie to win a Best Picture Oscar was the 1967 movie *The Heat of the Night*.

In 1962, 16-year-old actress Patty Duke became the youngest person to win an Oscar. She won the Best Actress Oscar for her role in *The Miracle Worker*. Before that, child stars had been awarded special Oscars.

The 1942 movie *Mrs Miniver*, starring Greer Garson, was the first movie to receive five acting nominations. On the night, it won four Oscars—Best Picture, Best Director, Best Actress and Best Supporting Actress.

In 1943, Best Supporting actors and actresses received full-sized Oscars. Up until that time, they had received miniature Oscars attached to a wooden plaque.

James Cagney was the first actor to win an Oscar for a musical role in the 1942 movie *Yankee Doodle Dandy.*

James Dean was the first actor ever to be nominated for an Oscar posthumously.

In 1939, Vivien Leigh won the Academy Award for Best Actress in *Gone with the Wind*, making her the first non-American to ever win Best Actress.

The Silence of the Lambs was the first Oscar-nominated movie to be released on video, before winning an Oscar for Best Picture in 1991.

Adam Sandler made his first appearance in a TV sitcom on the *Cosby Show.*

Lucille Ball was the first woman to wear long trousers in public in her birthplace of James Town, New York. She caused quite a stir with her bold fashion statement.

The first guest on *Johnny Carson's Tonight Show* was Joan Crawford on 1 October 1962.

In the 40-year history of Bond movies, Halle Berry is the first Oscar winner to become 007's big-screen love interest as sexy secret agent Jinx in the 20th Bond movie, *Die Another Day* (2002).

The first porn movie with a script, a musical score and a sense of humour was *Deep Throat*, starring Linda Lovelace and Harry Reems. The movie was shot on a budget of $25,000 over six days in Miami. It premiered at the New York Times Square New Mature World Theatre in June 1972, and fast became the X-rated sensation of the decade. Over the years the movie has made over $900 million.

In 1910, *Little Nemo* was the first animated cartoon to be released.

Penny Marshall (who played Laverne in the hit TV series *Laverne and Shirley*), was the first Hollywood woman director to have a movie bring in more than $10 million at the box-office. She cracked it with the 1988 movie *Big* starring Tom Hanks.

Hollywood's youngest movie producer was Steven Paul, who directed and produced *Falling in Love Again* (1980) at the age of twenty.

When *The Wizard of Oz* was first released in England in January 1940, it was labelled 'adults only' by the English censors because of Margaret Hamilton's expertly terrifying performance as the Wicked Witch.

Twenty-three-year-old *'N Sync* singer Lance Bass went through months of space training all for nothing. In early September 2002, the Russian Space Agency organisation planning the pop star's space voyage rejected his place on the next space mission because he failed to pay the required $20 million fee. Lance was to blast off to the International Space Station on October 28 in a Russian capsule along with two professional astronauts, which would have made him the first show-business celebrity space tourist in history. In late August, he received the news that US space agency NASA had cleared him for the trip after an intensive training course at the Johnson Space Centre in Houston, Texas. His space trip was to be sponsored by a number of major companies along with Hollywood producer David Krieff.

At the age of 12, Steven Spielberg made his first short movie, using his dad's 8-mm Kodak camera. The movie featured his toy trains, which he crashed into each other with drama and amazing precision.

The 1991 performance that Samuel L Jackson gave as a crackhead in the movie *Jungle Fever* won him the first-ever Supporting Actor Award given by the Cannes Film Festival.

Grammy Award-winner Bono, was the first winner ever to use the 'F' word during the show's live telecast in 1994.

Ellen Degeneres's TV character Ellen became the first female TV character to declare herself a lesbian. A few weeks before the episode aired in the US, Ellen herself came out. She was also the first female comic to be invited by TV chat-show king Johnny Carson to sit on his couch on her first appearance on his show. This is something that Johnny usually decided himself after he'd seen the guest's on-camera performance.

The first actress to appear nude on the screen in a commercial public movie was Australian swimmer and dancer Annette Kellerman. She appeared naked in the movie *Daughter of the Gods*, (1916). Esther Williams portrayed her in the 1952 movie, *Million Dollar Mermaid.*

Cuba Gooding Jr was 16 when he landed his first professional job; he was a breakdancer during Lionel Richie's number at the 1984 Olympic Games.

The first cartoon to appear on prime-time TV in the US was *The Flintstones* in 1960.

The first Smell-O-Vision movie was a Canadian thriller called *Scent of Mystery*, (1959). Special scents were released into the theatre at the required moment. John Walters attempted Smell-O-Vision in the 1981 movie *Polyester*, starring Divine. Every audience member was given a scratch and sniff card; when a number came up on the screen you scratched and sniffed the number on your card. Most of the smells this time were less pleasant than the *Scent of Mystery* movies.

The first movie with a Dolby stereo soundtrack was Ken Russell's controversial 1975 movie *Lisztomania*.

One hundred and thirty-five women appeared in MGM's *Little Women* (1939) making it the first movie with an all-female cast of this size.

The first all-dwarf cast appeared in the 1938 movie *The Terror of Tiny Town* in 1938.

MGM produced *Broadway Melody* (1929) making it the first Hollywood movie musical. *The Jazz Singer* (1927) did have songs but was not considered a genuine musical.

The first 3-D feature movie was produced in Italy in 1936, and was titled *Nozze Vagabond*. In the 1920s, a number of shot-test 3-D shorts were made. Hollywood's first 3-D movie was called *Bwana Devil* (1952), an African adventure starring Robert Stack, Barbara Britton and Nigel Bruce.

In 1979, Paramount Studios released the first Trek feature movie, *Star Trek—The Motion Picture*, starring the original TV cast. The box-office taking was a whopping $82 million.

The first public screening of a movie was when brothers Auguste and Louis Lumiere presented *La Sortie des Ouvriers de L'Usine Lumiere*, which was made in 1894. The brothers gave the first screening for a paying audience on 28 December 1895 at the Grand Café on the Blvd des Capucines in Paris; the entrance fee was 1 franc.

Diane Keaton played Kay, Al Pacino's screen wife, in all three *Godfather* movies. She's one of the first actresses to play an ongoing female role in sequel movies.

In August 2000, Nicole Kidman shot her first TV commercial for El Corte Ingles, Spain's ubiquitous department store. The location was a 1920s Beverly Hills house, where films like *The Witches of Eastwick* were shot.

To date Clark Gable is the first and only actor to play a role in one movie, *Red Dust* (1932), and then play the same role in the movie's remake; some 20 years later in *Mogambo*.

In 1985, Emilio Estevez was the youngest Hollywood actor to write his own script. The movie was called, *That Was Then, This Is Now.* Not long after, he entered the Hollywood history books at 23 years old as the youngest writer/director/star of a movie, which was called *Wisdom*.

Val Kilmer became the youngest student ever admitted (at the time) to the drama division at Julliard, in New York.

The silent movie version of *The Lodger*, made in London in 1926, was the first suspense thriller to be directed by Alfred Hitchcock.

It's thought that George Lucas's 1977 movie, *Star Wars*, was Hollywood's most commercially successful movie.

In late August 2002, *Lord of the Rings: Fellowship of the Ring* achieved the UK's biggest-ever first week DVD and video sales, sinking the previous record set by the movie *Titanic*. The epic movie version of the first part of the J R R Tolkien fantasy, sold 2.5 million copies during the first seven days in UK shops. That put sales some 700,000 ahead of *Titanic*'s total in 1998.

Courtney Cox-Arquette was the first person on American TV to utter the word 'period' in a Tampax commercial.

Robin Williams made his first appearance as Mork in a one-shot stint on TV's *Happy Days*, after executive producer Gary Marshall's nine-year-old suggested that a space creature should visit the Cunningham family on *Happy Days*. So great was the American viewer response, that a Morkan spin-off was created in a few weeks. On 14 September 1978, ABC premiered *Mork & Mindy*.

In September 1983, Vanessa Williams (Miss New York) became the first black Miss America. In July of the following year, she was ordered to relinquish her title after sexually explicit poses with another woman were published in *Penthouse* magazine.

Janet Jackson and her brother Michael were the first siblings to both have number-one hits as solo rock-and-roll artists.

Never before in the history of Hollywood has one sequel, let alone two sequels, been filmed before the first movie had been released. This happened when *Lord of the Rings: The Fellowship of the Ring* was released in 2002.

Psycho was the first film ever to show a flushing toilet.

Paul McCartney was the first Beatle to release a solo album after the Fab Four broke up. George Harrison was the first Beatle to have a number one hit single after they broke up with *My Sweet Lord*.

The first movie fan magazine in the US was *Motion Picture Story Magazine* published in February 1911. In October the same year, the first English movie magazine was published. It was titled *Pictures Weekly* and cost 1 penny.

In 1913, the London West End Cinema was the first movie theatre to erect a neon sign. It was 10 years before another theatre did the same.

Traffic Crossing Leeds Bridge (1888) was the first motion picture film. It was made by Frenchman Louis Aime Augustin Le Prince.

The Lost World was the first in-flight movie; it was shown on an Imperial Airway's flight between London and the continent in April 1925.
The Wizard of Oz was shown for the first time in East Germany on 31

December 1989 at East Berlin's historic Babylon Theatre. The movie was first released in America in 1939, the year war broke out in Europe.

Hollywood captured the first screen kiss, lasting 30 seconds, in the 1896 movie aptly named *The Kiss*. This scene, along with a couple of others, can be seen in *The Spiral Staircase* (1946).

Elvis Presley was the first star to be given his very own dressing suite at MGM studios.

On 3 May 1993, Dolly Parton was honoured by the unveiling of the Dolly Parton Blvd near New York's Radio City Music Hall. She said she was now a street ahead of any other singer.

Hollywood's very first movie premiere was held at the Egyptian Theatre in 1922. The movie was *Robin Hood*, starring Wallace Beery, Alan Hale and Douglas Fairbanks Sr.

1933 saw the first teaming of Fred Astaire with Ginger Rogers in *Flying Down to Rio*.

The first movie shot in Hollywood was *The Straw Man*, made in 1913 by Cecil B De Mille, Samuel Goldwyn and Jesse Lasky. It cost $15,000 and earned more than $250,000, which was then a great deal of money.

Sam Lucas was the very first black actor to play a lead in a movie. It was *Uncle Tom's Cabin* (1914), a silent movie.

Who's Afraid of Virginia Woolf? (1966) was the first Hollywood movie to use four-letter words and go out on general release. Elizabeth Taylor won an Oscar for Best Actress in it. It is listed in the Oscar Pictorial History as the film that broke Hollywood taboos for adult material.

On the Beach was the first film to premiere simultaneously in major cities throughout the world on 17 December 1959.

Spencer Tracy narrated the first Cinerama fiction movie *How the West Was Won* (1963).

The stage show *Oh, Calcutta* opened off-Broadway in 1969, and brought full-frontal nudity to the American stage for the first time.

Omar Sharif's second movie, in 1953, was the Egyptian production *The Blazing Sun* and was the first Arabic movie to show two people kissing.

Dr No (1964) was the first James Bond movie with Sean Connery as superspy 007.

CARTOONS

In 1955, the Catholic Church was adamant in its condemnation of the cartoon movie *Lady and the Tramp*. The reason was the dogs portrayed an unwed couple; the movie went on to be one of that year's biggest movies at the box-office.

Hollywood dancer Marge Champion was used as the human model for Snow White in the movie. Her every dance movement was transferred to the cartoon character.

It's believed that every day 5 million Americans and tourists buy items modelled on Mickey Mouse.

Originally the 1960s–70s TV hit *The Beverly Hillbillies* was written to be a cartoon; that's why most of the characters looked and sometimes acted like cartoon characters.

One of the first TV couples to be seen sharing the same bed on TV were cartoon husband and wife team Fred and Wilma Flintstone.

Donald Duck comics were once totally banned in Finland, simply because he didn't wear any pants.

The American TV cartoon character duo *Rocky and Bullwinkle* represented a number of General Mill's cereals in the US from 1959–1970: Cheerios, Cocoa Puffs, Jet and Trix.

As a young man, *Peanuts* cartoonist Charles Schulz took a correspondence course in cartoon drawing. He then applied for a job as a cartoonist at the Walt Disney Studio and was turned down.

In the 1998 animated feature movie *The Brave Little Toaster Goes to Mars*, the voice of the tap was the voice of Farrah Fawcett. The joke being that Americans call taps faucets.

In June 2002, US *TV Guide* magazine named Bugs Bunny the greatest cartoon character of all time. He beat out Fred Flintstone and Homer Simpson along with a host of other animators' delights. Long-time cartoon favourite Mickey Mouse finished in 19th place, just behind Snoopy and Charlie Brown.

Ricky Martin sang the Spanish-language version of the theme to Disney's *Hercules*.

Walt Disney made his very first cartoon film when he was 22, in 1923. He invented Mickey Mouse when he was 26, the same year he made his first 'sound' cartoon film. Mickey, who turned 60 on 18 November 1988, is one of the most popular cartoon characters ever created. Even today he receives more fan mail than any other human movie star in the history of moviemaking. Not bad for a character who was originally dreamed up after Walt Disney found mice nesting in his waste paper basket!

In the 1951 Bugs Bunny cartoon, *Operation: Rabbit* the Road Runner spoke for the first and last time.

Walt Disney's *Snow White and the Seven Dwarfs* was the first full-length animated feature film ever made by the Disney studios. It's rumoured that Walt had to cut a scene in which the little fellows were making up a bed for Snow White. The Hays Code thought the audiences might deduce she was sleeping with them. The movie took 750 artists over three years to complete at a cost of $1.5 million; the movie premiered on 21 December 1937 at the Carthay Circle Theatre in LA.

Walt Disney took a trip to New York in 1927 to negotiate a new contract for an animated series he'd created about a character called Oswald. On arrival, Walt found that the name Oswald had already been copyrighted, so he re-named Oswald Mortimer, who eventually became Mickey Mouse, the world's favourite rodent.

Mark Hamill, who rocketed to stardom as Luke Skywalker in *Star Wars*, was the voice of Flipper and the genie, in the *I Dream of Jeannie* cartoon TV series.

Walter Lanz created the cartoon drawings of Woody Woodpecker. His wife Grace is Woody's voice, which is speeded up a little on tape. Woody's laughter comes from Mel Blanc's voice.

In the early 1930s, a drawing of Mickey Mouse by Walt Disney sold for $1,100, a huge fortune for the time, which made it the third most expensive animation art drawing ever sold. It was sketched in black ink on a large sheet of white paper and signed 'Best Wishes from Mickey Mouse and Walt Disney.' He did the sketch at a Hollywood party in a matter of a few seconds to amuse his guests.

Marilyn Monroe was the actual model type that Walt Disney used for his cartoon character, Tinkerbell, in *Peter Pan* (1953).

Mel Blanc, the voice of Bugs Bunny since his first cartoon *A Wild Hare* (1940), was allergic to carrots all his life.

The TV cartoon show *The Flintstones* is seen around the world in 22 different languages, and syndicated in 80 countries. Not bad for a 1960s series they said would never last.

Donald Duck's girlfriend made her debut in *Donald Duck* (1937), and was billed as Donna Duck. It was not until a few years later that she changed her name to Daisy Duck.

The most used voice in Hollywood belonged to the late Mel Blanc. He's the voice of Bugs Bunny, Daffy Duck, Porky Pig, Barney Rubble, Sylvester, Tweety Pie and over 200 more characters. He worked right up until the day he died in 1989.

In May 1989, at Christies East Auction Rooms, a cel (with a production background) from a 1934 Walt Disney short was auctioned for $286,000 to an anonymous Canadian collector. Back in 1934, how many people who saw the black-and-white movie *Orphan's Benefit*, which features Mickey Mouse, and one of the first appearances of an irritable, frequently victimised duck named Donald, could have known that a single moment of it would be worth so much in 1989?

During the movie slump of 1938, Hollywood's most outrageous sex siren Mae West commented, 'The only picture to make money recently was *Snow White and the Seven Dwarfs*, and that would have made twice as much if they had let me play Snow White.'

When cartoonist Bob Clampett saw Clark Gable eat a carrot in *It Happened One Night* (1934), it gave him the inspiration for the cartoon character of Bugs Bunny. Prior to Bugs's debut in *A Wild Hare* (1940), he was called Happy Rabbit.

In 1928, Walt Disney made his first Mickey Mouse movie in colour. In the early days little Mickey was banned from the screen in Russia, Germany and Italy. Mickey's voice during the first 20 years of his life was Walt's.

In *Anchors Aweigh* (1945), Gene Kelly danced with a cartoon mouse as his partner; the first human and cartoon dance segment filmed.

FOUR-LEGGED FRIENDS

How do you replace one of America's favourite male actors? That's easy—in Hollywood they sign up the son. In late 2002, four-year-old Enzo replaced Moose, the Jack Russell terrier who was almost 13 that's 91 years in human years. Moose played Eddie for 10 years in the US sitcom *Frasier.*

The LA Pet Memorial Park, which was established back in 1928, is a final resting place for many celebrities' four-legged friends. Out of the 40,000 animals buried there, are the pets of Hollywood celebrities including: Charlie Chaplin, Tori Spelling, Steven Spielberg, Faye Dunaway, Tony Orlando, William Shatner, Kate Capshaw, Humphrey Bogart, Bob Barker, Diana Ross, Bob Newhart and Jim Nabors to name but a few.

The pug dog that played Frank in the 1997 movie *Men in Black* was the same pug that played three years later in *Men in Black II*. Over those three years, he became quite grey, so they used special makeup to cover his grey hair.

In the Hollywood epic *Quo Vadis*, shot in 1925, one of the lions killed an extra on the set. The attendants were very reluctant to shoot the beast because the cameras were rolling and they did not want to spoil the scene. But when the lion started to eat the extra, the producer gave the order to shoot.

A 10-year-old Jackie Cooper found it very hard to cry profusely on cue in the 1931 movie *Skippy,* which was about two boys and a loveable dog. Towards the end of the shooting schedule, Jackie was feeling very tired and a little cranky to say the least. The movie was very much a family affair as Jackie's uncle, Norman Taurog, was the director. At one point he told Jackie if he didn't start crying as soon as the cameras rolled, he would take the dog off the set and shoot him. Unfortunately, Jackie couldn't start crying on cue when the cameras rolled, so Norman took the dog outside the studio where moments later a gunshot was fired. A very upset Jackie began sobbing uncontrollably—the cameras rolled and Norman got his shot. As soon as the scene was completed the dog was brought back to the set, when Jackie sobbed again uncontrollably; this time it was tears of happiness. Believe it or not, Norman won an Academy Award for Best Director for *Skippy*.

You'll never see Lyle Lovett around horses, one kicked him as a boy and he's never forgotten it.

Around the World in 80 Days (1956) holds the record for the movie using the most animals: 3,800 sheep, 2,448 buffalo, 15 elephants, 6 skunks, 4 ostriches, 800 horses, 512 monkeys, 950 donkeys and 17 bulls. The movie also had 42 cameo appearances by well-known actors and actresses.

Rock wild man Alice Cooper always performed on stage with his favourite boa constrictor Monty, until Monty died after being bitten by the mouse he was eating for breakfast. A few weeks later, Alice's other snake, Yvonne, disappeared down a hotel lavatory.

To date only two animals have their own star on Hollywood's Walk of Fame: dogs Rin-Tin-Tin and Lassie.

Ricky Martin has two pet dogs, a golden retriever and a chihuahua. Their names are Ikaro and Pitagne.

There were three Totos used in *The Wizard of Oz*. First was a female Cairn terrier named Terry, accidently injured when one of the Wicked Witch's guards stepped on her. A second dog filled in for several days, and the third was supposedly a stuffed toy dog used for extensive camera and lighting test shots.

In 1926, Rin-Tin-Tin was voted most popular movie star. At the first Academy Awards ceremony, the dog scooped the pool with the most votes for Best Actor Oscar. The panel of judges eliminated him, making way for a German actor called Emil Jannings, who won the first Academy Award for Best Actor in 1928.

The dog Lassie was receiving $1,000 a week at the height of its career. In Lassie's contract it was stated that there be a fully air-conditioned kennel on standby 24 hours a day, along with a personal hairdresser. Lassie was really a he, but he was replaced with a she in *Lassie Come Home* (1943).

In *The Wizard of Oz*, a dozen actors played the flying winged monkeys. Clever camera work and hundreds of miniature rubber monkeys made it seem as if there were thousands of them.

For *Planet of the Apes* (1968), the makeup budget came to $1 million, 17 per cent of the total production cost. Seventy-eight makeup artists worked on the movie, and head makeup man John Chambers won a special Oscar for his ape makeup design.

While filming *Doctor Doolittle* (1967), Rex Harrison was bitten by a chimp, a duck, a dog and a parrot. After the movie, he became a strong believer in never working with animals or children.

The animal most often seen in Hollywood movies and TV series is a dog. Second most common is a horse, third a cat, and then come chimps, lions, tigers and then seals.

In an episode of TV's *MacGyver,* they sawed off the horn of a rhino. The TV Production Company received thousands of letters complaining that this was illegal. Then the truth came out; it was a very realistic-looking mechanical rhino-head, which cost the production company $40,000.

Elvis Presley's favourite pet was a collie named Baba that appeared with him briefly in the 1966 movie *Paradise, Hawaiian Style*.

In the 1972 movie *The Godfather* the horse's head in the bed was a real one and not a movie prop.

The dashing, snow-white stallion Topper, who galloped his way through the *Hopalong Cassidy* movies years ago, is buried in the LA Pet Memorial Park in a specially made casket 9 feet long and 7 feet wide. William Boyd, who played Hopalong, gave specific instructions about where his beloved horse should be buried. Over the years, a number of visitors to the pet cemetery say they have seen Topper trotting through the tombstones. The caretaker says the sightings and stories are more than just wild imagination; he too has seen Topper more than once.

OSCARS, RECORDS AND OTHER AWARDS

January 2003 saw Nicole Kidman join a handful of Australian entertainers with her star on the world famous Hollywood Walk of Fame, in pride of place outside the Kodak Theatre, home of the Academy Awards ceremony. Hers was the 2,211th star to be honoured since its inception in 1958. Only a few Australians: Errol Flynn, Olivia Newton-John and the *Bee Gees* have won a place on Hollywood Blvd.

In 1986 Halle Berry was first runner-up in the Miss USA Beauty Pageant. In high school, she was prom queen as well as the editor of the school paper and class president.

Queen Latifah wore a $3 million Harry Winston designer necklace to the 2003 Academy Awards consisting of 1,055 pure white diamonds.

Anna Paquin made history when she presented the 1994 Best Supporting Oscar at the Academy Awards ceremony, making her the youngest person ever to present an oscar she; was 12 years old.

In April 2003 the UK magazine *Hello* asked their readers to vote for their all-time 'Oscar-Winning Golden Boy' with a rare combination of talent, sex appeal and charisma most personifies the ultimate leading man. Some 13,000 readers in the UK voted online. *Hello* magazine readers' Top 10 Oscar-winning Leading Men:

1. Russell Crowe
2. Nicolas Cage
3. Paul Newman
4. Denzel Washington
5. Daniel Day-Lewis
6. Robert De Niro
7. James Stewart
8. Gregory Peck
9. Clark Gable
10. Marlon Brando

On 10 September 2000, the stage show *Cats* played its final performance at the Winter Garden Theatre in New York. To that date, it had played 7,485 performances, a record for any show ever produced on Broadway.

At the age of eight, Justin Henry became the youngest Oscar nominee for his role in the 1979 movie *Kramer vs Kramer.*

In 1978, actress Maggie Smith won herself the Best Supporting Oscar for playing the role of an actress who was up for an Oscar but lost, in the movie *California Suite*.

Alfred Hitchcock only received one Oscar; it was the Thalberg Memorial Oscar in 1967.

The 1958 movie *Gigi*, starring Louis Jourdan and Leslie Caron, received nine Oscars. At the time this was a record for a single movie.

In 1956, the Oscar for the Best Screenplay was awarded to the French movie *The Red Balloon,* which never had a single line of dialogue.

In 1987, not one American movie director was nominated for an Oscar.

The first time the envelopes were sealed at an Academy Awards ceremony was in 1940.

In 1986, Paul Newman and his wife actress Joanne Woodward became the second married couple to win acting Oscars. The other married couple was Vivian Leigh and Laurence Olivier.

Four days before the 2002 Oscars, thieves stole Angelina Jolie's $10,000 gown, along with another one-off designer gown by British designer Scott Henshall, hours before hers was to be flown to her in LA. 'I would offer a cash reward to anyone who returned them in time,' Scott told the *London Evening Standard* after the incident. 'There were 20 outfits in the collection and now the two most glamorous have gone. There is no way I can remake Angelina's or the other in time.' Scott was shopping in Knightsbridge when thieves slashed through his parked BMW soft-top roof and stole the one-off gowns, accessories and jewellery worth worth about $90,000.

When *Schindler's List* won the Best Picture Oscar in 1993, it marked the first time a black-and-white movie had won Best Picture since 1960, when *The Apartment* won.

In 1993, Holly Hunter took home the Oscar for Best Actress in the movie *The Piano*. This marked the seventh Oscar awarded for a completely non-speaking movie role.

When Susan Sarandon accepted her Oscar in 1995, she made history by becoming the first actress to win the Best Actress Oscar for playing a nun—the movie was *Dead Man Walking*.

When Roberto Benigni took the Best Actor Oscar for the 1998 movie *Life Is Beautiful*, it marked the first time a foreign actor in a foreign-language movie had won. Up to that date, only Sophia Loren had won Best Actress Oscar for her role in *Two Women* back in 1961.

On 16 December 2002, Michael J Fox was awarded his own star on the Hollywood Walk of Fame—number 2,209. It also marked the opening day of his starring role in the 1985 movie *Back to the Future* with a release of the movie on DVD.

John Huston is the only person to direct both his parent and his child to winning Oscars. John directed his dad, Walter, in *The Treasure of the Sierra Madre*, 1948, and his daughter, Anjelica, in *Prizzi's Honour*, 1985. Both won Best Supporting Oscars for their roles.

It's been said that Russell Crowe keeps his Oscar in a chicken barn on his Australian farm; he says it increases the size of the eggs his hens lay.

Composer, singer, pianist and arranger Randy Newman was nominated 16 times for an Oscar before winning his first in 2002 for Best Song *If I Didn't Have You* from *Monsters Inc*.

Alfred Uhry is the only Pulitzer Prize and Oscar winner to win for adapting his own work. It was for his play *Driving Miss Daisy*, which won the Pulitzer Prize for drama; his adaptation won best adapted screenplay in 1989.

The only blind person to receive an Oscar was Stevie Wonder for the song *I Just Called to Say I Love You* from the movie *The Woman in Red* (1984).

To date, Luise Rainer and Jodie Foster are the only actresses to receive two Oscars before turning 30.

At the 2002 Governor's Ball, held every year after the TV Emmy Awards show, 2,100 bottles of wine were drunk. In the press tent, 600 cans of Diet Coke were drunk, and over the Emmys weekend rehearsals and live telecast, 40 producers drank 1,282 cups of coffee and tea. There were 14 metal detectors at the LA Shrine Auditorium where the Emmys took place.

In a run-up to the 2001 Academy Awards, Russell Crowe became the target of an abduction, during which he received protection from the FBI.

In the 1930s, Edward G Robinson held the record for being the most shot-at actor. He was shot to death at the end of *Little Caesar* (1931), *Silver Dollar* (1932), *I Love a Woman* (1933), *Barbary Coast* (1935), *Bullets or Ballots* (1936) and *Kid Calahad* (1937). In fact, the record still stands.

In 1978, reggae singing legend Bob Marley was awarded the United Nations Medal of Peace.

In September 2002, Brad Pitt and Angelina Jolie were voted the celebrities with the sexiest lips.

Susan Sarandon keeps her Oscar on a pedestal in the guest bathroom, right next to her two anatomically correct Italian Oscars.

The 2003 Oscars were meant to mark the final showbiz appearance of double Oscar winner Dame Elizabeth Taylor, one of Hollywood's greatest legends. She was to take part in the line-up featuring previous Oscar winners as part of celebrations to mark the Academy's 75th anniversary. It would have been her goodbye to her millions of fans via TV. Days before the ceremony she decided not to attend because of the war in Iraq. She said her appearance would have been disrespectful to the people in the war who had lost or were going to lose their lives.

When actress Halle Berry was handed the Oscar for her role in the 2002 movie *Monster's Ball,* Oscar history was made. She was the first African-American woman to win Best Actress. At the same ceremony, Denzel Washington was the first African-American man to win Best Actor for *Training Day.* Some say that Sidney Poitier, was the first, however, this is not true because he was of Jamaican heritage.

Matt Damon's date at the 1997 Oscars was his mum. That night he won the Oscar for *Good Will Hunting.*

In July 2002, Steven Spielberg was awarded a Bachelor of Arts degree. He graduated from the California Film School 33 years after he dropped out before finishing the course.

September 2002 saw Oprah Winfrey become the first recipient of the prestigious Bob Hope Humanitarian Award at the 54th Annual Primetime Emmy Awards. The award is presented to individuals in the industry whose humanitarian efforts have had a lasting impact on society. Tom Hanks presented her with the high-profile award.

In Florida 1990, Kurt Russell, driving a boat owned by fellow actor Don Johnson, finished only in seventh place in the Key West Offshore Professional Tour World Championship after the boat broke down.

Bo Derek holds the record for receiving the most fan mail in the 1980s—about 50,000 letters and cards a week.

Canadian actor Martin Short has received the Order of Canada, which is the equivalent of receiving a British Knighthood.

In 1981, Henry Fonda won the Oscar for playing the dying octogenarian Norman Thayer in *On Golden Pond*. He was too ill to attend the glittering ceremony but did watch the live telecast from his sickbed at home. His daughter Jane accepted the trophy on his behalf, telling her dad she was leaving the theatre immediately and bringing the Oscar to him.

At the 2002 Billboard Awards, Beyonce's skirt was so tight she had to be lifted onto the stage.

In August 2002, Paul Simon replaced Sir Paul McCartney as one of the recipients of the Kennedy Centre Honours. Sir Paul was unable to attend, due to a personal obligation. According to the Kennedy Centre, Sir Paul would be on the list of honourees for 2003.

In August 2002, Oscar winner Russell Crowe got an unexpected award—the *Autograph Collectors* magazine put him top of their award list as the worst autograph signer. The magazine said that Russell is rude to autograph hunters. Britney Spears was a close runner-up.

In August 2002, the BBC polled more than 30,000 people to come up with the A list of 100 celebrities. There were only 15 entertainers on the list: Julie Andrews, David Attenborough, David Bowie, Richard Burton, Charlie Chaplin, Michael Crawford, Bob Geldof, George Harrison, John Lennon, John Lydon (Johnny Rotten), Paul McCartney, Freddie Mercury, Eric Morecambe, George O'Dowd (Boy George) and Robbie Williams.

English actor John Cleese won an Emmy Award for his guest appearance on the hit American TV series *Cheers*.

At the 1989 Oscar ceremony in LA, Rob Lowe poked fun at himself singing *Proud Mary* with Snow White. The worldwide televised prank backfired big time, when Disney sued the Academy for breach of copyright.

The day after Cher won the Best Actress Oscar for her role in *Moonstruck*, her ex-husband Sonny Bono was elected mayor of Palm Springs.

Hollywood costume designer Edith Head was nominated for 35 Oscars during her long career in the movies, which started in 1938. She won eight Oscars, from *The Heiress* in 1950 to *The Sting* in 1974. A title she earned for herself was 'The First Diva of Hollywood Design'.

In 1998, when Gwyneth Paltrow won the Academy Award for the Best Actress for the role of Viola in *Shakespeare in Love*, she was likened to a modern-day Grace Kelly.

Kevin Spacey bought the 1945 Oscar presented to composer George Stoll for the movie *Anchors Aweigh* at an auction. He then donated it back to the Academy.

Ricky Schroder won a Golden Globe at the age of nine for his role in the 1979 movie *The Champ*.

Running for 849 performances, musician/comic Victor Borge has the record for the longest-running one-man show ever to play on Broadway.

Sean Penn didn't attend the 1996 Oscar ceremony, even though he was up for an Oscar for *Dead Man Walking*. The reason was his wife Robin needed to have an emergency gall-bladder operation that night.

Up until 1931, the Academy Award trophy, a figure of a man with a Crusader's sword standing on a reel of film, was simply called the Statuette. Then in January 1931, Margaret Herrick, an Academy librarian, just chanced to remark, 'He looks a lot like my Uncle Oscar', and from that minute on the nickname stuck.

Susan Lucci was nominated for an Emmy 19 times for Best Actress in a Daytime TV series; the curse ended in 1999 when she won. The following year, she hosted the Emmy telecast, but was overlooked for a nomination.

In 1996, David Bowie didn't turn up for his induction into the Rock and Roll Hall of Fame.

Russell Crowe's grandfather was a cinematographer of war documentaries, for which he was awarded Member of the Order of the British Empire. Russell wore the medal to the 2001 Academy Awards in honour of his memory, to accept the Best Actor Oscar for his role in *Gladiator*. He later found out that the medal must technically be worn only by the person on whom it was bestowed.

In June 1991, New York's Sixth Avenue was renamed 'Minnelli Way' for a day in Liza Minnelli's honour as she performed at Radio City Music Hall.

In 1978, *The Wizard of Oz* was voted the third-best movie ever made by the American Film Institute.

The very first Academy Awards presentation was held in the Blossom Room of the Roosevelt Hotel, Hollywood on 16 May 1929. Tickets were $10 each.

Walt Disney received the most Oscars in the history of the Academy Awards. In all, he was presented with 26 gold statues.

Eddie Murphy holds the Hollywood award record for the highest number of swear words in a movie. *Harlem Nights* has 262 dirty words—one every 33 seconds.

On 12 September 1991, LA mayor Tom Bradley proclaimed it to be Freddy Krueger Day, in honour of the fictional serial killer who has rampaged through the gruesome *Nightmare On Elm Street* movie series. Robert Englund, who played Freddy, was on hand to accept the proclamation.

Movie art director Cedric Gibbons designed the Oscar Award in 1928. It stands 13½ inches high, and is cast in solid Britannia metal, electroplated with 18-carat gold—it weighs 8½ pounds. The Dodge Trophy Company in California makes the statuettes at a cost of $200 per Oscar. No Oscar is ever meant to be sold; it must first be offered back to the Academy of Motion Picture Arts and Sciences.

On 26 October 1965, the *Beatles* received their MBEs at Buckingham Palace. Then on 23 November 1969, John Lennon returned his MBE in protest against British involvement in Biafra, and British support of US involvement in Vietnam.

When Groucho Marx was in Cannes, France, to receive a decoration (the French Commandeur des Arts et Lettrs) from the French President, he received an invitation to appear at a Royal Command Performance in England. Groucho said that he was very honoured to have been asked to perform in front of Queen Elizabeth. He was about to accept the invitation when he was told that all the night's proceeds, including the fees of the performers, went to charity. The palace emissary was told, 'Tell the Queen that Groucho doesn't work for nothing.'

The Best Picture Academy Award in 1927 went to *Wings*, the only silent movie to win the award.

Liza Minnelli and Rita Moreno, over their respective careers, have been awarded an Emmy, Oscar, Tony and a Grammy Award.

In 1926, the uncle of Grace Kelly, George Kelly, won a Pulitzer Prize for drama.

One of the most touching moments at any Oscar ceremony was when Louise Fletcher signed along with her moving acceptance speech. She is the daughter of deaf parents, and said she wanted to tell them of her 'special gratitude'. Jill Ireland presented Louise with the Oscar for Best Actress for *One Flew Over the Cuckoo's Nest* (1975).

At the age of six, Shirley Temple won a special Oscar Award for her outstanding contribution to screen entertainment during 1934. But Tatum O'Neal is the youngest person to receive a regular Academy Award; she was nine when she won the Oscar for Best Supporting Actress for her role in *Paper Moon* (1973).

The Grammy Award is one of the music world's most prestigious awards, and over the years it has also honoured the spoken word, documentary, children's stories, comedy and poetry. Among the winners have been: Martin Luther King Jr, Orson Welles, Garrison Keillor, Eddie Murphy, Jim Henson's Muppets and Bob Newhart.

Stars who have won a Tony, an Oscar and an Emmy Award are: Jack Albertson, Paul Scofield, Melvyn Douglas, Thomas Mitchell, Ingrid Bergman, Shirley Booth, Helen Hayes, Liza Minnelli, Cloris Leachman and Rita Moreno.

To date the only tie for Best Actress Oscar was in 1968, between Barbra Streisand for *Funny Girl* and Katharine Hepburn for *The Lion in Winter.*

When the nodules on Frank Sinatra's throat brought his singing career to a temporary standstill, he accepted a small fee of just $8,000 to star in *From Here to Eternity* (1953). The role gave him an Oscar for Best Supporting Actor.

At 29, actor Adrien Brody became the youngest person to win the Best Actor Oscar, in 2003, for his lead role in Roman Polanski's movie *The Pianist*.

In 1942, Greer Garson won an Oscar for Best Actress in *Mrs Miniver.* But what people remember the most is her 40-minute acceptance speech, which is still a record today.

Jane Wyman in *Johnny Belinda* (1948), John Mills in *Ryan's Daughter* (1970) and Patty Duke in *The Miracle Worker* (1962) all won Oscars for roles as mutes. Jane Wyman's acceptance speech went like this: 'I accept this very gratefully for keeping my mouth shut. I think I'll do it again.' When John Mills stepped up to receive his award, he did not say a word.

Up to 1989, *Bewitched* star Elizabeth Montgomery had never won an Emmy award despite nine tries for five different TV programmes after some 30-odd years in TV.

In 1966, the Golden Turkey Award for the worst performance in a movie went to singer Tony Bennett for his role in *The Oscar.*

In 1984, Robert Jacobsen, internationally renowned sculptor, designed the first Danish Film Academy's Oscar, which he called Alta. He would not take any fee for the design, but asked for, and got, a free pass for life to every movie theatre in Denmark.

Acting sisters Joan Fontaine and Olivia de Havilland were both born in Tokyo. Joan won an Oscar in 1941 for Best Actress in *Suspicion*; Olivia won an Oscar in 1949 for Best Actress in *The Heiress*. They are the only sisters to have won Oscars. The only brother and sister to win Oscars were Lionel and Ethel Barrymore.

Clint Eastwood took his 85-year-old mother as his partner to the 1992 Academy Award. That year he won Best Director for *Unforgiven*.

Walter and John Huston, father and son, both won Academy Awards for *The Treasure of the Sierra Madre* (1948); Walter for Best Supporting Actor, and John for Best Director. This is the only time family members have won Oscars on the same evening.

Jack Benny was to co-star with Walter Matthau in *The Sunshine Boys* (1975), but he died just months before the movie was to go into production. George Burns stepped into his shoes at the 11th hour, which gave him his only Oscar for Best Supporting Actor. It made him the oldest star to receive this award; he was 80 at the time.

In 1971, Jane Fonda won a Best Actress Oscar for her role in *Klute*, making her the first member of the Fonda family to win an Oscar.

John Lennon and Paul McCartney won an Oscar for Best Original Song Score in 1970 for the movie *Let It Be*.

To date, American actress Meryl Streep has been nominated for 13 Oscars, giving her the title of the most nominated actress in the history of the Academy Awards.

The Turning Point (1977) and *The Colour Purple* (1986) were both nominated for 11 Academy Awards, but neither movie received an Oscar, making them the most nominated movies to receive no awards.

During World War II, all the Oscars given out were made of wood sprayed with gold paint. This was done to conserve metal.

Melvyn Douglas, John Gielgud, Ruth Gordon, John Houseman, Helen Hayes and Dame Margaret Rutherford were all over 70 years old when they won Oscars for supporting roles.

Hollywood's Entertainment Hall of Fame was opened in 1974. Elected as its first 10 members were: George Bernard Shaw, Eugene O'Neill, Tennessee Williams, Charlie Chaplin, Judy Garland, Katharine Hepburn, Irving Berlin, Laurence Olivier, George Gershwin and D W Griffith.

Gregory Peck won an Oscar for *To Kill a Mockingbird* (1962), which made him the first native Californian to win an Oscar.

At the 1974 Academy Award live telecast, David Niven walked onto the stage to announce his co-presenter Elizabeth Taylor, when the phantom streaker dashed behind him across the stage. 'Isn't it fascinating that probably the only laugh that man will ever get is by stripping off his clothes and showing his shortcomings', said David, dismissing the streaker. He had accomplished his 'streak' so quickly and smoothly that hundreds in the audience weren't quite sure what they had just seen. His name was Robert Opel, and he was shot to death in the San Francisco sex paraphernalia shop he owned on 9 July 1979. Two men armed with sawn-off shotguns burst through the door of his shop, called Fey Way, and killed him. All they got was $5 out of the till, a used camera and a bit of stock.

Judy Garland was the favourite to win an Oscar for her great comeback performance in *A Star Is Born* (1954), but she lost the award to a newcomer called Grace Kelly for her role in *The Country Girl*. Judy never won an Oscar.

Edith Head, who won eight Academy Awards for her movie fashion designs, to date she still holds the Hollywood record for the most Oscars for a costume designer. Before she got into the movie industry she taught French and Spanish at a girls' school.

The children of Henry Fonda, Judy Garland, Kirk Douglas and Ryan O'Neal have all won Oscars.

When Helen Hayes saw herself in her first movie, *The Sin of Madelon Claudet*, she was so upset at her performance that she attempted to buy the movie original from the studio so that she could destroy it. The studio wouldn't hear of it, and just as well. In 1931, Helen won the Best Actress Oscar for this role.

Katharine Hepburn has won four Oscars as Best Actress: for *Morning Glory* (1933), *Guess Who's Coming to Dinner* (1967), *The Lion in Winter* (1968) and *On Golden Pond* (1981).

In 1990, *My Life As a Dog* was the most rented foreign movie in the US; it was rented out 1.6 million times.

In 1948, Laurence Olivier directed the movie *Hamlet*. He also played Hamlet, and won the Oscar for Best Actor. Talk about directing yourself to stardom!

The equivalent of the Academy Award in Germany is the Bambi; in Finland they have the Snosiki.

In 1959, Shelley Winters won an Oscar for Best Supporting Actress for *The Diary of Anne Frank*. Shelley was so touched by Anne's story that she gave the Oscar to the Anne Frank Museum in Amsterdam. The museum is in the very building where Anne hid for 25 months.

Jacqueline Kennedy won a TV Emmy award while she was First Lady, for her TV tour of the White House in the early 1960s.

Angelina Jolie and Will Smith pulled out of the 2003 75th annual Academy Awards ceremony protesting against glitz in the face of the war in Iraq. *Lord of The Rings* actress Cate Blanchett said she would be uncomfortable flying from London to the US and gave the ceremony a miss. It wasn't only the actors who were boycotting the show—fashion designers Donatella Versace, Georgeo Armani and Matthew Williamson were not on hand to personally dress the stars as they didn't want to take the risk of flying to the US. Many of the stars wore peace dove badges. Rumour was many of the stars arrived at the Oscars in bullet proof limousines. Up to and including 2003 the Academy Awards have been postponed only three times in the Academy's history. For the 1938 floods in Los Angeles, in the wake of the assassination of Martin Luther King Jr and after the 1981 attempted assassination of President Ronald Reagan. Otherwise, the show has always gone on!

Hollywood Composer Victor Young,was nominated 19 times for an Academy Award, but won only one. In 1956, he was awarded the Oscar for Best Scoring of a Dramatic or Comedy Picture for *Around the World in 80 Days*. Sadly, Victor died four months before the ceremony, never knowing he'd won an Oscar.

Spencer Tracy, Peter Finch and James Dean were all nominated for Oscars posthumously.

Writer Dudley Nichols who was a militant member of the American Screenwriter's Guild, was the first person to refuse an Academy Award. He refused to accept the Best Writing Award for *The Informer* (1935).

In May 2000, when Elizabeth Taylor (68) flew to London to receive her Damehood from Queen Elizabeth II, she packed 24 pieces of luggage for her two-week stay. At the airport and on arrival at the Savoy Hotel, two porters needed two large carts to move the baggage, enough for at least 10 first-class passengers.

John Avildsen won the Best Director Oscar in 1976 for *Rocky.* A low-budget movie, it was nominated for nine Academy Awards and won three, for Best Picture and Best Film Editing as well as Best Director. Writer/leading actor Sylvester Stallone was nominated for two awards but won neither.

In November 1989, a US judge ruled that anyone could own an Oscar statuette, Hollywood's most coveted prize. Judge Laughlin Waters ruled that the copyright on the famous figure was invalid because it had been distributed without the necessary mark from the first Academy Award's ceremony in 1929 until 1941. This final ruling was made in a lawsuit brought by the Academy of Motion Pictures Arts and Sciences against a Chicago firm, which makes Oscar-like 'Star Awards' statuettes for American corporations.

The only sequel to win a Best Film Oscar is *The Godfather Part II* (1974). The original *Godfather* (1972) also won the award.

Paul Newman was nominated six times for an Oscar before he finally won an honorary one in 1985 for his combined work. Ironically, he won a 'real' one the next year for his role in *The Colour of Money.*

In 1978, British actress Maggie Smith became the only person to win an Oscar by playing a woman who loses an Oscar, in the movie *Californian Suite*.

The first black person to win an Oscar was Hattie McDaniel in 1939, for her wonderful performance as Mammy in *Gone with the Wind.*

Alfred Hitchcock never won an Academy Award for Best Director of a movie.

Gone with the Wind (1939) was the first colour movie to win the Best Picture Oscar.

When Spencer Tracy won an Academy Award for his role in *Captains Courageous* (1937), he found his Oscar was engraved with the name Dick Tracy. Spencer never had the engraving changed; he always thought it was very funny.

One Oscar was unclaimed for 40 years. It was the first Academy Award for a documentary, won by *Krakatoa* (1932). Joe Rock was the producer, but at the time the Awards were announced he was in England, so there was nobody to accept the Oscar. When he returned to America some years later, he was unable to prove his entitlement to the award, as he didn't get a credit on the movie. It wasn't till mid 1973, that a document was found proving that Joe did produce the movie, and he picked up his prize.

In 1991, Sinead O'Connor was staying at New York's Plaza Hotel when she received a fan letter from Raquel Welch applauding her Grammy boycott. After reading the letter Sinead said, 'I'm going to give the letter to my dad. He's a big fan of hers.'

Linda Hunt is the only actress to win an Oscar for playing a man. She got the 1983 Best Supporting Actress award for portraying a male photographer in *The Year of Living Dangerously*. Then in 2000, Hilary Swank won the Best Actress award for playing a boy in the movie *Boys Don't Cry*.

In 1938, actress Alice Brady broke her ankle, which kept her from attending the Oscar Night presentation. She was announced as Best Supporting Actress for her role in the movie *In Old Chicago*. A mystery man very graciously accepted on her behalf, then vanished with it. They never found him or the Oscar, but Alice received another statuette.

Best Actress (*Norma Rae*, 1979) Sally Field, stepped forward to accept her award, having the last laugh on co-nominees Jill Clayburgh, Jane Fonda and Marsha Mason. You see, all these actresses turned the role down.

Despite being one of Hollywood's hottest stars in her heyday and making more than 25 movies, Marilyn Monroe was never once nominated for an Academy Award.

In 1991, the *I Love Lucy* TV series and its co-star, the late Desi Arnaz, were inducted into the 'Television Academy Hall Of Fame'. At the ceremony their two children accepted the award.

Charlie Chaplin's movie *Limelight* was banned for 20 years in America, simply because of Charlie's political stance. It premiered on American screens in 1972, and won an Oscar.

Oscar-winning actress Marlee Matlin was 18 months old when she lost her hearing as a result of roseola, which is a form of measles.

In 1992, at the 34th Annual Grammy Awards, Barbra Streisand received a special Grammy Legend Award for lifetime achievement.

In 1992, Hollywood movie director/producer Hal Roach was honoured at the 64th Academy Awards. He walked on stage unaided at the age of 100.

Oscar Hammerstein II is the only Oscar to win an Oscar.

By the time she was 27, Barbra Streisand had won a Tony, Grammy, Emmy, Oscar and a Golden Globe.

Sylvester Stallone was named worst actor of the 1980s in the 1989 10th annual Golden Raspberry Awards.

When *From Here to Eternity* (1953), won eight major Academy Awards, the movie tied the record held by *Gone with the Wind*. This record stood for six years, until *Ben Hur* won 11 Oscars then in 1989 *Titanic* equalled *Ben Hur* by winning 11 Academy Awards. On accepting his Oscar, the movie's co-producer, screenwriter, co-editor and director James Cameron added a very serious touch to the night's glitzy black-tie proceedings as he asked for a moment of silence for the 1,500 people who died on the 'ship that could not sink' on its maiden voyage in 1912.

On 30 March 1989, at the Academy Award ceremony, Kurt Russell proposed marriage to the love of his life Goldie Hawn on stage in front of a televised audience of 1.5 billion going out to 91 countries. Goldie was not amused.

August 1998 saw Aussie singer Kylie Minogue awarded one of the worst songs of the past three decades in a music poll held by the British newspaper *The Evening Standard*. The song was her dance standard, *I Should Be So Lucky*. Mind you, she was in very good company – pop icon Sir Paul McCartney took two spots in the worst 20 list for *Frog Chorus* (which featured noises from frogs), and for his *Ebony and Ivory* collaboration with Stevie Wonder.

On accepting her Oscar for Best Supporting Actress in the 1965 movie *A Patch of Blue*, Shelly Winters said, 'I want to thank my director Guy Green who understood the role better than I did.' She played a lush and a whore in the movie.

Russell Crowe's 14-year-old New Zealand niece, Chelsea, partnered her uncle to the 2000 Academy Awards in Los Angeles.

Mae West left the silver screen after starring in *The Heat's On* (1943), and did not appear in another movie until *Myra Breckenridge* (1970). She holds the record for the longest gap in a career. Her last movie was in a 1978 romp called *Sextette* a version of one of her old plays from the 1930s, which has become a camp classic. She played the starring role of a bride trying to consumate her sixth marriage—to a much younger man played by Timothy Dalton. At the time she was in her late 80s and had trouble remembering her lines. The director came up with the idea of having someone off camera reading her lines to her through an earpiece. If you watch the movie you can often see her hesitate before speaking her lines, waiting for them to be relayed to her. In the middle of a take, and to everyone's astonishment she blurted out an LA traffic report. Her earpiece had picked up the frequency of an LA police traffic report. Oblivious to what she had said she carried on acting as if nothing had happened, of course that take never got to the screen.

In 1997 Joan Collins received the OBE from the Queen, she said how proud she was to receive the honour. 'To me, it's one of the reasons why I will always be British. I've lived in America for a long time and my friends ask me why I haven't become an American citizen. It's because I love everything British and this is one of the things that makes me so proud.'

Sir Andrew Lloyd Webber's *Phantom of the Opera* marked its 7,000th performance in London on 19 August 2003. The musical has grossed $2.6 billion worldwide.

GETTING TECHNICAL

The tattoos on Ralph Fiennes's back, in the movie *Red Dragon*, took between seven and eight hours to apply. Five people mapped out the tattoos on his back legs and butt while he lay naked on a massage table. They were painted with a special fixer, but after three days they had to be completely redone.

The number of crew members that worked on the movie *Stuart Little* included 136 in visual effects, 23 in the art department, 29 in the sound department and 26 in the special-effects department.

Daniel Day-Lewis spoke with a New York accent during the entire production of the movie *Gangs of New York*—even when he wasn't on set. Daniel is an actor who becomes totally absorbed in his character. He kept fighting during a scene with Leonardo DiCaprio and accidentally broke his nose.

Tobey Maguire, star of the *Spider-Man* movies, doesn't drink or smoke.

Gary Burghoff, who played 'Radar' in the smash-hit TV series *M*A*S*H*, was the only actor to appear in both the movie and the TV series. In the 1970 movie, director Robert Altman allowed the actors to improvise most of their dialogue. It didn't do the movie any harm because it won an Oscar for Best Screenplay.

A special version of the 1970 movie *Patton* was released for the Italian market. All of the scenes set in the German Military Headquarters, and any appearances of German officers were cut, making the movie 21 minutes shorter.

So he could do the raspy voice of a 120-year-old man in the 1970 movie *Little Big Man*? Dustin Hoffman would scream at the top of his lungs for hours before he went in front of the cameras.

George Lucas, who directed the 1973 movie *American Graffiti*, looked at over a thousand cars before he settled on the 300 pre-1962 cars he needed for the movie.

A fan of the 1961 movie, *One Hundred And One Dalmatians*, supposedly counted frame-by-frame, all the black spots in the movie, and came up with a grand total of 6.5 million spots.

There are no women with speaking roles in the 1962 movie, *Lawrence of Arabia*.

Over 100 makeup artists and hair stylists were used in the 1968 movie *Planet of the Apes*. It was so hot on location for the actors in their ape makeup and costumes that they had to wait in specially designed refrigerated trailers.

Over 3,500 extras were used in the chariot race sequence in the 1926 movie *Ben Hur*. During the naval-battle scene, two ships collided and three crew-members were drowned. In the 1959 *Ben Hur* movie, they used 15,000 extras in the chariot-race scene. The movie's location catering service had to feed around 5,000 cast and crew every 20 minutes during the day and night shoots.

The 1973 movie *Last Tango in Paris*, starring Marlon Brand and Maria Schneider, was the first mainstream feature movie to explicitly depict sexual situations. America and France were the only countries in the world that screened the movie in its uncut format. For many years, it was completely banned in Italy, the home of its producer Alberto Grimaldi.

Hollywood screenwriter Erich Segal adapted the 1970 movie *Love Story* into a novel while the movie was in production. The book was launched around the same time as the movie and became a best-seller; the movie was the biggest-grossing movie for Paramount Studios at that time.

Olivia Newton-John was sewn into her extremely skin-tight, sexy black leather outfit for the final scene with John Travolta in the 1978 movie *Grease*.

In the 1988 movie *Die Hard*, starring Bruce Willis, the German version had its terrorists come from 'Europe' instead of Germany.

Demi Moore insisted her feet were covered with makeup in the *Charlie's Angels 2* movie, because she wanted to look tanned all over.

It's rumoured that Jean-Claude Van Damme had to stand on a box for close-ups with his tall co-star Dolph Lundgren while shooting the movie *Universal Soldier.*

In the 2002 movie *Gosford Park*, the cast was instructed to read books like *The Book of Etiquette* for the movie's authenticity. It contained such tips as: 'Remember that you must not go to bed when you choose, however tired you may be. It is the hostess's duty to make the first move.'

Ben Affleck and Samuel L Jackson were so cold during shooting of the movie *Changing Lanes* in New York's bitter winter months that they both wore wet suits under their clothes to keep warm.

It's rumoured that Sean Connery is terrified of spiders. In *Dr. No*, the spider scene was shot with a stuntman.

Rupert Grint, the red-headed kid actor in *Harry Potter* who played Ron Weasley, said: 'The slugs that I threw up in one scene were my favourite, because we had three different flavoured slugs. We got them in lemon, chocolate and peppermint.'

Tom Cruise did most of his own trick billiard shots for the 1986 movie, *The Colour of Money.* The only shot he did not do was the one where he had to jump two balls to sink the other—professional pool player Mike Sigel did that shot.

On Halloween night 2002, Robin Williams, who's a strong believer in dental hygiene, gave out toothbrushes instead of sweets to kids who came knocking.

When Dolly Parton is on tour and staying in hotels, she always requests that a large double-door refrigerator be installed in her hotel suite. The fridge is for her wigs, which need to remain at a certain temperature.

In April 2003 London's famed wax museum Madame Tussaud's unveiled a life-size model of Brad Pitt with a squeezable bottom. He was the first ever squeezable waxwork. Brad was very amused by the idea and provided sculptors with a mould of his rear, cast in a foam and silicone mixture for a more squeezable feel.

The reason *Star Trek*'s Mr Spock had green skin was because he had traces of copper and nickel in his blood.

The 29 body tattoos that Vin Diesel sported in the 2002 movie *XXX*, were all fakes. They were hand-printed adhesive designs by Christien Tinsley, the founder of the LA Tinsley Transfers.

Mark Wahlberg did all his own singing in the movie *Rock Star.* He trained with a professional vocal coach for six months to prepare for the role.

Matthew Lillard, who created Shaggy's scratchy voice in the movie *Scooby-Doo*, would start screaming before the take until his voice was hoarse. Towards the end of the movie he came down with laryngitis.

The house in the *Psycho* movie, which stood behind the Bates Motel, was a replica of a house which still stands in Kentucky, Ohio.

Russell Crowe learnt to play the violin for his role in the 2003 movie *Master and Commands.*

The radioactive spider that bit Peter Parker, played by Tobey Maguire, in the 2002 movie *Spider-Man*, was actually a black widow spider which was painted red and blue.

When the James Bond movie *From Russia with Love* was released in China it was re-named *007 Averted the Spy Plot.*

When Matt Damon prepared himself for the role in *Courage Under Fire*, he lost 40 pounds in just three months. He did this by running 12 miles every day, and only eating chicken, egg whites, baked potatoes and broccoli.

When Big Bird from TV's *Sesame Street* visited President and First Lady Patricia Nixon at the White House, the Secret Service's radio frequency crossed into Big Bird's microphone frequency. This meant the Secret Service was picking up Big Bird's lines all over the White House!

In 1949, top Hollywood model Robin Roberts brought a lawsuit against Humphrey Bogart for snatching a giant toy panda out of her hands at the El Morocco nightclub. In court, Humphrey told the judge that the toy panda was his. She said he had given it to her as a gift; the case was dismissed.

In 1990, the Berlin Wall was being called the 'Wall of Fame'. Here are a list of stars that made a pilgrimage to the crumbling Cold War symbol: Michael Douglas, Julia Roberts, Oliver Stone, Sally Field, Daryl Hannah, Denzel Washington, Neil Young, Liza Minnelli and Billy Graham.

Joan Collins concedes to being famous, but says it does have a few drawbacks. She can cope with the eternal curiosity about her private life, and living-in-the-goldfish-bowl syndrome, but while she was visiting the loo in a very exclusive restaurant a woman shoved a scrap of paper under her door for her autograph. Joan thought this was going a bit far!

Charlie Chaplin once entered his own look-alike competition and did very well—he came third.

On 27 June 1984, in order to quell complaints over violence in the PG-rated hits *Gremlins* and *Indiana Jones and the Temple of Doom* Hollywood invented a brand-new rating category: PG-13.

Mae West was one of the few stars listed in the LA phone directory. It was one of her little quirks; she believed her fans should always be able to contact her.

Cary Grant never said the words, 'Judy-Judy-Judy' in any movie; it was something invented and used by imitators as a characteristic Cary Grant exclamation.

In *The Man Who Never Was*, Peter Sellers was the voice of Sir Winston Churchill.

Marcel Marceau, the world's greatest mime artist, was the only actor to utter a word in Mel Brooks's silent movie. All he said was 'No'.

In the movie *Look Who's Talking* (1989) you didn't see Bruce Willis; he simply did the voice of the baby. He took no pay for his speaking role, just a percentage of the profits.

The most-quoted Hollywood movie line of 1938 was an over-the-top imitation of Charles Boyer: 'Come wiz me to the Casbah', which he is meant to have said to Hedy Lamarr in *Algiers*. In fact, this line was never spoken in the movie, and nobody quite knows where it came from.

Rumour has it that if Yul Brynner didn't get a standing ovation when playing the king in the stage production of *The King and I* he refused to make a final curtain call.

In the 1960s, miniskirts were all the rage in Hollywood and in the movies, but they were banned at Disneyland. The gatekeepers measured the distance from a woman's knee to her hemline, and didn't allow entrance to the mini-wearers unless they ripped down their hems.

The sinking of the *Devonshire*, in the 1997 Bond movie *Tomorrow Never Dies*, was shot in the same tank that was used to sink the *Titanic* in the same year. The enormous water tank is at the Baja Studios in Mexico.

Who could forget the green vomit that gushed out of Linda Blair's mouth in the 1973 movie *The Exorcist*. It was nothing more than a simple mixture of split pea soup and oatmeal.

When Dustin Hoffman played Dorothy Michaels in the movie *Tootsie*, he said that he had based the role on his mother, Lillian, who, at 72, had 'the spirit of a chorus girl'.

Robin Williams had no trouble playing a gay role in the movie *The Birdcage*, a movie about a family where both parents are men. 'I grew up in the most gay neighbourhoods of San Francisco, so I've seen everything', he said.

Anjelica Huston and Gene Hackman demanded that extra scenes be written for the *Royal Tenenbaums* to give their characters more depth.

The boots eaten by Charlie Chaplin in the 1924 movie *The Gold Rush* were made out of licorice.

In the 1941 movie *Suspicion*, director Alfred Hitchcock put a light bulb in the glass of milk that Joan Fontaine suspected was poisoned, giving the milk an unearthy glow.

Glenn Close dubbed over all of Andie MacDowell's dialogue in *Greystoke: the Legend of Tarzan*.

The 1975 movie *One Flew Over the Cuckoo's Nest* was shot in the Oregon State Hospital.

In the 1983 movie *FlashDance*, Jennifer Beals's dancing gymnast movements were doubled by a male gymnast, because the dance scenes were so demanding.

The hit movie *Harry Potter and the Sorcerer's Stone* is known everywhere, except in the US as *Harry Potter and the Philosopher's Stone*. The studio shot every scene in which the 'Philosopher's Stone' was mentioned twice, once with the actors saying 'Philosopher's' and then again with the actors saying 'Sorcerer's'.

Sean Connery has a phobia about spiders. Even with a thick piece of plate glass separating the spider from his leg, he still couldn't do the tarantula scene in *Dr.No*. The producers ended up using a mechanised tarantula; even then it still gave Sean the willies.

Mark Wahlberg freaks out about sharks. In the movie *The Perfect Storm* he had to work with one, and even though it was an animatronic shark it still freaked him out. During filming, Mark got his foot in the mouth of the amazingly realistic looking shark, but the mechanism grabbed his toe and wouldn't let go. The technicians powered up the mouth trying to release his toe. His screams were so realistic that the movie director kept shooting.

Allowing a boa constrictor into a snake-free New Zealand for the 1982 Bo Derek movie *Eve and that Damned Apple* would damage the country's image, said the then Labour MP for Sydenham, John Kirk. In the end, Bo Derek and her husband John came to New Zealand for a promotional trip, but the movie was canned along with the boa.

Despite playing James Bond in seven movies, Roger Moore never once ordered a Martini 'shaken not stirred'.

Lord of the Rings: the Fellowship of the Ring, plus the two sequels, were shot at more than 100 locations and included more than 350 sets all over New Zealand. The 14-month shoot started on 11 October 1999, and finished on 2 December 2000. Peter Jackson struck a deal with New Zealand's Telecom that allowed him to use their satellites to view what was happening at all locations from any one site.

George Cukor was 82 years old when he directed the 1981 movie, *Rich and Famous*, starring Candice Bergen and Jacqueline Bisset. This made him the oldest director ever to be signed for a major American movie.

In the 1997 movie *Titanic*, most of the women's costumes were soaked in tea to make them look much older. Kate Winslet spent a lot of time in the water at the end of the movie—the wardrobe department has 28 copies of the dress she wore as the ship sank. The dress had to be made a few sizes bigger to hide a wet suit, so she wouldn't freeze. The movie featured 1,700 extras, which were mostly locals of Mexico, where most of the movie was filmed. A studio was specially built in Mexico for the movie; since then, movies like *The Mask of Zorro* and *Goldeneye* have used it. After shooting completed, they set up a *Titanic* museum on the lot in Mexico, which is now a major tourist attraction for movie buffs.

In the 1942 movie *Casablanca*, starring Humphrey Bogart, there's something that moviegoers never saw. Bogey strapped on large platform soles to his regular shoes, which made him appear taller on screen. The only picture of him wearing the strap-on platforms can be seen on display at a Frankfurt film museum. It's a secret the studio never wanted to get out.

In the movie *My Stepmother's an Alien*, the legs of Kim Basinger belonged to body-double Shelley Michelle. She also did the body-double for Catherine Oxenberg's love scene in *Over Exposed* because Catherine was too shy to appear nude in the scene.

In 1991, Lily Tomlin learned to smoke for her role in Woody Allen's movie *Shadows* and she became addicted to cigarettes. Soon after the completion of the movie, Lily recruited a hypnotist to help her kick the habit.

The greatest number of costume changes in a movie is credited to Elizabeth Taylor in the 1963 movie *Cleopatra*.

On 21 September 1962, in *The Hollywood Reporter* classifieds, this ad appeared under 'Situation Wanted Women Artist': 'Mother of three—10, 11 & 15—divorcee American 30 years' experience as an actress in motion pictures. Mobile still and more affable than rumour would have it. Wants steady employment in Hollywood. (Has had Broadway) Bette Davis, c/- Martin Baum, G.A.C. References upon request'. The next month, she opened in *Whatever Happened to Baby Jane?*, which was an immediate success.

The hat worn by Henry Fonda in the 1981 movie, *On Golden Pond*, was given to him by his co-star Katharine Hepburn on their first day of shooting. The hat used to belong to the late Spencer Tracy, the love of Katharine's life.

Devil's Tower National Monument, in Wyoming, is a dramatically exposed volcanic core, which was the central image in the movie *Close Encounters*. Steven Spielberg totally refused to shoot any studio mock-up; it was the real thing or nothing. Folks living around the area were so inhospitable to both Steven and his crew that they doubted real aliens would want to land there.

Cecil B DeMille was a stickler for accuracy in his movies. For his 1934 epic *Cleopatra*, he sent his art director William Menzies to Egypt to find out the real colour of the pyramids. William visited over 90 pyramids at a cost of $100,000, which in those days was a fortune. On his return to America, he reported to Cecil that all the pyramids were a sandy brown, which really didn't matter because the movie was produced in black and white.

On 18 March 1991, actress Nancy Seabrooke became the longest-serving cast member of the world's longest-running play. After 5,000 performances as understudy in *The Mousetrap*, 75-year-old Nancy has no idea just how many times she has actually appeared on stage as the bad-tempered Mrs Boyle. She has been in the show since 1979.

In *Singing in the Rain* (1952), milk was added to the rainwater so that it would film better.

For *The Wizard of Oz*, MGM imported over 120 midgets to play the Munchkins. In some of the long shots, children were also used to fill in, but this was always kept a secret, as they did not want to break the illusion.

Universal Studios holds the record for the most overused haunted castle in movies. The medieval castle has been the backdrop for many B-grade horror films, as well as being featured in such movies as *Gypsy Wildcat* (1944), *Son of Ali Baha* (1952), *The Golden Blade* (1953), *The Veils of Baghdad* (1953), *The Black Shield of Falworth* (1954) and *The Purple Mask* (1955). The castle has become an all-purpose prop at the studio, and has also appeared in quite a few TV series over the years.

E.T., the extra-terrestrial model, had 150 separate movements. He could wrinkle his nose, furrow his brows, close his eyes, smile, walk and speak. But his vocabulary was just 10 words in the movie and his sex has never been disclosed. E.T. was played by three models, designed and built for a total of approximately $3.5 million by Italian artist and sculptor Carlo Rambaldi.

1953 saw the first Cinemascope movie, *The Robe*, starring Jean Simmons. The first movie in colour was *Toll of the Sea*, which was made in 1922, beating the first full-length sound movie, *The Jazz Singer* (1927), by five years.

The 1964 movie *My Fair Lady* caused quite a problem for the costume department. The extra-large hats worn by the 100 female extras in the Ascot scene were so big that an army surplus Quonset hut had to be put up on the Warner Brothers lot to serve as a storage and dressing room for that one scene.

The most takes ever recorded for a single scene in a Hollywood movie were 342, for a sequence in Charlie Chaplin's *City Lights* (1931).

The scene of the busy Indian railway platform sequence in *The Jewel in the Crown* was shot thousands of miles from India, at a disused railway station in Buckinghamshire.

In *Psycho* (1960), Janet Leigh's blood in the shower scene was really chocolate sauce, the most realistic looking substitute on black-and-white film.

It seems everyone remembers the chariot-race scene from *Ben Hur* (1959), which only lasted 8½ minutes on the screen. The film won a Best Picture Oscar.

In *Halloween* (1978), there was an instant on-the-spot change of direction where they quickly needed a horror mask. The only one they could get was a William Shatner mask (Captain Kirk in *Star Trek*). The props department quickly sprayed it white, cut off the hair and used it as their horror mask.

Janet Leigh was not nude in her chilling shower scene in the 1960 thriller Psycho; she wore a flesh-coloured moleskin bikini.

The Kansas 'twister' in *The Wizard of Oz*, was actually a 35-feet-long canvas cone. It provided such effective footage that MGM used alternate takes of the Oz tornado in a couple of its later pictures.

In 1989, when *Steel Magnolias* was being filmed on location in Louisiana, they wanted the trees to be full of beautiful Magnolia blooms. But as it was the wrong time of year for flowers, the movie company had the blooms flown in and wired to the trees during shooting.

Crispin Clover played the father in *Back to the Future*, but when it came to making *Back to the Future II*, they had to use a stand-in for his character's long shots because the script had already been written when producers found out that Crispin didn't want to be in the sequel. They cleverly spliced in some of his scenes from the first movie along with his voice.

The first colour telecast of the Academy Awards was in 1966; the first Technicolour non-cartoon movie was *La Cucaracha* (1934).

Alfred Hitchcock always liked the unusual in his movies. He made *Spellbound* (1945) entirely in black-and-white, except for one scene of a gun being fired, which showed the colour red for one-twelfth of a second.

Alfred Hitchcock originally filmed *Dial M For Murder* (1954) in 3-D, but it was never shown as such.

The Abyss (1989) was the first movie to record scripted dialogue directly onto tape during underwater filming.

When Howard Hughes made *Hell's Angels*, he really got carried away with the amount of film he used. If the movie had been shown totally unedited, it would have run for 23½ days non-stop.

Movie director Cecil B De Mille wanted the greatest special effects in *The Ten Commandments* (1956) no matter how impossible they seemed. His special-effects team built a water tank so large that the brick wall between Paramount and RKO studios had to be pulled down to accommodate it. It held over 360,000 gallons of water, tinted slightly blue. This was poured from 15 manually controlled valves over a large concrete ramp, which was 32 feet high and 80 feet long. The effect took a little over two years to build and cost $2 million, which in 1956 was an amazing amount to spend on a movie prop.

In *The Bride of Frankenstein* (1935), Elsa Lanchester had to wear so much makeup that she had to be fed through a tube.

Cameron Diaz had her eyes digitally enhanced to make them bluer for the *Charlies Angels II* movie at a cost of $600,000.

WHOOPS!

In 2002, a Toyota car advertisement for the Asian market, featuring 39-year-old Brad Pitt, was banned in Malaysia because the country's authorities felt that Brad could make Asian people who looked at the advert feel inferior.

The 2002 movie, *The Lord of the Rings: The Two Towers*, has been listed as having some 75 mistakes. Here are a few:
Just prior to the attack scene from the Orc riders you can see Aragon's horse change from brown to white, then back to brown again. When Legolas is in Fangorn his brooch is the wrong way round, in the next shot it's back the way it should be. Soon after Gandalf has freed the king from the grip of Saruman, we see him outside. In this shot, his hair is noticeably greyer than his beard, whereas earlier everything was white. When he goes back inside, his hair is now much more white, and his beard is greyer. Look at Eowyn's hair when she is talking to Aragorn about being prepared to die. In the beginning of the scene her hair is down, but a couple of shots later, part of it is pinned back with a barrett.

This is one of my favourite movie stories true or false it's a good bit of gilt-edged Hollywood trivia gossip. Walt Disney had very high hopes for the opening night of his 1940 movie *Pinocchio* with a huge premiere at New York's Radio City Music Hall. He employed 11 midgets and had them all dressed as Pinocchio and had them placed on the Radio City marquee with an endless supply of food and wine. Their job was to wave at all the children arriving at the movie. Unfortunately by the middle of the afternoon the crowd outside the theatre were treated to the sight of 11 very drunk and half-naked midgets running around yelling obscenities. The New York police were called to bring long ladders and remove them, which they did, much to the amusement of the crowd. It's a premier that neither Walt nor the people of New York City will ever forget.

In May 2003 Ben Affleck called the pest-control experts after the horror of finding his new $7 million Georgia mansion was infested with cockroaches.

In the *Charlie's Angel's* movie, if you listen carefully, Drew Barrymore calls out 'Lucy!' to Lucy Liu, instead of 'Alex', which was Lucy's character's name.

Burt Reynolds became so nervous while making his footprints in the cement at Mann's Chinese Theatre in Hollywood that he misspelled his own name.

In the 1987 movie *Lethal Weapon*, you see Riggs and a businessman handcuffed ready to jump off the building. But when they leap off the building, the handcuffs have disappeared.

There was nine years' difference between husband and wife, Richard Ney and Greer Garson. In the 1942 Oscar winning movie *Mrs Miniver*, he played her son.

During a take in the1953 movie *Gentlemen Prefer Blondes*, Jane Russell accidentally fell into the swimming pool after singing *Ain't There Anyone Here for Love*. When director Howard Hawks saw the take in the dailies, he liked it so much he kept the scene in the movie.

After winning the 1979 Best Supporting Actress Oscar, Meryl Streep went off to the A-List party at the Governor's Ball. Some 30 minutes after her arrival she realised she'd misplaced her Oscar; then she remembered she'd left it in the ladies' loo, which caused great excitement and amusement among the celebrity guests.

During filming the movie *Gladiator*, Russell Crowe broke a bone in his foot, punctured his cheek and fractured his hip.

On accepting her Oscar for Best Actress in the 2000 movie *Erin Brockovich*, Julia Roberts completely forgot to thank the real Erin Brockovich. Later that evening when she was reminded of her boo boo she said, 'I'll send her something special.'

Keep your eyes peeled for the beach scene towards the end of the Beatles' movie *Help!* An actor stood in for John Lennon, as he was not available for filming on that day.

During the filming of *The Talented Mr Ripley*, Jude Law fell backwards in a dramatic murder scene on a boat and suffered a couple of broken ribs.

In late 2002, rapper Snoop Dogg was completely cut out of the Muppets' Christmas movie. Rumour has it that Snoop's forays into adult movies before the Muppet movie came out, meant he was not the best person to be seen alongside the squeaky clean Muppets.

Take a look at all of the clocks in the movie *Pulp Fiction.* They are all set on 4.20 p.m.

In early October 2002, Halle Berry was doing a love scene with Pierce Brosnan for their James Bond movie, *Die Another Day,* when she choked on a piece of fruit. Brosnan told *Esquire* magazine that the two of them were in the middle of their love scene when he made a joke. He says Berry laughed, and then started gagging. Brosnan says it became serious when Berry was unable to make a sound—a sign that a person is choking. He says he started banging on her back, and eventually the piece of fruit came out. He says it was a good thing, since both of them were basically naked at the time and he was 'in no position' to do the Heimlich manoeuvre on her. Watch out for the quick-dry Halle Berry—she has a two-second transformation from dripping wet to bone dry as she emerges from the sea. In another scene, Rosamund Pike, who plays Miranda Frost, turns her hair from blonde to brunette between the time she goes to bed with James Bond and wakes with him the next morning. Just before James Bond plunges into the ice, he removes his jacket, but when you see him emerge he takes off the same jacket again. When James steals Gustav Graves's rocket-powered ice vehicle, look closely, and you will see a wire pulling the ice vehicle along. In one of the car chases, James's wing mirror falls off; later it's magically back.

In the movie, *The Lord of the Rings: the Fellowship of the Ring* (2001), there are quite a few whoops moments. When Arwen and Aragorn are talking on the bridge, you see Arwen's lips moving while Aragorn is speaking. After the battle with the cave troll, Aragorn rushes over to injured Frodo and brushes past quite a few large rocks, which wobble, clearly letting everyone know they are made of fake lightweight material. Take a close look at the two portraits in the oval frames hanging above the fireplace in Bag End; they are of Peter Jackson, the movie's mastermind director and his partner Phillipa Boyens. Watch out for a car cruising past in the distance from right to left in a scene where Sam and Frodo are in the field with the scarecrow. When Frodo awakes in bed in Rivendell, you can see his shirt is open, and his sheet is pulled down on the bed. The very next shot his shirt is closed, and the sheet is pulled up a lot higher. When

Boromir walks towards Merry and Pippin to rescue them, a brief shot shows that his elven cloak is open. The very next shot his cloak is perfectly closed with the broach again. Once Frodo stops rolling down the hill in the snow, watch just before the shot of Boromir picking up the ring—the place where Frodo's makeup latex hobbit foot and real leg meet is visible; it's usually covered by the leg of his trousers.

In the 1990 movie *LA Story*, as Victoria Tennant's car starts rolling away, she jumps into the driver's seat and Steve Martin gets into the passenger side. A few minutes later, you see Steve getting out of the driver's side—there was no mention of them ever stopping to change sides.

In Walt Disney's *The Story of Robin Hood*, Maid Marian wears a gown with a zip in the back. Zips weren't invented until many years later.

In the 1985 movie *St. Elmo's Fire*, there's a scene where Demi Moore and Rob Lowe are making out in a jeep. Watch very carefully, and you'll see her dangling earrings come and go several times.

The 1997 blockbuster movie *Titanic* was handsomely praised for its recreation of the disaster, and swooped 11 Oscars. But there were a number of so-called blunders right through the smash-hit movie. During the memorable scene between Jack and Rose's 'I'm flying' scene on *Titanic*'s bow, we see the sun setting off the giant ship's port side. Now in reality, if this were true, the ship would be steaming north, instead of west heading to New York, where it was going. Passengers at the service are heard singing from a hymn *Eternal Father, Strong to Save*, but that hymn wasn't written until 1937 some 25 years after the disaster. The Picasso painting *Les Demoiselles d'Avignon* is seen among the artworks Rose and her fiancé Cal were taking to New York. All the artwork went down with the ship and was lost, but that painting is on display today at the New York Museum of Modern Art. Watch out for the some of the movie crew and equipment, which are reflected in the glass door as Jack enters the dining room, and in the brass panel on the front of the Renault car in the cargo hold. The hands sketching Rose nude are clearly those of a man much older than Jack—they are actually the hands of the movie's director James Cameron. At one point, Jack tells Rose that he used to go fishing on Lake Wissota, Wisconsin, which wasn't created until five years after the ship sank. Rose as an old woman tells the salvage crew that six people were plucked from the sea. In fact, there were 13 people. Butlers used halogen lamps to look for Rose and Jack, but that kind of lamp didn't exist in 1912.

In the movie, it's stated that the third-class passengers, which Jack was, are barred from any of the services in the ship's first-class dining room. In fact, all religious services were open to everyone on board, no matter where they were classed on the ship. As the ship was sinking, First officer William Murdoch shoots a passenger, and then turns the gun on himself. History reports that First Officer William Murdoch only fired warning shots from his gun and went down with the ship. The movie's executives were forced to apologise to the residents of Murdoch's Scottish hometown, where to this day he's been hailed as a hero for his efforts to help save as many of the passengers on board that fateful night. If you look very closely, you can see a digital wristwatch on a man getting into the lifeboat—remember the year was 1912!

Keep your eyes peeled in the movie *The Two Jakes*, which stars Jack Nicholson and is set in the 1940s. In one scene, Jack walks past a very 1990s automatic bank teller.

Watch out for the waitress in the diner in the movie *Erin Brockovich* (2000), who's wearing a name badge 'Julia'. This is the real Erin Brockovich it's not a whoops but just something to keep an eye out for. When Ed loosens his tie, there's a quick cut to Erin and back to Ed, to find his tie back around his neck, and he's taking something out of his breast pocket. Then when they cut back his tie is off altogether. Watch for Erin standing in the doorway talking to someone, keep your eyes on the TV set next to the door, and you'll spot the cameraman shooting the scene in the blank TV screen. When Erin is collecting the water samples, she's seen wearing a T-shirt then a tank top that keeps changing back and forth.

In the movie *Batman*, his henchman defaces a Rembrandt painting in a gallery, but when the henchman dances by the painting a moment or two later the painting is still untouched.

In the movie *Jagged Edge* (1985), Glenn Close's outfit changes three times in just a few minutes. When she enters the courtroom with Jeff Bridges, she is wearing a grey suit. Then she gets up and makes her opening arguments standing before the judge wearing a dark blue suit with a white blouse. Then, just a few minutes later, without leaving the courtroom, she's seen questioning a witness wearing a dark brown suit and a light brown blouse.

As agents K and J interview the farmer's wife, you can see a boom mike creeping into the scene in the 1997 movie *Men in Black*.

There's a fight in a nightclub dressing room in the movie *The Man with the Golden Gun*, starring Roger Moore as James Bond. During the scuffle, a dressing-table mirror is knocked over, and for a brief second or two you catch a glimpse of the camera crew in its reflection. The next moment, the mirror is back in its original place on the dressing table!

In the movie *Forrest Gump*, an early scene recreates the integration of the University of Alabama. A newscaster announces, 'Here by videotape is the encounter...'. Videotape? In 1963? Then Gump and Dan Taylor go shrimp fishing and reel in a Mello Yello drink can. Remember, this is the mid 70s—Mello Yello wasn't manufactured until 1979. After President Reagan's assassination, Gump calls on his sweetheart Jenny, and she shows him her scrapbook on Gump, which includes a clipping from the American newspaper *USA Today* dated 1978—*USA Today* wasn't published until 1982. Then, when Gump visits Jenny's grave, he says, 'You died on a Saturday', but the headstone is marked March 22 1982, which happened to be a Monday.

When Captain Kirk plunges off a cliff in *Star Trek V*, a wire supporting him around his waist is clearly visible.

Keep your eyes peeled in the 1989 *Batman* movie when Batman, played by Michael Keaton, starts up the Batmobile automatically from the outside. You can see a helping hand on the steering wheel of the Batmobile, which is supposed to drive itself.

Harry Potter may be a kid wizard, but even he couldn't stop some whoops moments in his movie. His eyes change from blue to green as he grows up: Watch in the flashback scene, when the evil Lord Voldemort tries to kill one-year-old Harry, who has blue eyes. The 11-year-old boy, played by Daniel Radcliff, has green eyes. During a scene in the school dining room, Harry starts out sitting next to Ron. But when the food is served, he's sitting next to Hermione on the other side of the table. All of this happens without him ever getting up. Harry's seen reading by lantern light in the library, but his shadow is on the wrong wall. In one scene, he walks through a door to find the magic Mirror of Erised. Later, the door disappears, and is replaced by a solid wall. After Harry's battle with Lord Voldemort, he's left with a rather large scratch on his chin. In the hospital it disappears, but ,hey presto, like magic it comes back bigger than ever in a later scene.

In *Star Wars* (1977), way towards the end of the movie, when Princess Leia (played by Carrie Fisher) rushes to welcome Luke Skywalker (played by Mark Hamill) back from the final battle, you can hear Luke shouting through the noisy tumult, 'Carrie' instead of Leia.

In the 1989 movie *Born on the Fourth Of July,* set in 1968–69, Don McLean's hit number, *American Pie,* is playing in the background. The song was released in 1979.

There is a huge blooper in the 1988 movie *Twins*, starring Arnold Schwarzenegger and Danny DeVito. Watch out for the bottle of beer, which is standing on the left-hand towel dispenser. Like magic it moves to the one on the right during a restroom visit from the twins.

Watch out for the reflection of the crew as C3PO's head travels along the conveyor belt in Cloud City in the 1980 movie *The Empire Strikes Back.*

Richard Harris plays the role of King Arthur in the 1967 movie *Camelot*. In the movie, you can see a piece of sticking plaster clearly visible on his neck.

In the 1956 movie *The King and I*, you can clearly see Yul Brynner's earrings move from one ear to the other in the same scene.

In Alfred Hitchcock's classic 1954 movie, *Rear Window,* the plaster cast on James Stewart's leg jumps from his left leg to his right for an entire scene.

In the 1990 movie *Ghost*, Patrick Swayze and Demi Moore are covered in potter's clay during one scene, but hey presto the clay magically disappears from their hands and clothing when they turn away to make love.

In *Pretty Woman* (1990), Julia Roberts removes Richard Gere's tie. The suddenly, the next shot shows him wearing the tie, only to have it disappear again a few seconds later.

A reporter shoves a tape recorder in front of Harrison Ford as he leaves the courtroom in the 1990 movie *Presumed Innocent*. It's easy to see that the tape recorder didn't have a tape in it.

When McCauley Culkin's mum, played by Catherine O'Hara, leaves Paris in *Home Alone* (1990), she departs on an American Airline's flight 767. But when she arrives she on an American flight numbered 757—how did she change planes in mid air?

You can clearly see the reflection of a cameraman in the metal of Merlin's helmet towards the end of the 1981 movie *Excalibur.*

In the 1957 movie *Jailhouse Rock*, Elvis Presley is seen standing between two policemen wearing his prison uniform #6239; in another scene it magically becomes #6240.

In the 1986 movie *Black Moon Rising*, Tommy Lee Jones is shot at seven times from a six-shooter gun.

Near the end of the 1983 movie *Risky Business*, you see a removal truck outside the house fully loaded with furniture. A few minutes later the removal truck drives away empty; the furniture has mysteriously vanished.

In 1990, when Audrey Hepburn visited Auckland, New Zealand as UNICEF's goodwill ambassador in front of a huge outdoor rally, kiwi radio DJ Danny Watson, who was the master of ceremonies, welcomed her as 'Katharine Hepburn'. She never blinked or stirred a muscle. Then in 1992, history repeated itself—in San Francisco she was being presented with the keys of the city when Mayor Frank Jordan called her 'Katharine'. Again she never blinked.

At the start of *E.T.* (1982), Drew Barrymore and her mother, played by Dee Wallace, are eating their dinner. Keep your eye on Drew's hamburger as it goes from half eaten to a whole new hamburger, and then completely vanishes.

Chevy Chase impersonates a doctor during a scene in the 1985 movie, *Fletch*. During the front shots, Chevy is seen wearing his stethoscope in his ears; when he's seen from the back it's hanging around his neck.

Lou Diamond Phillips wears silver-tipped cowboy boots for most of the 1990 movie, *The First Power.* When he climbs through a church window he is wearing sneakers, but the shot of him jumping back out of the church window and running down the road shows him once again wearing his silver tipped cowboy boots.

In *The Silence of the Lambs*, Clarice (played by Jodie Foster) examines the room of the first murder victim. The girl's dad tells Clarice that the room has been left exactly the same since the day she died. There's a poster for Debbie Harry's *Def, Dumb & Blonde* album, which wasn't released until 1989, and according to the movie's script, three years after the girl's death.

In one episode of *Star Trek*, Captain Kirk walks onto the bridge wearing a brilliant gold shirt. A few seconds later, when the TV camera switches to another angle, Captain Kirk is suddenly wearing a green V-neck top.

In 1959, Otto Preminger directed Lee Remick in *Anatomy of a Murder.* It was a serious movie, but he overlooked a point, which has become more famous than the film. Lee Remick is seated in a café wearing a snow-white dress; a couple of seconds later she emerges from it in a pair of pants.

In the 1977 movie poster *Wings of the Dove*, it features the three protagonists, played by Helena Bonham Carter, Linus Roache and Alison Elliot, on a gondola in Venice. Despite the period setting (1910), a motorised waterbus can be glimpsed bobbing in the background. These weren't invented until well after World War II.

To settle squabbles, ads and posters for the movie *Outrageous Fortune* were reversed in different parts of America, so that the stars Bette Midler and Shelly Long both shared top billing.

When English actor Oliver Reed died of a sudden heart attack at 61, on 2 May 1999, he was playing Proximo, a warrior trainer in the movie *Gladiator.* After his death, they needed to complete the last few scenes in the movie, so the post production magic went into overdrive. $3 million later, the computer had scanned Oliver's face onto a body-double, and recreated his character.

In *Dance, Fools, Dance* (1930), actor Cliff Edwards was murdered in a subway entrance in Chicago. But there were no subways in Chicago until many years later.

In *The Wrong Box*, which is set in Victorian times, you can easily see a number of TV aerials on the roofs of the houses.

After only a couple of weeks shooting on *Elephant Walk* (1953), its star Vivien Leigh had a breakdown. Elizabeth Taylor instantly replaced her, but if you look carefully you can spot Vivien in a number of long shots, which were never retaken with Elizabeth.

Emma Hamilton was set in the year 1804 in London. In the movie, you hear Big Ben strike, but Big Ben wasn't built until 50 years later.

911 calls are free from all phones in America. So why did Linda Hamilton, in the 1984 movie *Terminator*, insert a quarter before dialling 911 when she suspected that she was being followed?

In the Oscar-winning movie *It Happened One Night* (1934), Clark Gable leaves his motel room at 2.30 a.m., drives around New York, writes a story for his newspaper and returns to his room, where the clock still reads 2.30 a.m.

In the movie *Smokey and the Bandit* (1977), Burt Reynolds clocks up mile after mile as he drives his Trans-Am truck all over the place. But watch the speedo it never changes throughout the entire movie.

The Prisoner of Zenda (1979) was set in the Victorian era, but as men on horseback ride towards a castle, a truck and two Volkswagen Beetles drive through the back of the shot.

If you look closely at the major love scene in *The Sheik* (1921), starring Rudolph Valentino, you will see a Cartier watch on his wrist. What sheik back then owned a Cartier watch, indeed, who had even heard of watches in that era?

The movie about the great volcanic explosion of Krakatoa in 1883 was entitled *East of Java*. Unfortunately, Krakatoa is west of Java.

In *The Sound of Music* (1965), which is set in the 1930s, you can clearly see a number of orange boxes stamped 'Produce of Israel' in a market scene. The story took place more than a decade before the founding of the state of Israel.

In *Triple Cross*, set during World War II, there is a scene where Christopher Plummer opens a newspaper with the bold headline 'Cost of Concorde Rises Again'. In 1943, we hadn't heard of supersonic passenger planes.

In *Decameron Nights*, Louis Jourdan is seen standing on the deck of his 14th-century pirate ship, while in the background a white delivery truck slowly makes its way down a hill.

When the Wicked Witch of the East was killed in *The Wizard of Oz*, all the Munchkins were seen singing out so that the entire land could hear. But at the first screening of the movie, it was discovered they had sung 'Ding, dong, the bitch is dead'. Within 24 hours, they had dubbed in the word 'witch' and removed 'bitch'.

If you look carefully at *Son of Ali Baba* (1952), you will see one of the corpses in the battle scene move his arm quickly; just before somebody stands on it.

In *Rich and Famous* (1981), Jacqueline Bisset boards a flight on a Boeing 747. The year is 1969, quite a few years before the 747 was launched. In 1969, the plane was still on the drawing board.

In *Raiders of the Lost Ark*, on the map marking Indiana Jones's journey, one country is clearly marked 'Thailand', but the film is set in 1936 when Thailand was officially named Siam.

In *The Viking Queen*, set in the time of Bodicea, a leading character is seen to be wearing a wristwatch in one scene.

Singer Tony Orlando made his debut singing *Tie a Yellow Ribbon Round the Old Oak Tree* in the 1970s on American TV. He was very well dressed except for one thing—he forgot to do up his fly.

Stagecoach, the classic 1930s Western starring John Wayne, was set in the 19th century, but if you look carefully you will see car-tyre tracks clearly visible in the desert sand during a couple of scenes.

In *Cain and Mabel* (1936), during the big production number starring Clark Gable and Marion Davies, a stagehand wearing dirty overalls wanders onto the set, and exits very sheepishly after a few seconds. The producer didn't notice his screen appearance until the movie had been out for quite a few years, and it is still there.

In *Carmen Jones*, the camera tracks its star, Dorothy Dandridge, down a street. If you look in the shop windows you will see the entire movie crew reflected in them.

Gladiator was supposedly an accurate historical epic set during the reign of Marcus Aurelius; he ruled the Roman Empire until 180 AD. That's about 800 years before the crossbows, maces, saddles and stirrups that were used by the movie's soldiers were invented. Watch carefully when hero Maximus—played by Russell Crowe—and the evil emperor Commodus fight over a knife near the end of the movie. Just for a split second the knife bends in the middle because it was a prop knife made of rubber.

Watch out in *The Godfather* movie when Michael and Kay see the newspaper announcing Don Corleone has been shot—parked right by the news stand is a Volkswagon Beetle. The movie was set in 1945 but the Volkswagon didn't arrive in the US until 10 years later. They also fly an American flag in the movie with 50 stars on it—in 1945, there were only 48 states.

When Helen Hunt's character in *As Good As It Gets* waves goodbye to her son, you can clearly see one of the movie cameras reflected in the window behind her.

At the beginning of the Bond movie *Goldeneye* watch as Pierce Brosnan scrambles out of a manhole, then leans against a stonewall to contemplate his next move. Look closely and you'll see the 'stone' wall bend.

In the *Die Hard* movie actor Alan Rickman comes across a dead body in a lift, when he slaps the corpse on the cheek, it blinks.

There were a few embarrassing bloopers in the 2003 blockbuster *The Matrix Reloaded.* When Neo stabs a thug with a sword, watch carefully and you'll see the sword doesn't actually penetrate him, it goes under his arm. Near the end of the movie Morpheus is sitting in a chair giving his 'war and fate' speech. You can easily see a microphone and camera reflected in his sunglasses. During the car chase, the twins shoot out most of the windows of the car that Morpheus and Trinity occupy. Seconds later they cut to a shot of Morpheus and Trinity inside the car, the windows are intact and no shattered glass can be seen anywhere. A cut on Trinity's right arm during the freeway scene keeps appearing and disappearing.

DEATH—CELEBRITY STYLE

The epitaph on Frank Sinatra's headstone reads, 'The best is yet to come.'

In 1989, when movie and TV icon Lucille Ball died, fans put up a huge billboard in Hollywood, which read 'Heaven needed a laugh!' There has been talk of moving Lucy's ashes from Forest Lawn Memorial Park in LA to her hometown of Jamestown, New York, where the Lucy–Desi Museum is located.

In June 1995, six months after his five-year romance with Renée Zellweger had ended, Sims Ellison inflicted a fatal gunshot wound to his head. Just before his death his heavy-metal band, *Pariah*, had lost its recording contract.

A matter of weeks before Chinese actor Leslie Cheung, 46, committed suicide on the 1 April 2003 he'd been nominated for best actor in the Hong Kong Film Awards, for his role in the horror film *Inner Senses*. Cheung played the role of a man possessed by a dead girlfriend who tries to lure him into jumping to his death, though he was saved by a female lead who urged him to stay alive. The star plunged from the gym on the 24th floor of the five-star Mandarin Oriental Hotel in Hong Kong's Central Business district. Police said they found a note on the body saying Cheung was plaqued by 'emotional problems'. Wreaths from fans lined the hotel's entrance within hours of his death and the website of Cheung's Internet fan club proclaimed him a 'legend forever'. 'Leslie, we will always remember you.' The site said.

Clark Gable, American movie heart-throb of the 1940s, left very strict demands that his coffin must be kept closed during his funeral. He once said, 'I don't want a lot of strangers looking down at my wrinkles and my belly when I'm dead.'

In October 1994, illusionist David Copperfield donated $10,000 for repairs on the vandalised New York grave of the legendary magician Harry Houdini.

When Richard Harris died in November 2002, it was discovered he had a Rolls Royce stored in a garage in New York, which had been there for 25 years. Friends and family had no idea it was there; they even thought Richard had forgotten he owned it.

Michael Landon appeared on three consecutive covers of the American *TV Guide* in July 1991, the month in which he died.

Romantic movie hero Douglas Fairbanks insisted on having his grave monument built like a Greek temple set in its own lake. When it was erected in 1939 it cost around $250,000. Today, it would cost well over $1 million.

On 16 August 2002, the 25th anniversary of Elvis Presley's death, more than 35,000 of his fans from all over the world braved the rain to visit his grave at Graceland. Organisers said it was the largest turnout ever for the vigil that's become an annual event.

Elvis Presley's co-star in the movie *Jailhouse Rock* was Judy Tyler. Unfortunately, both she and her husband were killed in a car accident just before the movie was released.

Director/producer Bruce Paltrow, the father of Gwyneth Paltrow, died of a heart attack in Rome on 4 October 2002; he was 58. He had travelled from LA to Italy for his daughter's 30th birthday; his last public appearance was at the Italian premiere of *Minority Report*. His death came as a surprise, even though he had been suffering from throat cancer. He directed his daughter in *Duets* in 2000, a story about a father and daughter who come together through a shared love of karaoke.

Larry Hagman revealed exactly what he wants to happen to his body after his death. No freezing, no cremation, not even a donation to medical science. He wants to be served as dinner to his friends. Speaking to the *New York Post* in July 2002, he said, 'When I die, I want my friends to eat me. I want to be fed through a wood chipper, then be spread over a wheat field, then have a cake backed from the crop for all my pals to lunch on.' He also says he wants some marijuana added to the mix for good measure. 'It makes people so much less violent than booze,' he added. I sincerely hope that he's joking—I'm sure he has a great sense of humour.

Dominique Dunne, who starred in the movie *Poltergeist*, was the daughter of American author/journalist Dominick Dunne. In 1982, she was strangled to death by an ex-boyfriend.

Western movie hero John Wayne was adamant that he be buried wearing his best cowboy boots. His wish was carried out.

Kate Blanchett's dad died of a heart attack when she was 10 years old.

A five-year-old boy drowned in Tommy Lee's swimming pool in 2001. The boy was a guest at Tommy and Pam's son Brandon's birthday party.

Lauren Holly's brother died in a house fire when he was fourteen.

Jeff Goldblum's brother, Rick, died from a rare virus after returning from a trip to North Africa. He was twenty-three.

Unknown to any of his friends and family, Peter Sellers had arranged his own funeral music, Glenn Miller's *In the Mood*.

Janis Joplin, Landmark Hotel, (later renamed Highland Gardens) Hollywood, California 4/10/70.

Jimi Hendrix, a London hotel, 18/9/70, overdose of sleeping pills and wine.

Jim Morrison ended his life in a Paris hotel, 3/7/71, suffocation after taking barbiturates.

Michael Hutchence of *INXS*, a Sydney hotel, Australia, 22/11/97, found hanged.

Leon Wilkeson, bassist for *Lynyrd Skynyrd*, Ponte Vedra Beach Hotel in Florida, 27/7/01, autopsy revealed chronic lung and liver disease.

Stuart Adamson, lead singer Scottish rock band *Big Country*, Honolulu, Hawaii, hotel, 16/12/01, from apparent suicide.

Jonathan Melvoin, keyboardist of *Smashing Pumpkins*, New York hotel room, 12/7/96, heroin and alcohol overdose.

Rob Pilatus, half of *Milli Vanilli*, a German hotel room, 3/4/98, after consuming large amounts of pills and booze.

Elvis Presley's body was buried in Forest Hill cemetery, but after a body-snatching attempt his body was taken to Graceland and laid to rest in the Meditation Gardens beside his beloved mother.

Weeks before her fatal car crash on September 1982, Princess Grace unwittingly composed her own epitaph: 'I'd like to be remembered as a decent and caring human being.'

River Phoenix's autopsy confirmed there was a presence of valium in his system along with marijuana and ephedrine. There was no doubt that it was the massive doses of heroin and cocaine that killed him after he left the Viper Room on Sunset Strip in LA in 1993. There were no needle marks on his body and nobody knew just how he took the drugs. His mother spoke the final tribute and laid his memory to rest at a small private memorial service in Hollywood. His dad, John, chose to remain at home in Florida with River's ashes. He'd been cremated the week before.

Freddie Mercury kept his illness a total secret from all the members of *Queen*. They learned he had AIDS 24 hours before the end, when Freddie released the following statement. 'I wish to confirm that I have been tested HIV-positive and have AIDS. I felt it correct to keep this information private to date in order to protect the intimacy of those around me. However, the time has now come for my friends and fans around the world to know the truth. I hope everyone will join with me, my doctors and all those worldwide in the fight against this terrible disease.' His parents didn't even have time to get to see him before he died unexpectedly on Sunday, 24 November 1991 at 45 years old.

'They shot and killed my parents! My mom and dad. My mom and dad!' An irate Lyle Menendez on the phone reporting to the Beverly Hills 911 emergency line on 20 August 1989 that intruders had just murdered his wealthy parents. Seven months later, both Lyle and his brother Eric were charged with the killings, after embarking on a spending spree that came close to depleting every cent of their fathers $15 million estate. They were convicted in 1996.

Both Kelsey Grammer's father and sister were murdered, and his two half brothers died in a scuba accident. As if that wasn't enough, his unborn child died when his ex-wife attempted suicide.

'Elvis seen in Miami supermarket!' This was a headline, which ran in the US tabloid *The Weekly World News*, four years after Elvis's death. Since that date its become a 'joke saying' around the world.

When Judy Garland died, she left nothing in her will for her children—the star died broke. In fact, she owed more than $1 million, which her daughter Liza Minnelli paid off in memory of her mother.

Nearly 50 years after actress Hattie McDaniel's death, the Oscar winner very nearly got her last wish. Hattie, the first black person to win an Academy Award, asked in her will to be buried at the Hollywood Memorial Park Cemetery, the final resting place of other great stars. However, when she died back in 1952, the LA cemetery did not take black people and she was buried elsewhere. But in November 1999, to celebrate the 47th anniversary of her death, the new owners of the Hollywood cemetery, now called Hollywood Forever, installed a memorial to Hattie. The monument has a view of the landmark Hollywood sign.

When Marilyn Monroe's agent Johnny Hyde died in 1950, it's rumoured that she spent the night before his funeral lying beside him in the coffin. In her grief, she overdosed on pills, one of several suicide attempts.

In 1980, Peter Sellers's three children were stunned to learn that their dad had left them a mere $200 each, from his $10 million estate. His 26-year-old fourth wife, Lynne Frederick, got the bulk of his estate.

At the age of 13, Katharine Hepburn went in to wake up her 15-year-old brother, Tom, who she adored. She found him dead, hanged by a braided sheet tied to a rafter. He and Katharine, the two oldest of the six children, had been on a pleasure trip to New York and were staying at their aunt Mary's house.

On 21 June 1991, only three days after his 39th birthday, American TV chat-show host Johnny Carson's second son Rick, was driving his Pathfinder near the scenic coastal town of Morro Bay, California, when his car plummeted 125 feet down an embankment, killing him instantly.

The ghost of John Belushi has appeared more than once to several people who have been in his bungalow at LA's Chateau Marmont. Guest bungalow three is where he died in March of 1982.

In 1982, on the fifth anniversary of Elvis Presley's death, an advert appeared in two Memphis daily newspapers. 'Elvis official autopsy table for sale, best offer'. Hospitals in the Memphis area denied that this particular souvenir was available.

Barbra Streisand's father died when she was just 15 months old.

In 1959, Robert Redford and wife Lola lost their first child to Sudden Infant Death Syndrome.

Richard Harris has had the last rites administered to him twice.

Carmen Electra's mother and sister died within a week of each other.

Peter O'Toole once said he keeps fit by 'following friends' caskets'.

Marilyn Monroe and Jean Harlow both made their last movies with Clark Gable.

Kristin Scott Thomas's dad was a naval pilot. When she was five, he was killed in a flying accident. Years later, her stepdad, who was also a naval pilot, was killed in a nearly identical air crash.

Yoko Ono said she would like her late husband, John Lennon, to be remembered on the anniversary of his birthday, 9 October 1940, rather than on the date he was killed, 8 December 1980.

It's said that Richard Carpenter keeps his sister Karen's clothes at a warehouse near his home. He gave some of them away, but he couldn't bring himself to part with all of them. Karen died of anorexia in 1983.

Sharon Tate's last interview took place just two weeks before her death. During the interview, European journalist Enrico di Pompeo asked her if she believed in fate. 'Certainly', she said. 'My whole life has been decided by fate. I think something more powerful than we are decides our fate for us. I know one thing—I've never planned anything that ever happened to me'. One thing is for sure, she never planned the ghastly fate that befell her at her Hollywood home two weeks later on 9 August 1969.

Movie star Peter Lawford was friends with everyone in Hollywood. He was always on the A list, and he was also a close friend to President Kennedy. Unfortunately, when he died his friends deserted him; in fact, his wife Patricia spent all her savings to give him a simple funeral. She didn't even have a suit to bury him in on Christmas Day 1984. She went to a tailor that Peter had patronised in his better days, when he was one of the best-dressed men in America.

Over the years, Hollywood safety rules have got stricter, but back in the 1980s there were a string of disasters on many movie sets:
The 1982 movie *Twilight Zone*, must go down as the most notorious of all set disasters. Actor Vic Morrow, along with two young child actors were killed when a crashing helicopter hit them. While shooting the 1984 movie, *Rambo: First Blood Part II*, in Mexico, a special-effects man slipped and fell to his death over a waterfall in the dense Mexican jungle. A stuntman was killed in the 1986 movie *Million-Dollar Mystery*; his motorbike went off a 40-foot embankment and he was gored by a sagebrush limb. Chuck Norris was starring in the1987 movie *Braddock: Missing in Action III*, when disaster struck. A helicopter crashed into Manila Bay, killing four Filipino soldiers outright. While clowning around on the set of his 1984 hit TV show, *Cover Up*, Jon-Erik Hexum fatally shot himself in the head with a blank-loaded .44-calibre handgun. The intense force of the blast drove a skull fragment directly into his brain. The 1980 Burt Reynolds comedy *Cannonball Run* turned into a real life drama when a stuntwoman was paralysed from the waist down. She also lost the use of both hands when her car crashed. A helicopter was taking off during the 1989 filming of *Delta Force 2* when it crashed, killing the pilot and four others.

A stuntman was critically injured in the 1990 movie *The Rocketeer.* A cable dragged him headfirst into a tree for a scene depicting flight with a rocket backpack.

A stuntman was killed in the 1990 movie *Bikini Island*; he landed very badly on an airbag and smashed into the rocks while practising a 60-feet cliff jump. This all happened in a split second on location in Malibu, California.

In 1969, during the making of a movie called *Catch-22: Hired to Kill* (which went straight to video, and starred Oliver Reed), a helicopter crashed into a medieval fort on a Greek island. The crash killed one stuntman and injured five others. A second-unit director was killed falling out of a vintage B-25 bomber, plummeting 4,000 feet.

In November 1986, Patrick Duffy's mother and father were gunned down in cold blood at their Boulder Mountain bar. His mum and dad, Terry and Babe, welcomed two strangers who walked into their bar; within seconds they were both shot dead for a mere $90 the robbers had stolen from their till. The killers were caught and will be eligible for parole around the year 2030.

For Elizabeth Taylor's fourth movie, she was loaned out from MGM to 20th Century-Fox for the 1944 movie *Jane Eyre*, which starred Margaret O'Brien and Peggy Ann Garner. Although she was the hottest Hollywood child star at the time, she never even got a mention in the credits. In her one big scene, prophetically perhaps, she died of tuberculosis.

Yul Brynner's final resting place had always been a mystery, but then 11 years after his death, it was located in the countryside of Central France, on the grounds of an ancient monastery. The secret site is marked only by a simple tombstone, which reads 'Yul Brynner, 11 Juillet (July) 1920–10 October 1985'. After he died at the age of 65 after a long battle with lung cancer, he was cremated and his ashes were removed from New York to his beloved chateau home in Normandy, France. When the chateau was sold by his fourth wife, Kathy Lee (a former dancer in his show), Yul was without a final resting place. At this point, Kathy was leaving France, but wanted Yul's ashes to remain in the country he loved most. For months, she searched for a Russian Orthodox Church—the religion in which he was raised—that would agree to accept his remains. After many months, she finally found the tiny Abbey de Bois Aubry, an Orthodox monastery near the city of Tours. The nine monks who inhabit it agreed to become the caretakers of his ashes. In death, Yul Brynner's acting talent is completely lost on the caretakers of his final resting place—they've never been to the movies or to see a stage show.

The James Dean Crash Site Memorial is a modern, angular, chromium cenotaph; it indicates the spot where he was killed. The memorial was installed in 1983 by Japanese businessman Seita Onishi, who personally commissioned a 120-ton, $200,000 wall sculpture for the site. Embedded around the entire monument are small James Dean medallions; avid souvenir seekers have pried some of them loose. The memorial is maintained by the adjacent Aggie's restaurant, which sells James Dean sunglass visors, postcards etc.

Ex-airline pilot Gene Roddenberry, who created the *Star Trek* science-fiction TV series, died in 1991 at the age of 70. Paramount Studios in Hollywood, where the TV series and a series of *Star Trek* movies were shot, named a sound stage after him.

Audie Murphy was only 46 when in May 1971, on a flight to North Carolina, the plane carrying him and some business associates crashed into a mountain.

The first wife of American actor Henry Fonda took an overdose of barbiturates when she believed she was going deaf; she was 49 years old.

Sammy Davis Jr died on May 16 1990, at the age of 64 after an eight-month battle with throat cancer. In respect, the lights went dark for 10 minutes in Las Vegas where he'd played many times.

In 1962, Clara Blandick, who played Auntie Em in the *Wizard of Oz*, put a plastic bag over her head in the Shelton Apartments at 1735 Wilcox Avenue and killed herself. It was the very same room where Jenny Dolly of the famous *Dolly Sisters* had hung herself with a red scarf back in 1941.

Demi Moore was only 15 when her dad committed suicide at the age of thirty-seven.

For 28 years after Rudolph Valentino's death in 1926 at the age of 31, a woman in black would appear at his grave on 23 August to place flowers. The woman in black's name was Ditra Flame. The story goes that Rudolph made her promise that if he died first, she would bring flowers to his grave on his anniversary. Ditra kept her promise until her death in 1985 at the age of seventy-eight.

For 29 years after rock star Buddy Holly was tragically killed in a plane crash in Iowa, his glasses had never been found. But then some 20 years later someone came across a pair of black-rimmed glasses without lenses in what would have been the crash area. Three weeks later, they were identified as Buddy's.

American TV star Tony Danza was totally devastated when his father died of lung cancer and a brain tumour at sixty-two. He said in a magazine interview, 'Toward the end I slept under his hospital bed because I wanted to be near him.'

Michael Palin based the stammerer he played in the movie *A Fish Called Wanda* on his father, Edward, who passed away in 1981.

On 24 September 1991, the Muppet's creator, the late Jim Henson was honoured with his own star on the Hollywood Walk of Fame. Two hundred celebrities and fans turned out for the star's unveiling, on what would have been Jim's 55th birthday; he died in May 1990.

The English actress Estelle Winwood lived to be 100 years old; she scandalised New York in 1919 by wearing lipstick offstage as well as on. She appeared in over 40 Broadway plays, along with a great number of movies. At the age of 100, living in California, she smoked 60 cigarettes a day, ate most nights at fashionable 'in' places, drank sherry and played bridge three times a week. She was married four times; she once said that even being 100 she was still 'waiting for something wonderful to happen'. She died in 1984.

In 1978, Charles Chaplin's coffin was stolen from a Swiss cemetery, three months after burial. It was later found 10 miles away on 17 May 1978. Today, it's buried under a ton of cement.

In 1925, thin was the hot new look for many Hollywood stars. When movie queen Barbara LaMarr died from a drug overdose, her studio was very anxious to avoid any kind of scandal which could be attributed to her stringent dieting. Back in those days, the studios owned the stars lock stock and barrel, and controlled every word through their PR department.

Every year on 14 March, which is the anniversary of Hollywood movie star Susan Hayward's death, a memorial notice appears in *Variety* magazine anonymously: 'Susan Hayward, Academy Award Winner Actress. 30 June 1918–14 March 1975. A Star, Is a Star, Is a Star'.

When James Dean died back in 1955, Warner Brothers received thousands of letters from his fans. The following year, the studio received some 6,000 letters of mourning, and 4 million people became paying members of the James Dean posthumous Fan Club.

August 1998 saw O J Simpson's infamous Brentwood mansion at 360 N. Rockingham Avenue reduced to a pile of rubble. The American gossip tabloid the *Globe* was quick to jump on the bandwagon, giving their millions of readers around the world an exclusive competition. In their 18 August issue, a headline read: 'A Brick from Rockingham in a Free Contest. You can win a piece of history salvaged from O J Simpson's bulldozed estate simply by entering *Globe's* great O J giveaway contest. When the walls came tumbling down at Simpson's former home in Brentwood, *Globe* was there to retrieve six pieces of stone from his patio and four bricks from his driveway. To win, just answer correctly: What type of car did O J make his infamous getaway in? (a) Green Ford Explorer (b) Blue Jeep Cherokee, (c) White Ford Bronco (d) Red Chevy pickup truck.'

In April 1990, secrecy surrounded the funeral arrangements for Greta Garbo, exactly the same as it did in her life. Swedish diplomatic sources believed that her remains should be flown home to her native Sweden. A spokeswoman for the New York medical examiner said relatives had received permission to have her cremated. She died at the age of eighty-four. On 20 April 1990, a Swedish nephew of Greta's came forward to claim half her estate. Garbo's niece, Grey Reisfield, who lived in New Jersey, had earlier been reported in the Swedish media as the sole heir to an estate estimated to be worth millions. But the ex-Hollywood movie goddess also had a nephew, 64-year-old Ake Fredriksson, the illegitimate son of Grey's father Sven, Greta's oldest brother.

American actress Colleen Dewhurst won her fourth Emmy Award two days before her death on 29 August 1991. She was voted 'Outstanding Guest Actress in a Comedy TV Series' for her recurring role as Murphy Brown's mother in the CBS series.

On 6 June 1992, on the set of the movie *The Bodyguard*, starring Kevin Costner and Whitney Houston, a worker was crushed to death. William Vitaglian was using a remote-control cable to guide a scissor lift down a ramp when he became trapped between the lift and another at the bottom of the ramp. Kevin was on the set filming at the time, although he didn't see the accident.

In 1922, Hollywood actress Mary Miles Minter's career was ruined when leading man and director William Desmond Taylor was found dead under mysterious circumstances—his closet was filled with feminine underwear marked MMM.

In November 1981, American movie legend William Holden was discovered lying in a pool of blood in his lounge room. He had been dead for several days. The coroner's report stated that he had fallen, struck his head on the coffee table and bled to death too drunk to call for help.

Teen pop idol singing star David Cassidy's father Jack Cassidy was killed in a fire in 1976, which was probably started by a cigarette. His body had to be identified by medical records.

In 1942 American movie star Carole Lombard was killed in an air crash returning from a war bond rally in her home town.

John Candy died of a massive heart attack in March 1994 while shooting the movie *Wagons East* in Durango, Mexico. The movie was released as a tribute to his memory.

It was a huge Hollywood scandal when one of its hottest comedy stars of the time, Roscoe 'Fatty' Arbuckle, faced criminal charges on 5 September 1921, for the rape and manslaughter of a beautiful young 25-year-old starlet called Virginia Rappe. It all took place at a 'wild' orgy party held in a leading San Francisco hotel, in which Virginia suffered a ruptured bladder—allegedly sustained because of Fattie's amorous advances. Virginia was found lying on the bed semi-nude, covered in blood and in great pain. She was admitted to hospital, and it's here that she claimed that Fatty had raped her. Five days later she died of peritonitis. There were three trials; two with hung juries. Finally, he was acquitted, but his career was totally ruined. He died in mid 1933, at the age of 46, broken-hearted and alone.

When Ricky Nelson was killed in a plane crash on New Year's Eve 1985, his twin boys, Gunnar and Matthew, were listening to their car radio, when they heard their dad's 1972 hit single *Garden Party* being played. Then the DJ made an announcement: 'This has been a tribute to Ricky Nelson, who was killed earlier today in a plane crash'. This was how the twins first heard of their father's death.

On 2 July 1966, the decomposed body of actress Margaux Hemingway was found in her apartment in Santa Monica, California. They had to use dental records to identify the body; the coroner's report stated that she had committed suicide by taking an overdose of drugs. No suicide note was found she was the fifth member of the Hemingway family believed to have committed suicide.

On 18 July 1989, a young man arrived at the front door of the apartment of actress Rebecca Schaeffer (she played a lead in the American TV series *My Sister Sam*), carrying a gun and a picture of her. He'd tracked down her home address through the Department of Motor Vehicles, and thought it was time to pay the star some flattering one-on-one compliments. He was totally convinced that after introducing himself to her she would fall instantly in love with him. Rebecca was very nervous at this unwarranted intrusion and tried to shut the door in his face. Immediately, the young man pulled the trigger and fired several bullets into Rebecca, killing her instantly. He then fled the scene. The next day, he was apprehended by the LAPD, and is now serving time behind bars. This was the first stalker, Hollywood celebrity-type murder; today stalking is a major hazard of celebrities around the world.

The three-foot-seven-inch high English actor David Rappaport attempted suicide in March 1990. He was rescued by a friend, and sought psychiatric help. But that suicide attempt further damaged his sagging career, because he was then rendered uninsurable. Two months later he ended his life by shooting himself.

Cass Elliott, from the group *The Mamas and Papas*, suffered a heart attack in a Mayfair apartment in 1974. At the time of her death she was thirty-two. She did not choke on a ham sandwich as the myth goes.

In 1988, singer Roy Orbison went home to visit his mother in Hendersonville, Tennessee. While he was there, he died from a heart attack; he was 52.

The MGM movie mascot Leo the Lion, who roared into the movie theatres around the world for nearly 75 years, died some 60 years ago. Leo was buried in the front yard of a Gillette, New Jersey farmhouse. The property was owned by Hollywood animal trainer Volney Phifer, who died in 1974. Out of all the animals he trained, over many years in Hollywood, Leo was always his favourite. It was Volney who arranged to have a newborn lion cub shipped from the Nubian Desert in Sudan. After six months in Hollywood, he turned the scraggliest ugly duckling lion cub into the King of the movie-making jungle—Leo quickly grew to trust Volney and blossomed into a 731-pound magnificent animal. Leo and Volney became the best of friends, and when Leo retired he romped freely on Volney's 13-acre New Jersey farm, where there were monkeys, alligators, buffaloes and even an elephant. Leo died in the 1940s and was buried on his farm; over his grave Volney planted a small tree in his honour. When Volney died his family inherited the farm, but the animals' burial sites were totally forgotten. In 1986, a man called Pearce bought the run-down property. He had wonderful childhood memories of the farm being filled with animals, and two years later both the farm and house looked a million dollars. He then commissioned a local tree-carver and sculptor to carve a monument for Leo out of the now giant pine tree on top of his grave, which, when finished, will mark the grave of one of Hollywood's true legends.

Weeks before Groucho Marx died on 19 August 1977, at 87, he said he wasn't impressed by funeral services. 'It doesn't do any good. When you're dead, you're dead. I don't want a lot of people at my funeral. I want them to go out and find a Marx Brother's film and laugh a lot.' Zeppo Marx was not invited to either the Bel Air funeral service or the burial itself. He learned of Groucho's death from a radio report.

Ramon Navarro was one of Hollywood's hottest stars of the 1920s, 30s and early 40s a romantic hero from the heyday of Hollywood films. But he was to endure a ghastly death on Halloween night, 1968. Two brothers, Paul and Tom Ferguson, arrived in Hollywood from Chicago; they had no job and existed as best they could by breaking into houses, mugging the elderly and stealing from shops. So long as they got cash they didn't care what they did. They found out that an old-time movie star called Ramon Navarro lived alone in his beautiful Hollywood Hills mansion surrounded by thousands of dollars of antiques. The two brothers found the mansion, and decided it would be an easy break-in. Because they were already well known to the LA Police, they didn't want to be spotted so they opted for grotesque Halloween costumes and masks. They smashed their way into the mansion, and found 70-year-old Ramon alone in the house. They demanded he give them money, which he refused. This angered the two brothers who went on a ransacking tour of the mansion, viciously attacking Ramon as they went. They roughly stripped the movie idol, and mercilessly and relentlessly beat him almost to a pulp. Even when he collapsed on the floor unconscious, they both continued to beat him while screaming for money, which they thought he had hidden in the house. Ramond's nude body was found the next day on his bedroom floor with a black phallus forced into his mouth and half way down his throat. He'd finally choked on his own blood and died. The black Art Deco phallus was a gift from his good friend (some say lover), and fellow Hollywood star Rudolph Valentino, which had his signature embossed in silver on the base. It was always kept by his bedside. The brothers left the mansion with $5,000 in cash—leaving a multitude of clues behind them. LA Police soon picked them both up. They were both convicted of murder and sent to jail for life.

The 1956 movie *The Conqueror* did exactly that to its leading stars and some crew members that worked on the movie, which was shot on location in Mexico – they all died from cancer. Within a few years of the movie hitting the screens, the deaths began. The Mexican actor, Pedro Armendariz, was diagnosed with lymphatic cancer; the pain became too much for him and he shot himself while still in hospital. Some five months later, Dick Powell died of lung cancer, as did actress Agnes Moorehead. Carroll Clark, the art director on the movie, developed prostate cancer. Webb Overlander who was the movie's head makeup artist had a cancerous lung removed. Both Susan Hayward and John Wayne died from cancer, and character actress Jeanne Gearson developed skin cancer.

Marilyn Monroe was and still is the best-known Hollywood movie star that ever lived. In death, Marilyn became much more famous than she had been in life. To date, there have been more books written about her than any other movie star in the history of Hollywood. There have been over a dozen TV shows, three feature movies and 10 plays on her life. Her grave is visited, photographed and has more flowers delivered to it daily than any other celebrity grave in America. Here's a full account of her life from the cradle to the grave: Norma Jean Mortensen was born in 1926 to Gladys Baker Mortensen on 1 June in the charity ward at the LA General Hospital, 1200 South State Street. Twelve days after her birth, she was placed in a foster home at 4201 West, 132nd Hawthorne. She was baptised in November at six months old at the Four Square Church at 4503 West Broadway, Hawthorne. In July 1927, her grandmother Della Grainger nearly suffocated her with a pillow. In 1931, she started kindergarten school at Washington Elementary at 4339 West 129th Street. She moved to Hollywood with a new foster family in 1932, and was enrolled in the Vine Street School at 955 North Vine Street. In 1934, she attended the Selma Street School in the third grade. In October that year, her mother bought a home on Arbol Street, and Marilyn moved into the first real family home she had ever known. Then in February 1935, her mother was sent to a mental asylum. Neighbours looked after Marilyn for a few months, but then in October she was placed in an LA orphans' home. In late August 1936, she moved into the foster home of 'Aunt' Ana Lower. She went to the Lankershim School at 5250 Bakeman, North Hollywood. She did well at sport by winning two first-place track awards in jumping and running. In December, she moved in with Grace Goddard who was her mother's best friend—Grace now lived at 14753 Archwood, Van Nuys. At the start of 1937, she moved back in with 'Aunt' Ana Lower in West Hollywood. From September of 1938 through till June, she attended the Sawtelle Elementary School at 1730 Corinth Avenue, West LA. In September 1939, she entered Junior High School, attending Emerson Junior High at 1650 Selby, West LA where she graduated in June 1941. That same month, she moved back to Van Nuys to live with her guardian Grace Goddard.

She met her first husband, Jim Dougherty, in September at the Van Nuys High School. Their first date was at the Adel Precision Products employee Christmas Party. She was 15, and the party was held at 231 South Olive Street, Burbank. In January 1942, she moved with 'Aunt' Ana Lower to 11348 Nebraska West LA where she attended the University High School at 11800 Texas, West LA. On 19 June, she married James Dougherty at the home of friends at 432 South Bentley, West LA; she was just 16. Their wedding reception was held at the Florentine Gardens, 5951 Hollywood Blvd. After the wedding, they moved into a one-room apartment at 4524 Vista Del Monte, Sherman Oaks. Early in 1943, she moved in with her husband's parents when James joined the Service—their house was at 14747 Archwood, Van Nuys. In 1944, she signed with the Blue Book Modelling Agency at the Ambassador Hotel at 3400 Wiltshire Blvd. In April 1945, she tried to kill herself by gas, then in the May she tried again with pills. In June, she had her hair bleached blonde for the first time at a beauty salon located at 6513 Hollywood. In July 1946, she changed her name to Marilyn Monroe when she signed with 20th Century-Fox Studios. Three months later, she moved into room #307 at the Hollywood Studio Club located at 1215 North Lodi. In 1948, she moved back for a short time and lived in room #334. 20th Century-Fox let her go in August 1947, so she started collecting unemployment. In December, she moved in with Hollywood actor John Carroll and his wife at 8491/99 Fountain Apt #F, West Hollywood. She signed a six-month contract with Columbia Studios in March 1948. She tried to commit suicide in September at the apartment she then shared with her drama coach, Natasha Lytess, after being dropped by Columbia. In May, the following year, she was paid $50 to pose nude in the studio of Hollywood photographer, Tom Kelly. In July, she moved in with 72-year-old Joseph Schenck, who was the co-founder of 20th Century-Fox, at his beautiful Holmby Hills mansion. In October 1950, she was evicted by the family out of the home she had shared with her 53-year-old lover/agent Johnny Hyde who'd died of a heart attack in December. She moved back in with her old friend, Natasha Lytess, at 611 North Crescent Drive. In February 1951, she shared an apartment with actress Shelley Winters at 8573 Holloway. She met Joe DiMaggio on a blind date at the Villa Nova Restaurant in March 1952, which was located at 9015 Sunset Blvd. In May, her former guardian and her mother's best friend, Grace Goddard, killed herself. In August, Marilyn put her mother, Gladys, in the Rockhaven Sanatorium at 2713 Honolulu, Glendale. She stayed there until she died in her sleep on 11 March 1984. On 26 June 1953, Marilyn placed her hand- and footprints in cement at Graumanns on Hollywood Blvd.

She lived with Joe DiMaggio from January to October 1954 at 508 North Plam. In July 1956, she married Arthur Miller in New York. Their divorce was granted in January 1961. In July 1962, she entered Cedars of Lebanon Hospital, reportedly to abort a child of Jack Kennedy. Two days before her death, she had dinner with her good friend, actor Peter Lawford, at the La Scala 9455 Santa Monica. Marilyn had prescriptions for Nembutal and Phenergan filled at Vaccinate Pharmacy two days before her death at 12025 San Vaccinate Blvd. Marilyn was found dead of a suspected drug overdose on 5 August, at her home on 12305 Fifth Helena Drive, Brentwood, California. On 8 August 1962, 36-year-old Marilyn Monroe was dressed in a green sheath dress with a green silk scarf draped around her neck. Her hair had been freshly dyed, and she lay clutching a small bouquet of mature pink roses, which came from Joe Di Maggio; she was buried in a wall crypt in Westwood Memorial Park Cemetery. Marilyn didn't like the idea of being buried in the ground. The crypt next to Marilyn's has been bought by Hugh Hefner, the founder of *Playboy* magazine. Marilyn graced the very first cover of *Playboy* and was its first centrefold, in December 1953. In 1982, for no reason at all, Marilyn's ex-husband Joe DiMaggio cancelled his 20-year-old order for fresh flowers to be placed regularly on her tomb. No matter who the culprit, or the culprits, or the instigator of the cover-up of Marilyn Monroe's death was or were, her death will always remain one of the most controversial of all Hollywood's unsolved mysteries.

The ghost of novelist Ernest Hemingway terrified Cuban employees at his former estate-turned-museum outside Havana. In April 1998, one former employee said how the ghost would emerge at full moon and chase him down a path. A week later, three workers quit because of the Hemingway ghost.

Mel Blanc, the 'man of 1,000 voices', got the last laugh on his gravestone when he died at the age of 81 in 1989. He did the voices for Bugs Bunny, Daffy Duck and dozens of other Looney Tune's characters. But his most famous voice is right at the end of the cartoons when stuttering Porky Pig says, 'Tha, tha, tha, tha, that's all folks'. And that's exactly what Mel has on his head stone—'That's All Folks'.

The 26th President of the United States, Theodore Roosevelt, opened the Roosevelt Hotel, Hollywood at 7000 Hollywood Blvd on 15 May 1927. It was built at a cost of $2.5 million, which was a tremendous price in those days. It quickly became the 'in' place, and the centre of the glamorous social whirl for all of Hollywood's biggest stars. The first Academy Awards presentation was held in the Blossom Ballroom on 16 May 1929. Then the awards were called Merit Awards, and were given not for one performance, but for work covering a two-year period. Douglas Fairbanks was host for the evening, presenting awards to Janet Gaynor as Best Actress, Emil Jannings as Best Actor, and to *Wings,* starring Buddy Rogers, as Best Picture. Marilyn Monroe posed for her first advert, for suntan lotion, on the diving board at the pool. She stayed at the hotel often over the years, preferring a second-floor Cabana Room overlooking the pool. Over the years, my favourite hotel of all time has gathered hundreds of stories of ghosts, spirits and other things that go bump in the night. Here are just a few of them; true or not, these stories are all part of yesteryear Hollywood. In mid December 1985, two weeks prior to the big re-opening of the Roosevelt Hotel, Hollywood, the first ghost spirits were discovered. As the big day came closer, all the staff from management pitched in to help. Alan Russell, who was assistant to the general manager, offered to sweep the Blossom Ballroom before the carpeting was put down. He swept the entire ballroom, noticing one area that seemed a lot cooler than the rest of the room, but he never really gave it much thought. Later, as he swept the width of the room, the cool spot was still there. At that point, he called Kelly Green and together they tried to figure it out. They looked for open doors but there were none open the air conditioners had not been hooked up at that point and there was no trap door in the floor, so there appeared to be no reason for the cool spot. They measured the cool spot to be about 30 inches in diameter and about 10 degrees cooler than the rest of the room. Since 1985, two different respected psychics have said that it is the spirit of a man, wearing black and that there is a lot of anxiety there. Could it have been the spirit of a man attending the first Academy Awards dinner? Nobody knows. On the same day, staff member Suzanne Leonard was dusting the general manager's office. As she was dusting the tall dark-framed mirror, she saw the reflection of a blonde girl. When she turned around to speak to the girl, there was no-one there, yet when she looked back at the mirror, the reflection was still there. Suzanne was puzzled, so she asked the manager about the mirror. He told her that the mirror had belonged to Marilyn Monroe and had been removed from the suite that Marilyn had often occupied out by the swimming pool. The mirror stood outside the hotel lift on the lower-level landing for many years. Up on the ninth floor, maids were making up the beds while other hotel employees stocked the rooms with towels. A waitress was helping out by setting out the towels, and she went into room 928; she felt a cool breeze against her arms but didn't pay much attention to it. Workmen were still in the hall and doors were open, so she thought it was just a draft. As she went into the room the door slammed shut however; these doors have compression hinges, which means they can't slam. That startled her, but she continued placing the towels. As she came out of the room, she again felt a very definite coldness; it was like someone in a rush brushing past her in the hall. Later that day, two housemaids who also worked on the ninth floor said, 'There was something strange there', and that they would not work anywhere near the room again. Later it was learned that Room 928 was where Montgomery Clift had lived for three months. While filming the movie *From Here to Eternity,* he used to pace up and down the hall, rehearsing his lines and sometimes blowing a bugle. The hotel opened, welcoming its first guests on 30 December 1985, but during the next few months a number of ghostly things happened. For the first couple of months, only the public areas of the hotel and floors three, four and five were completed and in full use. One night before the third floor was completed, and exactly at midnight, there was a call on the hotel's PBX from Room 1032. PBX responded, but there was nobody on the other end. The room, like the entire floor, was unfinished and unoccupied; there was also no phone in that room at the time of the call to the PBX. By May of the following year, work on the upper floors was being completed. Daniel Cichon, Assistant Director of Housekeeping, was inspecting the rooms prior to the opening of the 11th floor. After completing his full inspection in Star Suite 1101/1102, he turned off the lights, locked the door and went back to his office. Minutes later, he returned to the suite with an extra wastebasket, only to find all the lights on. He was the only one with a key to the Star Suite, yet 'someone' had turned on all the lights. In mid October 1989, a TV film crew wanted to do a story on the hotel's ghosts for a Halloween special. During shooting, outside Room 928, the house lights went out, their sound equipment broke down and the film jammed in the camera ... it took almost four hours to do a one hour shoot. When they tried to shoot Marilyn's mirror, the smoke alarm went off and they couldn't complete the shoot. The cold spot in the ballroom affected the audio equipment—I guess they really stirred up the ghosts that night! On 15 December 1990, the LA County District Attorney's Office held a holiday dinner dance at the hotel. After the party, one of the invited couples was looking at the pictures on the mezzanine. As they neared the doors that lead to the balcony, overlooking the Blossom Room, they heard beautiful piano music drifting out. They walked into the room and saw a man in a white suit. As they approached, they spoke to him but he didn't answer. As they got even closer, he totally disappeared! The couple told the night manager that the man didn't walk away; he simply vanished. The manager went upstairs with the couple, but there was no man in a white suit; in fact, the room was empty. The following Monday morning, Billy from Engineering was working on the third floor. He was walking south in the north/south hallway. As he came to the corner he looked to his left (east), and halfway down the hall he saw a man standing in the hallway. He called out, asking the man if he could help him. The man didn't answer, but continued to look from side to side as if he wasn't sure which way he should go. Bill came closer, within 3 feet of the man, and again asked if he could be of help. The man still did not reply, but turned and walked towards the fire exit at the east end of the hall. Then he walked 'through' the door. He didn't open it and go out—he walked 'through' the door! Billy tried to follow, but he found that his feet were rooted to the spot. He could not move for what seemed like five minutes, though he said it was probably only a few. When asked for details about the man, Billy said, 'He was wearing old shoes and a white suit'. Could it have been the same man in the white suit that the others saw two days earlier? The American TV show *Entertainment Tonight* came to do a piece about Montgomery Clift's room and even bought a psychic with them. The room had been vacant for three days, but when they went in, the heat was on full blast. The windows were wide open as the crew started setting up their equipment. The interviewer was very, very sceptical about a 'ghost' in the room. When the filming lamp suddenly blew, he laughed and said, 'Those things happen all the time'. Immediately the film crew corrected him, saying that those lights last forever, but he wouldn't admit that anything strange was going on. As he began the interview, he asked the psychic if she felt any ghosts in the room. She said, 'No, not really. Perhaps if I were alone I might, but with all these people (10 in all) all the lights, and your negative attitude ... no I don't!' At that moment the interviewer started to laugh, when suddenly a window slammed shut! There was no wind that night and no-one was near the window. It couldn't have closed by itself because it opens from side to side and not up and down; someone would have needed to push it. The interviewer was rather shaken at this point. When the crew finished in the room, they went next door to talk to the guests in that room. They didn't identify themselves as a TV crew, asking only if the girls had heard any noises in Room 928. They replied, 'Oh yeah, there were some bumping noises, but we didn't think anything about it. We were going out, and really forgot about it'. The room had not been occupied for three days. Room 1217, which is now Room 1221, has long been known to have 'something unique and magical' about it, so said Linda Goodman, author of the books *Sun Signs* and *Love Signs*. She stayed in Room 1217 for several months, back in 1959, while writing her first book. She said then that the room had 'a presence, a special quality' about it. In October 1989, that presence made itself known again, this time by telephone. Late one night, #1221 lit up on the hotel PBX switchboard. The operator responded, but there was no-one on the line. When the light lit up again, the operator checked the guest-list register and found that the room was not occupied. She called Security, explained the situation and asked that they check the room and put the phone back on the hook. They did, and that was that, until three nights later when it happened again. That night, the phone got off the hook by itself—three times in one hour. Each time, Security went up and replaced the phone, and the next time they went up ... the phone was off the hook. If you've never stayed at, or visited, The Roosevelt Hotel, you're missing out on a 'real' part of Hollywood. Believe me it's a must for a stay or just a visit—you will not be disappointed.

A helicopter was taking off during the 1989 filming of *Delta Force 2*, when it crashed killing the pilot and four others.

There's an urban legend about the man who bought the empty crypt above Marilyn Monroe's. It goes like this: When his body was placed in the crypt above Marilyn's, a few of his close friends stayed behind after the funeral so they could honour their friend's last request, which was to turn his body face down, so he would lie facing Marilyn for eternity. I'm not sure if there is anything in this urban myth, but the crypt above Marilyn's bears the name Richard F Poncher, and the inscription reads, 'To the man who gave us everything and more. You're one in a million, Freddie.' He was born in 1905 and died in 1986, which is when the so-called event would have happened, if indeed it ever did. If this urban myth is indeed a myth and therefore not true, one can only apologise to Mr Poncher's family, who undoubtedly suffer each time the story is repeated.

It's rumoured that when Sammy Davis Jr died on 16 May 1990, he was buried wearing so much jewellery that his coffin was bolted and locked shut and buried 12 feet underground. It is also rumoured that there is a ton of cement on top of the coffin.

Michael Caine only found out that he had an illegitimate half brother called David Burchell 10 months before David died of pneumonia at the age of sixty-six. He was shut away in a mental hospital for more than 40 years until Michael moved him to a luxury suite at an old people's home.

Grace Kelly's family kept her tragic death a secret from her ailing mother for seven years. She died on 6 January 1990, aged 91, thinking her beloved daughter was still alive. It's said that a granddaughter, Grace Levine, who looked like Princess Grace, occasionally visited Margaret Kelly and pretended to be the Princess. The family kept her death a secret from Margaret because they feared the truth would kill her.

On 2 August 1998, Aurelia Schwarzenegger, the 76-year-old mother of Arnold Schwarzenegger, had a heart attack while visiting her husband's grave in Weiz, Austria.

In August 1998, Ukrainian-born teenage immigrant Mikail Markhasev (19), was sentenced to life imprisonment by a court in Santa Monica, California, for murdering comedian Bill Cosby's son, Ennis Cosby, who was 27.

For years, the 'Hollywood' sign that use to read 'Hollywoodland' has withstood the onslaught of the elements and the degradation of vandals. Over the years, many stories have been told about it, but the most famous is the one about actress Peg Entwistle for whom the sign had a very special and tragic significance. Peg came to the US from the UK in 1929, with 'very' high hopes of breaking into the movies. After appearing in several Broadway plays, all of which were flops, she signed a contract with RKO Pictures in Hollywood, which at the time was the largest movie studio in California. She made several appearances in B-grade movies but did not achieve the stardom she craved. Then, in July 1932, the studio decided not to pick up her option. According to her uncle, with whom she lived on Beachwood Drive, the Hollywood sign fascinated Peg Entwistle. She would stand for hours at a time at the front gate looking at it. Peg would wait for the postman every morning in the hopes of receiving a letter telling her that the studio had second thoughts about her contract. Then, disappointed yet again, she would ride horseback in the hills beneath the sign. On the evening of 18 September 1932, Peg Entwistle told her uncle she was going out for some cigarettes. She never returned. Wearing a dress she had borrowed from Broadway's leading lady Effie Shannon, Peg climbed up the side of the mountain and onto the 50-foot-high letter H. From there, she jumped to her death. Her pitiful suicide note was found not far from her body. What Peg did not know as she climbed the sign on that Friday evening was that there was a contract in the mail from the Beverly Hills Community Players. They were offering her a lead role in their next stage production—that of a girl who commits suicide at the end of the third act. There have been reports over the years that many people have jumped to their deaths from the sign, but Miss Entwistle's is the only recorded suicide from the landmark.

Persis Khambatta, a former Miss India and Miss World, who played the navigator in *Star Trek: the Motion Picture*, died on 18 August 1998 from a massive heart attack.

Keith Relf, who was the lead singer of the *Yardbirds*, was electrocuted by his own guitar in London, 1976.

On the day of Judy Garland's death, 23 June 1969, a tornado touched down in Kansas.

Hollywood actress Lupe Velez was known as the tempestuous 'Mexican Spitfire'. She lived up to her name both on and off the screen. The petite Latin beauty was a very familiar personality in Hollywood's social scene back in the 1930s. From 1933–1938 she was married to Tarzan star Johnny Weissmuller. In 1944, she was pregnant and up to her ears in debt when she decided to end it all at the age of thirty-four. After finishing a good spicy Mexican meal, she dressed herself in the best evening gown she owned in her favourite colour silver. Then she lay down on a couch that was surrounded by fresh flowers and candles splaying out her gown and taking a pose like something in a fashion magazine—she then swallowed an entire bottle of strong sleeping pills. Her plan was to be found in a state of serene and peaceful beauty. But the red-hot Mexican spices and the sleeping pills just didn't mix—she got up, staggered to the toilet, slipped on the tiles and fell headfirst into the toilet bowl - and drowned! Believe me, this was not the way she'd planned to be found.

Carmen Miranda, the 'Brazilian Bombshell', suffered a heart attack while performing on the Jimmy Durante live TV show in 1955; she died hours later. Her death at 46 brought about national mourning in Brazil.

John Lennon, former *Beatle*, was shot to death in New York City on 8 December 1980 as he and his wife, Yoko Ono, were entering the Dakota, their residence. The shooting shocked the world. Even TV sport's announcer Howard Cosell announced the shooting during the live broadcast of the 'Monday Night Football' game on ABC-TV. Two fans committed suicide after hearing of the death.

The *Sex Pistols* punk rocker Sid Vicious died of a heroin overdose in New York back in 1979; he was twenty-one. In October, the year before, he was arrested in New York and charged with stabbing his American girlfriend, Nancy Spungen, to death.

Just a fortnight before he died in a car crash on 30 September 1955, James Dean filmed a road safety commercial, it ended with his saying, 'And remember, drive safely, because the life you save may be mine!'

The 60s singing star, Del Shannon, shot himself at his LA home on 8 February 1990. He hit the charts in 1963 with *From Me to You*, the first *Beatles* cover tune on the US charts. He also wrote *I Go to Pieces*.

Marvin Gaye sung the big hit, *I Heard It On the Grapevine*, and won two Grammys for his million-selling *Sexual Healing*, cut from his last album, *Midnight Love*. He was fatally shot on 1 April 1984, the day before his 45th birthday during a family argument. His 70-year-old father, Marvin Gaye Sr (an Apostolic minister), was charged with the shooting.

The *Rolling Stones* guitarist and founder member, Brian Jones, drowned in his swimming pool at his home in Hartfield, Sussex, England on 3 July 1969. He bought the home at the beginning of 1969; it was where A A Milne wrote *Winnie the Pooh*.

The gravel-voiced singer, Janis Joplin, whose biggest hit was *Me and Bobby McGee*, died of a heroin overdose in room 105 at the Landmark Hotel (renamed Highland Gardens) in Hollywood on 4 October 1970. She'd just finished recording her new album *Pearl*. There is a monument of her in Port Arthur, TX, dedicated in 1987 under protest from some townsfolk. In 1970, two months before her own death, Janis bought a headstone for the grave of Bessie Smith, 33 years after the blues and jazz singer died.

In 1991, Lady Oona, Charlie Chaplin's widow, was buried with half a ton of concrete poured over her coffin to protect it from grave robbers. Back in 1977, two men dug up Charlie's coffin and stole his remains from the same cemetery in Vevey, Switzerland. They were arrested as they attempted to sell the remains back to the family.

East of Eden was the only one of James Dean's movies to be released while he was still alive. A year before his death in 1955, James paid a visit to his hometown, and insisted that the photographer from *Life* magazine snap him in a coffin. He was the first actor to be posthumously nominated for a Best Actor Oscar for *Rebel without a Cause* in 1955. He was nominated again in 1956 for *Giant* but won in neither year.

In May 1991, Bing Crosby's son Dennis died of a self-inflicted gunshot wound to the head. He was the second of Bing's sons to commit suicide. Dennis, 56, was found dead in his California home. His brother Gary said in a book in 1983 that he grew up in a house of terror.

A statue to commemorate the life and death of Stan Laurel of the comedy team Laurel and Hardy was unveiled on 16 June 1990 in Tyneside, north-eastern England. The British actor, whose real name was Arthur Jefferson, was born in the town of Ulverston but his family later moved to Tyneside where his father ran a theatre. The statue marked the 100th anniversary of his birth.

In March 1958 Elizabeth Taylor had a very bad viral infection and stayed at home instead of flying with her husband, Mike Todd, to a promotional evening for his movie *Around the World in 80 Days*. That night his plane crashed, killing all on board.

Andy Warhol occasionally contemplated his death and once said, 'I do like the idea of people turning into dust or sand, and it would be very glamorous to be reincarnated as a big diamond ring on Elizabeth Taylor's finger.'

Ray Bolger, who played the Scarecrow in *The Wizard of Oz* (1939), was the last surviving leading actor in the cast. He died in 1987. He once told me he was sad that there was nobody left from the main acting core to speak at his funeral.

Author Jackie Collins says she intends to leave the real names of her book characters in a little black box, which is not to be opened till after her death. There could be a few red faces around Hollywood when that happens.

Freddie Prinze Jr is the son of the late Freddie Prinze, the Latino comic who shot to fame in the ground-breaking TV series *Chico and the Man*.

Unfortunately he couldn't handle his phenomenal success and fell into a non-stop spiral downward into booze and drugs. Back in 1977, he blew his brains out after his wife filed for divorce; he was 22 years old.

During a live interview on a TV chat show in New York, a rambling and very incoherent Truman Capote had to be taken off the air. Among other things, he said he had slept with all his psychiatrists and that he would eventually probably die from a mixture of booze and pills. These certainly contributed to his death.

After James Dean's death in September 1955, actor, Nick Adams dubbed James' voice in one uncompleted scene from *Giant* (1956).

TV star David Janssen dreamed he saw a coffin being carried out of his Beverly Hills mansion. When he asked who was in it, he was told, 'Some actor called Janssen'. A little less than 48 hours later he suffered a massive heart attack, and died at the age of 49 at his home; he was carried out in a coffin.

George Reeves, who played Superman on TV, died on 16 June 1959. He was buried in the grey double-breasted suit he had worn for years as Clark Kent in the smash-hit 1950s series.

When he was dying, Aristotle Onassis sent for Anthony Quinn and begged him to portray him in the movie, *The Greek Tycoon*. Aristotle thought Anthony was the only actor who could portray him favourably. The two had only met once—several months before the final script was completed.

A little over two years after his death, James Dean was still receiving fan mail; thousands of fans would not accept he was really dead. Some even wanted to dig up the body to prove it wasn't James. For weeks after his funeral police guarded his grave around the clock.

Jim Carrey's dad was an accountant, so while he was a struggling nobody Jim Carrey wrote himself a cheque for $10 million for 'acting services'. He kept this cheque with him right up till 1994, when he placed it in his father's coffin. Months after his dad's death, he was paid $20 million for the lead in *The Cable Guy*.

On 16 August 1956 Bela Lugosi died in his Hollywood apartment. As he had requested in his will, Bela was buried in the high-collared cape he wore in his many portrayals of Count Dracula. His final resting-place is at the Holy Cross Cemetery, just a few feet away from his old friend Bing Crosby.

A woman who bought a vacant vault right next to Marilyn Monroe in the LA Westwood Memorial Park decided to put it up for sale in 1980. One man thought the prospect of spending eternity beside Marilyn Monroe was too good to miss; he paid $30,000 for the vault, at the time about 10 times the normal price.

When Rudolph Valentino died in 1926, several women committed suicide and a whole nation mourned. He was buried in a magnificent silver-bronze coffin, wearing a slave bracelet given to him by his last wife, actress Natacha Rambova. He was placed in a temporary vault that belonged to his friend, the woman who first discovered him, writer June Mathis. Unfortunately grand plans for a huge marble monument were abandoned at the last minute, and to this day Rudolph rests in his borrowed wall crypt, no. 1205 in the Hollywood Memorial Cemetery. Ironically, when he was alive he stood many times in front of his own wall crypt to place flowers on the crypt of Miss Mathis's mother Virginia, who lies just below Rudolph. June Mathis died just 12 months after Rudolph, and now lies in the wall crypt on his left. In his will, Rudolph left his first wife $1, so that she could not contest the will.

Some of the cremated remains of the famous gay author Truman Capote disappeared in a macabre theft during a Halloween 57th birthday party thrown by Joanne Carson in her Beverly Hills home. Truman died in Joanne's home in 1984. Since they were close friends, she kept half his ashes; the other half went to his long-time lover Jack Dunphy. Joanne's party on Halloween fulfilled her promise to Truman that she would give a Hollywood version of the famous masked ball he had held in 1966 at the Plaza Hotel in New York. Among the 50-odd guests that night were: Sally Struthers, Valerie Harper, Judge Reinhold, Kelly McGillis, Phyllis Diller and Alan Thicke. In the morning, Joanne found the ashes missing. No report of the theft was ever filed with the LA Police Department, and to this day the ashes have not been returned.

The largest and most flamboyant grave of any movie star can be seen at Hillside Cemetery in LA. It's the grave of Al Jolson, which includes an enormous statue of him on his knees in his famous 'Mammy' pose at the top of a waterfall. He died in 1950 of a heart attack, aged sixty-four.

Walt Disney died of cancer on 15 December 1966. The actual cause of death was acute circulatory failure, following surgery one month earlier. There have been many stories that his body has been kept on ice, as he believed that they would find a cure for cancer some day and bring him back to life. This is totally untrue. His ashes are in the corner garden of Forest Lawn Cemetery in California. The 24 December issue of the French magazine *Match* marked Walt's passing with an evocative portrait of Mickey Mouse with a tear falling from his right eye, with the headline 'Adieu a Walt Disney'.

Liberace, music's most flamboyant showman, died in 1987. He is buried at Forest Lawn Cemetery in Burbank, California, in a tomb that also contains his mother and brother George. The tomb, embellished with his signature and grand piano, is located between two trees shaped like candelabras, which was his trademark.

Hollywood's most visited grave is Marilyn Monroe's, in the Corridor of Memories in Westwood Memorial Cemetery. Her crypt is very plain with a simple brass plaque reading: Marilyn Monroe 1926–1962.

If you've heard that movie star Jayne Mansfield's head was severed from her body in a car crash on 29th June 1967, at the age of 34, well it's not true. She was killed when her 1966 Buick Electra car rammed a truck at 2 a.m. on a rain-slicked highway, near New Orleans on her way to a TV engagement. There were six other passengers in the car including Jayne's three children, one of which is Mariska Hargitay, today a movie star in her own right. While the children survived, Jayne, her lawyer and boyfriend Sam Brody, driver Ronnie Harrison and the dog did not. It's a myth, says Louisiana funeral director, Jim Roberts, who prepared her body for burial. 'Her head was attached as much as mine is,' he says. 'What was thrown clear—and seen by those at the crash site—was her wig.' Her thousands of fans thought she should be buried in Hollywood, so they clubbed together and bought a plot and headstone at the Hollywood Memorial Cemetery. The headstone reads: 'Jayne Mansfield 1933–1967. We live to love you more each day'. She is buried in a heart-shaped grave, just like the pool in her Beverly Hills mansion in the Fairview Cemetery, Pennsylvania.

Grace Kelly's family kept her tragic death a secret from her ailing mother for seven years. She died on 6 January 1990, aged 91, thinking her beloved daughter was still alive. It's said that a granddaughter, Grace Levine, who looked like Princess Grace, occasionally visited Margaret Kelly and pretended to be the Princess. The family kept her death a secret from Margaret because they feared the truth would kill her.

Here are a list of stars who died or suffered fatal injuries doing what they love best—performing:
Irene Ryan who played the loveable granny on the hit TV series *The Beverly Hillbillies* was felled by a stroke while performing on Broadway in the musical *Pippin*. She died six weeks later on 26 April 1973, at the age of 69. Carmen Miranda who was known for her over-the-top, camp, fruity headgear collapsed on *The Jimmy Durante TV Show* after returning to her dressing room. A few days later at the age of 46 she died from heart failure at her Beverly Hills home on the 5 August 1955. Swashbuckling movie star, Tyrone Power, suffered a fatal heart attack in Madrid, Spain, during a fencing scene for the movie *Solomon and Sheba*. He was 44, and the date was 15 November 1958. His dad Tyrone Power senior died on the set of the 1931 movie *The Miracle Man*. Hollywood hunk, Jon-Erik Hexum, accidentally shot himself in the head with a blank from a .44 magnum on the set of the TV series *Cover Up* on 12 October 12 1984. The impact was enough to kill the 26-year-old. On 30 November 1996, Tiny Tim had a fatal heart attack while playing the ukulele and singing at a concert appearance in Minneapolis. Redd Fox, who was loved for his role as Fred Sanford on the hit American TV series *Sanford and Son*, suffered a fatal heart attack on 11 Ocotober 1991 on the LA set of his brand new TV sitcom, *The Royal Family*. Bruce Lee's son Brandon was killed in North Carolina during a shootout for his movie, *The Crow*, on 31 March 1993. A bullet, mistakenly mixed in with blanks, struck Brandon. He was 28. A helicopter accident on the California set of the movie *Twilight Zone*, claimed the life of Vic Morrow, the *Combat* star on 23 July 1982. He was 53.

Sex siren Mae West lived in Unit 611 of the Ravenswood Apartments in LA from 1932 until her death in 1980. 'As long as the building stands, I will never leave', she once said. Over the years, an occupant of the apartment believes Mae's sprit is still there. The TV works everywhere, except the bedroom, which Mae always felt should be kept for reading, sleeping and making whoopee. On numerous occasions, the phone in the apartment will ring when no one's calling, and the chandelier in the foyer flashes when someone Mae dislikes is present. A photo taken in the lounge showed a bosomy apparition in a mirror. Many psychics have visited the apartment and all believe there is a strong spirit of Mae West there.

If you're looking for that special celebrity gift for a friend, contact a shop called Starworld. The shop specialises in items like a lock of Marilyn Monroe's baby hair or her first wedding ring, from Jim Dougherty. If you're into something more macabre, they stock things like the blood stained pants Marvin Gaye was wearing when he was shot dead by his father.

SEX, NUDITY AND DRUGS

David Duchovny was taken aback when a female fan asked him to sign a photo for her of him in the nude. David told the fan the picture was definitely not him; it was a computerised fake. He could see that the fan was very disappointed and promised to send her a signed picture and asked her for her address. True to his word, he sent her a picture of him wearing nothing but his skimpy pants. He wrote, 'Dear Janice, sorry I'm not nude in this one, but this is the closest I can come with my wife hovering around.'

Christina Aguilera's raunchy video for her 2002 single *Dirty* was banned from TV in Thailand, but the problem wasn't about her near-naked bum-baring, tiny miniskirt or her sexy dance moves. The criticism came from a set of posters in the background. The Thai Government complained about the messages on the posters, which said 'Thailand's sex tourism' and 'Young underage girls' in Thai on the walls behind a boxing ring in the video. Christina's label, BMG, confirmed the controversial video wouldn't be screened in Thailand. 'We at the company feel we should not think of business only. We have to think about our country as well', said a spokesperson for BMG.

Verne Troy (who played Mini Me in the *Austin Power* movies) revealed that the drinking binge that almost killed him was triggered by the fear that his girlfriend was going to leave him. The little-person star was rushed to hospital in September 2002 suffering from alcohol poisoning.

In the late 1960s, Jennifer Aniston's mum, previously known as Nancy Dow, appeared in a soft-porn movie starring John Holmes titled *The Ice House*.

In May 2002, a judge let five-time Grammy-winner singer Dionne Warwick 'Walk On By' her drug bust when she was slapped with a

$250 fine, and an order to write a letter telling people not to take drugs. Dionne, who was 61 at the time, was arrested when baggage screeners found 11 suspected marijuana cigarettes in her bags at Miami International Airport.

In mid September 2002, Rod Stewart's then 22-year-old son Sean was sentenced to 90 days' jail and ordered to undergo drug rehab after pleading guilty to attacking a man outside a restaurant in Malibu, California. The police arrested Sean in December 2001, after he was seen kicking the man in the stomach and face area. Actor Dean Cain, who played TV's Superman in the 1990s, and his brother broke up the fight. When Sean took off in his car they followed him and reported the incident to the LA police. Sean was also sentenced to five years' probation and ordered to pay his victim $5,600. He faced the possibility of four years in prison. In a totally separate case, in June of 2002, a court ordered Sean to enter a drug rehab programme. He had pleaded guilty to possessing a controlled substance in West Hollywood.

According to a foot-fetish website, Geri Halliwell, Kylie, Britney and Shakira have the sexiest feet. Geri was thrilled. 'I always thought my feet were quite ugly', she said.

To learn more about his role as a male prostitute in the movie *My Own Private Idaho*, Keanu Reeves hung out with male street hustlers.

Ewan McGregor has demonstrated on more than one occasion in the movies that he's not afraid of appearing nude. As far as sex scenes are concerned he said, 'In real life, you don't get up with the sheet after you've had sex.'

Sylvester Stallone said he's ashamed of appearing in the 1970 soft-core porn movie *A Party at Kitty and Studs*. After Sylvester's success in the 1976 movie, *Rocky*, it was re-named *The Italian Stallion*. It's rumoured that he was only paid $200 for his full-frontal role.

Tommy Lee and Pam Anderson went water-skiing in the nude on Lake Mead not long after they were married.

Bo Derek, using her real name Kathleen Collins, appeared in John Derek's 1973 soft-core movie called *Fantasies*.

Chinese action actor, Jackie Chan, has a few rules when it comes to appearing in movies. He told his manager, 'No sex scenes, no making love. The kids who like me don't need to see it. It would gross them out.'

Diane Keaton starred in the stage musical *Hair.* She was the only cast member in any of the *Hair* production companies to refuse to take her clothes off for the nude scene.

At the age of six, and living in Flushing, New York, Mary Tyler Moore was molested by a family member. In her autobiography, *After All*, she gives an account of the incident saying, 'I was paralysed as I remembered where I was and who was making me feel this way. It had to be bad what he was doing, really bad … I was ashamed and scared because I couldn't stop him.'

In 2002, to prepare for her role in the movie *28 Days*, Sandra Bullock spent time at a rehabilitation clinic.

In 1999, Steve Tyler sued his ex-wife. He wanted her to return a set of nude pictures she had of him after reading in a magazine article that she intended to publish them.

Charlie Sheen told *Maxim* magazine that he guessed he's slept with 5,000 women.

Unlike most actors, Harvey Keitel is willing to do full-frontal nudity in his movies.

Don Johnson was 12 years old when he seduced his babysitter.

Stage and screen actor Yul Brynner posed nude for artists and photographers in his pre-Hollywood days. He was hurt in a trapeze accident in his youth as an acrobat; it's rumoured that he then started taking opium as a painkiller and became addicted to it.

Courtney Cox-Arquette keeps a box of clay bricks under her bed after hearing from a Feng Shui expert that it'll improve her orgasms.

It's rumoured that Robert Downey Jr took daily drug tests during the filming of 1997's, *Two Girls and a Guy.*

Demi Moore was voted the 'worst-dressed actress' at the 1989 Oscars. Two years later, she showed the world she didn't need clothes at all, by appearing totally naked and very pregnant on the cover of *Vanity Fair* magazine stirring up even more controversy.

Madonna wasn't always a material girl, no sir. She once rented by the hour as a nude model for artists. She also performed in an underground movie, again wearing no material. In late 1990, she draped herself in the American flag in a naughty US TV advert to promote free expression and voting. 'Dr King, Malcolm X, freedom of speech is as good as sex', she raps as a male dancer slapped her backside. She ended by flinging open the Stars and Stripes, flasher-style, and saying, 'If you don't vote, you're going to get a spanking.' Madonna did the TV advert for free to help an organisation called Rock the Vote. These days the TV advert has become a collector's item.

In 1990, pop star Billy Idol was totally surprised at a concert in Seattle when five men wearing nothing but masks marched on stage in a conga line during his last number. Watched by some 14,000 fans, Billy tried to keep a straight singing face, but burst into laughter. Since the men had been masked, nobody could identify the offenders. They were believed to be members of Billy's entourage.

In 1990, Lisa Marie Presley's then husband Danny Keough formed a new band with the odd name of *Ten-Inch Men*. Take from that as you will.

Drew Barrymore is remembered as the beautiful young girl in *E.T.* At a young age, she checked herself into an alcoholism treatment centre. She revealed that she had begun drinking at the age of eight and began using drugs at the age of eleven.

In 1989, the DA agreed not to prosecute Rob Lowe over his famous sex videotapes—Rob had to lecture in LA schools on the dangers of drugs. It turned out that the LA School Board didn't want any part of the young Hollywood star. The Board's president said, 'It appears on the surface he has, at minimum, dubious judgment.' After the much-publicized video sexcapades, hundreds of jokes circulated around the world; one was that Rob's next movie would be *Two Men and a Baby*. As the news of the sordid video sexcapades hit the front pages of every tabloid, Rob was in the middle of shooting a movie called *Bad Influence*—it was all about a drifter who secretly videotapes a businessman having sex with a woman.

The September 1998, US issue of *Movieline* featuring a near-naked shot of Liz Hurley wearing nothing but strategically placed fur was deemed far too risqué by the prudish Yanks. It was considered too raunchy for news-stands and magazine racks to display. Only the magazine subscribers got to see the original pic of Liz, while copies bought in the shops had her in a full-length dress.

Baywatch star David Hasselhoff peeled off to his birthday suit for the 25th anniversary issue of *Cosmopolitan* magazine. He followed in the footsteps of Arnold Schwarzenegger, Burt Reynolds, Jim Brown and John Davidson.

In 1969, Jim Morrison was fined for exposing himself during a Miami concert. In a bizarre 1970 white-witchcraft ceremony, Jim 'married' rock writer Patricia Kennealy. She later had an abortion when he made it clear he would have nothing to do with the child.

In the 1970 movie comedy *The Owl and the Pussycat*, Barbra Streisand did a nude scene only on the condition that she would have the full right to veto it if she didn't like the way it looked on the screen. She didn't like it at all so Barbra and the movie studio struck a compromise. They did use the scene but the detail was totally obscured in the final print. Years later a print appeared in which the nude scene had not been obscured. It was printed in a rather sleazy magazine called *High Society*. Barbra sued the magazine and won.

People magazine selected Tom Cruise as 'The Sexiest Man Alive' in 1990. Not bad for a young man, who at the age of just 14 spent one relatively stable year at a Franciscan seminary in Cincinnati.

Nude pictures of Brad Pitt and Gwyneth Paltrow (her beau at the time) were taken with a telephoto lens while they were on holiday in St. Barts. The pictures were published on the Internet and in the tabloids. Brad filed suit against the photographer.

Cher was once asked what she thought made her sexy: 'I don't know how to make sex appeal. If anyone asks me how I do it, I tell them I don't know how I do it, I just do it.'

Madonna laughed loudly when a reporter asked her about her habit of putting condoms into her tour staff's pay packets. She said that she didn't think that it was in any way kinky, just practical, as it encouraged safe sex.

In May 1998, singer George Michael was ordered to do 80 hours of community service after being found guilty of committing a lewd act in a public toilet in Beverly Hills. He was then on probation for a further two years.

Actress Kim Basinger posed nude for *Playboy* magazine back in 1983; the magazine was a sell-out.

On 14 August 1990, Kirstie Alley told interviewer Maria Shriver on national TV, 'I was a drug addict … I sold drugs'. She kicked drugs and then took up Scientology, followed by acting.

Back in 1978, Tim Allen served 28 months in jail for attempting to sell cocaine.

In 1986, American comedian Robin Williams was sued for $6.2 million by former companion Michelle Trish Carter, who claimed she got herpes during their two-year relationship. Robin countersued her for extortion. Both suits were settled out of court for an undisclosed amount.

On 26 August 2002, former *Baywatch* star Yasmine Bleeth married Paul Cerrito who was reportedly the same man with whom Yasmine was arrested with in September 2001 in Michigan, for possessing cocaine. Yasmine pleaded guilty to the charge and was sentenced to two years probation and had to submit to regular drug tests. The couple reportedly met while they were both in a Malibu, California, rehab centre.

Ben Affleck refuses to use a body-double in his movie love scenes. 'It's a point of pride with me. You'll always see my butt', says Ben.

In 1998, Hollywood heart-throb Leonardo DiCaprio sued *Playgirl* magazine to stop them from publishing nude shots of him from the movie *Total Eclipse*.

Less than a week after completing her 1990 movie *Total Recall*, Sharon Stone posed nude for *Playboy* magazine.

Sting claimed in a 1993 *Rolling Stone* interview that by practising meditation he can make love for more than five hours at a time.

In 1996, Jennifer Aniston posed nude in *The Rolling Stone* magazine. In

2000 she was snapped topless while sunbathing in her backyard. The pictures were published in *High Society* and *Celebrity Skin*, both of which she sued.

Julia Roberts refuses to do any kind of movie nude scenes; a double is used if her character has to appear nude.

In 1999, Nicole Kidman appeared nude on stage for approximately 12 seconds in a limited Broadway run of David Hare's *The Blue Room*. She later appeared in the London production to rave reviews.

Angela Lansbury says she lost her virginity at age 20 to 36-year-old Richard Cromwell, who was a homosexual—they married shortly after. She did not find out he was gay until after they separated.

In 2001, Ben Affleck checked himself into a rehabilitation facility for alcohol dependency.

Backstreet Boy AJ and Jason Priestley shared a room in rehab in the summer of 2002.

Ewan McGregor revealed he bonked his way into shape in preparation for nude scenes in the film *Down with Love*. The *Star Wars* star says, 'I do it by shagging. It's better than working out.'

In June 1967, Mick Jagger and Keith Richard were sentenced to three months and one year in jail respectively for drug offences, but after an appeal court hearing, their sentences were quashed.

In August 2002, Britney Spears burst into a fit of giggles when a cheeky flasher confronted her in an LA club. The unidentified man marched up to the singer, pulled his trousers down and gave her a good look at his crown jewels before calmly walking off and disappearing.

Don't get Tony Curtis started on the infamous kissing scene with Marilyn Monroe in the movie *Some Like It Hot* (1959) with his remark 'it was like kissing Hitler'. He is violent in his denial of this slur, claiming it was the studio trying to discredit Marilyn because she was so troublesome—late, distracted, etc.—during production. With great emphasis he says, 'It so offends me'.

In the 2002 Steven Soderbergh movie, *Full Frontal*, David Duchovny did just that—or did he? In one scene, David was in a state of what the *New York Post* saucily described as 'heightened awareness'. Insiders on the set say he used a fake piece of male anatomy for the shot, and most of it took place under a sheet. Censors fought for the scene to be cut, but Steven reportedly insisted on it staying in the finished movie.

In 1997, Hollywood actor Christian Slater was ordered by a judge to take an Aids test after biting a woman at a party.

In 1954, psychologist Frederick Werthman claimed that Batman and his buddy Robin, the Boy Wonder, were closer than they should have been! The comic, he claimed, encouraged youngsters to become homosexuals.

In August 2003 Justin Timberlake replaced David Beckham as the sexiest man in the world according to a UK *Company* magazine poll.

At 42, the stunning blonde actress Daryl Hannah bared all for the cover of the November 2003 *Playboy* magazine.

CELEBRITY BIRTHDAY LISTINGS

JANUARY

1st

Nicolle Dickson	1969
Michelle Holmes	1967
Frank Langella	1940
Cate Blanchet	1969

2nd

Gabrielle Carteris	1961
John Paul Jones	1945
Christy Turlington	1969
Cuba Gooding Jr	1968

3rd

Mel Gibson	1956
Robert Loggia	1929
Jason Marsden	1976
Victoria Principal	1950
Stephen Stills	1945

4th

Dyan Cannon	1937
Rick Hearst	1965
Michael Stipe	1960
Jane Wyman	1914

5th

Suzy Amis	1961
DJ Bobo	1968
Robert Duvall	1931
Diane Keaton	1946
Pamela Sue Martin	1953
Marilyn Manson	1969

6th

Rowan Atkinson	1955
Jack Jones	1971
Sylvia Sims	1933
Loretta Young	1913
Malcolm Young	1953

7th

Nicolas Cage	1964
Kate Couric	1957
Dustin Diamond	1974
Kenny Loggins	1948
Helen Worth	1951
Chris Rock	1966

8th

Shirley Bassey	1937
David Bowie	1947
Ami Dolenz	1969
Rachel Friend	1970
Paul Hester	1959
Steven Jacobs	1967
Elvis Presley	1935

9th

Joan Baez	1941
Bob Denver	1944
Clive Dunn	1919
Crystal Gayle	1951
Emma Roche	1976
Marco Sanchez	1970
Susannah York	1941
Alexander Mclean	1978

10th

Pat Benatar	1953
Ray Bolger	1904
Claire King	1963
Linda Lovelace	1950
Sal Mineo	1939
Marine Reece-Wilmore	1974
Frank Sinatra Jr	1944
Rod Stewart	1945

11th

Jason Connery	1963
Kim Hartman	1955
Naomi Judd	1946
Rod Taylor	1930

12th

Chynna Phillips	1968
Kirstie Alley	1955

Anthony Andrews	1948
Michael Aspel	1933
Per Gessle	1959
Andrew Lawrence	1988
Des O'Connor	1932
Howard Stern	1954
Melanie Chisholm	1974
13th	
Kevin Anderson	1960
Patrick Dempsey	1966
Nicole Eggert	1971
Michael Galvin	1966
LL Cool J	1968
Julia Louis-Dreyfus	1961
Penelope Ann Miller	1964
Richard Moll	1943
Charles Nelson Reily	1931
Robert Stack	1919
14th	
Jason Bateman	1969
Richard Briers	1934
Faye Dunaway	1941
David Grohl	1969
Warren Mitchell	1926
Carl Smith	1959
15th	
Lloyd Bridges	1913
Chad Lowe	1968
16th	
Debbie Allen	1950
John Carpenter	1948
David Chokachi	1968
Ethel Merman	1909
Kate Moss	1974
Sade	1959
17th	
Muhammad Ali	1942
Jim Carrey	1962
David Caruso	1956
Larry Fortensky	1952
Susannah Hoffs	1960
James Earl Jones	1931
Shari Lewis	1934
Sheree North	1933
Vidal Sassoon	1928
Betty White	1922
18th	
Kevin Costner	1955
Bobby Goldsboro	1941
Cary Grant	1904
Danny Kaye	1913
19th	
Desi Arnaz Jr	1953
Michael Crawford	1942
Phil Everly	1939
Shelley Fabares	1944
Tippi Hedren	1931
Robert Palmer	1949
Dolly Parton	1946
Katy Sagal	1956
Jean Stapleton	1923
Jodie Sweetin	1980
Micky Vitue	1957
20th	
Gary Barlow	1971
George Burns	1896
Kimberley Davis	1973
DeForest Kelly	1920
Lorenzo Lamas	1958
Mario Lanza	1921
David Lynch	1946
Patricia Neal	1926
Paul 'Kiss' Stanley	1949
Skeet Ulrich	1970
21st	
Robby Benson	1956
Geena Davis	1957
Placido Domingo	1941
Jill Eikenberry	1947
Eric Falconer	1959
Peter Kircher	1948
Billy Ocean	1950
Telly Savalas	1925
Emma Bunton	1978
Alicia Keys	1981
22nd	
Steve Adler	1965
Linda Blair	1959
Olivia d'Abo	1969
Balthazar Getty	1975
John Hurt	1940
Michael Hutchence	1960
Piper Laurie	1932

Nyree Dawn Porter 1936
Ann Sothern 1909
Abi Tucker 1973
Diane Lane 1965

23rd

Tatyana M Ali 1979
Richard Dean Anderson 1950
Humphrey Bogart 1899
Princess Caroline 1957
Earl Falconer 1960
Gil Gerard 1943
Rutger Hauer 1944
Jeanne Moreau 1928
Zack Morrison 1976
Tyrone Power Jr 1959
Chita Rivera 1933
Tiffani Amber Thiessen 1974
Alex Erkiletian 1974
Tracy Anne George 1968
Kathleen Trimble 1969
Geoffrey Wigdor 1982
Rick Youck 1970
Mariska Hargitay 1964

24th

John Belushi 1949
Ernest Borgnine 1917
Neil Diamond 1941
Ava Gardner 1922
Nastassja Kinski 1961
Aaron Neville 1941
Ray Stevens 1941
Sharon Tate 1943

25th

Anita Baker 1958
Dean Jones 1935
Richard Grieve 1970
Diana Manoff 1958
Leigh Taylor-Young 1944

26th

Michael Bentiner 1922
Wayne Gretzky 1961
Ellen Degeneres 1958
Norman Hassan 1957
Anne Jefferys 1923
Eartha Kitt 1928
Paul Newman 1925
Andrew Ridgeley 1963
Moira Shearer 1926
Eddie Van Halen 1955

27th

Mikhail Baryshnikov 1947
Troy Donahue 1937
Bridget Fonda 1964
Mark Owen 1974
Donna Reed 1921
Mimi Rogers 1956
Nic Testoni 1972
Alan Cumming 1965

28th

Alan Alda 1936
Barbi Benton 1950
Elijah Wood 1981
Nick Carter 1980
Joseph Fatone 1977

29th

Mathew Ashford 1961
John Forsythe 1918
Sarah Gilbert 1975
Ann Jillian 1951
Andrew Keegan 1979
Greg Louganis 1960
Jason James Richter 1980
Katharine Ross 1943
Tom Selleck 1945
Oprah Winfrey 1954
Heather Graham 1970

30th

Christian Bale 1974
Brett Butler 1958
Phil Collins 1951
Jeremy Giffins 1956
Tammy Grimes 1936
Gene Hackman 1931
Vanessa Redgrave 1937

31st

Carol Channing 1921
Norman Mailer 1923
Suzanne Pleshette 1937
John Lydon (Johnny Rotten) 1956
Jean Simmons 1929
Jessica Walter 1944
Minnie Driver 1970
Justin Timberlake 1981
Portia De Rossi 1973

FEBRUARY

1st

Don Everly	1937
Sherilyn Fenn	1965
Clark Gable	1901
Margaux Hemingway	1955
Jani Lane	1964
Lisa Marie Presley	1968
Pauly Shore	1970
Princess Stephanie	1965

2nd

Christie Brinkley	1954
Farrah Fawcett	1947
Bo Hopkins	1942
Jeffery Hughes	1944
David Jason	1940
Glenda McKay	1971
Elaine Stritch	1926

3rd

Thomas Calabro	1959
Morgan Fairchild	1950
Isla Fisher	1976
Nathan Lane	1956
Frankie Vaughan	1928

4th

Clint Black	1962
David Brenner	1945
Alice Cooper	1948
Michael Goorjian	1972

5th

Bobby Brown	1969
Red Buttons	1919
Russell Grant	1952
Barbara Hershey	1948
Jennifer Jason Leigh	1962
Rose McKaggan	1964
Frank Muir	1920

6th

Rick Astley	1966
Natalie Cole	1949
Fabian	1943
Mike Farrell	1939
Zsa Zsa Gabor	1917
Patrick Macnee	1922
Dennis Norden	1918
Ronald Reagan	1911
Axl Rose	1962
Jimmy Tarbuck	1940
Michael Tucker	1944
Mamie Van Doren	1931

7th

Garth Brooks	1962
Dame Dora Bryan	1923
Andrew Gillan	1966
Jerry Hall	1956
Alan Lancaster	1949
James Spader	1960
Ashton Kutcher	1978

8th

Gary Coleman	1968
James Dean	1931
Joshua Jacob	1975
Joshua Kadison	1965
Jack Lemon	1925
Nick Nolte	1941
Mary Steenburgen	1953
Lana Turner	1921
John Williams	1932
Seth Green	1974

9th

Mia Farrow	1945
David Gallagher	1985
Kathryn Grayson	1922
Carole King	1942
Brandon Lee	1965
Judith Light	1949
Carmen Miranda	1909
Joe Pesci	1943

10th

Peter Allen	1944
Laura Dern	1967
WC Fields	1879
Roberta Flack	1940
Briony McRoberts	1957

11th

Jennifer Aniston	1969
Brandy	1979
Sheryl Crow	1962
Matthew Lawrence	1980
Leslie Nielsen	1926
Burt Reynolds	1936
Sidney Sheldon	1917
Kelly Slater	1972

12th

Maud Adams	1945
Arsenio Hall	1959
Joanna Kerns	1953
Simon MacCorkindale	1952
Maxi Priest	1961
Jesse Spencer	1979
Franco Zeffirelli	1923
Christina Ricci	1980

13th

Ali Campbell	1959
Stockard Channing	1944
Kim Novak	1933
Oliver Reed	1938
George Segal	1934
Robbie Williams	1974
Jerry Springer	1944
Peter Gabriel	1950

14th

Dean Gaffney	1978
Florence Henderson	1934
Gregory Hines	1946
Meg Tilly	1960
Ken Wahl	1956

15th

Marisa Berenson	1947
Clair Bloom	1931
Josh Byrne	1984
Chris Farley	1964
Matt Groening	1954
Melissa Manchester	1951
Cesar Romero	1907

16th

Daniel Amalm	1979
Sonny Bono	1935
Ice T	1958
James Ingram	1956
William Katt	1955
John Schlesinger	1926
Andy Taylor	1961

17th

Billie Joe Armstrong	1972
Alan Bates	1934
Brenda Fricker	1945
Joseph Gordon-Levitt	1981
Hal Holbrook	1925
Barry Humphries	1934
Michael Jordan	1963
Julia McKenzie	1942
Lou Diamond Phillips	1962
Gene Pitney	1941
Rene Russo	1954

18th

Randy Crawford	1952
Andrew Daddo	1966
Matt Dillon	1964
George Kennedy	1925
Rachel Lindsay	1972
Juice Newton	1952
Yoko Ono	1933
Jack Palance	1919
Molly Ringwald	1968
Greta Scacchi	1960
Cybill Sheppard	1950
John Travolta	1954
Vanna White	1957
Adam Willits	1972

19th

Justine Bateman	1966
Jeff Daniels	1955
Cass Elliot	1943
Lee Marvin	1924
Stephen Nicols	1951
Gary Pinto	1975
Smokey Robinson	1940

20th

Edward Albert	1951
Charles Barkley	1963
Kurt Cobain	1967
Cindy Crawford	1966
Kimberly Davies	1973
Sandy Duncan	1946
Kelsey Grammer	1955
Jennifer O'Neill	1948
Sydney Poitier	1924
Andrew Shue	1967
Brian Littrell	1975

21st

Christopher Atkins	1961
William Baldwin	1963
Tyne Daly	1946
David Geffen	1943
Jennifer Love Hewitt	1979
Rue McClanahan	1934

Ann Sheridan	1915
Nina Simone	1933
22nd	
Drew Barrymore	1975
Jonathan Demme	1944
Bruce Forsyth	1928
Sheila Hancock	1933
Kyle MacLachlan	1959
Sir John Mills	1908
Julie Walters	1950
Robert Young	1907
23rd	
Sean Astin	1971
Peter Fonda	1939
24th	
Barry Bostwick	1945
James Farentino	1938
Edward James Olmos	1947
Helen Shaver	1952
Denis Waterman	1948
Billy Zane	1966
25th	
Jim Backus	1913
Tom Courtney	1937
George Harrison	1943
Sally Jessy Raphael	1943
Tea Leoni	1966
26th	
Michael Bolton	1953
Johnny Cash	1932
Fats (Antoine) Domino	1928
Jennifer Grant	1966
Betty Hutton	1921
Guy Leech	1964
Tony Randall	1920
Sandy Shaw	1947
27th	
Peter Andre	1973
Adam Baldwin	1962
Howard Hesseman	1940
Grant Show	1962
Elizabeth Taylor	1932
Joanne Woodward	1930
28th	
Stephanie Beacham	1949
Charles During	1923
Gavin MacLeod	1930
Vincente Minnelli	1913
Zero Mostel	1915
Bernadette Peters	1948
Mercedes Ruehl	1948
29th	
Antonio Sabato Jr	1972

MARCH

1st	
Catherine Bach	1954
Harry Belafonte	1927
Dirk Benedict	1945
Robert Conrad	1935
Roger Daltrey	1944
Timothy Daly	1956
Mark-Paul Gosselaar	1974
Ron Howard	1954
Glenn Miller	1904
David Niven	1909
Dinah Shore	1917
Alan Thicke	1947
Jasen Ackles	1978
2nd	
Desi Arnaz	1917
Karen Carpenter	1950
Jennifer Jones	1919
Jon Bon Jovi	1962
Hayley Lewis	1974
Jay Osmond	1955
Lou Reed	1943
3rd	
David Faustino	1974
Jean Harlow	1911
Ronan Keating	1977
Christian Oliver	1972
Miranda Richardson	1958
Jessica Bile	1982
4th	
Steve Bastoni	1963
Chastity Bono	1969
Evan Dando	1967
Emilo Estefan	1953
Pasty Kensit	1968
Jason Newstedt	1963
Patricia Heaton	1958
5th	
Jack Cassidy	1927

Samantha Eggar 1939
Andy Gibb 1958
Sir Rex Harrison 1908
Elaine Page 1952
James Sikking 1933
Dean Stockwell 1935
Niki Taylor 1975

6th

Tom Arnold 1959
Norman Coburn 1937
Kiki Dee 1947
Ben Murphy 1942
Shaquille O'Neal 1972
Rob Reiner 1945
Graham Steadman 1951
Dame Kiri Te Kanawa 1944
Mary Wilson 1944

7th

Clive Blurr 1957
Cameron Daddo 1965
Rik Mayall 1958
Daniel J Travanti 1940
Rachel Weisz 1971

8th

Jamie Lynn Baur 1949
Cyd Charisse 1922
Mickey Dolenz 1945
Chad Gabriel 1976
Camryn Manheim 1961
Freddie Prinze Jr 1976
James van der Beek 1977
Kathy Ireland 1963
Aidan Quinn 1959
Lynn Redgrave 1943
Carol Bayer Sager 1946
Salt 1964

9th

Barbie (the Doll) 1959
Linda Fiorentino 1960
Raul Julia 1940
Emmanuel Lewis 1970
Mickey Spillane 1918
Juliette Binoche 1964

10th

Neneh Cherry 1964
Jasmine Guy 1964
Chuck Norris 1940
Sharon Stone 1958

11th

Bobby McFerrin 1950
Lindsay McKeon 1982
Lawrence Welk 1903

12th

Barbara Feldon 1941
Steve Harris 1957
Liza Minnelli 1946
James Taylor 1948

13th

Adam Clayton 1960
Dana Delaney 1956
Donald Duck 1934
Deborah Raffin 1953
Neil Sedaka 1939
Tracey Wells 1971

14th

Chris Klein 1979
Michael Caine 1933
Jasper Carrott 1945
Billy Crystal 1947
Lochie Daddo 1970
Rick Dees 1951
Quincy Jones 1933
Taylor Hanson 1983

15th

Terence Trent D'Arby 1962
Fabio 1961
Judd Hirsch 1935
Bret Michaels 1965
David Price 1977

16th

Erik Estrada 1949
Jerry Lewis 1926
Leo McKern 1920
Kate Nelligan 1951

17th

Billy Corgan 1967
Nat 'King' Cole 1919
Cynthia Daniel 1976
Leslie-Anne Down 1954
Patrick Duffy 1949
Stephen Gately 1976
Rob Lowe 1964
Rudolf Nureyev 1938
Kurt Russell 1951

18th

Queen Latifah	1970
Irene Cara	1964
1959	
Kevin Dobson	1943
Peter Graves	1926
William Picket	1941
Charlie Pride	1938
Vanessa Williams	1963

19th

Ursula Andress	1936
Glenn Close	1947
Dalton James	1971
Larry Johnson	1969
Patrick McGoohan	1928
Bruce Willis	1955

20th

Holly Hunter	1958
William Hurt	1950
Spike Lee	1957
Hal Linden	1931
Vera Lynn	1917
Sir Michael Redgrave	1908
Carl Reiner	1923

21st

Ed Begley Sr	1910
Timothy Dalton	1944
Cynthia Geary	1966
Rosie O'Donnell	1962
Gary Oldman	1958
Janes Bittle Ryna	1977
Sarah White	1969
Roger Whittaker	1946

22nd

Karl Malden	1914
Marcel Marceau	1923
Matthew Modine	1959
William Shatner	1931
Sir Andrew Lloyd Webber	1948
Bob Costa	1952
Reese Witherspoon	1976

23rd

Joan Crawford	1904
Richard Grieco	1965
Chaka Khan	1953
Marti Pellow	1966
Amanda Plummer	1957
Keri Russell	1976

24th

Robert Carradine	1954
Kelly LeBrock	1960
Bob Mackie	1940
Steve McQueen	1930
Billy Warlock	1961
Lara Flynn Boyle	1970

25th

Cathy Dennis	1969
Aretha Franklin	1942
Paul Michael Glaser	1943
Elton John	1947
Peter O'Brien	1960
Frank Oz	1944
Sarah Jessica Parker	1965

26th

Matthew Broderick	1962
James Caan	1939
Leeza Gibbons	1957
Jennifer Grey	1960
John Hendy	1971
Vicki Lawrence	1949
Leonard Nimoy	1931
Diana Ross	1944
Martin Short	1950
Josh Lucas	1972

27th

Andy Brown	1949
Mariah Carey	1969
Bernard Curry	1974
Andrew Farris	1959
David Janssen	1931
Corey Page	1971
Gloria Swanson	1899
Quentin Tarantino	1963
Michael York	1942

28th

Sir Dirk Bogarde	1921
Ken Howard	1944
Reba McEntire	1955
Tracey Needham	1968
Michael Parkinson	1935
Dianne Wiest	1948
Lucy Lawless	1968
Julia Stiles	1981

29th

Jennifer Capriati	1976
Julie Goodyear	1942
MC Hammer	1963
Eric Idle	1943
Christopher Lambert	1957
Elle Macpherson	1964

30th

John Astin	1930
Warren Beatty	1937
Tracey Chapman	1964
Eric Clapton	1945
Celine Dion	1968
Matt Doran	1976
Richard Dysart	1929
Rolf Harris	1930
Steve Oinder	1960
Paul Reiser	1957
Ian Ziering	1964

31st

Her Alpert	1935
Richard Chamberlain	1935
Angela Marie Dotchin	1974
Ed Marinaro	1950
Jim Hutton	1934
Shirley Jones	1934
Mark McClure	1957
Paul Mercurio	1963
Ewan McGregor	1971
Paul Norton	1961
Rhea Perlman	1948
Christopher Walken	1943
Angus Young	1959
Colin Farrell	1976

APRIL

1st

Ali McGraw	1938
Jane Powell	1929
Michael Praed	1960
Debbie Reynolds	1932
Philip Schofield	1962
Andrew Vlahov	1969
Kym Wilson	1974

2nd

Buddy Ebsen	1908
Marvin Gaye	1939
Sir Alec Guinness	1914
Emmylou Harris	1947
Linda Hunt	1945
Penelope Keith	1940
Todd Woolbridge	1971
Christopher Meloni	1961

3rd

Alec Baldwin	1958
Eric Braeden	1941
Marlon Brando	1924
Doris Day	1924
Jennie Garth	1972
Marsha Mason	1942
Eddie Murphy	1961
Wayne Newton	1942
Tony Orlando	1944
David Hyde Pierce	1959

4th

Jane Asher	1946
Anthony Clark	1964
Robert Downey Jr	1965
Steve Gatlin	1951
Andrew Hill	1975
Ashley Judd	1968
Christine Lahti	1950
Patti Lupone	1949
Nancy McKeon	1966
Paul Nicholls	1979
Anthony Perkins	1932
William Tarner	1941
Sean Wilson	1965
Heath Ledger	1979
Natasha Lyonne	1979

5th

Bette Davis	1908
Nigel Hawthorne	1929
Gregory Peck	1916
Spencer Tracy	1900
Andrew Williams	1966

6th

Candice Cameron	1976
Marilu Henner	1953
Jason Hervey	1972
John Ratzenberger	1947
George Reeves	1914
Billy Dee Williams	1937

7th

Jackie Chan	1954
Francis Ford Coppola	1939
Sir David Frost	1939
James Garner	1928
Billie Holiday	1915
Gordon Kaye	1941
John Oates	1949
Lynne Perrie	1931
Wayne Rogers	1933
Russell Crowe	1964
Jack Black	1969

8th

Patricia Arquette	1968
John Gavin	1928
Sonja Henie	1912
Julian Lennon	1963
Mary Pickford	1893
John Schneider	1954
Melody Thomas Scott	1956
Taran Noah Smith	1984
Izzy Stradlin	1962
Robin Wright Penn	1966

9th

Ward Bond	1903
Hugh Hefner	1926
Michael Learned	1939
Keshia Knight Pulliam	1979
Dennis Quaid	1954

10th

Chuck Connors	1921
William Jayne	1969
Harry Morgan	1915
Steven Segal	1951
Omar Sharif	1932
Max Von Sydow	1929
Charlie Hunnam	1980
Mandy Moore	1984
Haley Joel	1988

11th

Jill Gascoine	1937
Joel Grey	1932
Lisa Stansfield	1966

12th

Jeremy Beadle	1948
David Cassidy	1950
Claire Danes	1979
Shannen Doherty	1971
Andy Garcia	1956
Susan Hampshire	1942
David Letterman	1947
Ann Miller	1923
Ed O'Neill	1946
Tiny Tim	1922
Magda Szubanski	1961

13th

Jonathan Brandis	1976
Peabo Bryson	1951
Peter Davidson	1951
Edward Fox	1937
Howard Keel	1917
Ron Perlman	1950
Rick Schroder	1970

14th

Julie Christie	1941
Sir John Gielgud	1904
Loretta Lynn	1935
Rod Steiger	1925
Sarah Michelle Gellar	1977

15th

Claudia Carinale	1939
Samantha Fox	1966
Elizabeth Montgomery	1933
Linda Perry	1965
Robert Walker Jr	1939
Emma Watson	1990

16th

Kareem Abdul-Jabbar	1974
Ellen Brakin	1954
Sir Charles Chaplin	1889
Jon Cryer	1965
Martin Lawrence	1965
Dorothy McGuire	1919
Henry Mancini	1924
Spike Milligan	1918
Jimmy Osmond	1963
David Pirner	1964
Dusty Springfield	1939
Sir Peter Ustinov	1921
Bobby Vinton	1935

17th

William Holden	1918
Olivia Hussey	1951
Liz Phair	1967

Michael Treanor	1987
Victoria Adams	1975
Jennifer Garner	1972
18th	
Barbara Hale	1922
John James	1956
Hayley Mills	1946
Rick Moranis	1954
Conan O'Brien	1963
Eric Roberts	1956
James Wood	1947
Melissa Joan-Hart	1976
19th	
Don Adams	1927
Tim Curry	1946
Ashley Judd	1968
Jayne Mansfield	1932
Dudley Moore	1935
Dick Sargent	1919
Ruby Wax	1953
Hayden Christensen	1981
20th	
Paul Asher	1961
Michael Brandon	1945
Jessica Lange	1949
Joey Lawrence	1976
Harold Llyod	1893
Ryan O'Neal	1941
Luther Vandross	1951
Carmen Electra	1972
21st	
Tony Danza	1951
Nicolas Lyndurst	1961
Andie MacDowell	1958
Iggy Pop	1947
Anthony Quinn	1915
Robert Smith	1959
22nd	
Eddie Albert	1908
Joseph Bottom	1954
Glen Campbell	1938
Salvatore Coco	1975
George Cole	1925
Peter Frampton	1950
Daniel Johns	1979
Jack Nicholson	1937
Charlotte Rae	1927
Aaron Spelling	1923
John Waters	1946
23rd	
Valerie Bertinelli	1960
Shirley Temple Black	1928
David Brinkley	1938
Judy Davis	1955
Sandra Dee	1942
Joyce DeWitt	1949
Lee Majors	1940
Simon Matthews	1964
Roy Orbison	1936
Herve Villechaize	1943
Judy Davis	1955
24th	
Jill Ireland	1936
Shane McDermott	1967
Shirley MacLaine	1934
Barbra Streisand	1942
Paula Yates	1960
25th	
Joey Andrews	1979
Jonathan Angel	1977
Al Pacino	1940
William Roache	1932
Renée Zellweger	1969
Daniel MacPherson	1981
26th	
Carol Burnett	1933
Michael Damian	1962
Bobby Rydell	1942
Koo Stark	1956
27th	
Judy Carne	1939
Howard Donald	1970
Sheena Easton	1959
Casey Kasem	1932
Jack Klugman	1922
Walter Lantz	1900
David Lascher	1972
Kylie Travis	1969
28th	
Ann-Margaret	1941
Jimmy Barnes	1956
Carol Jones	1933
Jay Leno	1950
Alexandra Paul	1964

Nate Richard	1988
Penelope Cruz	1974
Nate Richert	1978
29th	
Daniel Day-Lewis	1957
Anita Dobson	1949
Celeste Holm	1919
Rod McKuen	1933
Kate Mulgrew	1955
Michelle Pfeiffer	1957
Jerry Seinfeld	1955
Uma Thurman	1970
30th	
Kirsten Dunst	1982
Jill Clayburgh	1944
Michael Elder	1931
John Galecki	1975
Perry King	1948
Cloris Leachman	1926
Al Lewis	1923
Willie Nelson	1933

MAY

1st	
Judy Collins	1939
Rita Collidge	1945
Glenn Ford	1916
Joanna Lumley	1946
Charlie Schlatter	1966
Una Stubbs	1937
2nd	
Christine Baranski	1952
Bing Crosby	1901
Larry Gatlin	1948
Lesley Gore	1946
Bianca Jagger	1945
Donatella Versace	1955
The Rock	1972
3rd	
James Brown	1928
Christopher Cross	1951
Ben Elton	1959
Engelbert Humperdinck	1936
Frankie Valli	1937
Sally Whittaker	1963
4th	
Michael Barrymore	1952
Audrey Hepburn	1929
Jackie Jackson	1951
Randy Travis	1959
Pia Zadora	1956
Lance Bass	1979
5th	
Annette Bening	1958
Dieter Brummer	1976
Danielle Fisher	1987
Vincent Kartheiser	1979
Michael Palin	1943
Tyrone Power	1913
Sage Stallone	1976
Tammy Wynette	1942
6th	
George Clooney	1961
Stewart Granger	1913
Bob Seger	1945
Rudolph Valentino	1895
Orson Wells	1915
7th	
Anne Baxter	1923
Teresa Brewer	1931
Gary Cooper	1901
Julian Escott	1972
Richard O'Sullivan	1944
Peter Reckon	1955
8th	
Sir David Attenborough	1926
Melissa Gilbert	1964
Gary Glitter	1964
Ricky Nelson	1940
Toni Tennille	1943
Alex van Halen	1955
Enrique Iglesias	1975
Gary Wilmont	1954
Darren Hayes	1972
9th	
Candice Bergen	1946
James L Brooks	1940
Albert Finney	1936
Glenda Jackson	1936
Billy Joel	1949
Joan Simms	1930
Hank Snow	1914
10th	
Fred Astaire	1899

Bono	1960
Donovan	1946
Meg Foster	1948
Maureen Lipman	1946
Nancy Walker	1922
11th	
Bryan Adams	1959
Irving Berlin	1888
Jonathan Stevens Jackson	1982
Austin O'Brien	1981
Natasha Richardson	1963
Dame Margaret Rutherford	1892
Phil Silvers	1912
12th	
Burt Bacharach	1929
Stephen Baldwin	1966
Bruce Boxleitner	1950
Teddy Dealcourt	1972
Emilio Estevez	1962
Kim Fields	1969
Katharine Hepburn	1907
Wilfred Hyde-White	1903
Pam St Clement	1944
Jason Biggs	1978
13th	
Bea Arthur	1926
Harvey Keitel	1939
Julianne Phillips	1962
Dennis Rodman	1961
Stevie Wonder	1950
14th	
David Byrne	1952
Bobby Darin	1936
George Lucas	1944
Robert Zemeckis	1951
15th	
David Charvet	1972
Lainie Kazan	1942
Trini Lopez	1937
James Mason	1909
Jamie-Lynn Sigler	1981
16th	
Pierce Brosnan	1952
Henry Fonda	1905
Tracey Gold	1969
Janet Jackson	1966
Lenny Kravitz	1964
Liberace	1919
Tori Spelling	1973
David Boreanaz	1971
17th	
Enya	1961
Dennis Hooper	1936
Maureen O'Sullivan	1911
Trent Reznor	1965
Bob Saget	1956
Debra Winger	1955
18th	
Perry Como	1912
Nancy Kwan	1939
Martika	1969
Robert Morse	1931
Pernell Roberts	1930..
George Strait	1952
19th	
Steven Ford	1956
James Fox	1939
Grace Jones	1952
James Ryne	1957
Pete Townshend	1945
Victoria Wood	1953
20th	
Cher	1946
Joe Crocker	1944
Tony Goldwin	1960
Bronson Pinchot	1959
Ron Regan Jr	1958
James (Jimmy) Stewart	1908
21st	
Raymond Burr	1917
Mr T	1952
Judge Reinhold	1957
Harold Robbins	1916
Leo Sayer	1948
22nd	
Richard Benjamin	1938
Naiomi Campbell	1970
Lord Olivier	1907
Barbara Perkins	1942
Susan Strasberg	1938
Bernie Taupin	1950
23rd	
Rosemary Clooney	1928
Joan Collins	1933

Nigel Davenport	1928
Douglas Fairbanks	1883
Tamara Kennedy	1962
Artie Shaw	1910
Drew Carey	1958
24th	
Gary Burghoff	1943
Roseanne Cash	1955
Bob Dylan	1941
Patti La Belle	1944
Kristin Scott Thomas	1960
Lilli Palmer	1914
Priscilla Beaulieu Presley	1945
Jon & Jeremy Torgerson	1982
Kym Valentine	1946
25th	
Frank OZ	1944
Dixie Carter	1939
Jeanne Crain	1925
Hal David	1921
Mike Myers	1963
Connie Selleca	1955
Beverly Sills	1929
Lesile Uggams	1943
Anne Heche	1969
Lauryn Hill	1975
Sir Ian McKellen	1939
26th	
James Arness	1923
Helena Bonham Carter	1966
Ray Dotrice	1925
Genie Francis	1962
Al Jolson	1886
Peggy Lee	1920
Patsy Palmer	1972
Stevie Nicks	1948
Phillip Michael Thomas	1949
John Wayne	1907
Hank Williams Jr	1949
27th	
Cilla Black	1943
Todd Bridges	1965
Wayne Carey	1971
Pat Cash	1965
Neil Finn	1958
Louis Gossett Jr	1936
Christopher Lee	1922
Vincent Price	1911
Bruce Weitz	1943
Peri Gilpin	1961
Joseph Fiennes	1970
28th	
Paul Bradley	1955
Faith Brown	1944
Dame Thora Hird	1913
Gladys Knight	1944
Sondra Loke	1947
Kylie Minogue	1968
Gary Stewart	1945
29th	
Helmut Berger	1944
Melissa Etheridge	1961
Rupert Everett	1959
Anthony Geary	1947
Bob Hope	1903
LaToya Jackson	1979
Francis Rossi	1949
30th	
Mel Blanc	1908
Benny Goodman	1909
Wynnona Judd	1964
Michael Pollard	1939
Clint Walker	1927
31st	
Tom Berenger	1950
Diesel	1966
Clint Eastwood	1930
Chris Elliott	1960
Sharon Glass	1943
Anthony Harrell	1977
Gregory Harrison	1950
Joe Namath	1943
Brooke Shields	1965
Lea Thompson	1961

JUNE

1st	
Pat Boone	1934
Jason Donovan	1968
Morgan Freeman	1937
Andy Griffith	1926
Lisa Hartman/Black	1956
Bob Monkhouse	1928
Marilyn Monroe	1926

Alanis Morissette	1974
Robert Powell	1944
Ron Wood	1947
Edward Woodward	1930
2nd	
Dana Carvey	1955
Cy Chadwick	1969
Charles Haid	1943
Marvin Hamlisch	1944
Stacy Keach	1941
Sally Kellerman	1937
Johnny Weissmuller	1904
3rd	
Tony Curtis	1925
Colleen Dewhurst	1926
Paulette Goddard	1911
Benjamin Mitchell	1965
Suzi Quatro	1950
Tristan Rodgers	1946
4th	
Angelina Jolie	1975
Gene Barry	1922
John Drew Barrymore	1932
Bruce Dern	1936
Michelle Phillips	1944
Rosalind Russell	1908
Parker Stevenson	1952
Dennis Weaver	1924
Dr Ruth Westheimer	1928
Noah Wyle	1971
Scott Wolf	1968
5th	
Chad Allen	1974
Moira Anderson	1940
Kenny G	1956
Mark Wahlberg	1971
6th	
Sandra Bernhardt	1955
Harvey Fierstein	1954
Staci Keanan	1975
Toni Michelle	1972
Amada Pays	1959
Toni Pearen	1972
7th	
Jenny Jones	1946
Tom Jones	1940
Liam Neeson	1952
Larisa Oleynik	1981
The Artist Formerly Known as Prince	1958
Cassidy Rae	1975
Jessica Tandy	1909
Mick Foley	1965
8th	
Kathy Baker	1950
James Darren	1936
Griffin Dunne	1995
Mick Hucknall	1960
Taryil Jackson	1975
Julia Margulies	1966
Robert Preston	1918
Nick Rhodes	1962
Joan Rivers	1937
Boz Scaggs	1944
Nancy Sinatra	1940
Alexis Smith	1921
Bonnie Tyler	1953
Keenan Ivory Wayans	1958
9th	
Tony Britton	1925
Johnny Depp	1963
Michael J Fox	1961
Les Paul	1916
Cole Porter	1892
Natalie Portman	1981
10th	
Linda Evangelista	1965
Judy Garland	1922
June Haver	1926
Elizabeth Hurley	1965
Lionel Jeffries	1926
Hattie McDaniel	1895
Elisabeth Shue	1963
Andrew Stevens	1955
Bill Waddington	1916
Leelee Sobieski	1982
11th	
Chad Everett	1936
Joshua Jackson	1978
Richard Todd	1919
Gene Wilder	1935
Hugh Laurie	1959
12th	
Timothy Busfield	1957

Vic Dammone	1928
Ann Kirkbridge	1954
Jim Nabors	1932
13th	
Tim Allen	1953
Mary Kate & Ashley Olsen	1986
Ethan Randall	1968
Ally Sheedy	1962
Richard Thomas	1951
Jamie Walters	1969
14th	
Boy George	1961
15th	
James Belushi	1954
Courtenay Cox Arquette	1964
Ice Cube	1969
Helen Hunt	1963
Waylon Jennings	1937
Malcolm McDowell	1943
Jim Varney	1949
Josh Walker	1973
16th	
Stan Laurel	1890
Laurie Metcalf	1955
Joan van Ark	1946
Tupac Shakur	1971
17th	
Mark Linn-Baker	1954
Barry Manilow	1946
Dean Martin	1917
Joe Piscopo	1951
Jason Patric	1966
Beryl Reid	1920
Greg Kinnear	1963
18th	
Kathy Bates	1948
Paul Eddington	1927
Carol Kane	1952
Sir Paul McCartney	1942
Jeanette MacDonald	1901
Isabella Rossellini	1952
Delia Smith	1941
19th	
Paula Abdul	1962
Louis Jourdan	1919
Simon O'Brien	1965
Phylicia Rashad	1948
Gena Rowlands	1934
Kathleen Turner	1954
20th	
Chet Atkins	1924
Wendy Craig	1934
Olympia Dukakis	1931
Errol Flynn	1909
John Goodman	1952
Martin Landau	1934
Nicole Kidman	1967
Cyndi Lauper	1953
Audie Murphy	1924
Anne Murray	1945
Lionel Ritchie	1949
Tina Sinatra	1948
Brian Wilson	1942
21st	
Meredith Baxter	1947
Ron Ely	1938
Michael Gross	1947
Mariette Hartley	1940
Judy Holiday	1922
Anne Kirkbridge	1954
Bernie Kopell	1933
Juliette Lewis	1973
Jane Russell	1921
Doug Savant	1964
Maureen Stapleton	1925
Scott Richard Wolf	1973
22nd	
Bill Blass	1922
Kris Kristofferson	1936
Chris Lemmon	1954
Michael Lerner	1941
Allen Osmond	1949
Tracy Pollan	1960
Freddie Prinze	1954
Prunella Scales	1932
Meryl Streep	1949
Lindsay Wagner	1949
Billy Wilder	1906
23rd	
Bryan Brown	1947
June Carter Cash	1929
Adam Faith	1940
Bob Fosse	1927
24th	

Nancy Allen	1950
Mick Fleetwood	1942
Michele Lee	1942
Sherry Stringfield	1967
Solange Knowles	1986
25th	
Gary Grosby	1933
Tim Finn	1951
June Lockhart	1925
George Michael	1963
Carly Simon	1945
26th	
Georgie Fame	1943
Chris Isaak	1956
Aaron Jackson	1973
Chris O'Donnell	1970
Elanor Parker	1922
27th	
Yasmine Bleeth	1969
Shirley Anne Fields	1938
Lorrie Morgan	1959
Tobey Maguire	1975
28th	
Kathy D Bates	1948
Danielle Brisebois	1969
Mel Brooks	1926
John Cusack	1966
Bruce Davidson	1946
John Inman	1935
Mary Stuart Masterton	1966
Gilda Radner	1946
Adam Woodyatt	1968
Gill Bellows	1967
29th	
Gary Busey	1944
Amanda Donohoe	1962
Nelson Eddy	1901
Robert Evans	1930
Sophie Formica	1971
Sharon Lawerance	1962
Richard Lewis	1947
John McCook	1945
Samantha Smith	1972
Ruth Warrick	1947
Abs Breen	1977
30th	
Melanie Alexander	1974
Florence Ballard	1943
Nancy Dussault	1936
Susan Hoyward	1918
Lena Horne	1917
Buddy Rich	1917
Vincent D'Onofrio	1959

JULY

1st	
Dan Ackroyd	1952
Daryl Anderson	1951
Karen Black	1942
Leslie Caron	1931
Olivia DeHavilland	1916
Diana Princess of Wales	1961
Johnny Farnham	1949
Jamie Farr	1934
Deborah Harry	1945
Charles Laughton	1899
Pamela Lee	1967
Jean Marsh	1934
Sydney Pollack	1934
John Tesh	1953
Liv Tyler	1977
William Wyler	1902
2nd	
Polly Holliday	1937
Cheryl Ladd	1951
Jimmy McNichol	1961
Ron Silver	1946
Tom Springfield	1936
Ashton Kutcher	1978
3rd	
Laura Branigan	1957
Betty Buckley	1947
Vince Clarke	1961
Tom Cruise	1962
Taylor Dayne	1963
Pete Fountain	1930
Shane Lynch	1976
Ken Russell	1927
George Sanders	1906
Jan Smithers	1949
Tom Stoppard	1938
4th	
Gina Lollobrigida	1927
Scott Major	1975

Geraldo Rivera	1943
Eva Marie Saint	1927
Neil Simon	1927
5th	
Huey Lewis	1951
Warren Oates	1928
6th	
Allyce Beasley	1954
Ned Beatty	1937
Merv Griffin	1925
Nancy Griffith	1953
Shelly Hack	1952
Bill Haley	1925
Janet Leigh	1927
Della Reese	1932
William Schallert	1922
Sylvester Stallone	1946
Burt Ward	1946
Geoffrey Rush	1951
7th	
Pierre Cardin	1922
Shelly Duvall	1949
Vince Edwards	1929
Jessica Hahn	1959
David Duchovny	1960
Bill Oddie	1941
Jon Pertwee	1919
Ringo Starr	1940
Dame Flora Robson	1902
Joe Spano	1946
8th	
Kevin Bacon	1958
Nathan Harvey	1971
Anjelica Huston	1951
Milo Ventimiglia	1977
9th	
Ed Ames	1929
Brian Dennehy	1939
Scott Christopher Grimes	1972
Tom Hanks	1956
Courtney Love	1964
Kelly McGillis	1957
Fred Savage	1976
O J Simpson	1947
Jimmy Smits	1955
Michael Williams	1935
10th	
Ron Glass	1945
Fred Gwynne	1926
Thomas Ian	1980
Sue Lyon	1946
Jason Orange	1970
Neil Tennant	1954
Jessica Simpson	1980
11th	
Giorgio Armani	1934
Tab Hunter	1931
Mark Lester	1958
Bonnie Pointer	1951
Richie Sambora	1958
Suzanne Vega	1959
Sela Ward	1956
Lisa Rinna	1963
12th	
Milton Berle	1908
Leah Brechnell	1964
Yul Brynner	1915
Bill Crosby	1937
Mel Harris	1957
Jennifer Saunders	1958
Jason Simmons	1971
Richard Simmons	1948
13th	
Bob Crane	1928
Cameron Crowe	1958
Harrison Ford	1942
Louise Mandrell	1954
Cheech Marin	1946
Patrick Stewart	1940
14th	
Polly Bergen	1930
Missy Gold	1970
Nancy Olson	1928
Harry Dean Stanton	1926
15th	
Willie Aames	1960
Brian Austin Green	1973
Ken Kercheval	19635
Brigitte Nielsen	1963
Linda Ronstadt	1946
Jan-Michael Vincent	1944
Forrest Whitaker	1961
Aden Young	1972

Scott Foley	1972
Forest Whitaker	1961
16th	
Corey Feldman	1971
T J Jackson	1978
Ginger Rogers	1911
Barbara Stanwyck	1907
Will Ferrell	1967
Phoebe Cates	1963
17th	
Lucy Arnaz	1951
James Cagney	1899
Diahann Carroll	1935
Spencer Davis	1942
Phyllis Diller	1917
David Hasselhoff	1952
Billy Myers	1971
Donald Sutherland	1934
Brandy Alexander	1964
Tim Brooke-Taylor	1940
Gale Garnett	1942
Jane Hazlegrove	1968
Melanie Thierry	1981
Alex Winter	1965
18th	
James Brolin	1940
Hume Cronyn	1911
Audrey Landers	1959
Elizabeth McGovern	1961
Martha Reeves	1941
Ricky Skaggs	1954
Red Skelton	1913
Vin Diesel	1967
19th	
Vicki Carr	1941
Anthony Edwards	1963
David Goldsmith	1969
20th	
Donna Dixon	1957
Wendy Richard	1946
Dame Diana Rigg	1938
Natalie Wood	1938
Gisele Bundchen	1980
21st	
Leah Bracknell	1964
Don Knotts	1924
Jon Lovitz	1957
Kay Starr	1922
Cat Stevens	1948
Mollie Sugden	1922
Robin Williams	1952
Josh Hartnett	1978
22nd	
Albert Books	1947
Willem Dafoe	1955
Danny Glover	1947
Jason Robards	1922
Bobby Sherman	1945
Terence Stamp	1939
Alex Trebek	1940
Carson Daly	1973
23rd	
Bert Convy	1934
Gloria DeHaven	1925
David Essex	1947
Woody Harrelson	1961
Eriq LaSalle	1963
Eddie McClurge	1951
Stephanie Seymour	1968
Slash	1965
Michael Wilding	1912
Monica Lewinsky	1973
Rebecca Cartwright	1983
24th	
Ruth Buzzi	1936
Jennifer Lopez	1969
Linda Carter	1951
Robert Hays	1947
Lori Loughlin	1964
Michael Richards	1949
Chris Sarandon	1942
Anna Paquin	1982
25th	
Estelle Getty	1923
Barbara Harris	1935
Iman	1955
Matt Le Blanc	1967
Brad Renfro	1982
26th	
Sandra Bullock	1964
Blake Edwards	1922
Susan George	1950
Mick Jagger	1943
Stanley Kubrick	1928

Helen Mirren	1945
Kevin Spacey	1959
27th	
Bobby Gentry	1944
Norman Lear	1922
Maureen McGovern	1949
Julian McMahon	1968
Sasha Mitchell	1967
Betty Thomas	1948
Jerry van Dyke	1931
Toby Maguire	1975
28th	
Elizabeth Berkley	1972
Sally Struthers	1948
Michael Hayden	1963
Linda Kelsey	1946
Barbara la Marr	1896
Rudy Vallee	1901
Joe E Brown	1892
29th	
Robert Fuller	1937
David Warner	1941
Wil Wheaton	1972
30th	
Paul Anka	1941
Peter Bogdanovich	1939
Delta Burke	1956
Kate Bush	1958
Ed Byrnes	1933
Larry Fishburne	1961
Lisa Kudrow	1963
Arnold Schwarzenegger	1947
31st	
Dean Cain	1966
Geraldine Chaplin	1944
Wesley Snipes	1962
Daniel Radcliffe	1989

AUGUST

1st	
Tempest Bledsoe	1973
Dom DeLuise	1931
Joe Elliott	1959
Stuart Wade	1971
2nd	
Edward Furlong	1977
Myrna Loy	1905
Carroll O'Connor	1924
Peter O'Toole	1932
Alan Whicker	1925
3rd	
Tony Bennett	1926
Victoria Jackson	1958
John Landis	1950
Jay North	1951
Martin Sheen	1940
Terry Wogan	1936
4th	
Marques Houston	1981
Billy Bob Thornton	1955
5th	
Loni Anderson	1946
John Huston	1906
Tawny Kitaen	1961
Maureen McCormick	1956
Holly Palance	1950
John Saxon	1935
Jonathan Silverman	1966
Robert Taylor	1911
6th	
Lucille Ball	1911
Frank Finlay	1928
Soleil Moon Frye	1976
Melissa George	1976
Catherine Hicks	1951
Stephanie Kramer	1956
Robert Mitchum	1917
Geri Halliwell	1972
Olver Tobias	1947
Andy Warhol	1927
Barbara Windsor	1937
7th	
Billie Burke	1886
Lana Cantrell	1943
Bruce Dickson	1958
Stan Freberg	1926
Alexei Sayle	1952
B J Thomas	1942
Charlize Theron	1975
8th	
Richard Anderson	1926
Keith Carradine	1950
Dino DeLaurentis	1919
Brian Harvey	1974

Dustin Hoffman 1937
Connie Stevens 1938
Sylvia Sydney 1910
Mel Tillis 1932
Peter Weir 1944
Larry Wilcox 1947
Esther Williams 1923
Joshua Scott Chasez 1976
Mary-Louise Parker 1964

9th

Gillian Anderson 1968
Amanda Berse 1958
Sam Elliott 1944
Melanie Griffith 1957
Whitney Houston 1963
Andrew Mackintosh 1960

10th

Rosanna Arquette 1959
Patti Austin 1948
Antonio Banderas 1960
Eddie Fisher 1928
Rhonda Fleming 1923
Annie Jones 1967
Paul Kelly 1955
Kate O'Mara 1939
Norma Shearer 1900

11th

Arlene Dahl 1928
Mike Douglas 1925
Will Friedle 1976
Hulk Hogan 1953

12th

Cecil B DeMille 1881
John Derek 1926
George Hamilton 1939

13th

Danny Bonaduce 1959
Quinn Cummings 1967
Dan Fogelberg 1951
Sir Alfred Hitchcock 1899
Don Ho 1930
Buddy Rogers 1904

14th

Halle Berry 1966
David Crosby 1941
Alice Ghostley 1926
Jackee 1957
Gary Larson 1950
Steve Martin 1945
Susan Olsen 1961
Susan Saint James 1946
Danielle Steel 1947
Gillian Taylforth 1955

15th

Ethel Barrymore 1879
Julia Child 1912
Mike Connors 1925
Jim Dale 1935
Abby Dalton 1935
Michael Graham 1972
Dame Wendy Hillier 1912
Rose Marie 1925
Vincent Poletto 1970
Ben Unwin 1977
Jimmy Webb 1946
Ben Affleck 1972

16th

Angela Bassett 1958
Ann Blyth 1928
Robert Culp 1930
Eydie Gorme 1932
Timothy Hutton 1960
Donovan Letich 1968
Madonna 1958
Julie Newmar 1935
Fess Parker 1925
Lesley Ann Warren 1946

17th

Belinda Carlisle 1958
Robert DeNiro 1943
Samuel Goldwyn 1882
Maureen O'Hara 1921
Sean Penn 1960
Donnie Wahlberg 1970
Mae West 1892

18th

Max Factor 1904
Martin Mull 1943
Roman Polanski 1933
Robert Redford 1937
Christian Slater 1969
Madeleine Stowe 1958
Patrick Swayze 1954
Malcolm Jamal Warner 1970

Edward Norton	1969
19th	
Coco Channel	1883
Kevin Dillon	1965
Jonathan Frakes	1952
Peter Gallagher	1955
Gerald Moore	1902
Debra Paget	1933
Matthew Perry	1969
Gene Roddenberry	1921
Jill St John	1940
John Stamos	1963
Percy Miller	1989
20th	
Connie Chung	1946
Rudy Gatlin	1952
Isaac Hayes	1942
21st	
Count Basie	1904
Kim Cattrall	1956
Kenny Rogers	1938
22nd	
Howie Dorough	1973
Tori Amos	1963
Honor Blackman	1928
Ray Bradbury	1920
Valerie Harper	1940
Debbie Peterson	1960
Cindy Williams	1947
Shelley Winters	1922
23rd	
Barbara Eden	1934
Gene Kelly	1912
Shelley Long	1949
Vera Miles	1929
Keith Moon	1947
River Phoenix	1970
Richard Sanders	1940
Rick Springfield	1949
Rich Neville	1979
24th	
Stephen Fry	1957
Steve Guttenberg	1958
Marlee Matlin	1965
Joe Regalbuto	1971
Rupert Grint	1988
25th	
Anne Archer	1947
Leonard Berstein	1918
Clara Bow	1905
Tim Burton	1958
Elvis Costello	1955
Billy Ray Cyrus	1961
Sir Sean Connery	1930
Mel Ferrer	1917
Val Johnson	1916
Ruby Keeler	1909
Bryan Mosley	1931
Gene Simmons	1949
Tom Skerritt	1933
Blair Underwood	1964
Claudia Schiffer	1970
26th	
Chris Burke	1965
Macaulay Culkin	1980
27th	
Barbara Bach	1947
Pee-Wee Herman	1952
Martha Raye	1916
Tommy Sands	1937
Tuesday Weld	1943
28th	
Windsor Davies	1930
Michael Galeota	1984
Ben Gazzara	1930
Nancy Kulp	1921
Donald O'Connor	1925
Wayne Osmond	1951
Jason Priestley	1969
Leann Rimes	1982
Emma Samms	1960
David Soul	1943
Daniel Stern	1957
Shania Twain	1965
29th	
Sir Richard Attenborough	1923
Ingrid Bergman	1913
Richard Gere	1949
Elliott Gould	1938
Lenny Henry	1958
Michael Jackson	1958
Robin Leach	1941
Rebecca De Mornay	1962

Isable Sanford 1933
30th
Elizabeth Ashley 1939
Timothy Bottom 1951
Peggy Lipton 1947
Fred MacMurray 1908
Cameron Diaz 1972
Kimberley Joseph 1973
Rich Cronin 1975
31st
James Coburn 1928
Debbie Gibson 1970
Buddy Hackett 1924
Van Morrison 1945
Jack Thompson 1940
Chris Tucker 1971

SEPTEMBER

1st
Yvonne de Carlo 1922
Gloria Estefan 1957
Barry Gibb 1946
Sir Jack Hawkins 1910
Lily Tomlin 1939
Conway Twitty 1933
2nd
Marge Champion 1923
Mark Hermon 1951
k.d. Lang 1961
Keanu Reeves 1964
Salma Hayek 1966
3rd
Eileen Brennan 1937
Tiffany Chapman 1979
Pauline Collins 1940
Katrina Hobbs 1961
Alan Ladd 1913
Valerie Perrine 1943
Charlie Sheen 1965
4th
Mitzi Gaylor 1930
Judith Ivey 1951
Kevin Kennedy 1961
Ione Skye 1971
Damon Wayans 1960
Beyonce Knowles 1981
5th
Kristian Aldonso 1965
Johnny Briggs 1935
William Davane 1937
Carol Lawrence 1932
Freddie Mercury 1946
Bob Newhart 1929
Raquel Welch 1940
Darryl F Zanuck 1902
Dweezil Zappa 1969
6th
Jane Curtin 1947
Jeff Foxworthy 1958
Swoosie Kurtz 1944
Jo Anne Worley 1937
7th
Corbin Bernsen 1954
Michael Feinstein 1958
Samuel Goldwyn Jr 1926
Buddy Holly 1936
Noah Huntley 1974
Chrissie Hynde 1951
Julie Kavner 1951
Elia Kazan 1909
John Philip Law 1937
Peter Lawford 1923
Anthony Quayle 1913
Richard Roundtree 1942
Devon Sawa 1978
8th
Sid Caesar 1922
Patsy Cline 1932
Sir Harry Secombe 1921
Peter Sellers 1925
Jonathan Taylor Thomas 1981
Heather Thomas 1957
Henry Thomas 1972
9th
Angela Cartwright 1952
Hugh Grant 1960
Rachel Hunter 1970
Michael Keaton 1951
Kirsty McNichol 1962
Sylvia Miles 1932
Pepa 1969
Otis Redding 1941
Cliff Robinson 1925

Adam Sandler	1966
Tom Wopat	1951
10th	
Chris Columbus	1958
Jose Feliciano	1945
Colin Firth	1960
Judy Geeson	1948
Amy Irving	1953
Jennifer Tilly	1958
Fay Wray	1907
Ryan Phillippe	1974
Guy Ritchie	1968
11th	
Harry Connick Jr	1967
Brian DePalma	1940
Lola Falana	1943
Joe Jackson	1955
D H Lawrence	1885
Virgina Madsen	1963
Ariana Richards	1979
Brad Fischetti	1975
12th	
Maurice Chevalier	1888
Linda Gray	1940
Margaret Hamilton	1902
Patrick Mower	1940
Peter Scolari	1954
Rachel Ward	1957
13th	
Barbara Bain	1932
Jacqueline Bissett	1944
Neil Carter	1948
Claudette Colbert	1905
Bert Lahr	1895
Ben Savage	1980
Jean Smart	1959
Mel Torme	1925
Shane Warne	1969
14th	
Amanda Barrie	1939
Mary Crosby	1959
Faith Ford	1964
Joey Heatherton	1944
Walter Koenig	1936
Clayton Moore	1914
Sam Neill	1947
Joe Penny	1956
15th	
Agatha Christie	1890
Jackie Cooper	1921
Tommy Lee Jones	1946
Margaret Lockwood	1916
Oliver Stone	1946
Jay Whitmore	1975
16th	
Lauren Bacall	1924
Ed Begley Jr	1949
George Chakiris	1933
David Copperfield	1956
Peter Falk	1927
Ann Francis	1930
Alan Funt	1914
BB King	1925
Richard Marx	1963
Mickey Rourke	1950
Susan Ruttan	1948
Alexis Bledel	1982
17th	
Anne Bancroft	1931
Paul Benedict	1938
Kyle Chandler	1965
Elvira	1951
Charles Lawson	1959
Roddy McDowall	1928
John Ritter	1948
Rita Rudner	1956
Austin St John	1974
Hank Williams	1923
18th	
Frankie Avalon	1939
Robert Blake	1933
Rossano Brazzi	1916
Agnes De Mille	1905
Greta Garbo	1905
Holly Robinson	1964
Jack Warner	1920
Jada Pinkett Smith	1971
James Gandolfini	1961
19th	
Brian Epstein	1934
Frances Farmer	1913
Kevin Hooks	1958
Jeremy Irons	1948
Joan Lunden	1950

David McCallum	1933
Freda Payne	1945
Rex Smith	1956
Twiggy	1949
Adam West	1928
Paul Williams	1940
James Fallon	1974
20th	
Gary Cole	1957
Sophia Loren	1934
Gunnar & Matthew Nelson	1969
Rachel Roberts	1927
Tim Rogers	1969
21st	
Dave Coulier	1959
David James Elliott	1960
Liam Gallagher	1972
Larry Hagman	1931
Stephen King	1947
Ricki Lake	1968
Joseph Mazello	1983
Rob Morrow	1950
Bill Murray	1950
Alfonso Riberio	1971
H G Wells	1866
Luke Wilson	1971
22nd	
Bree Desborough	1979
Scott Baio	1961
Shari Belafonte	1954
Debby Boone	1956
Nick Cave	1957
John Houseman	1902
Catherine Oxenberg	1961
Rob Stone	1962
Eric Von Stoheim	1885
Andrea Bocelli	1958
23rd	
Jason Alexander	1959
Ray Charles	1930
Lesley Fitz-Simons	1961
Julio Iglesias	1943
Walter Pidgeon	1897
Mickey Rooney	1920
Bruce Springsteen	1949
Erik Michael Estrada	1979
24th	
Jim Henson	1936
Shelia MacRae	1924
Linda McCartney	1942
Anthony Newley	1931
Kevin Sorbo	1958
25th	
Ronnie Barker	1928
Michael Douglas	1944
Mark Hamill	1952
Felicity Kendall	1946
Heather Locklear	1961
Juliet Prowse	1936
Christopher Reeve	1952
Will Smith	1968
Robert Walden	1943
Barbara Walters	1931
Anson Williams	1941
Catherine Zeta-Jones	1969
26th	
Melissa Sue Anderson	1962
Carlene Carter	1955
Donna Douglas	1935
T S Elliot	1888
Bryan Ferry	1945
George Gershwin	1898
Linda Hamilton	1957
Olivia Newton-John	1948
Patrick O'Neal	1927
George Raft	1895
Anne Robinson	1944
Christina Milian	1981
27th	
Wilford Brimley	1934
Shaun Cassidy	1958
Michele Dotrice	1948
Sophie Jeffery	1984
Adolph Larrue Martinez II	1948
Meat Loaf	1951
Jane Meadows	1926
Greg Morris	1934
Cheryl Tiegs	1947
Robb Weller	1949
Gwyneth Paltrow	1972
28th	
Brigitte Bardot	1934
Peter Finch	1916

Janeane Garufalo	1964
Sylvia Kristal	1952
Marcello Mastroianni	1924
Ed Sullivan	1902
Moon Unit Zappa	1968
Mira Sorvino	1967
29th	
Gene Autry	1907
Anita Ekberg	1931
Greer Garson	1908
Patricia Hodge	1946
Trevor Howard	1916
Madeline Kahn	1942
Stanley Kramer	1913
Jerry Lee Lewis	1935
Larry Linville	1939
Emily Lloyd	1969
30th	
Crystal Bernard	1963
Truman Capote	1924
Lacey Chabert	1982
Angie Dickinson	1931
Fran Drescher	1957
Deborah Kerr	1921
Rula Lenska	1946
Johnny Mathis	1935
Marilyn McCoo	1943
Ian Ogilvy	1943
Eric Stoltz	1961
Victoria Tennant	1953
Barry Williams	1954
Jenna Elfman	1971
Monica Belluci	1968

OCTOBER

1st	
Julie Andrews	1935
Tom Bosley	1927
Stephen Collins	1947
Keith Duffy	1974
Richard Harris	1932
Laurence Harvey	1928
Walter Matthau	1920
George Peppard	1928
Randy Quaid	1950
Stella Stevens	1936
James Whitmore	1921
2nd	
Bud Abbott	1900
Lorraine Bracco	1971
Simon Gregson	1974
Don McLean	1945
Groucho Marx	1890
Thomas Muster	1967
Rex Reed	1938
Sting	1951
Tiffany	1971
Lene (Aqua)	1973
3rd	
Neve Campbell	1973
Chubby Checker	1941
Tommy Lee	1962
Sir Jimmy Savile	1926
Gore Vidal	1925
Kevin Richardson	1972
India Arie	1976
Gwendolyn Stefani	1969
4th	
Jackie Collins	1941
Charlton Heston	1924
Buster Keaton	1895
Patti LaBelle	1944
Chris Lowe	1959
Anneka Rice	1958
Susan Sarandon	1946
Alicia Silverstone	1976
5th	
Karen Allen	1951
Josie Bissett	1969
Diane Cilento	1933
Jeff Conway	1950
Sir Bob Geldof	1954
Glynis Johns	1923
Donald Pleasence	1919
Scott Weinger	1975
Kate Winslet	1975
Bernie Mac	1957
6th	
Eileen Derbyshire	1930
Britt Ekland	1942
Janet Ganor	1906
Amy Jo Johnson	1970
Carole Lombard	1909
Anna Quayle	1936

7th

June Allyson 1917
Toni Braxton 1967
Clive James 1939
Al Martino 1927
John Cougar Mellencamp 1951
Jane Torvill 1957
Simon Cowell 1959

8th

Shane Ammann 1979
David Carradine 1936
Chevy Chase 1944
Martin Henderson 1974
Paul Hogan 1939
Karyn Parsons 1966
Sara Purcell 1948
Laura Vazquez 1975
Sigourney Weaver 1949
Stephanie Zimbalist 1959
Matt Damon 1970

9th

Scott Bakula 1955
Jackson Browne 1948
Zachary Ty Bryan 1981
John Lennon 1940
Sean Ono Lennon 1975
Michael Pare 1959
Donald Sinden 1923
Randy Spelling 1978

10th

James Clavell 1924
Charles Dance 1947
Helen Hayes 1900
Harold Pinter 190
David Lee Roth 1955
Tanya Tucker 1958
Ben Vereen 1946
Wendy Wasserstein 1950
Bradley Whitford 1959

11th

Joan Cusack 1962
Daryl Hall 1949
David Morse 1953
Luke Perry 1966
Jerome Robbins 1918

12th

Susan Anton 1950
Kirk Cameron 1970
Luciano Pavarotti 1935
Adam Rich 1968
Angela Rippon 1944

13th

Lenny Bruce 1952
Tisha Campbell 1970
Art Garfunkel 1941
Beverly Johnson 1952
Yves Montand 1921
Marie Osmond 1959
Kelly Preston 1962
Paul Simon 1941
Cornel Wilde 1918
Ashanti Douglas 1980

14th

Harry Anderson 1952
Greg Evigan 1953
Lillian Gish 1953
Roger Moore 1927
Sir Cliff Richards 1940
Usher 1978

15th

Richard Carpenter 1946
Tito Jackson 1953
Linda Lavin 1937
Penny Marshall 1942
Tanya Roberts 1955

16th

Peter Bowles 1936
Max Byqraves 1922
Barry Corbin 1940
Linda Darnell 1921
Jeremy Jackson 1980
Gary Kemp 1959
Angela Lansbury 1925
Kellie Martin 1957
Tim Robbins 1958
Suzanne Somers 1946
Wendy Wilson 1969

17th

Sam Bottoms 1955
Montgomery Cliff 1920
Michael French 1962
Beverly Garland 1926
Rita Hayworth 1918
Alan Jackson 1958

Margot Kidder 1948
Evil Knievel 1938
Dolph Lungren 1959
Michael McKean 1947
Arthur Miller 1915
Howard Rollins 1950
Irene Ryan 1903
Vincent Van Patten 1957
George Wendt 1948
Christopher Kirkpatrick 1971
Marshall Mathers III—Eminem 1972

18th

Chuck Berry 1926
Pam Dawber 1951
Sean Patrick Flanery 1965
Wynton Marsalis 1961
Erin Moran 1961
George C Scott 1927
Inger Stevens 1934
Jean-Claude Van Damme 1960

19th

Divine 1945
Jennifer Holliday 1960
John Le Carre 1931
John Lithgow 1945
Robert Reed 1932
Jeannie C Riley 1945
Simon Ward 1941

20th

Snoop Dogg 1971
Earl Hindman 1942
Bela Lugosi 1882
Melanie Mayron 1952
Dannii Minogue 1971
Jerry Orbach 1935
Tom Petty 1952
Susan Tully 1967
Timothy West 1934

21st

Carrie Fisher 1956
Manfred Mann 1940
Jeremy Miller 1976
Judith Sheindlin 1942

22nd

Patti Davis 1953
Catherine Deneuve 1943
Michael Fishman 1982
Joan Fontaine 1917
Annette Funicello 1942
Jeff Goldblum 1952
Alan Ladd Jr 1937
Christopher Lloyd 1938
Zac Hanson 1985

23rd

Johnny Carson 1925
Michael Crichton 1942
Diana Dors 1931
Lauren Tewes 1946
Weird Al Yankovic 1959
Dwight Yoakam 1956

24th

F. Murray Abraham 1939
Doug Davidson 1955
Kevin Kline 1947
David Nelson 1936
Bill Wyman 1936

25th

Billy Barty 1924
Ben Gould 1980
Tracey Nelson 1944
Pablo Picasso 1881
Helen Reddy 1941
Marion Ross 1928

26th

Jackie Coogan 1914
Bob Hoskins 1942
Marla Maples 1963
Natalie Merchant 1963
Jaclyn Smith 1947
Dylan McDermott 1961

27th

William Christopher 1932
John Cleese 1939
Nanette Fabray 1920
Simon Le Bon 1958
Fran Lebowitz 1950
Carrie Snodgrass 1946
Roberto Benigni 1952

28th

Jane Alexander 1939
David Dimbleby 1938
Wayne Fontana 1945
Dennis Franz 1945

Jamie Gertz 1965
Dody Goodman 1929
Edith Head 1907
Bruce Jenner 1949
Cleo Laine 1927
Elsa Lanchester 1902
Leaf Phoenix 1974
Joan Plowright 1929
Annie Potts 1952
Julia Roberts 1967
Daphne Zuniga 1963
Lauren Holly 1963
Andy Richter 1966

29th

Fanny Brice 1891
Richard Dreyfuss 1947
Kate Jackson 1948
Randy Jackson 1961
Melba Moore 1945
Mark Stevens 1971
Joely Fisher 1967
Winona Ryder 1971

30th

Ruth Gordon 1896
Harry Hamlin 1951
Louis Malle 1932
Henry Winkler 1945

31st

John Candy 1950
Dale Evans 1912
Barbara Bel Geddes 1922
Lee Grant 1927
Deirdre Hall 1947
Vanilla Ice 1967
Michael Landon 1936
Sally Kirkland 1944
Dan Rather 1931

NOVEMBER

1st

Rick Allen 1962
Tina Arena 1967
Robert Foxworth 1941
Anthony Kiedis 1962
Lyle Lovett 1957
Marcia Wallace 1942

2nd

Peter Amory 1962
Burt Lancaster 1913
Stephanie Powers 1942
Ann Rutherford 1920

3rd

Adam Ant 1954
Charles Bronson 1921
Kate Capshaw 1953
Lulu 1948
Roseanne 1953

4th

Malandra Burrows 1966
Art Garney 1918
Walter Cronkite 1916
Tonicha Jeronimo 1977
Ralph Macchio 1961
Matthew McConaughey 1969
Markie Post 1950
Kate Reid 1930
Doris Roberts 1930
Will Rogers 1897
Loretta Swit 1937
Yanni 1954
Gig Young 1913

5th

John-Erik Hexum 1958
Vivien Leigh 1913
Andrea McArdle 1963
Corin Nemec 1971
Peter Noone 1947
Tatum O'Neal 1963
Roy Rogers 1912
Sam Shepard 1943
Elke Sommer 1940
Ike Turner 1931
Danniella Westbrood 1973
Frankie Muniz 1985

6th

Brad Davis 1949
Peter DeLuise 1967
Nicole Dubuc 1978
Sally Field 1946
Nigel Havers 1949
Ethan Hawke 1970
Lance Kerwin 1960
Mike Nicholes 1931

Maria Shriver	1955
Lori Singer	1962
7th	
Melissa Bell	1972
Al Hirt	1922
Jeremy Michael London	1972
Christopher Knight	1975
Gordon MacArthur	1961
Joni Mitchell	1943
Barry Newmand	1938
Dana Plato	1964
Su Pollard	1949
Johnny Rivers	1942
Dame Joan Sutherland	1926
Mary Travers	1937
8th	
Elizabeth Dawn	1939
Leif Garrett	1961
Mary Hart	1950
June Havoc	1916
Rickie Lee Jones	1954
Norman Lloyd	1914
Margaret Mitchell	1900
Patti Page	1927
Bonnie Raitt	1949
Esther Rolle	1933
Courtney Thorne-Smith	1968
Alfred Woodard	1953
9th	
Dorothy Dandridge	1922
Marie Dressler	1869
Lou Ferrigno	1952
Hedy Lamarr	1913
Claude Rains	1889
Clifton Webb	1891
Ed Wynn	1886
Nick Lachey	1973
10th	
Richard Burton	1925
Mackenzie Phillips	1959
Roy Scheider	1935
Sinbad	1956
11th	
Leonardo DiCaprio	1975
Stubby Kaye	1918
Demi Moore	1962
June Whitfield	1927
Jonathan Winters	1925
Calista Flockhart	1964
12th	
Tevin Campbell	1976
Grace Kelly	1929
David Loeffler	1972
David Schwimmer	1966
Jo Stafford	1918
Neil Young	1945
13th	
Whoopi Goldberg	1949
Richard Mulligan	1932
Camilla Power	1976
Dack Rambo	1941
Tracey Scoggins	1959
14th	
Barbara Hutton	1912
Brian Keith	1921
Veronica Lake	1919
Dick Powell	1904
Ray Sharkey	1952
McLean Stevenson	1929
15th	
Edward Asner	1929
Petula Clark	1932
Beverly D'Angelo	1953
Sam Waterston	1940
16th	
Lisa Bonet	1967
Tricia Cast	1966
Griff Rhys Jones	1953
David leisure	1950
Burgess Meredith	1907
Martha Plimpton	1970
17th	
Brett Blewitt	1976
Brandon Call	1976
Kate Ceberano	1966
Peter Cook	1937
Danny DeVito	1944
Rock Hudson	1925
Lauren Hutton	1924
Gordon Lightfoot	1938
Dino Martin	1951
Martin Scorcese	1942
Jonathan Ross	1960

Stuart Stone	1977
Lee Strasberg	1901
18th	
Imogene Coco	1909
Linda Evans	1942
David Hemmings	1941
James parker	1950
Elizabeth Perkins	1960
Susan Sullivan	1944
Brenda Vaccaro	1939
Kim Wilde	1960
19th	
Dick Cavett	1936
Tommy Dorsey	1904
Jodie Foster	1962
Dan Haggerty	1941
Larry King	1933
Calvin Klein	1942
Kathleen Quinlan	1954
Meg Ryan	1961
Ted Turner	1938
20th	
Kaye Ballard	1926
Alistair Cook	1908
Richard Dawson	1932
Bo Derek	1956
Veronica Hamel	1943
Gene Tierney	1920
Sean Young	1959
21st	
Goldie Hawn	1945
David Hemmings	1941
Lorna Luft	1952
Harpo Marx	1893
Juliet Mills	1941
Eleanor Powell	1912
Nicollette Sheridan	1963
Marlo Thomas	1938
22nd	
Tom Conti	1941
Jamie Lee Curtis	1958
Rodney Dangerfield	1921
Mariel Hemmingway	1961
Robert Vaughn	1932
Ray Walston	1917
23rd	
Maxwell Caulfield	1959
Boris Karloff	1887
Steve Landesberg	1945
Sue Nicholls	1943
David Rappaport	1951
24th	
Bill Connolly	1942
Denise Crosby	1957
Dan Falzon	1974
Dwight Schultz	1947
25th	
Christina Applegate	1971
Kathryn Crosby	1933
Amy Grant	1960
John F Kennedy Jr	1960
John Larroquette	1947
Roy Lynnes	1943
Ricardo Montalban	1920
26th	
Robert Goulet	1933
Shawn Kemp	1969
Rich Little	1938
Jamie Rose	1959
Charles M Schulz	1922
Tina Turner	1939
Marcy Walker	1961
27th	
John Alderton	1940
Robin Givens	1964
Jimi Hendrix	1942
Bruce Lee	1940
Eddie Rabbitt	1941
Jaleel White	1976
Ernie Wise	1925
28th	
Ed Harris	1950
Hope Lang	1931
Judd Nelson	1959
Randy Newman	1943
Kristian Schmid	1974
Paul Shaffer	1949
29th	
Busby Berkeley	1895
Jonathan Rashleight Knight	1968
Diane Ladd	1939
Howie Mandell	1955
Andrew McCarthy	1962
Cathy Moriarty	1960

Gary Shandling	1949
30th	
Dick Clark	1929
Richard Crenna	1927
Robert Guillaume	1937
Billy Idol	1955
Mandy Patinkin	1952
Virgina Mayo	1920
June Pointer	1954
Paul Stookey	1937
Efrem Zimbalist Jr	1923

DECEMBER

1st	
Woody Allen	1935
Carol Alt	1960
Kenneth Branagh	1960
Mary Martin	1931
Bette Midler	1945
Gilbert O' Sullivan	1946
Richard Pryor	1940
Lou Rawls	1936
Charleen Tilton	1958
Treat Williams	1951
Mark Winger	1961
2nd	
Steve Bauer	1956
Maria Callas	1932
Cathy Lee Crosby	1949
Julie Harris	1925
Eileen McCallum	1936
3rd	
Melody Anderson	1955
Anna Chlumsky	1980
Daryl Hannah	1960
Paul Nicholas	1945
Ozzy Osbourne	1948
Natalie Robb	1974
Mel Smith	1952
Andy Williams	1930
4th	
Max Baer Jr	1937
Tyra Banks	1973
Jeff Bridges	1949
Ronnie Corbett	1930
Deanna Durbin	1921
Pamela Stephenson	1950
Marisa Tomei	1964
Patricia Wettig	1951
5th	
Morgan Brittany	1951
Jose Carreras	1946
Walt Disney	1901
Carrie Hamilton	1963
Billy Hufsey	1960
Little Richard	1932
Otto Preminger	1906
6th	
Dave Brubeck	1920
Ufl Ekberg	1970
Ira Gershwin	1896
Jonathan King	1944
Agnes Moorehead	1906
Janine Turner	1963
7th	
Priscilla Barnes	1955
Ellen Burstyn	1932
C. Thomas Howell	1966
Ted knight	1932
8th	
Gregg Allman	1947
Kim Basinger	1953
David Carradine	1936
Lee J. Cobb	1911
Sammy Davis Jr	1925
Teri Hatcher	1964
Jim Morrison	1943
Sinead O'Connor	1967
Stan Richards	1930
John Rubinstein	1946
Maximilian Schell	1930
Flip Wilson	1933
Katherine Holmes	1978
9th	
Joan Armatrading	1950
Beau Bridges	1941
Dame Judi Dench	1934
Kirk Douglas	1916
Morton Downey Jr	1933
Douglas Fairbanks Jr	1909
Hermione Gingold	1879
John Malkovich	1953
Dina Merrill	1925
Donny Osmond	1957

Dick Van Patten	1928
10th	
Susan Day	1952
Dorothy Lamour	1914
Gloria Loring	1946
Raven Symone Peerman	1985
Tommy Rettig	1941
Jill Summers	1910
11th	
Teri Garr	1944
Jermaine Jackson	1954
Brenda Lee	1944
Donna Mills	1943
Rita Moreno	1931
Carlo Ponti	1913
Rider King Strong	1979
12th	
Ana Alicia	1957
Mayim Bialik	1957
Connie Francis	1938
John Osborne	1929
Edward G Robinson	1893
Frank Sinatra	1915
Dionne Warwick	1941
13th	
Jim Davidson	1953
John Davidson	1941
Chelsea Hereford	1981
Anissa Jones	1958
Robert Lindsay	1949
Christopher Plummer	1927
Dick Van Dyke	1925
Johnny Whitaker	1959
Paula Wilcox	1949
14th	
Dan Daily	1915
Patty Duke	1946
Bridget Hall	1977
Abbe Lane	1943
Lee Remick	1935
Charlie Rich	1932
15th	
Jeff Chandler	1918
Dave Clark	1942
Tim Conway	1933
Don Johnson	1949
Micheal Le Vell	1964
Helen Slater	1963
16th	
Steve Bochco	1943
Nicholas Cochrane	1973
Noel Coward	1899
Liv Ullmann	1939
17th	
Richard Norton	1970
Tommy Steele	1936
18th	
Betty Grable	1916
Ray Liotta	1955
Leonard Maltin	1950
Brad Pitt	1963
Keith Richards	1943
Steven Spielberg	1947
19th	
Jennifer Beals	1963
Limahl	1958
Alyssa Milano	1972
Tim Reid	1944
Sir Ralph Richardson	1902
Kirsty Swanson	1965
Robert Urich	1946
Cicely Tyson	1933
20th	
Irene Dunne	1898
21st	
Tristan Bancks	1974
Phil Donahue	1935
Jane Fonda	1937
Khrystyne Haje	1968
Josh Mostel	1957
Ed Nelson	1928
Jack Noseworthy	1969
Kiefer Sutherland	1966
Mike Vitar	1978
Frank Zappa	1940
Andy Dick	1965
22nd	
Lauralee Bell	1968
Paul Byatt	1971
Nicola Charles	1968
Noel Edmonds	1948
Ralph Fiennes	1962
Maurice & Robin Gibb	1949

Diane Sawyer 1945

23rd

Corey Haim 1972
Susan Lucci 1950
Dave Murray 1958
Eddie Vedder 1964
Adrien Brody 1976

25th

Cab Calloway 1907
Annie Lennox 1954
Barbara Mandrell 1948
Gary Sandy 1945
Sissy Spacek 1949

26th

Steve Allen 1921
Alan King 1927
Jared Leto 1972
Phil Spector 1940
Richard Widmark 1914

27th

John Amos 1941
Gerard Depardieu 1948
Marlene Dietrich 1901
Adrian Lee 1966
Anna Russell 1911

28th

Lew Ayres 1908
Richard Clayderman 1953
Alex Dimitriades 1973
Nigel Kennedy 1956
Dame Maggie Smith 1934
Denzel Washington 1954

29th

Ted Danson 1947
Marianne Faithfu 1946
Inga Swensen 1932
Mary Tyler Moore 1937
Jon Voight 1938

30th

Bo Diddley 1928
John Hillerman 1932
Davey Jones 1946
Jack Lord 1930
Michael Nesmith 1942
Del Shannon 1939
Noel Stookey 1937
Russ Tamblyn 1934
Tracey Ullman 1959

31st

John Denver 1943
John Diamont 1962
Sir Anthony Hopkins 1937
Val Kilmer 1959
Ben Kingsley 1943
Joe Mclntrye 1972
Sarah Miles 1941